GAMES AND GREAT IDEAS

GAMES AND GREAT IDEAS

A Guide for Elementary School Physical Educators and Classroom Teachers

Edited by
Rhonda L. Clements

GREENWOOD PRESS
Westport, Connecticut • London

Library of Congress Cataloging-in-Publication Data

Games and great ideas : a guide for elementary school physical
    educators and classroom teachers / edited by Rhonda L. Clements.
        p.   cm.
    Includes bibliographical references and index.
    ISBN 0–313–29460–7 (alk. paper)
    1. Physical education for children.   2. Group games.
    3. Educational games.   I. Clements, Rhonda L.
    GV443.G28   1995
    372.86—dc20   94–13200

British Library Cataloguing in Publication Data is available.

Library of Congress Catalog Card Number: 94–13200
ISBN: 0–313–29460–7

First published in 1995

Printed in the United States of America

♾️™

The paper used in this book complies with the
Permanent Paper Standard issued by the National
Information Standards Organization (Z39.48–1984).

10 9 8 7 6 5 4 3 2 1

Contents

Illustrations

Acknowledgments

The editor is greatly indebted to the many professionals who have contributed their works to this book. She is very grateful to Margaret Maybury, Elizabeth Leiba, and Sylvia J. Giallombardo for their valuable criticisms and helpful suggestions concerning the editing process, as well as Alexej Ugrinsky, Natalie Datlof, Athelene A. Collins, and the entire Hofstra Cultural Center staff for their continued advice and support throughout the project.

Acknowledgment is gladly given to Judith M. D'Angio and Nancy Lucas, who performed the typing and formatting for this manuscript; Teresa Rooney, who computerized the book's tables and figures; and G. H. C. Illustrations for the intricate pen and ink drawings that accompany the text.

Introduction

Rhonda L. Clements

The elementary school physical educator and the classroom teacher of today are very fortunate to be able to choose from any number of excellent references containing games and sport activities for all age levels. One could even conclude that the abundance of game literature makes it unnecessary to add one more title to the list. However, the decision to develop this resource seemed very logical. It was based on the fact that on any given day, at any given time, and in any given country in the world, elementary school age children organize themselves for the purpose of playing a favorite game.

These children may meet in community centers, local parks, open fields, sandlots, on one child's back or front lawn, and even on abandoned streets and sidewalks. They sometimes bring balls in a variety of sizes, shapes, and materials. Several will clutch striking implements like rackets, paddles, or softball bats, or they may agree to play chase and flee activities that do not require equipment. Individuals within the group will vary in age, height, weight, hair color, racial background, physical skill, and previous experience at game play.

Choosing which game to play will most likely become a point of discussion. Recalling previous game encounters, some children will urge their friends to consider new approaches or strategies aimed at increasing the group's success (Part I). Others will suggest that the group choose a game that incorporates new roles, story themes, or concepts learned in the classroom for an inventive experience (Part II). Still others will propose a game frequently played by their neighbors or family members who have lived in foreign countries (Part III). Several children might remind the group of a promise made earlier to change or modify previously used rules to decrease the possibility of arguments (Part IV), and several others will express their feelings concerning the benefits of playing a vigorous versus a nonvigorous game (Part V). The children will likely state several viewpoints before engaging in the decided upon activity. The values inherent in this type of childhood gathering provide essential opportunities for positive peer interactions and the sharing of ideas.

These inherent values were also evident at the East Coast Regional Games Conference, which took place at Hofstra University. The theme was "Games Children Play," and over 600 participants from more than thirty states and several foreign countries were able to choose from seventy-three sessions and special events. Each lecture and demonstration was designed to offer participants purposeful information, professional enrichment, and overall enjoyment. For many demonstrations, elementary school children from neighboring states and local schools were present to reinforce the explanation of specific points.

Much of this book's content was drawn from selected information delivered at that interdisciplinary conference. It represents the thoughts of elementary physical educators, elementary classroom teachers, early childhood teachers, school administrators, and university and college specialists. Additional works are included from preservice teachers; also, several teacher trainers responded to a letter sent to institutions of higher learning requesting original or modified games for inclusion in this resource.

Although it was possible to categorize each essay into one of five parts, the five themes had not been predetermined. Rather, the themes emerged naturally only after a thorough review of all accepted papers. Each chapter is more or less complete in itself. This is not a volume to be read once and then laid aside; instead, it is a resource to be referred to time and again for ideas on the nature, value, and implementation of games for children in preschool through grade eight. Brief summaries of the contents of each section of the book are provided to guide the reader. I hope this volume will help insure that future generations of children will assemble beyond the instructional setting to establish the ideals, experience new knowledge, and participate in the physical skills common to childhood games.

Part I

Theoretical Considerations for Teaching Games

Part I begins with a chapter by Beverly Nichols that presents a strong rationale supporting the value of games. She stresses that games give children a way to use motor skills creatively, not just practice them, shedding new light on old issues for teacher trainers and other professionals responsible for the selection and implementation of developmentally appropriate games. Philip Duhan Segal conveys information related to Pieter Bruegel's sixteenth-century painting, *Children's Games*, which shows children participating in eighty-seven games. He notes factors that motivated children to play these games and the significance of this historical masterpiece for teachers today. Amelia Mays Woods focuses on how to prepare students for complex game play by organizing learning experiences into four developmental stages. Similarly, Sarah Doolittle reinforces the need for cognitive understanding to increase the likelihood of student success. She includes a progression of activities designed around key concepts that help the child to discover how, where, and when to move in traditional games. Birger Peitersen identifies how the Teaching for Understanding approach is being implemented in several Scandinavian countries to bridge the gap between game skills and athletic sports. Susan M. Schwager discusses critical thinking as a tool for increasing the child's game playing abilities. Specific strategies for using higher order thinking skills are offered. Gary T. Barrette and Leah Holland Fiorentino describe a conceptually integrated decision-making pedagogical action model for physical education, designed to achieve appropriate and personalized student learning outcomes through an innovative teaching strategy in games and sports. Suzanne Mueller offers a games assessment instrument that can be used to make educationally sound and developmentally appropriate game choices for students. The chapter focuses on how to select games that increase student participation, self-concept, social interaction, fitness opportunities, and intellectual development. Svea Becker and Pat Huber provide teacher trainers with selected student worksheets to analyze several of the movements and motor skill principles involved in game activities and sport skills. Finally, Carol L.

Alberts explores several areas of teacher vulnerability related to planning appropriate games and sport activities toward ensuring a safe environment and a positive learning experience for all participants.

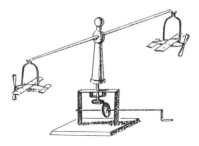

1

Games: The Means or the End?

Beverly Nichols

Situation Number 1: It is a warm afternoon in May. Children getting off the school bus agree to meet in the neighborhood park for a pick-up game of softball. Shortly after arriving home they reassemble in the park, girls and boys, younger and older children. They quickly select teams, adjust the rules for the youngest and most inexperienced players, and begin play.

What do we know about the games of children? Are games a means, affecting important aspects of the present and future lives of the participants, or are they ends in themselves?

In observing children on the playground or in the neighborhood, one notes that they invent games of many descriptions, some for one person, others for groups varying in number, age, and ability. The games differ in complexity according to the ability of the creator, but generally rules are minimal, limited to those needed at that particular moment. Rules are often modified as the game progresses to offer the most favorable opportunity for success by everyone, with special rules applied occasionally on an individual basis as differences in ability are considered by the group.

Children play games without adult supervision, choose teams that provide equal competition (although we might not consider their methods to be in the best interests of all the players), abide by the rules set by the group, and work out most differences of opinion in a reasonable manner. Scoring may be given little importance, and when the game ends, no real winners are declared. Children's personal satisfaction comes from being physically active and having given their best efforts in the play just completed.

When used effectively, games can make a substantial contribution to the objectives of physical education and consequently to the development of elementary school children. Games provide an opportunity for children to (1) use a variety of motor skills and their adaptations; (2) analyze a situation and use creative thinking in developing strategy; (3) share ideas and to work together in leadership and follower roles to meet challenges in achieving the game objectives;

(4) learn about themselves—their strengths and weaknesses—as they attempt to find appropriate solutions to game challenges based on their individual skill repertoire; (5) take risks in a fun way as they move into areas of uncertainty and insecurity without the real threat of failure, since the outcome of the game is not a life and death matter; and (6) experience self-discipline in playing within the parameters of rules and boundaries, including assuming responsibility for the enforcement of rules by acting as the leader or official.

To be meaningful for children, the cognitive, social, and motor aspects of the game must match the developmental needs of the participants. To achieve this, it may be necessary to alter the size of the playing space, the skills used, and the equipment available to adjust for the physical/motor needs of the group; to change the number of players and player relationships to meet the social development needs of the children; and to modify rules to further meet the cognitive needs of the children who will play the game. Games should challenge children within their capability for play and prepare them for game play independent of adult supervision.

Situation Number 2: The children enter the gymnasium. The teacher introduces the rules for a running game which the children play. Later in the class a second game, a ball game, is introduced. The group is reorganized, equipment is distributed, and play begins. The class period ends with the equipment being collected as the children leave the gymnasium on their way back to the classroom.

Are these games a means or an end? Games may be included for a number of reasons, not all of them related to learning. They may be used to appease children who perceive physical education as a time to play games, to reward work well done, or to celebrate special occasions when the lesson material has been developed and some time remains in the period. They may be introduced because they are a favorite of the teacher or because the teacher is eager to add a new activity to the children's game repertoire. Games used in this manner are ends in themselves.

Ideally, the majority of games incorporated into a lesson should be used as a means. These games are selected not because children like them, the teacher knows them, or facilities and equipment are available, but for their possibilities in furthering learning in physical education and adding to the lesson's objectives. A game may offer a series of possibilities for learning, so it might be used on a number of occasions, with different elements stressed each time the game is played.

DEVELOPING MOTOR SKILLS

Situation Number 3: The fifth grade soccer class begins by practicing dribbling. Prior to practice the teacher asks the students what points are important in executing the skill. The teacher then moves the students to a new activity in which they must protect the ball as they dribble throughout the playing space. Halfway through the practice the teacher stops the class to ask what they did to protect the ball. Following the dribbling practice the class reviews passing. A passing activity follows in which the students move with a partner in the activity area while dribbling and passing. Receivers call "yes" when they are open to receive a pass. Following a brief discussion of how they anticipated and moved to an open space to receive a pass, the students quickly review and are organized for small group soccer lead-up games. Play begins with the teacher moving from group to group coaching the students on their dribbling, passing, and movement to open spaces.

One of the primary uses of games is to provide the opportunity for children to use, not just practice, the motor skills they are learning in an activity. In selecting appropriate games to meet this goal, we need to examine games carefully to look at motor skills use and to answer the following questions:

1. What motor skills do I wish the students to use?
2. How are they used in the game to meet the game goals successfully?
3. Is the skill performed singly or in combination with other skills?
4. Is the potential receiver or opponent stationary, or is he or she moving in a manner requiring further judgment?
5. What technique modifications are needed for success under the varying game conditions? These might include a change of direction or pathway, a varying level of projection or receipt, or a shift in force or speed.

Once these questions are answered, the next step is to give each student maximum opportunity to practice the necessary skills as near to game conditions as possible. A series of practices may emerge, each adding to the complexity of the use of the skill. For instance, a game requiring a change in direction, pathway, or speed while running might be preceded by an activity in which the children respond to the teacher's instruction concerning a movement in space, avoiding others and moving in different directions, pathways, or speeds on a designated signal.

DEVELOPING COGNITIVE SKILLS

Games offer a number of different opportunities for enhancing cognitive skills, including developing game strategy, problem solving, and creating new games.

Situation Number 4: The fifth grade class is focusing on using space offensively in basketball. The class is divided into small groups with a designated space for each. Two players work against a third player, trying to pass and dribble to get the ball over an end line, the idea being to create a space for the player with the ball. As the children work the teacher poses such questions as, How can you position yourself so the defense has a large space to defend? How can you move to create the biggest open space within which to move the ball? After the activity a short discussion is held as groups demonstrate strategies that worked. With these in mind the group is organized for some small group games of sideline basketball. The teacher moves from group to group coaching students on their use of space, stopping them when it is necessary to raise questions about what needs to be done or to point out good play.

The application of movement concepts is important in developing game strategy. Usually a large number of movement concepts can be identified for each game, with the teacher having to decide which are most pertinent, given the ability and experience of the players. A number of factors in games determine the complexity of these applications, including the game's physical setup, the relationship of teammates and opponents, the number of participants, and the amount of space used.

Games in which each team is active on a different part of the court, such as many net games, offer a simpler structure than those in which players of opposing teams share space, such as hockey or basketball. Games with large numbers of players are often, but not always, more complex than games with fewer players, since they often involve the delegation of different responsibilities for players in the game.

Game concepts primarily fall under the category of space concepts. They may involve the relationship of the player to the space, such as moving within boundaries and using the space available; the relationship of the player to others or objects in space; recognition of and creation of open spaces on offense; or closing space on defense. They may also include anticipating the direction or pathway of others or objects.

Time is another concept important for game success. Anticipating the speed of a person or object to be intercepted is one application of time. Others involve timing movements, such as picking up the pin in Snatch The Club or in leaving first base in a softball game.

The application of concepts to games is dependent first upon the students' understanding of the concepts themselves and their game experience. What is learned in one game can be transferred to others when these applications are carefully taught.

Identifying and developing concepts in the context of games is an important first step. The game needs to be broken down into the smallest element where a concept can be used. A means of practicing it is devised, and then the concept can be used in the game with appropriate coaching.

PROBLEM SOLVING

Problem solving is an important part of the game experience and involves the application of the movement content in solving games challenges. Teachers can easily structure the game so that the desired application will result. However, the best chance for problem solving lies in the teacher's ability to structure the game in a way that allows problems to result and then raising questions with the children to help them find solutions. In our haste to get the class playing the game successfully, we often structure the lesson in such a way that problem solving is minimal or nonexistent. The measure of a lesson's value is not that the children have instant success but what the children can learn in the games experience. As teachers we must be patient, structuring a learning situation so that problems will occur.

The steps in problem solving include understanding the problem, planning and reaching a solution, thinking about the process, and evaluating what happened. Each step includes questioning and discussion to clarify the thinking. The first phase includes defining the problem and identifying all important information relating to the problem. The second phase involves looking for more than one way to solve the problem. The final phase is evaluating the solutions, with the pitfalls identified in each. Finally, it is helpful to relate the problem to similar ones students have encountered in class or in real-life situations. These solutions are not always easily discovered. As teachers we must be willing to take time to question and experiment until workable solutions result.

The satisfaction that comes in thinking through solutions to game problems, trying them out, and evaluating the results is an important outcome of the games experience.

Situation Number 5:   The teacher begins the lesson with a small group ball game previously played by the children. Following a short period of play, the teacher asks the children to create a new game based on the game they have just played. Each group works together to make up a new game, altering rules, skills, player relationships, and so on. After they have had a chance to try out their games they present them to the class. The other groups try out each of the new games and discuss what they like about each.

Creating games has only recently become a part of the games experience. In the early stages of game invention students may suggest changes in a known game to make it more challenging.   Adding more equipment, reducing or increasing the number of participants, changing the amount or shape of the space used, or using different skills or equipment may be some of the modifications tried. Children could be asked to record the rules of the new game as a writing assignment and to teach their new game to the class.

At a higher level, children of varying ability levels might be grouped together, then asked to create a game in which all have a chance to play their best.

DEVELOPING UNDERSTANDING AND SOCIAL SKILLS:
THE MULTICULTURAL EXPERIENCE

Situation Number 6: To make the games lesson a multicultural experience, the teacher selects a series of games from various cultures to be played individually and in small groups in stations scattered in the playing area. The teacher carefully describes each activity for the group and shares information available at each station to help them understand the culture and the games so that they can play independently. Play begins. After a period of time the children move to a new station. At the close of the lesson the teacher asks questions about each game, with emphasis on understanding the equipment used and the context in which the game was played.

The games experience can also broaden students' understanding of other people and cultures. Many activities, such as rope jumping and hopscotch, originated in other countries. As children are introduced to games they should also be exposed to the cultural heritage behind each game. This approach also fosters children's pride in their own heritage.

The United States is beginning to look at the many cultures that make up our society, including those of the native Americans or aboriginal peoples, with a new sense of their contributions to our way of life. Physical education is a natural setting for a closer look at other cultures. We are now beginning to see the potential for furthering cultural understanding through games as well as dance. We need to make a special effort to investigate the games of native peoples before they are lost to us forever and to teach the games of other people of the world.

PLAYER INTERACTIONS

Situation Number 7: The sixth grade teacher has structured a learning activity in which two students work together to develop a strategy to pick up a duckpin being guarded by another student without being tagged. Following a discussion of the activity and the strategies they tried, the class is divided into two teams for a game of capture the flag. Each group determines who will assume which responsibilities in the game, and play begins. Throughout the game the teacher poses questions to the offense as they work together to determine how to get the flag and then to try out the strategies they have developed.

While this may sound like a problem-solving activity, it is an activity in shared decision making as well. The interaction of players must be a consideration in selecting games. Often games are unsuccessful because children lack the necessary interaction skills. Unfortunately, these skills are most often overlooked as we select games for a group of children. As we look at the games played in the elementary school we see a logical progression in the skills needed, which match children's developing social skills.

Early games require very little social interaction, with some involving a simple individual response to the leader's signal as children play alongside rather than with others. Later games add a simple one-on-one encounter as children even in large group games move against one opponent.

As the children become ready, games are introduced involving more cooperation by players and a beginning team effort, such as covering space on defense. As socialization into games improves, increasingly complex games are introduced, requiring more group interaction and delegation of different player responsibilities for game success. These games gradually introduce more complex offensive and defensive strategies to meet game goals.

Games in which only one or two players from each team are active at a time are much simpler than those in which six or more from each team are active. An important aspect of a lead-up games progression is the gradual introduction of more and more players to gradually increase the complexity of the game as players are ready. In this way the type of interactions can be planned to meet the needs of individual children in the group.

Another aspect to consider is the nature of the interaction—cooperative or competitive. In some cases it may be helpful to modify game rules to enhance cooperation. Take snowball, for example: Each team works to have fewer balls on its side rather than competing with the other team. You win if you have fewer balls on your side than you did last time. (Other modifications for games might include awarding points for the number of passes completed rather than goals scored.)

Children also need to learn how to compete. However, since the competitive situation can so easily get out of control, certain safeguards need to be considered:

1. Players need to be matched if competition is to be successful. If players play one-on-one they should be playing against an opponent who also has a fifty-fifty chance for success. Teams need to be equal as well. If the competition turns out to be unequal, steps should be taken quickly to reorganize the groups so that fairer competition results.
2. Cooperation is an important element in competition, and teachers need to help children develop the cooperative skills needed for the group to be successful in a competitive situation.
3. Games should be relatively short in length, allowing teams to play many other teams in a short time. Competitive games may also be structured so that players change teams, as well as opponents, so that all are winners.
4. Keeping score should not be emphasized, although it is important for the teacher to keep track of the score to ensure the best possible experience for all children.
5. In cooperating and competing, children should be encouraged to be supportive of one another. Adding points at the end for good team effort goes a long way in enhancing favorable behavior in games.

The games lesson has the potential for providing participants with valuable experiences in the use of motor, cognitive, and social skills. Our success in this endeavor is dependent upon our creative talents as teachers and games leaders.

REFERENCES

Lever, Janet (1979). Sex Differences in Games Children Play. In A. Yiannakis et al., *Sport Sociology: Contemporary Themes*, 2nd ed. Dubuque: Kendall/Hunt.

Nichols, B. (1990). *Moving and Learning: The Elementary School Physical Education Experience,* 2nd ed. St. Louis: Times/Mirror/Mosby.

Polgar, Sylvia K. (1976). The Social Context of Games: Or When Is Play Not Play? *Sociology of Education*, 49 (October).

Thorpe, R., D. Bunker, and L. Almond (1989). A Change in Focus for the Teaching of Games. In *Sport Pedagogy*, ed. M. Peron and G. Graham. Champaign: Human Kinetics.

Wessinger, Nancy (1988). *The Child's Experience of Games in Physical Education.* Doctoral dissertation, University of Michigan.

2

Bruegel's *Children's Games* (1560): Implications for Today's Teachers

Philip Duhan Segal

Why do children play games? What inner resources do they use when participating in games? What do games teach the players? What can teachers learn from observing children at play? In brief, children enjoy the physical and mental activity that a game situation provides. They take pleasure in movement and gratification of the senses, in chasing, catching, seeking, hunting, racing, dueling, exerting, daring, guessing, acting, and pretending. Games also develop strength, agility, grace, and coordination, along with the ability to think. Children learn how to cooperate and display tolerance; they become socialized and resourceful.

Inner resources are used and developed. Intelligence, creativity, and curiosity grow, along with young bodies. Generosity, such as giving up one's turn or giving to others, is balanced by aggression and competition. Children learn about fair play, sportsmanship, and the values of working together in groups. In games, they realize the importance of coordinating the mind with the physical strength of the body, and steps toward knowing and liking themselves.

Children have always played games. In the 1560 painting *Children's Games* by Pieter Bruegel (c. 1525–1569), we see a town square devoted to children for their amusement. No adults are visible. Eighty-seven games may be counted, including boys and girls playing with hobbyhorses, tops, hoops, and masks. They amuse themselves with leapfrog, piggyback, blindman's buff, and walking on stilts—both short and long. They stand on their heads, climb trees and fences, swing, ride, and swim. Girls play at a wedding and with a doll's house. About two-thirds of the eighty-seven games are played in pairs or groups, while about one-third are solitary play. What can we learn from Bruegel's painting?

About two-thirds of the activities are easily recognized as games children play in pairs or groups today, and probably have played from time immemorial: playing jacks (with knuckle-bones), giving piggyback rides, carrying each other in hand seats, playing buck-buck or saddle-the-nag, building castles, playing leapfrog, competing in tug of war, choosing sides with odds or evens, spinning tops, digging ditches, jousting with windmills, playing on fences, building pyramids, pulling and heaving. The children enjoy blindman's buff, hide-and-seek, keep-away (saluggi), a fisherman cord game, the fish, bowling (bocci), drop the handkerchief, king of the mountain, mulberry bush, taw (marbles), bombardment (forerunner of balloon warfare), bottoms up (potchi), hunt the fox, horsey, and tag. Some children are clearly taking "time out" for rest and relaxation.

Another third of the activities are solitary. Individual children play with dolls, shake rattles, whirl windmill toys, blow bubbles, play with pet animals, ride hobbyhorses, make mud pies, roll hoops (some with bells), inflate animal skins (forerunner of blowing up balloons), tumble in somersaults, wear masks, turn cartwheels, do headstands, spin around, swim, wade, skinny dip, wave flags, balance brooms, and play games with cord.

Some adult activities are mirrored as the children play church and clergy, pretend to be doctors, act as doorkeepers, play store, carry home bread or cakes, form a wedding procession, march with fife and drum. A few children display naked aggression and mean spirits: pulling hair (*haarken plunken*), running the gauntlet, swatting flies, shooting pop-guns, hitting stones, throwing a girl off a fence, annoying an innkeeper. Other youngsters perform daring and dangerous feats and stunts, such as balancing on rolling barrels, walking on high stilts, climbing trees, and climbing walls and fences.

Bruegel may have been aware of the writings of physician and Franciscan-turned-Benedictine monk François Rabelais (1490–1553), who advanced a number of revolutionary theories on education. Rabelais emphasized the need for physical exercise and games, singing, dancing, modeling and painting, nature study, and manual training. His account of the education of Gargantua makes considerable use of play as an exercise for mind and body.

"Rabelais plays with words," wrote Anatole France, "as children do with pebbles; he piles them up into heaps." The *Histories of Gargantua and Pantagruel* recounts how Gargantua was sent to Paris on a huge mare (Chapter 16) and took the great bells from the church of Notre Dame as a plaything (Chapter 17). Chapter 22 catalogs Gargantua's games, about 220 of them. Many have salacious and earthy titles. "Very few artists or writers observed and depicted children as they really were," writes Robert Delort (1972). This observation increases our appreciation of the records left to us by artists such as Bruegel and writers such as Rabelais.

Three hundred years after Bruegel's painting, Louisa May Alcott (1832–1888) gives us a glimpse of games played by American children. In *Little Women* (1868), fifteen-year-old Jo writes and directs plays for her sisters Meg, Beth, and Amy to perform. Tomboyish, daring, and creative, she climbs trees to read about the world: "Jo spent the morning on the river with Laurie, and the afternoon reading and crying over *The Wide, Wide World* up in the apple tree." Later, in *Little Men* (1871), Jo and her husband Professor Bhaer run a school that encourages wayward boys to become civilized through creative play:

The children of Holland take pleasure in making,
What the children of Boston take pleasure in breaking.

Pursuing their individual interests, one boy collects and mounts bugs and butterflies; another develops as a carpenter; a third becomes a juvenile entrepreneur. From these activities, which they choose themselves and regard as play, they learn valuable lessons.

Games teach lessons useful in future life. For example, poet Yevgeny Yevtushenko (born in 1933) tells us about a street bully who disastrously pummels him. He gears himself for the next encounter and overcomes the aggressor. He uses this example as a goal for the rest of his life.

Similarly, our own Henry Adams (1838–1918) describes a snowball fight in New England in *The Education of Henry Adams* (1918). "One of the commonest boy-games of winter, inherited directly from the eighteenth century, was a game of war on Boston Common," he writes. In 1850 it was a battle of the Latin School, including boys of the west end, against all comers. "As the Latin School grew weak, the roughs and young blackguards grew strong." Stones, sticks, and slingshots, "as effective as a knife," multiplied the danger. As night came on, "only a small band was left, headed by two heroes, Savage and Marvin." They were rushed by "a swarm of blackguards from the slums, led by a grisly terror called Conky Daniels, with a club and a hideous reputation." Most of the Latin School boys fled, except for Savage and Marvin, Henry Adams and his older brother Charles, and a few others. "The terrible Conky Daniels swaggered up, stopped a moment with his bodyguard to swear a few oaths at Marvin, and then swept on." He chased those in retreat, leaving the few boys untouched who stood their ground. The obvious moral was that "blackguards were not so black as they were painted." Ten or twelve years later, when these same boys were falling on the Civil War battlefields of Virginia and Maryland, Henry Adams wondered "whether their education on Boston Common had taught Savage and Martin how to die."

IMPLICATIONS

What lessons can be drawn by teachers today? By observing children carefully, as Bruegel did in the process of artistic composition, teachers can learn to capitalize on natural inclinations, drives, and motivations. They can learn to channel these drives into socially acceptable habits of cooperation, tolerance, and good sportsmanship. They can become aware of socially destructive aggression and selfishness, so that they can devise strategies to combat these negative tendencies.

Games are essential for a child's development. One of the benefits of examining people of other times and other places is to remind us that these beings are human like ourselves, with feelings, urges, and preoccupations comparable to our own. They tell us about our universal selves.

NOTES

Bruegel was fascinated with how everyday things looked and worked. This lifetime interest resulted in a steadily fattening encyclopedia of details. *Children's Games* is a catalog of juvenile amusements. The painting hangs in the Kunthistorisches Museum in Vienna. It is 46 1/2" by 63 3/8" (118 by 161 centimeters), about four feet high and five feet long.

The technique Bruegel used to compose his pictures is called *wimmelbild* (literally, "teeming figure picture"). Masses of small figures are presented on a large painting surface, usually seen from above. To achieve this effect, Bruegel combined older approaches with newer techniques of perspective.

Authentic contemporary references to Bruegel's life are few. Known as "Peasant Bruegel" for his choice of subjects, or "Bruegel the Droll" for his approach, he was born about 1525 in a village named Brueghel, a name he took for himself. The *h* was dropped later. He did much work in the manner of Hieronymus Bosch and produced many spookish scenes. Bruegel delighted in observing the droll behavior of the peasants as they ate, danced, drank, capered, or made love.

An intriguing 1,200-word account of Bruegel's life, published thirty-five years after his death, appeared in *The Book of Painters* (*Het Schilder-Boeck*, 1604). In it, Karel van Mander chronicles some three dozen Flemish and Dutch artists in a frequently fanciful, sometimes inaccurate mixture of classical learning and chatty anecdotes.

REFERENCES

Adams, Henry (1918). *The Education of Henry Adams*, chapters 1-4. In *The Great Books Reading and Discussion Program*, Fifth Series, Vol. 3. Chicago: Great Books, 1985.

Alcott, Louisa May (1868). *Little Women*. Ed. Elaine Showalter. New York: Penguin, 1989.

——— (1871). *Little Men*. Garden City, N.Y.: Doubleday, 1955.

Benarde, Anita (1970). *Games from Many Lands*. New York: Savre.

Delort, Robert (1972). *Life in the Middle Ages*. Trans. Robert Allen. New York: Greenwich House.

Foote, Timothy (1968). *The World of Bruegel*. New York: Time-Life.

Gluck, Gustav (1936). *Pieter Bruegel the Elder*. Trans. Evaline Byam Shaw. New York: Art Book Publications.

Grossman, Fritz (1952). *Bruegel: The Paintings*. Complete Edition. London: Phaidon Press.

——— (1960). *Encyclopedia of World Art*, s.v. "Bruegel, Pieter the Elder." New York: McGraw-Hill.

Kraus, Richard (1971). *Recreation and Leisure in Modern Society*. New York: Appleton-Century-Crofts.

——— (1977). *Recreation Today: Program Planning and Leadership*. 2nd ed. Santa Monica, Calif.: Goodyear.

Milberg, Alan (1976). *Street Games*. New York: McGraw-Hill.

Opie, Iona, and Peter Opie (1969). *Children's Games in Street and Playground*. Oxford: Clarendon Press.

Prelutsky, Jack (1983). *The Random House Book of Poetry for Children*. New York: Random House.

Rabelais, François (1955; orig. pub. 1532–1534). *The Histories of Gargantua and Pantagruel*. Trans. J. M. Cohen. Five books published in one volume. New York: Penguin.

Storr, Francis (1948). *Encyclopedia Britannica*, s.v. "Games, Classical."

3

The Developmental Stages of Game Play

Amelia Mays Woods

The curriculum in physical education is comprised of games, dance, gymnastics, and physical fitness. Games or sports commonly taught in physical education include basketball, volleyball, soccer, hockey, softball, tennis, and badminton. To help students become proficient in these games, physical educators attempt to design appropriate developmental experiences for learners. When students fail to become skillful game players, it is typically because they have not been taught all of the skills needed for successful participation. According to Siedentop, Herkowitz, and Rink (1984), physical educators frequently expect learners who have the ability to control an object to know automatically what to do with that object in offensive and defensive relationships. An example of this would be a grade six basketball unit that focuses on dribbling a ball between cones or making chest passes with a partner in the first lessons, then rushes into five-on-five basketball one or two classes later. Students with the prerequisite abilities for basketball find the full game challenging and appropriate. The majority of the less skilled students, however, gain little from the experience.

When games are taught effectively, the teacher does much more than merely provide opportunities for students to practice individual skills and then participate in the game. Preparing learners to take part in complex game play requires that they be able to combine skills, use skills in challenging ways, and utilize effective offensive and defensive strategies (Rink, 1993). The evolution of game play can be conceived as consisting of four stages of development.

STAGE ONE

The first stage focuses on the ability of the learner to control body parts, total body movements, and objects. Progressive experiences are designed so that learners are involved in single movements and are encouraged to perform these movements with consistency. The primary objective of successful experiences in

Stage One is to have the learner manage him or herself and objects under defined conditions.

In Stage One, activities involving sending objects (i.e., throwing or striking) should focus on controlling the objects so that the appropriate placement and force are achieved consistently. For catching, trapping, and other collecting actions, the practice should be structured so that the learner becomes proficient at receiving objects that are moving at varying speeds, directions, pathways, and levels. With carrying and propelling activities, learners should be able to maintain control of an object while moving with versatility. For example, the learner would control a dribbled soccer ball while changing pace, or carry a football while moving in varying pathways (Rink, 1993).

Experiences in Stage One need to begin under very simple conditions and progress gradually, making the achievement of control more difficult by manipulating the conditions of practice. For instance, after learners are successful at receiving objects sent directly to them at a consistent speed, they should have experiences in moving at various levels and positions to catch objects sent from different locations and at different forces.

STAGE TWO

The teacher adds complexity by challenging students to combine skills. Control of self and objects continues to be important, but now the student is asked to work with another classmate in cooperative or competitive ways. A learner in a Stage Two softball experience might be working on fielding and throwing to a base, or hitting and running to first. In soccer, students are dribbling and passing the ball as they move down the field. Rules that confine the way a skill can be performed, such as traveling in basketball and lifting in volleyball, are added at Stage Two.

STAGE THREE

In Stage Three the students are challenged to use skills in an increasingly complex game play. The focus of activity shifts from working on skill combinations to applying those combinations in offensive and defensive situations. Learners are involved in making active decisions to gain an offensive advantage and properly defend their own space. Rink (1993) notes that in keep-away activities, such as soccer, football, or basketball, the emphasis is placed on obtaining and maintaining possession of objects. With tennis, volleyball, and other net activities, the learners concentrate on offensive placement in the opponent's court and defending their own space.

The basic one-on-one relationship is the simplest level for the teacher to introduce offensive and defensive strategies. As learners gain experience, offensive and defensive players are gradually added, as are boundaries, additional rules, and scoring.

STAGE FOUR

Practice in this stage combines skills in complex ways, leading to full game play. The point at which Stage Three ends and Stage Four begins is not easily defined. In most activities, when the players become more specialized and the game is played with more rules, scoring, and boundaries, the activity is considered a Stage Four experience. Stage Four includes the use of specialized rules for starting games, rules infractions, out of bounds plays, technical rules, and the gradual addition of the full-size playing area and number of players.

As learners move to more complex Stage Four play, teachers should continue to ensure that practice is appropriate for the learners. If some aspect of play continuously inhibits the flow of the game, then modifications should be made.

PROGRESSING THROUGH THE STAGES

It is important to recognize that students do not totally master one stage before moving to the next. Instead, a basic level of competency must be demonstrated before students proceed to a higher stage. For example, a learner may be skilled enough to benefit from experiences in the next stage, yet will often need to return to the previous stage(s) for skill refinement. Even Olympic athletes include experiences at all four stages in their practice. An Olympic volleyball team would spend a great deal of time in Stages Three and Four concentrating on effective strategy, but would not neglect the practice of the fundamental skills in Stages One and Two.

There is a tendency for teachers to limit the experiences common to Stages Two and Three (Rink, 1993). This may be because some physical educators assume that offensive and defensive strategy skills will be automatically acquired through participation in full game play. They are unaware that game strategy, like all other skills, must be taught developmentally for learning to occur. Strategy skills should initially be taught in much more simple conditions than full game play.

In helping learners to increase their understanding of offensive relationships, the teacher may consider the following sequential conditions for practice designed for keep-away activities (e.g., basketball, soccer, hockey) and net activities (e.g., tennis, badminton, volleyball) (Siedentop, Herkowitz, and Rink, 1984).

KEEP-AWAY ACTIVITIES

One offense and one defense: Encourage quick gamelike movements; the offensive player is encouraged to elude the defender, and the defensive player should try to make the offender lose control.

Two offense and one defense (not goal-oriented): Entice offensive players to pass quickly, to move to an open space to receive, and to use the lead pass. Meanwhile, stimulate the defensive player to stay close to one receiver at the angle most likely to deflect the pass, and to move constantly.

Two offense and one defense (goal-oriented): Encourage offensive players to keep the object moving toward the goal and to pass a certain number of times to gain advantage before going for the goal. Meanwhile, entice the defensive player to defend a space instead of a player.

Two offense and two defense (not goal-oriented): Have offensive players make passes quickly, receive passes by quickly moving into open spaces, and send and receive passes on the move. Meanwhile, encourage defensive players to make passes difficult by constantly moving and placing themselves between the two offensive players.

Two offense and two defense (goal-oriented): Encourage offensive players to keep the object moving toward the goal, and defensive players to cover space, thereby gaining experience in playing zone defense. At the same time, encourage defensive players to cover each of the offensive players, thereby gaining experience in person-to-person defense.

Three offense and two defense (goal-oriented): Have all three offensive players take part in maintaining the object, yet stimulate the defensive players by encouraging them to use a person-to-person defense in forcing passes while defending the goal.

NET ACTIVITIES

One offense and one defense: Entice the offense player to hit to the open space, with varied force, in order to give him or her time to relocate on the court. Encourage the defensive player to position him or herself to best cover the entire court, to return to this position after each shot, and to anticipate the opponent's play.

Two offense and two defense: Offensive and defensive strategy is the same as one-on-one with larger space. Encourage both sides to communicate with partners about the individual responsibility for covering space, be it up and back or side by side positions.

Four offense and four defense: Have offensive players set the ball up to front line players, and have offensive and defensive players cover not only their assigned space but also that of teammates who are pulled out of position.

SUMMARY

Games play an important part in the physical education curriculum. The four stages of game development can be used by teachers as an organizational framework for designing game experiences. When the stages are utilized, students are provided with challenging opportunities and should become more skillful game players.

REFERENCES

Rink, J. (1993). *Teaching Physical Education for Learning*. St. Louis: Times Mirror/Mosby College.

Siedentop, D., J. Herkowitz, J. Rink (1984). *Elementary Physical Education Methods*. Englewood Cliffs, N.J.: Prentice-Hall.

4

Teaching Children to Understand Games

Sarah Doolittle

This chapter describes a set of generic games that can be used in many different sports units. The activities can make a contribution to physical education programs because they are fun for children of all skill levels, they incorporate either fundamental or specific sport skills, and they help to bridge the gap between playing low organization children's games and playing more complex traditional sports. They are similar to lead-up games in that they help students move from skill practice to using skills in games. The focus, however, is on knowing what to do, and not on simply performing motor skills. Hence, their primary purpose is to help children understand what to do when they play complex team sports.

Many traditional team sports can be classified as "invasion games." In brief, invasion games are those in which one team moves through another's area to send a ball, puck, or disk into a goal. Soccer, basketball, lacrosse, hockey, football, and ultimate frisbee, as well as other games played on a field or court with goals at the endlines, fall into this category. Invasion games dominate most traditional physical education programs. Three concepts are common to all invasion games: goal play, possession play, and invasion. Scoring goals and defending a goal (goal play) are the first fundamental problems that make these games a challenge. After students acquire solutions for scoring and defending against scoring, they are ready to learn about gaining and retaining possession of the ball or puck (possession). With possession, players then need to understand how to advance through defended areas toward a goal (invasion).

The games are designed to help students of all ages, from grade one through adult players. When players understand invasion game concepts, they know how and when to use their skills, they can make decisions about where and when to move or pass, and they know several different ways to try to score. In short, they learn "game sense" or the basic strategies of traditional sports, which are as important as motor skills to successful game play. In fact, it may be even more important to teach game sense than motor skills, since this kind of understanding is the foundation for becoming knowledgeable spectators. Since many children require more time than physical education classes allow to become proficient at specific sports, teaching them to be intelligent spectators may be a more reasonable goal for many of our programs.

ORGANIZATION

The games described below are designed as one-on-one or two-on-two games, with very simple rules and scorekeeping, and can be played with fundamental skills like beanbag tossing, or with specific skills and regulation equipment. Because they are partner or small group games and can be played in small spaces, all students play at the same time, and the classes are very active. Students select partners of approximately the same skill level. The teacher decides which equipment will best enable the group to concentrate on understanding the concepts of the game. They must work with equipment and motor skills they are able to control. In these games, keep the skill simple and focus on your students' understanding and developing confidence with the concepts of the game.

In the following games the only skills required are tossing and catching beanbags. Beanbags are recommended to increase the likelihood that the student will focus on the concepts to be learned and not on specific sport skills. Each game can be taught to children in a few minutes and emphasizes a particular concept presenting the basic problems of all invasion games to which students can find answers through game play.

During the game, the teacher's role is not to referee or to tell students what to do, but instead to pay attention to the students' motor responses, to see, first, whether they understand the problem, and second, whether their solutions are appropriate. After a short interval the teacher should ask questions that guide the students' thinking and assist individuals in discovering their own solutions to the problems of offensive and defensive play. Suggested questions and appropriate responses follow each game description. Each question and answer session should be followed by another interval of game playing so that students can try their classmates' ideas or repeat their own successful solutions.

Name of Game: Goal Play
Equipment Required: One beanbag, one hoop, and a restraining line that is approximately three to five feet in front of the hoop
Starting Formation: Two opposing players
Description: One player (offense) starts by standing behind the line and trying to toss the beanbag into the hoop. He or she scores one point for each successful goal. The second player (defense) tries to prevent the opponent from scoring. After each toss, whether a point is scored or not, the players switch positions. Players keep their own scores. Play for approximately five minutes.
Questions and Solutions for Goal Play:

1. What are some ways to toss the beanbag so that it lands in the hoop for a point?

Responses should include: Over the opponent's head, between the legs, or while performing a fake.

2. Where should you stand if you are trying to prevent your opponent from scoring? How should you stand?
   Responses should include: Stand between the opponent and the goal, in the ready position to move sideways, up or down.
3. What should you focus on when your opponent gets ready to toss?
   Responses should include: Keep the eyes on the beanbag.
4. How can you score if your opponent stands close to the goal?
   Responses should include: Trick him or her into moving by making a space in front of the goal.
5. How can you score when your opponent stands close to you?
   Responses should include: By dodging or faking to move away.
6. How can you trick your opponent into making an error while tossing?
   Responses should include: Guard him or her closely or use a fake.

Variation: Offensive players should begin by standing stationary behind the line. When they are more skilled, allow them to move (right, left, forward, and back) to attempt to score. If scoring is too difficult, add a second hoop next to the first to make a larger goal, or add a second offensive player (two-on-one). If defending the goal is too difficult, increase the distance from which the offensive player has to try to score, or draw a crease or "no-go" area around the goal.

Name of Game: Possession
Starting Formation: Three players with one beanbag
Description: Two players (offense) stand approximately fifteen feet apart, and try to pass the beanbag continuously five times. The third player (defense) tries to intercept. Players cannot run with the beanbag. If there is no interception within five passes, switch positions, or switch positions within two to three minutes.
Questions and Solutions for Possession Games:

1. Offense: When should you keep the beanbag? When should you pass?
   Responses should include: Pass only when threatened.
2. How should you pass?
   Responses should include: Use a variety of passes like underhand and overhead, or use fakes.
3. What should you do when you don't have the beanbag?
   Responses should include: Move into a safe space away from the opponents.
4. If you don't have the beanbag, when should you move? How should you move?
   Responses should include: Move when you are needed, move quickly, use fakes, show you are ready to receive the beanbag.
5. Where should you stand on defense? How should you stand?
   Responses should include: Between opponents. Be ready to move with hands up, and stay close to one opponent at all times unless you can intercept.

Variations: Add a five-second rule (e.g., "You must pass within five seconds") if the defense is too difficult. Later, add a goal area. This forces the defender to choose between defending the goal and trying to intercept. (The students should defend the goal if points are given for goals scored.) Offense chooses between shooting or passing first for a better shot.

Name of Game: Invasion

Equipment Required: Two hoops about twenty-five feet apart, one beanbag

Starting Formation: Each player stands in front of his or her hoop

Description: One player with the beanbag tries to score by tossing it into the opponent's hoop. Players may run with the beanbag. The other player tries to prevent the score by guarding the hoop or intercepting the shot. Players score one point for each successful toss into the hoop. After each toss, whether or not a point is made, the defending player grabs the beanbag, moves to the opponent's hoop, and attempts to score. Possession changes after each attempt on a goal, or whenever the defender can intercept a shot. Contact is not permitted.

Questions and Solutions for Invasion Games:

1. Where should you move to in order to score? How should you move?
   Responses should include: Run quickly toward the opponent's goal before the opponent can react.
2. What should you do if you miss your shot? What should you do as soon as you score?
   Responses should include: Return quickly to your own goal.
3. What should you do if your opponent has the beanbag?
   Responses should include: Run back to defend the goal.
4. What should you do when you get the beanbag?
   Responses should include: Run quickly to shoot for a goal.

Variations for Invasion Games: Since the Invasion Game can quickly fatigue the students, the teacher should be prepared to add two more players for a two-on-two variation. This game works best when you divide the court with a center line and restrict one player from each team to one-half of the court. This forces players into offensive and defensive roles, where they must pass to their teammate across the center line in order to score. The beanbag can be exchanged for a ball that is easy to pass and catch, and the type of goal may be modified as necessary. The teacher can decide to allow players to run or not run with the beanbag. The variation can be expanded to three-on-three when the students are ready.

Questions and Solutions for the Two-on-Two Invasion Game Variation:

1. When should you shoot the beanbag? When should you pass the beanbag?
   Responses should include: Shoot when you have a good chance of scoring; pass in order to move the beanbag closer to the goal when your teammate is ready to catch, and when he or she is in a good position to score.
2. What can you do when your opponent is in the way trying to prevent a good pass?
   Responses should include: Pivot away or use fakes.
3. When your teammate has the beanbag, where should you move?
   Responses should include: Move away from your opponents to be sure you can catch the pass, or try to position yourself near the goal so that you have a good chance of scoring.
4. How can you let your teammate know that you are ready for the pass?

Responses should include: Move to a safe space; signal your teammate, or use voice or gesture when you are ready to receive a pass.

5. How can you prevent your opponents from scoring?
    Responses should include: Defend the goal area when your opponent has the beanbag, or try to intercept a shot or pass by guarding your opponent, or try to intercept any pass coming to an opponent.

Additional Variations for Invasion Games: If the scoring situation is too easy, the following rules may be added: Players with the ball may not run, or may take only three steps; or make the goal smaller. If scoring is too difficult, the goal should be made larger or an additional offensive player may be added (i.e., three-on-two and three-on-two game running should not be allowed with the beanbag).

Pointers for Teaching Invasion Games:

- Teachers should stop the games frequently to give students a rest and to encourage them to think about the alternative strategies for goal play, possession, and invasion problems.
- Look for students' solutions in their actions and ask them to demonstrate or replay their ideas for their classmates.
- Listen carefully to the students' descriptions of strategies they have discovered. Encourage them to share their ideas with their classmates.
- If the students become frustrated, simplify the game by changing the equipment for simpler skill requirements, or by changing a rule, goal size, or playing area.
- If the students demonstrate that they understand the concept, challenge them with more difficult rules or playing areas, or increase the number of players on each team.
- Above all, the teacher should remember that he or she is looking for evidence of good thinking from the students, not just good skill performance.

REFERENCES

Doolittle, S. A., and K. T. Girard (1991). A Dynamic Approach to Teaching Games in Elementary P.E. *Journal of Physical Education, Recreation and Dance*, 62(4), 57-62.

Thorpe, R., and D. Bunker (1989). A Changing Focus in Games Teaching. In L. Almond (ed.), *The Place of Physical Education in Schools*. London: Kogan Page, 42-71.

Werner, P. (1989). Teaching Games: A Tactical Perspective. *Journal of Physical Education, Recreation and Dance*, 60(3), 97-101.

5

Teaching for Understanding: The Bridge between Games and Sports in Scandinavian Countries

Birger Peitersen

The Scandinavian countries (Norway, Sweden, and Denmark) have a special sociocultural sport setting. In Denmark leisure time sport is grounded in amateurism, and extracurricular sport activities are almost nonexistent in schools. Despite increasing financial support from the private sector, the freedom and independence of voluntary organizations are not only respected, but highly regarded as an important instrument of physical education. The local sport club forms the basis of the Danish sports structure. A recent sociological study reported that 78 percent of the Danish population above the age of fifteen take part in one or more sport activities, organized as well as unorganized. (Danish Sports Federation, 1991). Among children of primary school, 92 percent take part in some form of sport activities and 74 percent are engaged for at least three hours a week (Holstein et al., 1991). Similar levels of participation are reported in the other Scandinavian countries (Engstrom, 1990). Most of these activities are organized around local clubs that pursue competitive sport disciplines.

In Denmark approximately 85 percent of children between nine and twelve years of age are members of a sports club (Forchhammer et al., 1980). In Sweden, sports club participation by fifteen-year-old boys and girls reaches 70 percent and 50 percent, respectively (Engstrom, 1990). Tables 5.1 and 5.2 show the most popular sports activities for children in Denmark (Forchhammer et al., 1980) and Sweden (Engstrom, 1990).

The most popular sports club activities in Denmark and Sweden are shown in Table 5.3 (Danish Sports Federation, 1991) and Table 5.4 (Engstrom, 1990).

The data suggest that leisure time sports outside of the school context have a significant influence in the formation of sporting habits of young people and their outward sport behavior. Of course, inherent differences concerning motives, values, and norms are highlighted by the various types of organizations and disciplines. In the organized sector, competitive sport is the main characteristic of the activity, and systematic training is utilized. The basic values are success and achievement in relation to fixed international standards, although sport federations have initiated various projects to encourage balance in coaching strategies by stressing the value of fun and participation. But do these values correspond to the official aims of physical education in schools? And, if so, should they?

TABLE 5. 1

Most Popular Sport And Leisure Time Activities For 9-12 Year Olds
In Denmark (Multiple Responses Were Recorded)

Sport	%	Sport	%
Soccer	35	Badminton	15
Swimming	29	Table Tennis	10
Cycling	27	Horseback Riding	9
Handball	20	Track and Field	5
Gymnastics	19	Other Ball Games	15

TABLE 5. 2

Five Most Frequent Physical Leisure Time Activities At The Age Of
15 Years In Sweden (Multiple Responses Were Recorded)

Girls	%	Boys	%
Walking	37	Cycling	38
Cycling	34	Soccer	25
Jogging	16	Walking	22
Gymnastics	14	Jogging	17
Jazz-dancing	13	Strength Training	12

TABLE 5. 3

Ten Most Popular Club Sports For 9-12 Year Olds
In Denmark

1. Soccer	31%	6. Rifle Shooting	3%
2. Handball	16%	7. Table Tennis	2%
3. Gymnastics	16%	8. Horseback Riding	1%
4. Swimming	10%	9. Track and Field	1%
5. Badminton	7%	10. Tennis	1%

TABLE 5.4

Most Popular Club Sports Among 10-12 Year Olds In Sweden

Girls	%	Boys	%
Soccer	26	Soccer	45
Riding	13	Ice Hockey	17
Gymnastics	13	Swimming	8
Dance, ballet, etc.	8	Tennis	7
Swimming	4	Golf	5
Track and Field	4		

PHYSICAL EDUCATION IN THE SCHOOLS

Physical education is a required subject in both primary school (ages 6-16) and secondary or grammar school (ages 16-19). On average, students have two physical education classes a week. In the middle years at primary school, an additional physical education class is devoted to aquatic skills. In their last years at primary school, students can elect to take extra physical education classes. The objectives of physical education in the primary schools are to motivate students to become physically active and to promote physical, psychological, and social development.

In grammar school, students can choose advanced physical education courses in addition to the required classes. These advanced courses meet an additional four times a week and culminate with a final examination designed to assess both practical and theoretical elements.

ATTITUDES TOWARD PHYSICAL EDUCATION

Due to the prominent position of voluntary sport in Danish culture, school physical education programs have been strongly influenced by the traditions and coaching methods of the various sport organizations. Generally, Danish standards and attitudes toward sport are derived from experiences in leisuretime activities. The high level of involvement in youth sport clubs, therefore, challenges physical education programs to maintain the quality educational and didactical aims inherent in the subject matter. The fruitless struggle of some educators against competition and sport games loses strength if the values and dynamics of team sports are viewed as a vehicle for a new direction toward a cooperative effort between physical education programs and sports clubs.

THE TACTICAL APPROACH TO TEACHING TEAM GAMES

The most popular leisure time activities for both boys and girls in Sweden, as Table 5.5 shows (Holstein et al., 1991), are team oriented.

Some physical education curriculums are also comprised primarily of ball game activities. What are the educational arguments for the inclusion of ball games, and how do they correspond with the prevalence of the games during leisure time? The teacher's goals for team games are, first, to teach the basic skills involved in various games with a focus on developing lifetime participation commitments to those sport activities and, second, to stimulate the student's physical, social, and neuromuscular development. In reality, most teachers concentrate on the specific techniques of the various games and rarely reflect on the game as a means to achieve pedagogical aspirations. The teachers use an instrumental approach to teaching ball games, with their lessons mirroring the organizational style of the sport clubs. This style is widely accepted by the students and meets their expectations of physical education classes.

TABLE 5.5

Popularity Of Three Types Of Sports In Sport Clubs
Among 10-12 Year Olds In Sweden

Sports	Girls %	Boys %
Team Sports	27	47
Individual Sports	24	39
Non-competitive Sports	29	3

TEACHING FOR UNDERSTANDING

This traditional approach is slowly being replaced by a new mode of thinking centered around a concept-based curriculum. The primary focus of this approach is based on the concept of Teaching for Understanding (TU). This concept has been discussed recently in both Europe (Thorpe and Bunker, 1989) and America (Doolittle and Girard, 1991). In Denmark we use a different approach to implement Teaching for Understanding, although the basic idea and concept stressed by Thorpe remains intact. The approach concentrates on the underlying principles of the tactical factors and emphasizes a much broader and more meaningful education through ball games. The analysis of the tactical factors that team games have in common serves as the foundation for factual and declarative knowledge. In physical education, teachers are expected to have both a factual and declarative knowledge about movement, sport, and exercise, as well as the procedural methods necessary to communicate that knowledge to learners. Declarative knowledge represents the theoretical or foundational knowledge of a discipline frequently represented as content. An understanding of the relationship between the tactical elements and game structure leads to carefully planned educational sequences believed to make a significant contribution to the quality of the learning experience. Knowledge acquired under these guidelines is thus stored and is usable when particular nodes are activated. Recall of information depends on its structural organization within the network. The challenge is not just the design and maintenance of strong knowledge foundations, but also the development of structures that facilitate the addition of increasingly more complex knowledge also associated with expert teaching (Ennis et al., 1991).

This approach also encourages a wider integration and coordination between various disciplines. Therefore, socio-psychological aspects are viewed in a more practical setting, bringing a new educational dimension into a more formal framework for the teaching/learning of team games. With this in mind, the ball game context now suggests that students and teachers should bring their basic knowledge and experiences in tactical matters to the most popular games, especially basketball, handball, and soccer. In addition, this approach has a specific and dynamic function in building a bridge to the athletic field. The students instructed through this approach are equipped with a more diversified play competency (playing ability) and are able to make tactical game-oriented decisions and then incorporate their techniques and tactical knowledge in the game context, both individually and as part of a team. The greater playing ability of the students facilitates the addition of increasingly complex tactical game knowledge as well as other relevant components of team games. Simply put, the introductory learning aspects are shifted from "learning a game" toward "learning how to play."

THE DIDACTICAL MODEL

Figure 5.1 shows what our didactical model looks like. Our approach stresses the tactical aspects of ball games. Observation of tactical skills illustrates the individual actions of the player as well as the team as a whole when viewed in games situations in relation to (1) the fundamental idea of the game, (2) the development of the game, and (3) the objectives agreed upon before starting the game.

The tactical aspects in ball games can be interpreted mainly as movement solutions. Specifically, the students must first perceive the situation, then make a judgment; a decision is then made, and an action is eventually taken. The quality of the movement response in a game is analyzed using a method inspired by Laban's (1971) principles of movement. During the introductory phase, the analysis is primarily restricted to the concepts of time, space, force, and relationships.

Methodology

The teaching units are guided by an integrated model based on a sequential organization of open-ended game situations with variable requirements. Permanent groups of six operate as the essential vehicle for building group confidence as well as developing a sense of awareness for a wide range of possible solutions (see Figure 5.2).

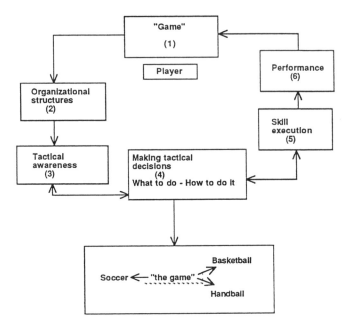

FIGURE 5.1: The Didactical Model

Methodology

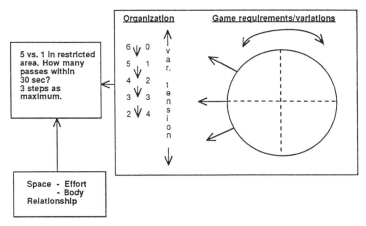

FIGURE 5.2: The Analytical Game Model: Example Game

What Is a Good Game?

When students learn to develop their own game, they transform it by adjusting the various game components. The component wheel depicted in Figure 5.3 is an essential tool for the players to use in their efforts to balance the challenges of the game and their skills.

By introducing this tool to the students, the teacher entrusts them with the responsibility for their own personal enjoyment. Initially the teacher guides the students' development, but the long-range goal is for the students themselves to assume this cognitive function. The "flow" experience is the ultimate reward (Csikszentmihalyi, 1988). This is the holistic sensation that occurs when players perceive the challenges (action opportunities) presented in a game as matching their skill level (action capabilities).

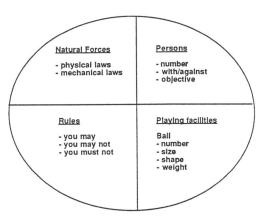

FIGURE 5.3: Game Components

A Brief Outline of the Stages of the Approach

As depicted in Figure 5.1, the model has two phases. The first phase is characterized by a more general perspective and requires a tactically dominated instructional strategy applied to games of a non-specific nature. During the second phase, the fundamental tactics are applied to major sport games (soccer, basketball, volleyball and handball). With reference to the game model (Figure 5.2), an example of the first phase will briefly be described.

The quality of passing in a game is considered a tactical theme. Critical to a beginner's understanding of the dimensions of accurate passing are proper speed, proper timing, and the proper positioning of feet, hands, or space. Starting with a very simple 6-on-0 task, the basic qualities of passing are discussed. The 6-on-0 situation is varied in different ways in order to give players experiences with a variety of objects (light or heavy balls, small or large balls, or even other throwing objects such as frisbees). The discussions are guided by the concepts of space, time, and force. The group then works to develop its own manner of interpreting the optimal conditions for a cooperative passing relationship.

For all the 6-on-0 games there is one common goal: to establish a smooth passing game within the group.

a. One ball is thrown caught between players. The ball must not touch the ground. How will you create a well-coordinated passing pattern when at least one player must move? Introduce various conditions.
b. Like the above activity, the group scores one point when the player receives the ball and touches a cone with it, without moving more than one step. All players move around. Four or five cones are spread in the game area. How many points can be made in 30 seconds?

From this stage the group moves to a 5-on-1 situation and implements their new tactical passing skills in a different game context. The intent is for the group to discover how the changing game context will affect their skills (how one opponent affects the passing patterns). The group discusses their expectations and writes them down before they try out any new strategies; they fully explore a range of possibilities based on their past experiences and draw conclusions as a group. The 5-on-1 situation offers the opportunity for other tactical concepts to be introduced, such as width and depth.

The presence of one opponent puts foward new tactical challenges.

a. Starting behind one goal line, the group must pass the ball to the other goal line. All players must have touched the ball. A three-step rule applies.
b. "Crossing Wall Street": Two groups, A and B, start behind their own goal line. Group A must pick up their ball from Group B's half of the field, and vice versa. After picking up the ball, the group passes the ball back to their own goal line. Who gets back first? All group members must be on the opponent's half of the field when the ball is picked up. The player who picks up the ball must pass immediately to a teammate and then stay on the opponent's half of the field, trying to prevent the opponent from catching their ball.

When using this approach, technical skill training can always be part of the lesson, but the guiding thread is always the identified tactical challenge. The progressive challenges that are evident in the transition from 6-on-0 through 5-on-1, 4-on-2, 3-on-3, and 2-on-4 dictate the direction of the lesson, but at various stages the nonspecific games (teacher-inspired or student-made) are replaced by periods of the major traditional ball games. This allows the students to make a direct link between the general tactical experiences and the more specific game tactics.

CONCLUSION

The Danish approach uses the symbolic interactionist perspective as the guiding didactical orientation. The perceived role of games in Danish schools is threefold: to experience an enjoyable activity, to develop competence in playing the specific game, and to promote the development of the "whole" child. This approach also encourages a much broader understanding and appreciation of ball games as both a player and, later on, as a spectator. The underlying dimensions of "fun" and "enjoyment" should be highlighted in each lesson, and become the crucial ingredient that helps the player understand his or her abilities in sport. Examples of these outcomes include application of knowledge, perceived choice, feelings of competence, and stimulation of support. An additional key element in the approach is the development of a common language for game analysis.

The concepts used to analyze games (time-space-force-relationship) serve as the immediate medium for bridging the two separate areas of games in the schools and games in local sport clubs. Coaches at the club sport level and many of the junior club players normally measure the quality of play in terms of motor skill performance. Rarely during coaching sessions are there sophisticated exchanges between coaches and players dealing with tactical matters. This shift in focus has led to the inclusion of tactical skills in coach-player dialogue. In addition, inexperienced players (those with only school experiences) are able to achieve greater success in club sport performances. At the same time, experienced club players become highly motivated in school lessons when they find that their personal resources are relevant and that they are being utilized in a new and exciting manner. Clearly, the Teaching for Understanding approach in this Danish variation breaks down the barriers between school physical education programs and the popular leisure time activities of sport clubs.

REFERENCES

Csikszentmihalyi, M., ed. (1988). *Optimal Experience*. Cambridge, U.K.: Cambridge University Press.

Danish Sports Federation. (1991). "Sport Towards Year 2000." Copenhagen: Danish Sports Federation.

Doolittle, S., and K. A. Girard (1991). A Dynamic Approach to Teaching Games in Elementary Physical Education. *Journal of Physical Education, Recreation and Dance* 62(4), 57-62. April.

Engstrom, L. M. (1990). Sport Activities Among Young People in Sweden. In *Physical Education and Life-long Physical Activity*. R. Telema, ed. Finland: University of Jyvaskyla.

Ennis, C., et al. (1991). Description of Knowledge Structures Within a Concept-Based Curriculum Framework," *Research Quarterly for Exercise and Sport* 62(3).

Forchhammer, I., et al. (1980). *The Children of Culture*. Copenhagen: Ministry of Culture.

Holstein, B., et al. (1991). Health and Social Conditions Among 11 to 15 Year Olds. Copenhagen Institute of Social Medicine, University of Copenhagen.

Laban, R. (1971). *The Mastery of Movement*. 3rd ed. London: Macdonald and Evans.

Peitersen, B., and H. Ronholt (1983). A Model For the Teaching of Games in Secondary Schools. In L. Spackman, ed., *Teaching Games for Understanding*. Cheltenham: College of St. Paul and St. Mary.

Thorpe, R., and D. Bunker (1989). A Changing Focus in Games Teaching. In L. Almond, ed., *The Place of Physical Education in Schools*. London: Kogan Page, 42-71.

6

Using Critical Thinking to Teach Sport Skills

Susan M. Schwager

The importance of critical thinking in education and the fostering of higher order thinking skills in children has received much attention in the education community. Definitions of critical thinking abound in the literature, and there are differences of opinion among scholars as to precisely what is meant by the term "critical thinking" (see McBride, 1991). Robert Ennis defines critical thinking as "reasonable, reflective thinking that is focused on deciding what to believe or do" (Ennis, 1987). Lipman's definition regards critical thinking as reflective thinking that is "sensitive to context, self correcting and reliant on criteria" (Lipman 1991, p. 3).

If one accepts these definitions of critical thinking, then many of the activities physical educators already teach encourage critical thinking in a variety of ways. In the context of what we know about skill learning, children are constantly reflecting on their attempts to perform a skill or play a game, and making decisions about subsequent actions (Schwager, 1991). In elementary physical education programs, I believe a conscious focus on teaching for critical thinking can be helpful in teaching sports and games skills as well as strategies to children. As children practice and acquire motor skills, they quite naturally engage in thinking processes that help them figure out what has to be done in order to be successful at performing the skills attempted. By encouraging children to focus on their thinking as they practice skills, teachers can facilitate the skill acquisition process. Here I offer a way of presenting skills that will encourage children to think about what they are doing, and some practical suggestions for how this emphasis on critical thinking for teaching sport and game skills might be implemented.

APPROACH

In general, I am suggesting that as we teach sports and games to children, we encourage our students to focus on their thinking processes in addition to the outcomes of their skill performance attempts. The teacher's role would be defined as follows:

Determine the goal (desired outcome) of the skill and communicate this clearly to the performers. Traditionally we have done this by explaining and demonstrating the skill. To encourage students to think about the skill, the teacher can identify the kinds of decisions that must be made for the skill to be performed successfully and ask students to think about how they will make those decisions.

Structure the environment to encourage goal attainment. Before a teacher can set up a practice situation that will be most helpful to children who are learning a skill, he or she should decide to what extent the skill is open or closed. The classification of skills as "open" or "closed" has to do with the factors in the environment relevant to goal attainment, and the relative predictability of these factors. There are theories of skill learning that emphasize the importance of the environment in which a skill is performed in determining the requirements for successful performance (see Schwager, 1991; Arnold, 1981). For example, if a child is throwing a ball to another child, it is important for the thrower to know if the receiver is standing still or moving. In addition, it is also important to know if there are other children (teammates and/or opponents) present to which the thrower must attend. If understanding the environment is necessary for goal attainment, then it is helpful for the learner to know the environmental constraints within which he or she must move. The teacher can help children here by verbally identifying those factors in the environment to which the students must attend, and asking the students questions about how they think the environmental conditions would affect their skill attempts. For example, when teaching throwing or catching skills to children, we usually have students throw at a stationary target or to a partner who is standing still before they attempt to throw to someone who is moving. Throwing to a stationary target would be an example of a closed skill, while throwing to a partner who is moving would be considered an open one. While the performer must make decisions regarding the force and direction of the throw for the closed skill, the timing of the throw is not crucial to successful performance since the target is not moving. In the open skill, however, the thrower must also decide when to release the ball, with the realization that the target is not where the catcher is at the moment the ball is thrown, but where the catcher will be when the ball reaches its destination. When the catcher is stationary, the teacher's questions would be aimed at getting the thrower to decide where the ball must be thrown. However, when the receiver is moving, the teacher can help the thrower think about where the ball must go and when it must get there for the throw to be successful.

Initially, structuring the environment appropriately may mean simplifying the practice conditions so that the performers can determine what has to be done. As children become more proficient, the environment should be structured to match, as nearly as possible, the conditions under which the skill is to be performed in a game setting. For example, we usually give children the opportunity to practice throwing and catching with stationary partners, before we have them throw and catch on the move.

Provide the learner with instruction and feedback. Children need information about the skill to be learned as well as feedback regarding their performance and the environment in which the skill is performed. The feedback should include statements of relevant information as well as questions to encourage the performer to focus on his or her practice attempts. For example, as children practice throwing and catching in pairs, the teacher may say, "Notice how far away from you your partner is. How much force do you think you will need to throw the ball so that your partner can catch it?"

A variety of teaching styles can be employed to teach sport or game skills in a way that encourages children to think. It should be recognized that even the traditional approach of explanation, demonstration, and teacher-directed group practice will require that students think critically about what it is they are doing. As mentioned earlier, theories of motor learning suggest that performers attempting motor skills naturally engage in problem solving and decision-making activities as skills are practiced. However, by utilizing alternative styles selectively, teachers can encourage children to think about their performance in a way that will enhance skill acquisition. Mosston's spectrum of teaching styles provide several alternatives to the traditional approach that can be very useful to the physical education teacher interested in encouraging his or her students to think critically about skills and game performance (Mosston and Ashworth, 1990).

SPECIFIC EXAMPLES

To illustrate how a teacher could encourage children to think critically about skills they are learning, I will outline a series of questions that would be appropriate for teaching throwing to children at two different proficiency levels.

Initially, provide different sized balls for children to throw, and provide different types of movement challenges (How far can you throw? Can you throw the ball against the wall so that it comes right back to you? Can you throw the ball into the basket? Through the hoop?). As children attempt to throw in different situations, ask them questions related to the force and direction of the throw to help them think about the kinds of decisions they have to make (What should you do to throw the ball far? What should you do when throwing at a target? What do you do if the ball does not hit the target?). When children can throw and catch successfully in closed settings using stationary partners, they can attempt throwing and catching on the move. In this situation, the questions would encourage the children to think about the timing of the throw, in addition to force and direction. For example, when you throw to a partner who is moving, how do you know when to release the ball? Where should you aim? How hard should you throw? What do you change about your throw if you are unsuccessful?

Skill learning is enhanced when children are encouraged to think critically about what they need to do to be successful. The teacher can facilitate skill learning by encouraging children to think about their performance, and make conscious decisions about how to change their performance to improve it. To provide this encouragement, the teacher can structure the activities to allow students to experiment with different ideas, and ask questions to get the children to think about the essential elements of the skill being practiced.

REFERENCES

Arnold, R. K. S. (1981). Developing Sport Skills: A Dynamic Interplay of Task, Learner and Teacher. *Motor Skills: Theory into Practice Monograph*. Newton, Conn.

Ennis, R. (1987). A Taxonomy of Critical Thinking Dispositions and Abilities. In J. Baron and R. Sternberg, eds., *Teaching Thinking Skills: Theory and Practice*. New York: W. H. Freeman.

Lipman, M. (1991). *Thinking in Education*. New York: Cambridge University Press.

McBride, R. (1991). Critical Thinking—An Overview with Implication for Physical Education. *Journal of Teaching in Physical Education*, 11, 112-25.

Mosston, M., and S. Ashworth (1990). *The Spectrum of Teaching Styles—From Command to Discovery*. New York: Longman.

Schwager, S. (1991). Thinking about Thinking in Physical Education. *Inquiry: Critical Thinking Across the Disciplines*, 8(2), 12-13.

7

The FIT SPORT Model
in Physical Education: The Premise,
the Promise, the Pay-Off

Gary T. Barrette and Leah Holland Fiorentino

Sport and sport-related activities comprise a large portion of the content of elementary and middle school physical education programs. These sport activities can be observed as early as the second or third grade as sport lead-up activities (as in a lead-up to volleyball, basketball, and soccer), and they bear witness to the traditionally close link between sport and physical education. Criticism over the last few decades has centered on the appropriate use of sport activities as vehicles to reach the objectives of physical education, especially for younger children and adolescents. Consequently, a number of alternative approaches to reconceptualizing the nature and substance of physical education curricula for these students have been suggested and explored. Proponents of these approaches, generally known under the rubric of movement exploration, have challenged physical education to broaden or reshape the structure, content, and process of traditional sport-based physical education programs. The alternatives they propose are focused at the apparent problems of sport-driven programs. These include excessive competition, exclusionary policies, gender segregation, biased teacher expectations, and stereotyping, which are viewed as inappropriate educational practices within school physical education. Their call has indeed had a strong impact on some physical education programs both here and abroad and has contributed to initiatives directed at curricular reform.

However, it also seems apparent that the inclusion of sport or sport-related activities in the curriculum is not the only problem faced in physical education programs. The nature of the instructional approach used by teachers has also detracted from the ability of sport-related programs to meet the physical education objectives for all students. More specifically, the instructional strategies employed by teachers (how teachers think about their roles and responsibilities and how they act) are incompatible with both the purposes of their programs and the principles and precepts of teaching and learning which have been part of their own professional training.

For example, dividing a class of forty students into four teams of ten and playing two cross-court basketball games in grade seven, with twenty students "participating" and twenty students "watching," excludes one-half of the class from meaningful activity. In addition, if the final score of the game is an important goal (which is a critical element in the sport competition physical education model), then the teacher can be assured that the best players will dribble, shoot, and control the distribution of the ball in a very selective manner, avoiding the inclusion of the less skilled. Therefore, the rich get richer and the poor get poorer, an all too familiar and continuing scenario in which teachers fail to construct and achieve personalized sport learning opportunities for all students.

THE PREMISE

What appears to be an irreconcilable dilemma between the objectives of physical education programs and the nature and structure of sport is reconcilable. We can have our sport and physical education, too. To do so, we must make a commitment to help students achieve sport education objectives that are in harmony with the objectives of physical education, as well as designing strategies and employing tactics that ensure their compatibility. The goal is to make sport a more appropriate part of our programs, with special concern for personalizing sport instruction by employing an integrative pedagogical strategy. The remaining portion of this chapter outlines important features of the FIT SPORT Model (Barrette, 1988) for curriculum and instruction.

THE PROMISE

The FIT SPORT Model is defined as a conceptually integrated decision-making and pedagogical action model designed to more realistically link curricular intent with teaching plans and actions. The overriding purpose of this model is to help *all* students achieve comprehensive, relevant, and appropriate educational objectives within that portion of the general physical education program devoted to sport education. This model in essence is a "promissory note," or a promise to deliver a positive personalized learning experience for all students within the context of sport education. The model is based on four critical assumptions (see Table 7.1). These assumptions, taken together, provide a powerful philosophical perspective that cuts across learning domains. In addition, they draw on the application of scientific principles of teaching and learning, and on a humanistic educational view which is grounded in both personal achievement and mutual respect.

The general criteria comprising the FIT SPORT Model are designed to help teachers focus on four critical pedagogical goals which, when achieved, effectively link curricular intent with responsible teaching actions (see Table 7.2).

TABLE 7. 1

Assumptions For Applying FIT SPORT Model In Sport Education

1. Student motivation in the practice of sport skills, concepts, and strategies can be greatly enhanced if students perceive that their practice efforts can be successfully integrated into sport play and game experiences.

2. Teachers can be encouraged to employ instructional strategies which maximize personalized instruction and minimize cohort instruction.

3. Integrated instructional strategies which optimize the concurrent achievement of physical education objectives for students are desirable and attainable in sport teaching.

4. Students can be amenable to modification in sport activities within the physical education context that are relevant and contribute to their own development and to the development of their peers.

TABLE 7. 2

FIT SPORT Model Criteria

1. High motor engagement time for each student directed at maximizing student opportunities to respond within sport play contexts.

2. Task relevancy for each student directed at high success rates in all learning domains.

3. Provisions for fitness activity related to the sport activity when lack of equipment, facilities, safety factors, and nature of the activity require such provisions.

4. Balance between cooperative and competitive sport play interaction.

THE PAY-OFF—AN EXEMPLAR

The FIT SPORT Model applied to sport modifications as exemplified in aerobic softball or aerobic kickball at the elementary level (see Figure 7.1) is not simply based on rule and equipment changes, which have traditionally been employed by teachers to provide diversity in activity routines for students; that is, changes that are essentially cosmetic, idiosyncratic, and not necessarily linked to meeting the objectives of physical education. On the contrary, the FIT SPORT Model is responsive to sport education instruction strategies directed at achieving physical education program objectives.

**Sport/Game Activity Modification
To Meet Physical Education Objectives**

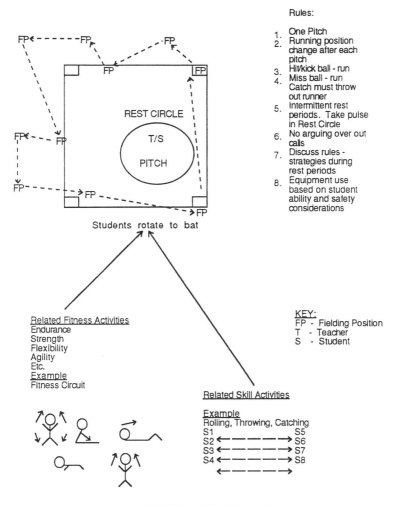

Rules:

1. One Pitch
2. Running position change after each pitch
3. Hit/kick ball - run
4. Miss ball - run Catch must throw out runner
5. Intermittent rest periods. Take pulse in Rest Circle
6. No arguing over out calls
7. Discuss rules - strategies during rest periods
8. Equipment use based on student ability and safety considerations

Students rotate to bat

Related Fitness Activities
Endurance
Strength
Flexibility
Agility
Etc.
Example
Fitness Circuit

KEY:
FP - Fielding Position
T - Teacher
S - Student

Related Skill Activities

Example
Rolling, Throwing, Catching

S1	S5
S2 ← — — — →	S6
S3 ← — — — →	S7
S4 ← — — — →	S8
← — — — →	

FIGURE 7.1: FIT SPORT Model

In this case, the instructional design maximizes the opportunity for all students to:

1. a) engage in more numerous skill performance opportunities and responses indigenous to the game of softball/kickball (running, fielding, swinging, kicking, and so forth);
   b) experience a greater array of rule, strategy, and situation applications naturally arising as a result of the increased and continuous flow of the game;
2. be appropriately challenged in skill through the teacher's employment of differing equipment (e.g., less lively and more lively balls, differing bats, and so forth) and

differing challenges (hitting to certain fields, running sideways, hopping, bounding, and so forth);

3. engage in a team sport activity in the context of an elevated aerobic level when students are continuously moving;

4. experience increased levels of positive teacher feedback, success, and positive experience under conditions of balanced cooperative and competitive play (i.e., a premium is placed on active participation, improvement, and accepting others' limitations rather than on winning the game. The focus is on the process of the game as a significant experience, while the outcome retains a natural unhyped status in the context of the larger experiences).

Similarly, a game we call challenge basketball can be used to meet more personalized and variable needs of students as they attempt to apply skills in a game. This is accomplished by the teacher assigning specific challenges to each player within the game format. For example, more talented players can be challenged to play defense without breaking the frontal plane of their body with their hands, dribble with their nondominant hand, and/or shoot from a minimal distance. Such limitations require these players to perform under more demanding and difficult conditions, thus challenging them to raise their level of play. Less talented players are given fewer restrictions (or none at all), which allows them to functionally participate in the game without being overwhelmed or intimidated by better players. This results in a more equitable personalized learning experience for each player within the context of a team sport. Players representing a wide range of ability levels are able to play together, and against each other, within a context appropriate and relevant to their developmental levels. Games constructed along these lines are (1) more flowing (allowing for a better feel for the nature and pace of the game); (2) more aerobic (less interruptions of play); (3) providing more skill attempts, thus giving the teacher the opportunity to provide more frequent feedback about skills and concepts (strategies); and (4) encouraging cooperative behavior among players (by playing within their specific challenge), which makes the game relevant, productive, and fun for all. Table 7.3 summarizes the application process.

The FIT SPORT Model design is not intended as an exclusive strategy and may be integrated with other instructional designs directed at other appropriate objectives (e.g., ability group designs for competition, skill practice designs, and/or combinations of instructional designs) that may be legitimate outcomes of the physical education program.

However, the FIT SPORT Model does emphasize the responsibility of the teacher to orchestrate those student learning experiences related to sport instruction that genuinely fulfill the learning needs in each learning domain for *all* students, as opposed to the few. It is the teacher's responsibility to transform sport in ways that benefit all students in physical education classes. The process of shifting to this model requires an orientation for students (explaining *why* and *how* to students) and time to adjust to the new format. It is advisable to approach the model slowly but steadily to increase the ease of implementation.

TABLE 7. 3

Additional Challenges And Guidelines For Challenge Basketball

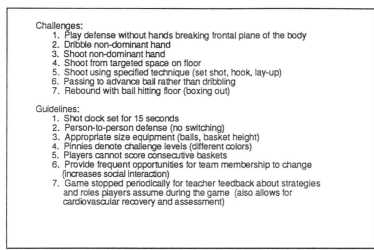

Challenges:
1. Play defense without hands breaking frontal plane of the body
2. Dribble non-dominant hand
3. Shoot non-dominant hand
4. Shoot from targeted space on floor
5. Shoot using specified technique (set shot, hook, lay-up)
6. Passing to advance ball rather than dribbling
7. Rebound with ball hitting floor (boxing out)

Guidelines:
1. Shot clock set for 15 seconds
2. Person-to-person defense (no switching)
3. Appropriate size equipment (balls, basket height)
4. Pinnies denote challenge levels (different colors)
5. Players cannot score consecutive baskets
6. Provide frequent opportunities for team membership to change (increases social interaction)
7. Game stopped periodically for teacher feedback about strategies and roles players assume during the game (also allows for cardiovascular recovery and assessment)

Finally, the FIT SPORT Model's application for other sport activity modifications (e.g., basketball, soccer, volleyball, and team handball) is equally achievable. What is required is an acceptance and belief in the FIT SPORT Model assumptions, an understanding of the criteria for teacher planning and action, an insight into the nature of the sport (its skills, concepts, and strategies), an accurate analysis of each student's needs, abilities, and potential, and finally, a commitment to thoughtful and deliberate teaching action. Try it; you'll like it and so will your students.

REFERENCES

Barrette, G. T. (1988). Collaboration for Instructional Improvement: A Strategic Sport/Movement Pedagogy Initiative. In *Humanisano y Neuvas Technologias en la Educacion Fisica y el Deporte*, J. Duran, J. L Hernandez, and L. M. Ruiz, eds. Proceedings of the AIESEP World Congress, Instituto Nacional de Educacion Fisica, Madrid, Spain, 165-69.

——— (1989). The Main(e) Physical Education Message: The Search for Professional Identity and Professional Practice. *The Easterner*, 13(1), 9-11.

National Association of Sport and Physical Education (1987). Position paper. American Alliance for Health, Physical Education, Recreation, and Dance, Reston, Virginia.

8

Games Assessment Instrument for Developmentally Appropriate Play

Suzanne Mueller

This chapter describes the Games Assessment Instrument for Developmentally Appropriate Play, which can be used by elementary physical education teachers to predetermine the developmental appropriateness of games for their students. The instrument encourages teachers to examine the performance demands as well as the inclusive and prosocial nature of the games they choose by examining six criteria: Does the game meet the stated purposes, match student abilities, and preserve self-esteem? Does it provide for maximum participation, prosocial behavior, and positive rewards?

Many physical education teachers use games from a large variety of elementary physical education games books to enhance skill development, lead up to a sport, improve cooperation, and develop fitness. They select the games at face value, assuming that the experience will be educationally sound. However, unless teachers examine games closely, they can make poor choices, resulting in conditions such as minimal student participation with the skills of the game, elimination of students based on skill failure, improper use of skills in a lead-up game for the context of the targeted sport, or promoting the value structure that "might makes right."

The Games Assessment Instrument instructs teachers to answer yes or no to each of six questions and invites them to make changes in the game by addressing the factor(s) that are developmentally appropriate (see Figure 8.1). A description and rationale for each of the six Games Assessment Instrument factors follows.

1. Do the Performance Demands of the Game Match Student Skill, Knowledge, and Social Abilities?

Can students consistently perform the mechanics of the game skills in dynamic skill situations or drills? Have they demonstrated the ability to use offensive skills cooperatively and defensive skills competitively? Have they experienced practical situations that have helped them learn how to use game strategies so that they can "play wisely?" For instance, have they demonstrated the ability to look for the open space and move or send a ball through it? Have they practiced keeping their bodies between the defense and the ball they are dribbling? Have they been able to make and carry out simple offensive strategies with peers? (For more information, see Nichols, 1990, Chapters 22 and 23.)

YES	NO	DOES THE GAME . . .	CHANGES
		1. MATCH STUDENT ABILITY? (Game performance demands match students' motor skills, concept development, and social interaction levels.)	
		2. PROVIDE MAXIMUM PARTICIPATION? (Frequent engagement in all skills by all children.)	
		3. PRESERVE SELF-ESTEEM? (Game is structured to promote success, and is free of elimination and punishment for skill failure.)	
		4. PROVIDE PROSOCIAL BEHAVIOR? (Game encourages mutual respect, fair play, cooperation, teamwork, and sportslike conduct.)	
		5. PROVIDE POSITIVE REWARDS? (If score is kept, points and advantages are awarded for skill success and prosocial behavior.)	
		6. MEET STATED PURPOSES? (Game uses the skills, develops the attributes, or leads up to the designated sport.)	

FIGURE 8.1: Games Assessment Instrument For
Developmentally Appropriate Play

Of course, to these questions you may reply, "Yes, *some* of the students can. What about those who are less capable?"

For all of us, mixed ability groups are the norm rather than the exception in physical education classes. Two common responses to mixed ability groups have been making up teams that are balanced with a cross section of less to more skilled students, or making homogeneous groups with same-skilled students competing against one another. Each response has its liabilities. In the first we set up the more skilled students for taking over the game and put less able students at risk for failure and the accompanying peer put-downs. In the second we segregate students and set them up for the rich getting richer and the poor, at best, remaining the same.

Another way of approaching mixed ability classes is to equalize groups by adjusting the demands of the game to meet individual needs. This could take the form of students choosing equipment appropriate to their size, strength, or ability (e.g., type of striking implement and object). It could mean adjusting the scoring system (handicapping) so that students are equitably challenged. It could also mean adjusting the way skills are used to provide developmentally appropriate challenges (e.g., some students are guarded, others are not; some may contact the ball twice, others once). All these adjustments reflect the idea that it is more educationally sound to adjust the game to match the children than to hold the game structure inviolate and sacrifice the children. This approach also assumes that the teacher values developmentally appropriate challenges for all in an environment that celebrates inclusion and acceptance.

When game performance demands are matched to student abilities, there is a much greater likelihood that the game will provide for skill refinement and be a positive rather than a frustrating experience for participants. Additionally, when students are feeling competent and experiencing success, they are more likely to demonstrate prosocial behavior.

2. Does the Game Provide for Maximum Participation?

Is it possible for all students for whom the game is intended to engage frequently in all game skills? Examine the game to determine if there are a few key positions (roles) that will most likely be active throughout the playing period, and other positions (roles) that will be inactive for long periods of time. If our goal in the instructional physical education program is to provide maximum use of skills by all students, then teachers must select games that provide for it.

There are a few situations in game descriptions that signal a potential setup for minimum participation by many in the class. One such setup is to divide the class in half. This usually means that few children get maximum skill participation time. In many games it is best to keep the number of individuals within each group small (i.e., two to five students) and add rules that require each person on the team to kick, strike, catch, or throw before a goal can be scored, or award points each time the desired skill or strategy is appropriately executed.

Another setup for minimal participation is having one team at a time up to bat (kick, etc.). Kickball, baseball, and softball are minimum participation activities for all students waiting for a turn to kick or bat. Additionally, most students in the field seldom interact with the ball. Since we value the attainment of skill in these cultural games, we need to find ways to engage children in skill and gamelike situations without sacrificing our instructional goals, which require frequent use of skills. (For more information, see Graham, 1987.)

3. Does the Game Preserve Positive Self-Esteem?

How will children feel about themselves and their abilities while they are playing the game? Will satisfaction and joy be the predominant emotions because they are experiencing success and accomplishment? Part of the groundwork for children experiencing positive feelings will come from an accurate match of their abilities and the performance demands of the game (see Question 2).

However, the teacher must also look at the structure of the game to determine if there are built-in punishments for skill failure. Are children eliminated from the game if they fail to respond or move quickly enough or fail to outmaneuver someone in pursuit? Are children labeled with a name (or a series of letters that lead to a name) for inaccurate skill performance? Do we advocate "feeling like a victim" as an affective goal of the game playing portion of the curriculum?

If we examine the children who are the victims of these punishments, they are usually the ones who are less skilled. They do not need less time using the skills of the game (elimination), and certainly do not need the embarrassment of a negative label (e.g., P-I-G, as in a basketball shooting game). Teachers need to find ways to include students throughout the games they play, provide appropriate specific feedback to help them improve performance, and choose games that match their performance abilities.

4. Does the Game Provide for Prosocial Behavior?

How will children interact with each other during the game? Does the game encourage mutual respect, fair play, cooperation, teamwork, and sportslike conduct as players try to outmaneuver opponents or work together to achieve a common goal? Or does the game structure promote overpowering one's opponent, hitting opponents with objects, or preying on the less capable? The popular bombardment, war ball, and killer ball games are examples of the latter. Where is the redeeming social value in promoting the aggressive behavior that permeates these games? Is "might makes right" the affective goal to which we ascribe in the games portion of our curriculum? (For a complete analysis of killer ball, see Zakrajsek, 1986.)

An environment conducive to prosocial behavior is also free of mocking, name calling, and other forms of derision. Helpful, supportive behaviors of students toward each other need to be encouraged, praised, and modeled by the teacher. Likewise, the emphasis of game outcome needs to shift from "Who won or lost?" to "How did I improve?" and "Did the team work well together?"

Additionally, the teacher needs to encounter children's put-down behaviors with the purposes of helping them identify with the feelings of the victim and finding alternative, supportive ways to handle their disappointments.

5. Does the Game Provide Positive Rewards?

If scoring is used, are points awarded or are scoring advantages given for successful skill or strategy demonstrations? Examine the scoring system. Are points awarded for successful offensive maneuvers? Are advantages given for successful defensive strategies? Most scoring systems are based on these positive premises rather than on the negative practices of taking points away for skill failure or, as in circle kickball (Pangrazi and Dauer, 1992), giving points when errors are made so that skill failure is highlighted.

However, one additional step would be to ask if the scoring system rewards fair play. Harris et al. (1982), in an effort to make winning more dependent on ethical behavior, suggested that scoring systems be amended in two ways: (1) give more points to teams with fewer violations, and (2) penalize players who do not call their own violations by doubling the penalty. (Players who call their own violations before the official calls them would receive the standard penalty.) Perhaps if we focus our students' attention on playing within the rules of the game, we will promote the expectation that ethical considerations are as much a part of their participation as skills and strategies.

6. Does the Game Meet the Stated Purpose?

Does the game actually meet all the claims made by the author? Does it use the skills, develop the attributes, and serve as a modified activity to the sport for which it was intended? Look carefully at the consistency between the purposes and the claims. For instance, soccer dodgeball is labeled a lead-up game for soccer. Students on the outside of a large circle pass, trap, and kick a soccer ball to each other and across the inside of the circle with the intent of hitting a few players in the middle with the ball. Inside players attempt to avoid being hit. Although players on the outside of the circle are using the soccer skills of passing, trapping, and kicking, they are kicking toward players who are trying to avoid contact with the ball. How does this realistically transfer to the game? When in soccer do players react to the ball by moving away from it? And don't offensive players try to find open spaces through which to pass the ball to teammates who are tying to move into the open space and converge on the ball?

Recently, games have been promoted for the fitness benefits students will accrue. Examine these claims carefully by comparing the duration and intensity of the activity with the nature of the specific fitness component being promoted. For instance, if a cardiovascular endurance benefit is claimed, are game participants moving at an intensity equal to their exercise heart rate for a minimum of twenty minutes? If an agility benefit is claimed, are the students moving quickly with changes in direction in touch and go activities?

In closing, the Games Assessment Instrument for Developmentally Appropriate Play provides elementary physical education teachers with a means for predetermining the suitability of games for their classes. The instrument is based on providing a developmentally appropriate, inclusive, and prosocial game environment that will promote positive and rewarding game experiences for students.

REFERENCES

COPEC (1991). Developmentally Appropriate Physical Education. (Draft)

Eisenberg, Nancy, and Paul Mussen (1989). *The Roots of Pro-social Behavior in Children*. New York: Cambridge University Press.

Graham, George (1987). Motor Skill Acquisition: An Essential Goal of Physical Education Programs. *Journal of Physical Education, Recreation and Dance*, 58(7), 44-48.

Harris, Janet, Kimberly Blankenship, Marie Cawley, Ken Crouse, Michael Smith, and William Winfrey (1982). Ethical Behavior and Victory in Sport: Value Systems at Play. *Journal of Physical Education, Recreation and Dance*, 53(4), 37, 98-99.

Nichols, Beverly (1990). *Moving and Learning: The Elementary School Physical Education Experience*. 2nd ed. St. Louis: Times Mirror/Mosby College.

Pangrazi, Robert, and Victor Dauer (1992). *Dynamic Physical Education for Children*. 10th ed. New York: Macmillan.

Zakrajsek, Dorothy (1986). Premeditated Murder: Let's Bump Off Killer Ball. *Journal of Physical Education, Recreation and Dance*, 57(7), 49-51.

9

Teaching Kinesiology through Movement and Games

Svea Becker and Pat Huber

The following information provides teacher educators with a means by which their students can learn kinesiology through movement and games. To do so, the educator prepares and introduces a checklist of selected movement concepts. This checklist can be displayed on an overhead projector and verbally described while participants follow movement cues for predetermined activities, such as the starting position for sprinting in track, the jump shot in basketball, the overhand throw, punting a ball (see Figure 9.1), as well as performing the side tilt, hinge, and spiral fall from educational dance and gymnastics.

The next step involves defining concepts on the professional teaching level that underlie motor skill development. These selected concepts should include body parts, short and long lever; body part relationship; a conscious awareness of the body through bony landmarks and patterns of organizing posture and movement; movements of body parts in the planes of motion; and body shapes, based on anatomical structure and function.

Worksheets with procedures and checklists of movement concepts can be created to guide the student in the process of problem solving (see Figure 9.2) and can be used to apply these kinesiological and movement studies concepts to specific movements and games in future physical education classes. Understanding how and why the body moves through developmental activities during childhood should help to form a foundation from which practicing teachers may analyze more advanced sport and dance activities.

Name of Motor Skill Observed: <u>PUNTING A BALL</u>
Procedure for Solving the Problem
1. Getting the idea of the movement - observe the child practicing the skill
2. Observation of movement - practicing toward movement of impact
3. What to look for:
   a. Describe the body shape(s)
      __X__ Elongated_____Wide_____Round_____Twisted
   b. Identify the body parts and joints emphasized in the movements

        BODY PARTS/LEVER
        _____whole torso; long
        _____head
        _____chest
        _____pelvis
        _____whole leg(s); long
        _____upper leg __X__ lower __X__ foot
        _____whole arm(s); long
        _____upper arm _____lower arm _____hand

        JOINTS/LOWER
        __X__ hip joint
        __X__ knee joint
        __X__ ankle joint

        JOINTS/UPPER
        _____shoulder joint
        _____elbow joint
        _____wrist joint

   c. Analyze the major kinesiological actions that occur;
     identify the planes of motion
        __X__ flexion __X__ extension __X__ sagittal/wheel plane
        _____abduction __X__ adduction __X__ frontal/lateral/door plane
        _____horizontal flexion _____extension _____horizontal/traverse/table plane
        _____turn/twist right __X__ turn/twist left __X__ horizontal traverse/table plane
        __X__ combination of three planes/diagonal plane

   d. Explain the body part relationship
        _____head & tailbone _____upper & lower body
        _____right or left body half __X__ opposition (upper right quadrant & lower
                         left quadrant or visa versa)
4. Rate the movement concept that is most important for executing the movement correctly.
   DIAGONAL ACTION IN HIP JOINT

5. How would you present these movement concepts to children? Apply movement concepts
   that you have learned today to specific sports and dance skills in your physical education classes.

<u>TEACHING APPLICATIONS:</u>
<u>1. PRIMARY GRADES: EXPLORATION OF FORCE, B. NICHOLS, PP. 153-155.</u>
<u>2. FOR INTERMEDIATE GRADES: FOOTBALL GAME, PUNTBALL, B. NICHOLS, P.493.</u>

FIGURE 9.1: Checklist Of Movement Concepts Worksheet

Directions: Practice, copy, follow, mimic the movement along with the instructor

1. Observation of movement

2. What a teacher should look for

    a. What are the body shapes?

    b. What body parts, joints, and kinesiological actions are included?

    c. What are the body part relationships?

    d. In what plane does the movement occur?

3. Application of concepts

    How could you present these movement concepts to pupils? Apply the movement
    concepts you've learned today to specific sports, dance, and/or gymnastic skills in
    your physical education classes.

FIGURE 9.2: Getting The Idea Of Movement Worksheet

REFERENCES

Bartenieff, I. (1980). *Body Movement: Coping with the Environment*. New York:
    Gordon and Breash.

Graham, G., et al. (1986). *Children Moving*. Palo Alto, Calif.: Mayfield Press.

Laban, R. (1950). *The Mastery of Movement*. London: Macdonald and Evans.

Maletic, V. (1987). *Body—Space—Expression*. New York: Mouton de Gruyter.

Minton, S. C. (1989). *Body and Self: Partners in Movement*. Champaign, Ill.: Human
    Kinetics Books.

Nicholas, B. (1990). *Moving and Learning: The Elementary School Physical Education
    Experience*. St. Louis: Times Mirror/Mosby College.

Parker, S. (1989). *The Skeleton and Movement*. New York: Franklin Watts.

Piscopo, J., and J. A. Baley (1981). *Kinesiology: The Science of Movement*. New York:
    John Wiley and Sons.

Preston-Dunlop, V. (1980). *A Handbook for Modern Educational Dance*. Boston: Plays,
    Inc.

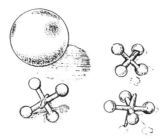

10

Liability and Games:
The Teacher's Responsibility

Carol L. Alberts

The purpose of this chapter is to provide the reader with the basic anatomy of a lawsuit, and to identify preventive measures and areas of vulnerability for teachers who supervise play, game, or sport activity on an informal or formal basis.

The legal system in our country provides opportunities for individuals to seek remuneration for "lack of ordinary care." Any individual who has a "duty," as it is legally defined, is vulnerable to a civil lawsuit if someone in his or her care is injured. The greater the degree of duty an individual has, the higher the standard of ordinary care legally required.

If a guest in someone's private home slips and falls on a broken step, for example, the owner can be sued for "negligence" or lack of ordinary care. Although the amount of care legally required for an adult guest in a home may be minimal, it is tenable that the owner could lose a lawsuit if an injury resulted from a preventable accident. The degree of legal duty that a teacher owes a student varies depending on the nature and circumstances of the relationship between the plaintiff (the party bringing the lawsuit) and the defendant (the party being sued). Any individual who organizes or supervises sport, play, or game activities in any capacity, from volunteer to paid professional, has a legal responsibility to exercise "reasonably prudent behavior." In general, the more formalized the relationship between the plaintiff and the defendant, the greater the duty is, and therefore the standard for what is considered reasonably prudent behavior is also higher.

For example, when a classroom teacher organizes an activity during recess and an injury occurs, the court's view assumes that the educator had a duty to provide reasonably prudent supervisory care. The precise nature of the supervisory care required would vary depending on a wide range of factors. A classroom teacher supervising students playing independently during recess may not have the same degree of duty as a physical education teacher who was conducting relay races up and down the monkey bars during recess. The area of certification of the teacher and the type of activity conducted are significant factors that are weighed by the courts. The courts will also take into consideration the age, size, and skill of the injured student relative to the nature of the activity being conducted. Generally, students younger than twelve years of age are not considered legally capable of responsibility for their own behavior as it relates to safety. High risk activities, or activities in which the risk of physical harm is inherently a part of the activity, often are required to have a higher degree of supervision than activities that are not considered high risk. For example, gymnastics, football, swimming, diving, and Project Adventure have all been considered high risk activities by the courts. In these cases, the courts have often scrutinized the credentials of teachers and supervisors for special training and certification to conduct these high risk activities. Classroom teachers who are not certified to teach physical education are particularly vulnerable to the court's scrutiny in this area. Even certified physical education teachers may need to demonstrate additional certifications or in-service training for specialized, high risk activities.

In addition to the qualifications of the supervisor and the age, size, and skill level of the participants, the courts have also examined whether the activity was voluntary, such as intramural, recreational, or interscholastic activities, or mandatory, such as an activity requirement for successful completion of a physical education class. Since in many states successful completion of physical education is a high school graduation requirement, mandated activities are usually more carefully examined by the courts. Under these circumstances, teachers may be required to justify the inclusion of the activity as a mandated activity for high school graduation. The courts have generally required teachers' supervisory duty to be highest when student nonparticipation or failure could result in the denial of a high school diploma.

In the event that the child's parents bring forth a lawsuit against this teacher, it is the court's responsibility to determine if the teacher was negligent in his or her supervisory care. The legal definition of negligence is given below, followed by a description of what the plaintiff must prove in order for an individual to be found legally liable, and therefore guilty of negligence.

ANATOMY OF A LAWSUIT

"Tort liability" is a breach of a legal duty (Gifis, 1975). It falls under the domain of civil law, which means that a guilty party is fined for damages rather than incarcerated, as would be the case in criminal law. The specific legal charge against a party whose breach of duty had resulted in an injury to another person is negligence. An expanded definition of *negligence* is failure to exercise that degree of care which a reasonably prudent person would have exercised under the same circumstances, or from failure to do an act which a reasonably prudent person would have done under the same circumstances (Gifis, 1975).

Burden of Proof

For a teacher to be found guilty of negligence, the injured party, the student, must prove that the teacher did not act as a reasonably prudent person would have done under the same circumstances. It is not the responsibility of the teacher to prove that he or she is not guilty. The burden of proof lies with the injured party bringing the suit. However, the teacher must be able to answer the charges and defend his or her actions or lack of action.

Foreseeability

For a teacher to be found guilty of negligence, there must have been a "foreseeable danger," and the conduct of the teacher must have been unreasonable in proportion to that danger. The exact occurrence or precise injury need not have been foreseeable, but an injury resulting from negligent conduct must be probable and not merely possible. In other words, if a reasonably prudent person could foresee injury, and his or her conduct was unreasonable given the circumstances, the teacher is very vulnerable to being found guilty of the charge of negligence.

Proximate Cause

In addition to being *foreseeable*, the teacher's action or lack of action must have been the *proximate cause* of the injury. In other words, the student must prove that the alleged negligent behavior of the teacher caused the injury. For example, if a student, while waiting quietly for his turn in a game, with the teacher present, suddenly turns to another classmate and hits him in the face, causing an injury to the eye, the teacher is only liable if his or her action or inaction directly led to the injury. If the student had a history of disruptive behavior, it might be argued that the teacher did not supervise that student appropriately. However, if there was no history of disruptive behavior, it is unlikely that the teacher's behavior proximately caused the injury.

What Must the Plaintiff Prove?

The plaintiff must establish four legal factors in order to prove that a teacher was negligent:

1. duty owed
2. duty violated
3. injury foreseeable
4. whether the teacher's behavior proximately caused the injury

In the case of teachers, duty is owed. By virtue of their position, teachers owe students a duty to provide ordinary care. Whether the duty was violated is dependent on whether the accident was foreseeable and whether the teacher's behavior proximately caused the injury. At trial, the judge reads to the jury the definition of negligence and identifies the four factors that the plaintiff must provide proof of in order to find the defendant guilty of negligence.

The Process of Being Sued

The defendant (teacher) will receive a claim letter or bill of particulars from the plaintiff's (student's) attorney. The teacher should contact his or her immediate supervisor and the principal, who will contact the school's insurance company. Personal insurance carriers should also be contacted. The school's lawyer will send an answer to the charges, in writing, to the student's attorney. Both parties with their lawyers are questioned regarding the facts and circumstances of the case. A court reporter documents the questions and answers. This documentation is considered sworn, legal testimony and can be used at the trial. The injured student is examined by a physician to ascertain the nature and extent of the injuries. Witnesses and documentation of facts are gathered by the defendant's attorney, and a decision is made to settle out of court or go to trial.

Increasing the Likelihood of Winning the Case

The teacher should obtain a copy of the accident report that details how the injury occurred and should identify the emergency procedures that were followed. He or she should also obtain a copy of the district's accident procedure, as well as a list of student witnesses to document the incident. The teacher should consult his or her attorney for guidance on the contents of student documentation. It is important that the teacher gather lesson and unit plans. If the activity stemmed from a state curriculum, the guide should be included with the unit and lesson plans.

AREAS OF VULNERABILITY AND PREVENTIVE MEASURES

Supervision

Supervision is an umbrella term that can encompass almost every aspect of teaching. When a claim letter or bill of particulars is sent to a defendant, the term *lack of supervision* often appears. Along with the general allegation of lack of supervision, usually a number of other more specific charges are listed. A perusal of the case law dealing with negligence and physical activity reveals a number of areas or issues central to the teaching and learning process that continually appear in cases. Based on the case law, areas of vulnerability can be gleaned which can serve as a guide for planning and conducting safe physical activity. There are no foolproof plans or steps a teacher can take to prevent a lawsuit. The facts and circumstances of every case are different. However, the following areas of vulnerability and specific suggestions for accident prevention should provide a framework for understanding the type and degree of legal duty owed a student during physical activity.

Instruction

- Conduct proper warm-up activities before every class.
- Require proper dress for the activity.
- Clearly review orally, and post in writing, any safety rules both general and specific to the activity being conducted every class.
- Clearly point out dangers inherent in the activity.
- Teach progressively. If students do not have prerequisite skills, do not allow them to try more advanced skills.
- Keep lesson and unit plans updated, and be sure to have rainy day activities that can be related to a specific educational purpose, preferably related to the current unit.

Selection of Activities

- Be sure you can justify the activity educationally, particularly if it is an inherently dangerous activity.
- If the activity requires greater supervision (e.g., golf, lacrosse indoors), be sure your facility and class size warrant using those sports to fulfill the educational objective they were designed to meet.
- Be sure you have knowledge of the activity you are teaching.
- Use a recognized source, such as a state curriculum guide or professional association suggested curriculum, as the foundation for your program curriculum. In New York State, for example, the "New York State Curriculum Guide and Syllabus" provides both justification and flexibility for almost any physical education program.
- Be sure the activities you cover are appropriate for the age, maturity, size, and skill ability of your students.
- Be careful not to encourage students to value competitiveness over safety (either through what you say or your attitude).

Protective Measures

- Provide and ensure that all participants are using safety equipment such as catcher's masks, shin guards, and so on.
- Be sure that all equipment is in good repair and worn correctly.
- Activities such as gymnastics require spotting. It is questionable whether student spotters are considered reasonable. If you use them, train them.
- Teachers are responsible for the safety of students. If you cannot eliminate a hazard, eliminate the activity.
- When pairing students (e.g., wrestling), match students in contact activities in terms of size, strength, and skill ability.

Control Measures

- Teachers are expected to have control over their students. Hazards created by students who break the rules may be interpreted as the teacher's inability to control the class. If a high degree of class control is needed, or if a class has a reputation for being disruptive, it may be hard to justify the selection of a potentially dangerous activity in court.
- Injuries that result from students fooling around or "having fun" may be interpreted as being caused by the teacher's lack of class control.

- If there is a history of allowing questionable behavior, and someone is injured under similar circumstances, it may be perceived as poor class control or judgment.
- Be sure your teacher-to-student ratio is appropriate for the nature of the activity you choose to fulfill curricular objectives.

Judgment

- Do not require students to try something they are afraid of to demonstrate "courage" if it could result in foreseeable harm.
- Be careful what you name modified activities or games. Activities named "suicides" and "bombardment" are difficult to justify educationally when someone has been injured.
- Be sure your certifications, such as first aid, are current. Do not over- or undertreat injured students.
- Do not ask students to move equipment or run errands that could result in injury. These tasks are not justifiable educationally.
- Maintain your composure. Loss of temper and excessive anger are not considered professional behavior. Likewise, being too lenient can be viewed as lacking good class control.

Facilities, Equipment, and Environmental Conditions

- If the facility has a defect, report it in writing, and keep students away from the area.
- Inspect all equipment before allowing students to use it.
- If students set up equipment, the teacher should make the final check.
- If broken bottles are on a playing field, the teacher is responsible for checking the area before allowing students to use it.
- Have regular safety checks of gymnastics and other large equipment that has a vendor who can sign a statement indicating that it is in good repair.
- Check weather conditions regularly for outdoor units. Lightning and thunder may be considered foreseeable if they have been forecasted.
- Check fields for mud, dew, or frost before allowing students to participate.

Waivers

In general, written release waivers do not protect the teacher or institution from potential liability. They are, however, helpful in the defense of negligence charges because they demonstrate careful planning and if worded correctly can be used as a written warning concerning the nature of the activity or field trip to be planned. Parents and students cannot sign away their right to bring a lawsuit against a teacher or supervisor for negligence. The educator may be more liable when waivers are not used, but educators are not less liable if their behavior was less than "reasonable" or "prudent." A waiver may only serve as a deterrent to a lawsuit.

CONCLUSION

The potential for physical injury is inherent, to some degree, in the nature of play, games, and sport. Even the most carefully planned and supervised activity can result in an accident that involves injury. The most prudent supervisor or teacher cannot eliminate all elements of risk for the participants in his or her care. Therefore, it is very important for supervisors to understand how reasonably prudent behavior has been defined by the courts. This knowledge can be used to guide teacher behavior in terms of the safe conduct of physical activities.

Nonetheless, juries are often comprised of parents, and all parents have a certain degree of empathy for a child who has been injured. Although the burden of proof lies with the child's lawyer to prove that the supervisor's negligence caused the injury, it can be difficult for juries objectively to evaluate the actions (or lack of action) of a supervisor, particularly if the injury is severe.

Because remuneration for injury is monetary, a prudent supervisor should check with the sponsoring organization to be sure that legal expenses and damages are covered by insurance. It is also prudent to secure additional liability insurance through the American Alliance for Health Physical Education and Recreation and Dance, which can be individually purchased for a nominal fee.

Finally, all teachers should think before they act. They should imagine themselves explaining and justifying their actions and decisions regarding an activity to a judge and jury. If a teacher can confidently justify his or her actions as "reasonably prudent" supervisory behavior, the chances are good that the judge and jury would agree.

REFERENCE

Gifis, Steven H. (1975). *Law Dictionary*. New York: Barron's Educational Series.

Part II

An Interdisciplinary Approach to Games

Part II demonstrates how physical skills and game activities can be used to reinforce academic learning experiences. The complexity of the learning experiences varies, beginning with Lisa M. Quirk's introduction to cognitive learning through the physical. Sample activities are included. Sheila L. Jackson designs a variety of innovative games to reinforce concepts in the academic areas of math and reading. Jim Stillwell also draws from the subjects of math and reading in his creation of exciting movement activities. Lynette C. Shott and Louise M. Gerbes present a variety of activities that stemmed from their efforts to create an integrated curriculum between the academic classes and the physical education program. Kara Christian describes a human board game that combines physical skills with environmental awareness concepts. Likewise, Nancy Woronowich and Lilka Lichtneger introduce environmental themes to games and movement obstacles to increase student involvement and awareness. Movement obstacles are also used by Ellen M. Kowalski and Susan O. Kennedy as a versatile means to enhance the child's imagination and creative movement performance, and Lorna J. Woodward makes use of simple concepts related to nutrition to expand the child's movement ability. Martha Owens and Susan Rockett explain the Every Child a Winner program. Developed in 1970, it has since been field-tested in more than five thousand school districts in Canada, the Virgin Islands, and the United States. This purposeful model reinforces the need for a developmentally appropriate scope and sequence in the curriculum. Lenore Sandel's chapter shows that very few materials are needed to design a purposeful teacher-made classroom game for instructional purposes. Similarly, Heidi Reichel challenges the reader to discover how unlimited subject matter can be put into a game format through a creative activity called Potpourri. Joyce A. Zucker's creative table board game responds to the child's love of hockey as a way to increase spelling skills.

11

Cognitive Learning through the Physical

Lisa M. Quirk

As the field of physical education evolves and changes under the pressures created by reduced budgets and a need to prove its accountability, new methods of presenting learning materials are surfacing. One of the ways the profession is expanding its value in education is through teaching and reinforcing cognitive concepts through physical activities. In some educational circles this idea is known as cognitive learning through the physical.

Cognitive learning through the physical is an innovative and creative approach to teaching that combines physical activities with cognitive knowledge. Through various activities (some of which are outlined in the next section), students are taught facts related to spelling, math, study skills, geography, anatomy, and languages. This approach can be used by all teachers to make subjects more enjoyable for students. Classroom and physical education teachers can work separately or together to accomplish goals combining physical activities and cognitive concepts.

SAMPLE ACTIVITIES

The five activities described below combine various academic themes that can be taught under the title of cognitive learning through the physical. These ideas stemmed from the author's desire to add this method of teaching to her existing repertoire of teaching strategies.

Name of the Game: Human Calculator
Suggested Grade Level: 3-6
Equipment Required: Floorspots with the numerals 0-9 and operation signs: + (plus), - (minus), x (multiplication), and ÷ (division).
Description: Students are individually assigned a number from 1 to 4. Some students will have the same number. Floorspots with numbers printed on them are scattered throughout the area. On the starting signal, students perform a specified locomotor skill (e.g., walking, jogging, skipping, or leaping) until they

are signaled to stop. Upon stopping, the teacher holds one or more operation signs above his or her head for the students. Individuals find a partner or a group to develop a math problem using the specified sign. Partners stand near the floorspot representing the solution to their problem and perform an exercise for the number of times indicated by the solution.

For example, if the operation sign was addition, two students with a Number 1 and a Number 3 would stand near a floorspot with a Number 4 on it. (Students should not stand on the floorspots, as two or more groups may be using the same answer to their problem.)

From this point, two actions can take place:

1. The teacher may check the students' answers.
2. Students can check each others' answers.

Variations: Continue the game, making problems more difficult if appropriate, that is, adding more operations, putting floorspots together to make bigger solutions, or giving students larger numbers to work with in the beginning.

Name of the Game: Skip and Spell
Suggested Grade Level: 3-6
Equipment Required: Floorspots or cardboard signs containing letters of the alphabet
Description: Floorspots are placed around the room or signs are hung on the wall at least five feet apart from each other. Divide the class into groups of three to ten students. The teacher identifies a word to spell. On the teacher's signal the students perform a specified locomotor skill while also traveling from one letter to the next in the correct sequence in order to spell the assigned word. Points are awarded for the correct spelling. The student's weekly list of spelling words can be used, or the teacher can reinforce sport terms from the current physical education unit. This is a great way to get the students to reinforce their movement vocabulary.

Name of the Game: Geography Quest
Suggested Grade Level: 3-4
Equipment Required: Various pieces of equipment depending on availability and students' choices
Description: Students perform a geographically themed obstacle course based on information from their geography class, the teacher's explanation, and a class discussion of the depicted region. Groups of three to six people are assigned to research a specific geographical region taken from their classroom text. Following this assignment, each group cooperatively builds an obstacle course including one or two items of interest in their assigned region (e.g., mountains, rivers, landmarks, or industries). Each group's selected items should be discussed. All obstacle items should be combined into one large course and be presented on the same day.

Name of the Game: Anatomy Busy Bee
Suggested Grade Level: 3-6
Equipment Required: None
Description: Students are introduced to several anatomical terms such as gluteals, biceps, and phalanges. On the teacher's signal, the students are directed to perform a locomotor skill. On the next signal, the teacher shouts a number from 1 to 8 while also shouting out the name of the body part. The students quickly get into groups of the designated number with the correct body parts touching. Each group that performs the task correctly within a certain period of time is awarded a point. For example, the teacher's command might be "six phalanges." The students' response would be to get into groups of six with their phalanges (fingers) touching.

A different command is given each time. Some common parts are quadriceps, metatarsals, cranium, ulna, femur, calcaneus, and patella.
Variation: Identify two or more body parts to make the game more challenging.

Name of the Game: Language Warm-Up
Suggested Grade Level: 2-6
Equipment Required: None
Description: Students perform exercises while counting in different languages (e.g., ten jumping jacks while counting in French, ten sit-ups while counting in Spanish, five push-ups while counting in Italian). Encourage students to compose a list of numbers from the languages they speak at home, such as languages their parents or grandparents may speak. Include words and phrases like *quiet!*, *ready?*, *listen*, *sit down!*, *stand up*, *please*, and *thank you* in these native languages.

EVALUATION

Teachers should consider the following when using the cognitive learning through the physical teaching approach.

Strengths:

- Students are using their minds and bodies in unison to solve problems.
- Students have an opportunity to create and improve games.
- Students assist each other's learning.
- Ongoing evaluation is taking place.
- Greater collaboration between physical educators and classroom teachers is created.

Weaknesses:

- Some equipment may need to be purchased.
- The activities require additional planning and preparation.
- Co-workers need to be cooperative and supportive for the program to reach its maximum effectiveness.

ADDITIONAL ACTIVITIES

The following games are appropriate for grades four through six, although they may be modified for younger children.

Name of the Game: Descriptive Scavenger Hunt
Description: Individuals are challenged to "hunt" for answers reflecting the group's descriptive characteristics.

- Find a classmate who was born in a different part of the country.
- Locate someone with two brothers.
- Identify someone that has the same birth month as you.
- Find someone with an unusual hobby.
- Identify two people with the same first name.
- Find someone who was born in another country.
- Find someone with the same initials as you.
- Identify someone who plays in a sports league. Where?
- Find someone who owns a cat. What's its name?
- Find someone who has a dog. What's its name?

Name of the Game: Group Problem Solving
Description:

- Count from 50 to 1 (together).
- Make a line starting with the shortest to the tallest student on your knees.
- Perform twenty jumping jacks in unison.
- Make two concentric circles.

Name of the Game: I Love Physical Education
Description: All students form a line along a line, a wall, or a fence. The teacher makes various statements such as:

Run if you love . . . biking.
Skip if you love . . . pizza.
Hop if you love . . . animals.
Gallop if you love . . . ice cream.

The students are given the opportunity to perform the prescribed motor skill when moving to a specific location and returning to the original line.

Name of the Game: Macaroni Soup
Description: The class stands in a circle with their palms facing upward. They rest each of their hands on the two players next to them (right hand on top of the neighbor's left). As the chant begins, each child, in turn, gently lifts his or her right hand and taps his or her neighbor's right hand. A rhythm is established by the leader. At the end of the chant, the player whose hand is tapped or the player who misses his or her neighbor's hand because it has been pulled away is "out." These students join another circle to remain active. The last remaining player is the champ.
The Chant:

Soup, Macaroni, Bologna,
Sliced Potato Chip, Chip, Chip
(the player taps his or her neighbor's hand three times)
Sliced Potato Chip, Chip, Chip
(three taps on "chip, chip, chip")
Fritos, Cheetos, Doritos, Pow!

On "Pow!" the person who is tapped on the hand or the person who misses his or her neighbor's hand is out.

Name of the Game: An Apple
Description: This game is played in a circle with one leader. The teacher sends around a beanbag, eraser, or some other small object, and prefaces it by saying "This is an apple." The other players pass it around and repeat what it is. Gradually more objects are added with different names. The children become very amused when two or more items cross paths.

Name of the Game: Land of the Lost
Equipment Required: Ten or more foam balls (7")
Description: This dodgeball-like game actually reinforces polite behavior, in contrast to less developmentally appropriate versions. The class is divided into two groups on opposite sides of the playing area. The objective of the game is to hit a player below the knees on the opposing side and send him or her to each team's designated area, called the "Land of the Lost."

After being hit, the player positions him or herself in order of arrival. Players are rescued when a member of their group catches a ball on the fly, rushes over to the "Land of the Lost," and hands the ball to the first player in line. When the player is handed the ball, he or she must say "thank you" and reenter the game. The person who handed the ball must respond by saying "you are welcome." The game continues.

Name of the Game: Snowball Melt
Equipment Required: Ten or more foam balls
Description: The class is divided into two groups. The objective is to hit an opposing player with a snowball (i.e., a soft foam ball). Once hit, the player melts to a sitting position and continues to play as if his or her legs have melted away. Melted snowpeople may continue to move around the playing area, but without the use of their legs. There are three ways a snowperson can regain the use of his or her legs. First, he or she may hit an opposing, standing snowperson; second, he or she may catch a ball on the fly; or third, in the event that one of his or her teammates catches a ball on the fly and gives it to the melted snow person. Challenge the students to develop additional game themes while maintaining similar rules.

Name of the Game: Invasion of the Ball Snatchers
Description: Cones are set in a large rectangle formation. A lane for jogging is designated around the outside. One half of the class is given a foam ball and

begins to foot dribble the ball inside the rectangle. The remaining students run one lap around the outside of the rectangle. After the lap, they may enter through a designated area and try to snatch the ball. If they are successful, the person who loses the ball takes a lap and then reenters and tries to snatch someone else's ball. Each time a ball is successfully snatched the student receives a letter. Letters are used to spell teacher designated words (e.g., H-A-L-L-O-W-E-E-N would equal nine successful snatches).

REFERENCES

Benton, Rudy (1986). *I Love Movement Education.* Carmichael, Calif.: Carmichael Publishing.

Carnes, Cliff (1983). *Awesome Elementary School Physical Education Activities.* Carmichael, Calif: Carmichael Publishing.

12

Games that Teach Academic Skills in Math, Spelling, and Geography

Sheila L. Jackson

The following games can be used by elementary classroom teachers to aid students in learning and practicing their skills in math, spelling, geography, and history. Some are variations of games that children may be familiar with, making it easy to adapt the specific academic skill to the game.

Name of the Game: Math Ball
Suggested Grade Level: K-3
Purposes: This game helps students to recognize and sequence numbers; do addition, subtraction, multiplication, and division; and improve hand-eye coordination.
Area and Equipment Required: Playground or area with a high ceiling; one ball of any type; index cards with appropriate numbers for each child; and index cards with math problems
Description: All players stand in a circle. Each player is given an index card with a number on it. One student, designated as "it," selects an index card with a math problem on it (e.g., 2 + 2), stands in the middle with a ball, and tosses the ball in the air while calling out the math problem. The child holding the number with the correct answer (i.e., 4) runs out and tries to catch the ball before it bounces. If successful, this child is now "it." Teachers may increase the number of bounces depending on the group's skill ability. In kindergarten or grade one the teacher may simply call out the numbers or letters or have students practice sequence of numbers or the alphabet. This game is an adaptation of Call Ball by Gallahue and Meadors (1979).

Name of the Game: Fractional Hoops
Suggested Grade Level: K-4
Purposes: This game helps students understand the concepts of fractions and division while promoting cooperation and practicing locomotor skills.

Area and Equipment Required: A large open area; hoops or bicycle tires or large, circular pieces of butcher paper (one per child); a radio, tape player, or record player

Description: In this activity the students are reminded that each child is a "part" or "fraction" of the "whole class." Place one hoop on the playing surface and have all the students (e.g., 24) place at least one foot in the hoop. Explain that the "whole class" is in one hoop, undivided, or that the hoop has divided the space into 24 parts. Then put down two hoops and tell the students to get the same number of students in each hoop (e.g., 12). Explain that the "whole class" divided by the two hoops is equal to 12 and that 12/24 is half of the class.

To begin the game, scatter several hoops throughout the playing area and have one child stand in each hoop. When the music plays, each student is to move outside the hoops and perform a specific locomotor skill. When the music stops, the class is challenged to quickly get an equal number of students in each hoop. The teacher should designate one hoop as the "leftover hoop" in case the number cannot be divided equally. Each time the music is playing the teacher should remove two or more hoops and tell the students how many hoops are left (e.g., 12). Before starting the game again, the teacher should reinforce that the "whole class" has been divided by 12 hoops, for example, and that 2/24 is 1/12 of the "whole class." This game is an adaptation of Musical Madness by Foster and Overholt (1989).

Name of the Game: ABC Throwing
Suggested Grade Level: K-3
Purposes: This game helps students learn their ABCs, number sequence, and spelling words, and it promotes cooperation.
Space and Equipment Required: A large enclosed playing area; marked tennis balls
Description: Give each child one tennis ball that has been marked with a letter of the alphabet or a number. The class is asked to form a side-by-side line on one end of the playing space. On the count of three, the students are challenged to throw their tennis balls to the other end of the area as hard as they can. When all balls have been thrown, each student quickly moves to retrieve his or hers. Returning with them, the group forms a line in alphabetical or numerical order according to each player's tennis ball. The students are asked to say aloud the number or letter on their tennis ball in order to reinforce the sequence.

Students can also be challenged to test their spelling ability. The teacher designates two or more teams and marks tennis balls with the letters of their weekly spelling list. To begin, each team is given a paper sack containing tennis balls with the letters of one of their spelling words. The tennis balls must have an additional mark denoting which team they represent. On the first count of three, each team member gets a tennis ball from his or her respective sack and looks at the letter on the ball while lining up side by side with her or his teammates. On the second count of three, the balls are thrown as the teacher says what the word is. After retrieving their tennis balls, each team runs back and lines up in the spelling word order as fast as possible and then sits down. They are not allowed to exchange positions or tennis balls after sitting down. Each team that correctly spells the word receives one point, and the game continues with the next word.

Name of the Game: Geography Tag
Suggested Grade Level: 2-4
Purposes: This game helps students correlate directions with various places and improves their dodging skills.
Space and Equipment Required: A large open area with four walls, with the four corners of the room marked off in sections large enough for the class to fit in; four large posters with north, south, east, and west designations taped to the appropriate walls
Description: One child is assigned the role of "it" in the middle of the room, with the remainder of the students in a designated "safe" region (e.g., NW corner). "It" then calls out either a direction (e.g., South) or a place which is in that direction (e.g., Texas). Following this announcement all the students must leave their previous safe place to go to the new safe place without being tagged by "it." The first person tagged by "it" exchanges roles.

Name of the Game: States and Capitals Chase
Suggested Grade Level: 4-6
Purposes: This game reviews and reinforces the correlation of states and capitals and improves the students' running and dodging skills.
Space and Equipment Required: A large open area with established boundaries; a box containing slips of paper with the name of each state; a second box of slips with the name of each capital; and a third box of slips with both the states and the capitals
Description: The class is divided into two teams. One team draws slips of paper from the state box, and the other team draws slips from the capital box. The teacher should check to see that for every state the corresponding capital has been drawn. The teams face each other about five to ten feet apart and rapidly take turns telling what they have drawn. The teacher then draws from the third box of slips with both the states and the capitals. If Little Rock is drawn, the student with the Little Rock slip chases and tries to tag the student who has Arkansas. In the event that a student does not remember what state Little Rock is the capital of, his or her teammates may yell out "Arkansas!" If the student gets tagged before crossing his or her boundary line, the capital team gets a point. The two students then go and pick out another state and capital from the appropriate boxes, and the game continues.

The same procedure can be used for historical dates and events, with one team having slips of paper naming famous historical events and the other team having the corresponding dates of these events. Math equations and answers can also be used.

REFERENCES

Foster, D., and J. Overholt (1989). *Indoor Action Games for Elementary Children: Active Games and Academic Activities for Fun and Fitness.* West Nyack, N.Y.: Parker.

Gallahue, D., and W. Meadors (1979). *Let's Move: A Physical Education Curriculum for Primary and Middle School Teachers.* 2nd ed. Dubuque, Iowa: Kendall/Hunt.

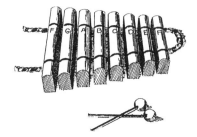

13

Acade-motion: Movement Activities Integrating Academic Concepts

Jim Stillwell

This chapter describes a variety of movement experiences designed to enhance the learning of selected academic concepts, including letter, number, and color recognition.

PRECLASS ORGANIZATION

To help with discipline, roll-taking procedures, and grouping, place spots on the gymnasium or multipurpose floor. The spots can be put on with tempera paint or colored marking tape. The shapes (circle, square, rectangle, triangle, etc.) need only be approximately one inch in size. They should be placed on the floor in rows about four feet apart and be different colors. Spot assignments can be made alphabetically or at random. Squads can be formed from the rows or columns of spots. They also can be formed from shapes or colors. If regrouping is necessary at any time during a class, the students may be asked to return to their spots.

ACADE-MOTION STRETCHES

Teachers can awaken the child's intellect by asking a variety of questions during warm-up sessions. For example, the teacher may ask that all children wearing a certain color or having a certain letter or a certain vowel sound in their name perform a selected exercise. Other examples include "If you are wearing red, perform ten jumping jacks," or "If you have an A in your first name, do five toe touches."

BODY LETTERS OR NUMBERS

Ask the children to use only their body to make a specific letter or number. This action can be performed in either a horizontal (lying) plane or a vertical (standing) plane. Teachers can also challenge groups of three, four, or five to make one letter or number. A greater challenge involves asking groups of three, four, or five to make a word or a date in history. As a finale, have the entire class make one huge letter.

ROPE ALPHABET

Challenge the students to make letters or numbers and geometric shapes using individual jump ropes. This can also be done with partners or in groups of three, four, or more.

VOWEL MOVEMENT

Teachers can challenge many students to move either in a high or a low plane depending on the vowel sound of a word. For example, for the word *cat* (short sound), the children must stoop and walk at a low level. For the word *cake* (long sound), the children must walk on tiptoe at a high level.

TOSS AND SPELL

Children can be challenged to spell words with a partner by stating a letter on each toss of a beanbag.

BODY PENCIL

Challenge the students to use the right hand as a large pencil to spell a word. Ask them to use the left hand to spell the word *day*. Greater challenges include having each child use the right leg to spell the words.

BODY POETRY

Teachers can challenge children to make the shape of something that rhymes with the words found in their spelling list. Examples might include stop (pop), car (star), truck (duck). To increase participation, have the students work in pairs.

EXPRESSING MOVEMENT

Teachers can read a poem and challenge the children to move freely as they listen to the key words. For example:

On a cold and windy day
The little puppy came out to play.
He jumped and skipped
So happy was he.
And he suddenly stopped to scratch a flea.
The flowers were blooming so bright and true.
And in the distance you could hear a cow say "Moo."
Things became so quiet, you could even hear a peep.
So the puppy sat down and went soundly to sleep.

14

Fitting Together: Activities Designed to Integrate Academic and Physical Education Curriculums

Lynette C. Shott and Louise M. Gerbes

Motivated by the belief that learning extends beyond the classroom walls, and that students can acquire the same knowledge through a variety of approaches, the Fitting Together centers approach was created. Similar to the stations approach used in physical education, our classroom centers focused on independent learning, required a minimum amount of space and materials, and included independent tasks ranging from movement and health-related fitness activities to academic skills such as charting, graphing, and reading.

Evaluation of our curriculum and current teaching methods led us to conclude that we needed a readily available method of instruction that stressed the importance of physical fitness to a generation of grade five students who are increasingly less physically fit, while enhancing the classroom curriculum. The length of each center was determined by the students' developmental level and the teacher's daily routine.

FITTING TOGETHER ACTIVITY ONE

The activity Games Written by Students can serve as one means of integrating language arts into the physical education curriculum. The activity began in the independent student center in the classroom and culminated as a whole group activity in the physical education class. Students were given books of games to serve as examples of the proper format. The children used one twenty-minute center to examine the books and observe the main components of a well-written game. A short class discussion was held after the entire class had rotated through this center, and a list was compiled of what needed to be included in the students' games. A sample outline was used to create a game (see Figure 14.1). After the games were developed we evaluated each one as a class to determine if the information was sufficient to play the game. If we could not comprehend the student's intentions, possible additions were suggested to make the game more developmentally appropriate. After our revisions were completed, the games were sent to the physical education teacher to review. Together, we chose three games that we believed the students could successfully play. The physical education instructor provided the necessary equipment and playing space. During the course of play, brief discussions were conducted to evaluate various aspects of the game.

1. TITLE OF GAME _____

2. NUMBER OF PLAYERS _____

3. EQUIPMENT NEEDED _____

4. SPACE REQUIRED _____

_____

5. RULES _____

_____

6. STEP BY STEP INSTRUCTIONS _____

_____

_____

7. HOW DO YOU WIN? _____

_____

_____

_____

8. DRAW A DIAGRAM OF HOW THE GAME IS PLAYED AND THE PLAYING AREA.

FIGURE 14.1: Games Written By Students

FITTING TOGETHER ACTIVITY TWO

The next activity demonstrates a center that began in the physical education class and was carried back to the classroom to enforce measurement and subtraction skills as well as completing a written chart. The students were involved in a fitness unit to prepare for the annual physical fitness test. Flexibility was one of the areas being assessed. We constructed a sit and reach box that was placed in a twenty-minute Fitting Together center in the classroom. Students measured their flexibility and recorded it on a pretyped chart (see Figure 14.2). To complete the activity, they performed a series of stretching exercises and retested their flexibility to see if improvement was made.

WHAT DO YOU THINK WILL HAPPEN TO YOUR MEASUREMENT AFTER EACH SECTION ON THE CHART?		
BEFORE EXERCISE	FLEXIBILITY AFTER 10 LEG STRETCHES	DIFFERENCE
BEFORE EXERCISE	AFTER 10 STRADDLE STRETCHES	DIFFERENCE

FIGURE 14.2: Flexibility Assessment

ADDITIONAL ACTIVITIES

Name of the Game: Word for the Week

Equipment Required: List of words related to your physical education curriculum

Description: This activity is designed to increase the student's vocabulary and word knowledge. Begin by giving the classroom teachers a list of words to use as spelling bonus words, in stories or sentences, and so on. Tell the students what the word of the week is at the beginning of each week. Have it announced during the school's morning report and ask students to find out what the word means and how it applies to physical education. Ask for the results later in the week.

Name of the Game: Daily Exercise

Equipment Required: Video capabilities

Description: The purpose of this activity is to provide students with a daily series of exercises to be performed in their classrooms. To begin, the physical educator videotapes a student or a group of students performing a ten to fifteen-minute exercise routine. Circulate the tape to the classroom teachers. Have this program aired daily to give the students an exercise break. Teachers can also request special airings to meet their schedule needs. Set the routine to lively music for an additional incentive to exercise.

Name of the Game: Mental Math

Equipment Required: None

Description: Many occasions arise during a physical education class that require computations on the part of the teacher (e.g., "How many more do we need?" or "How many has the class completed as a group?"). Simple computations can be given to the students to complete orally, or the teacher may play a game of softball and have the students at bat complete a math fact (or a spelling word) before they bat the ball.

Name of the Game: Letter People
Equipment Required: None
Description: This activity is designed to reinforce letter sounds and to introduce new vocabulary. While learning new vocabulary pertaining to physical education skills, the students are asked to identify the initial sounds of the words. They can trace these letters with their feet or make them as a group. During fitness testing, for example, discuss the word *fitness* with the younger children: "What letter sound do you hear at the beginning of the word?" "Can you think of another word that begins with the same sound?" Using every opportunity to remind the children of these sounds helps to build reading skills, and it reinforces that these skills are used outside the classroom.

Name of the Game: Pull-Up Challenge
Equipment Required: Pull-up bars, chairs, and pole
Description: Each month students are given a chance to demonstrate their improvement in pull-ups. The class is divided into several teams. Each team tries to improve on the number of pull-ups they are able to do each month. The team with the greatest number at the end of the school year is awarded a prize (e.g., an ice-pop party).

Classroom teachers are involved by giving the students an opportunity to practice at recess, by keeping individual records, or by having students practice in the classroom by providing a chair to do dips, or two chairs with a pole across them. In this arrangement the student lies on the floor between the two chairs, holds the pole, and pulls the body upward until the chin is over the bar. Heels remain in constant contact with the floor.

Name of the Game: Guest Speaker
Equipment Required: None
Description: The physical educator can invite a special guest to the physical education classes, for example, the president of your local American Heart Association, an exercise physiologist, a physical therapist, local square dance clubs, a United States Tennis Association pro, a professional sports figure, or the local sport news reporter.

These guests not only increase the interest level of the students, they can also be helpful to classroom teachers with their unit of study. For example, if the grade five classroom teacher is teaching about the human body and your physical education classes are studying aerobics, having an exercise physiologist or a representative from the American Heart Association as a guest speaker can enhance both areas of study.

Name of the Game: Fitness War
Equipment Required: Decks of playing cards (it is not necessary to have complete decks of fifty-two cards)
Description: In this activity, all students perform stretching exercises while practicing their math facts. The game begins by having students work in pairs or groups of four. Each group is given one deck of playing cards. Using the rules of

the card game War, students perform exercises when they lose the "war" on the cards drawn. Intermediate students can practice their multiplication facts by multiplying the cards that are drawn and performing that number of exercises. The younger students can practice addition facts. For example, the students divide the deck of cards between them. One student turns over a six; the other student draws a four. The student with the four has to do twenty-four of the designated exercises. The type of exercise can be chosen by the class or by the two students just before they drawn their cards. When two identical cards are drawn, the rules of the card game War apply, that is, both students turn over an additional four cards. The last card turned is used as the indicator.

Name of the Game: Calorie Counters
Equipment Required: Calorie counters, daily meal charts, pencils, paper, and calculators
Description: The students are challenged to keep a chart of their meals and snacks for one week. At the end of the week they can use calorie counters and calculators to add the amount of calories consumed each meal, each day, and for the week. The intermediate students can be challenged to calculate the number of calories burned by a variety of activities as well as the amount of exercise needed to burn a set number of calories.

Name of the Game: Create Your Own Square Dance
Equipment Required: Paper, pencil, and appropriate music
Description: This activity reinforces the knowledge of square dance steps and provides an opportunity to practice sequencing skills and writing using complete sentences. After the students have learned the basic steps of square dancing in their physical education classes, they can be challenged to write their own square dance. The dances can be performed in the physical education classes.

Name of the Game: Directional Treasure Hunt
Equipment Required: Objects for the children to hunt for, written directions, and a large area in which to hide the objects
Description: Divide the class into groups of four. Hide four objects in a spacious area. Give each group of children a set of written directions to follow in order to locate their object. For example: Start at the light pole. Take twenty-five steps northeast; take ten steps south; take thirty-five steps north. To add a greater challenge, have the physical education students write letters to famous explorers and send them to an eighth grade social studies class to answer. The older students reply as the character. The physical education teacher can hide the letters in the playing space and prepare the written directions. After the letters are found, individuals should share them with the entire class.

Name of the Game: Shape Up
Equipment Required: None

Description: Have the students create a variety of geometric shapes with their bodies. The number of students needed to create each shape should be the same as the number of sides.

Name of the Game: Human Place Value Chart

Equipment Required: Masking tape, paper plates, yarn

Description: This activity teaches or reinforces the concept of place value. To begin the activity, design a place value chart on the ground with masking tape. On paper plates write the numbers 0 to 9. Attach yarn to the plates so that children can put them around their necks. Call out numbers such as 642 and have the children stand in the proper column on the chart to make the number.

Another variation includes having some children represent ones, tens, and hundreds. Put the children on the chart to show a number like 14. Add six more ones on the chart and then make a trade for a ten.

Name of the Game: Action Stories

Equipment Required: An action picture from the sports section of the newspaper, paper, and pencil

Description: This activity lets students demonstrate their ability to compose a complete sentence, a paragraph, and a story. Begin by providing a selection of pictures from the newspaper that show vigorous actions. The students can compose a newspaper story of their own, write a humorous caption for the picture, or tell a story about the picture. Sentences that stress the use of verbs, adjectives, and adverbs can be placed on index cards, and a student-created matching game can be made. For a greater challenge, laminate the cards and the pictures and have the students play Action Memory.

Name of the Game: Fitness Survey

Equipment Required: A teacher-prepared survey, pencil, and form for students to write a fitness goal

Description: This game is designed to alert students to their fitness level and to motivate them to set a reasonable fitness goal. Graphing skills and language arts competencies are also used.

To begin the activity, students complete a teacher-prepared fitness survey to evaluate their daily exercise and eating habits. After the surveys are completed, the class results for each question can be displayed in a bar graph. Following a unit on healthy eating habits and good fitness practices, the survey can be administered again and the results graphed to see if the class has improved its habits. Following the initial survey, the students can set a personal fitness goal. At the end of the unit they can determine whether or not they achieved their goal.

Name of the Game: Graphing Results from Sporting Events

Equipment Required: Newspapers, paper, pencils, colored writing instruments (crayons or markers)

Description: After a basic graph has been created, the students use a current newspaper to chart the winning percentages of three to five sports teams over a given period of time. The charts can then be used to compare results. The students can also create their own word problems to be shared with the class. The type of chart used should vary with the age level and purpose of the activity. For younger children, a picture chart could be used to compare the number of wins and losses.

CONCLUSION

The Fitting Together centers approach has been beneficial for both students and teachers. It has helped students to have a clearer understanding that physical education has a broad knowledge base and goes beyond sports oriented activities. The students' cognitive awareness is increased through activities that are stimulating both mentally and physically. The students' self-esteem is enhanced through this fitting together method of self-improvement.

Curriculum goals are more fully realized in a cooperative manner. Finally, the act of communicating and sharing with other educators is the mission of all schools. An interdisciplinary approach strengthens the delivery of instructional services to meet the needs of all students.

15

Environmental Awareness Human Board Game

Kara Christian

By nature, environmental awareness is a subject that lends itself to being taught using an interdisciplinary approach. The Environmental Awareness Human Board Game incorporates physical education, reading, math, science, music, art, and writing in the learning activities. This combination of the psychomotor and cognitive domains increases the student's interest, appreciation, and respect for environmental awareness. In other words, the game uses the psychomotor and cognitive domains of several subject areas to help make positive changes in the affective domain. The greatest of these affective changes is demonstrated in environmental awareness. An example of this would be a class starting a recycling club after meeting the game's objectives.

DIRECTIONS

During the set induction of the game, the students read or listen to the following story adapted from Wilde Wood Creative Products (1984).

Concealed in the deep center of the universe, beyond the span of time, lies the everlasting planet Tourmaline. Within the glowing caverns of Tourmaline grow brilliant, soft edged crystalled Space Tubes™. Suspended in the liquid rain which collects inside the crystal walls are tiny newborn suns, moons, stars, and planets which one day will take a place among the other celestial bodies in the vast universe. At the appropriate moment in its growth each of the living crystals is gently pulled from the cavern walls by an ancient race of creatures called Hatchabies™ and sent by their special messengers to other planets throughout the universe. There the Space Tubes will be cared for by people living on the planet. If cared for properly, the Space Tube may one day be used by the Hatchabies to further enrich the never ending universe.

Next, the students play the game. Each square of the Environmental Awareness Human Board Game has a cognitive and a pyschomotor task for the students to complete. Each task is given a point value, and the students accumulate points as they progress around the board. The point value may range from two to six depending on the student's developmental level. Students accumulate points with the goal of earning the greatest score and having the honor of caring for the Space Tubes. This is possible by performing the cognitive and psychomotor tasks that represent squares 1 through 15. The cognitive square (C) task is always listed before the psychomotor square (P) task. Students play the game as individuals, as pairs, or in small groups depending on class size.

Each game square is made from one sheet of newspaper and numbered (see Figure 15.1). Index cards and pencils are used to record the answers and point values.

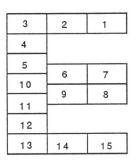

FIGURE 15.1: Environmental
Awareness Human Board Game

Square 1

2-5 pts.

C: Describe the type of environment where fish live, worms crawl, penguins live, and lizards grow.

1 pt. per successful attempt

P: Toss and catch the ball 6 times.
Materials: 2 paper balls made from newspaper. 2 plastic catchers made from bleach bottles.

Square 2

3-6 pts.

C: Describe what you see.
Materials: Triangle shapes cut from newspaper.

3-6 pts.

P: Move as if you are standing in deep mud; as if you are standing in a stream.

Square 3

Read: Plant cover helps to keep rain where it falls. An inch of rain on an acre of land amounts to more than 25,000 gallons of water. Roots lead some of the rainfall underground. Brooks, springs, wells, crops, and natural vegetation benefit from such water storage.

| 1-2 pts.
per answer | C: List 3 ways to save water. |

2-6 pts.   P: Demonstrate 2 ways (without using your hands) to carry
the 2 beanbags *over* the stream.
Materials: 2 beanbags and 2 parallel lines to represent
a stream.

Square 4

Read: Pretend you are in charge of the family dinner one
night this week. You are allowed to prepare only
foods that come in recyclable containers.

4-6 pts.   C: List the foods you would prepare.

0-10 jumps 2 pts.   P: Jump rope 40 times.
11-20 jumps 4 pts.   Materials: 4-6 jump ropes.
21-40 jumps 6 pts.

Square 5

4-6 pts.   C: Describe 4 ways to stop air pollution.

2 pts. per successful   P: Air volley each ball 10 times.
volley   Materials: 4-6 lightweight balls of various textures.

Square 6

Read: Not long ago a *Tucson Weekly* staffer was driving
down Arizona's Route 86 at well over the legal
speed limit. The hapless lawbreaker flew past a
patrolman who flicked on his lights, pulled the
speed demon over, and whipped out the dreaded
ticket book. Imagine said road runner's surprise
when the trooper cited her for "waste of a finite
energy source."

2-6 pts.   C: Explain why speeders should or should not be ticketed
for environmental waste.

2 pts. per completed   P: Dribble the ball: as fast as you can (record the number);
task   as slowly as you can (record the number).
Materials: 4-6 playground balls.

Square 7

Read: Throughout the history of man land has usually
shown evidence of previous dwellers and how these
people made use of the available natural resources.

4-6 pts.   C: Explain 2 ways to stop land pollution.

1 pt. per climber, jump

P: Perform 20 mountain climbs and 20 ski jumps.
Materials: Taped floor pattern for ski jumps.

Square 8

2 pts. for correct answer

C: The average American uses 7 trees a year. How many trees would a family of 4 use in 6 years?

1 pt. per can

P: Knock down as many cans as you can using the beanbag (2 tries).
Materials: 14 stacked cans in a pyramid formation, 2 bean bags.

Square 9

1 pt. per sound listed

C: List 5 sounds you like and 5 sounds you don't like. Explain why you like or dislike the sounds you have listed.

2-6 pts. for "why"; 3 pts. per completed task

P: Bounce the ball as high as you can 4 times. Does it make a loud or soft sound when you bounce it? Bounce the ball as low as you can four times. Does it make a louder or softer sound than when you bounced it high? (Record answers.)
Materials: 4-6 basketballs or rubber playground balls.

Square 10

3 pts. per correct entry

C: Define the word *environment*.

4 pts.

P: Dribble the ball (with your feet) along the pathway marked.
Materials: Taped pathway along the floor.

Square 11

Read: "The Earth does not belong to man, man belongs to the earth. All things are connected like the blood that unites us all. Man did not weave the web of life, he is merely a strand in it. Whatever he does to the web, he does to himself."—Chief Seattle, 1852

4-6 pts.

C: Relate the quote to a basketball team.

1 pt. per pass/lay-up

P: Bounce pass, with mechanical efficiency, 10 times. Perform 10 lay-ups with mechanical efficiency.
Materials: 4-6 basketballs.

Square 12

Read: Beginning in 1984, the nonprofit Surfrider

Foundation documented more than 40,000 violations of the federal Clean Water Act by 2 California paper companies which were dumping 40 million gallons a day of untreated waste into the waters off northern California. The result: The companies agreed to pay $5.8 million in fines and tens of millions more for new waste-treatment facilities and better waste-disposal equipment.

4-6 pts.   C: State how you can help clean beaches.

1 pt. per ball   P: See how many paper balls you can hit into the garbage sack.
                                  Materials: Paper balls, garbage sack, and striking implement.

Square 13

4-6 pts.   C: Make a poster that communicates your feelings on pollution.

4-6 pts.   P: Perform a dance routine using at least 3 elements of dance.
                                  Materials: Posterboard and markers.

Square 14

4-6 pts.   C: Describe how Goodwill Industries uses the concept of recycling.

4-6 pts.   P: Design and demonstrate a game using the equipment at this square. Extra points if the game teaches environmental awareness.
                                  Materials: Beanbags, hula hoops, cones, tennis ball, and frisbee.

Square 15

4-6 pts.   C: Describe an invention you could make to help clean the environment.

1 pt. per catch   P: Catch the paper ball in the "helmet catcher" 10 times.
                                  Materials: Paper balls and recyclable paper cups.

Note: Some tasks may be completed as homework.

REFERENCES

Goodwill Industries of America (1991). *Everyone Can Help Their Community—Through Goodwill*. Bethesda, Md.: Goodwill Industries of America.
Texas Water Quality Board (n.d.). *On Promoting Responsible Involvement in Water Quality Management*. Austin, Texas: Texas Water Quality Board.

Wilde Wood Creative Products (1984). *Enter the Enchantment*. Denver: Wilde Wood
    Creative Products.

16

Games that Teach Children to H.O.P.E. (Help Our Polluted Earth)

Nancy Woronowich and Lilka Lichtneger

This chapter explains how games that teach children to H.O.P.E. (Help Our Polluted Earth) can be used within the school environment by elementary physical educators, classroom teachers, and other school professionals who wish to develop an awareness of critical environmental issues among their students.

The H.O.P.E. Project is a multifaceted environmental curriculum involving grade four and grade five gifted students, classroom teachers, and their physical education teacher from the Tooker Avenue Elementary School, West Babylon, New York. The purpose of the project was to help young people become aware of the environmental issues facing our planet. The children were asked to develop ways that they could make a small improvement in three areas: their home, their school, and their community.

Throughout the school year the children were involved in numerous activities to meet these goals. In their home they actively tried to reuse items instead of disposing of them, and they participated in a recycling program. In their community, they participated in National Beach Clean-Up Day. They also planned and organized the clean-up of a neighborhood lake. Local community leaders received letters from the students inviting them to visit. Central to the H.O.P.E. Project were the school activities. The children arranged a schoolwide garbage reducing contest in which every class participated. They planned a toy and book exchange to encourage their peers to share their used toys and books instead of disposing of them. They wrote a play about their own environmental concern, which was performed on Earth Day. Finally, they worked together with their physical education teacher to create the games that teach children to H.O.P.E.

The following four themes are based on the need for environmental awareness, and include learning experiences in the community, school, home, and physical education setting.

THEME ONE: CLEANING UP THE ENVIRONMENT

Concepts: Discuss ways that individuals can stop pollution.

Reduce: Use less quantity of certain items whenever possible.
Reuse: Use materials again instead of throwing them away.
Recycle: Buy products that can be used again and again.

Community Activities: Participate in an annual National Beach Clean-up or other large-scale projects. Work with a local environmental group, allowing students to make the arrangements. Write letters to environmentally conscious politicians and community leaders, inviting them to speak to your class, and visit local recycling facilities.

School Activities: Recycle class waste paper by having each student attach a bag to his or her desk to hold paper that can be recycled or reused. Weigh the garbage thrown out at lunch and discuss waste reduction, then have a contest to see which group can make the greatest reduction in the amount of garbage thrown away. Have a book and toy exchange wherein children bring in items to be exchanged with other students.

Home Activities: Have students survey their homes and note the amount of plastic products used. Have a Ten Can Day when each student brings in ten deposit cans. Use the money to buy library books or join an environmental group.

Physical Education Game: Trashketball
Equipment Required: Several clean trash containers, three or more cones, and a variety of throwing objects, such as whiffle balls, sponge balls, yarn balls, beanbags, or crumpled paper balls
Starting Formation: Divide the group into relay formation, arrange the containers at one end of the gymnasium and the cones six to eight feet in front of the containers, and then scatter the balls in the middle of the gymnasium (see Figure 16.1).

FIGURE 16.1: Trashketball

Description: The objective is to clean up the gymnasium by picking up the trash (e.g., paper balls) and throwing it into a trash container. The first person in line is given a ticket (i.e., a rip flag or a slip of paper), and on signal picks up one piece of trash, runs to the cone, and throws it in the trash container. This person returns to his or her team's line and gives the next person the ticket. The game is over when the trash has been cleaned up. The team with the most trash in their container wins.

Rules:

1. Pick up only one paper ball.
2. One must throw from behind the cone.
3. Do not pick up balls that miss the trash container.
4. Students can run only when they have a ticket.

Discussion: Since litter is everyone's problem, keeping the environment clean is very important, especially in one's own neighborhood, school, and community.

THEME TWO: ENDANGERED ANIMALS

Concepts: Discuss why animals become endangered or extinct (e.g., hunted for sport, fur, hides, and ivory). Explain that animal habitats are being lost due to commercial projects and land development. Talk about why dolphins are being caught in tuna nets.

Community Activities: Visit a local ecology center. Adopt an animal from a zoo by helping to pay for the cost of caring for it.

School Activities: Learn how to attract birds by setting up bird feeders constructed by students. Identify local endangered species.

Home Activities: Encourage students to talk to their parents about not purchasing things made from endangered animals. Snip plastic bags and six-pack rings before throwing them away, for they endanger the lives of animals.

Physical Education Game: Jungle Juice

Equipment Required: Twenty stuffed animals donated by children, seven cones, and a jungle leaf cut from foam or paper

Starting Formation: Organize the children into a relay formation of three to four lines. Use cones to create an animal cage in the shape of a square. Place the stuffed animals inside the cage. Select two hunters who guard the animals.

Description: The objective is to have animal savers remove them from the cage without being tagged. The first person in the relay line holds the jungle leaf (gives energy) and runs to the animal cage to rescue an animal. The hunters try to tag the rescuers, who cannot be tagged while in line or in the animal cage. If a rescuer is tagged on the way to the cage, he or she must return to the line and pass the jungle leaf to the next person in line. If the rescuer is tagged on the way back from the cage, he or she must return the animal to the cage and pass the jungle leaf to the next person in line. The game is over when all the animals are rescued. The team with the most animals rescued wins.

Rules: No hunter is allowed in the cage, and students can rescue only one animal at a time.

Discussion: Discuss local endangered animals, world endangered animals, and the difference between being extinct and being endangered.

THEME THREE: AIR POLLUTION

Concepts: Discuss the causes and effects of air pollution. Car exhaust causes much of it, but coal-burning factories also put harmful gases into the air. Acid rain occurs when chemicals mix with the rain and form a weak acid, a substance very harmful to plants, animals, and people. Some propellants used in aerosol sprays destroy the ozone layer, allowing harmful rays from the sun to reach earth, and air pollution hurts people with respiratory diseases.

Community Activities: Invite local politicians to speak about the action being taken by the government to reduce air pollution. Invite local officials responsible for cleaning up toxic waste areas. Visit resource recovery centers to learn about the levels of toxins that are being emitted from burning garbage.

School Activities: Collect air samples by putting petroleum jelly on index cards and placing them high up on the school walls; after several days, view the results under a microscope.

Home Activities: Plant seedlings at home that are donated to students by local communities. Discourage the use of aerosol cans by purchasing substitutes.

Physical Education Game: Dirty Dudes Chemical Company

Equipment Required: Three or four large fold-up mats, twenty or more blown-up balloons (air pollution), two containers (large boxes or balloons), ten cones, four rip flags, and ten plastic bowling pins

Starting Formation: Select a president and vice president of a chemical company. Divide the rest of the class into two groups: the government's Environmental Protection Agency (EPA) and the Dream Green (DG), a local environmental group. Stand up large mats to form a circle, with an opening for the chemical company. Surround the mats with bowling pins (the company's security system), and surround the bowling pins with cones as a security fence.

Description: The objective is to have the EPA and DG remove all of the air pollution from the chemical company. Two people from the EPA and DG, each person holding a rip flag, try to get inside the chemical company and remove the balloons. The president and vice president guard the chemical company and try to tag people entering and leaving with balloons. The game is over when all balloons are removed from the chemical company.

Rules: The president and vice president remain between the boundary line and the security fence. Any EPA or DG team member tagged on the way to the company returns to the line and passes the rip flag to the next person, but when the EPA and DG representatives are inside the company's security area, they are safe and cannot be tagged, whereupon the president and vice president are not allowed inside the security area or the company. If a bowling pin is knocked down by an EPA or DG person, he or she returns to the line and passes the rip flag to next person. If an EPA or DG person removes a balloon and is tagged on the way back, the balloon must be returned to the company.

Discussion: Discuss the value of riding a bike or walking instead of using a car. Identify the value of using sun protection on clear days, and the value of having a company reduce the amount of pollution it puts into the air. Complain to your local governmental agencies about air pollution.

THEME FOUR: SAVE THE RAINFORESTS

Concepts: Discuss the importance of saving the rainforests. Rainforests contain many of the world's animals and birds. These forests should be preserved because they are sources of drugs, medicines, and other natural resources such as fibers and rubber. Yet the rainforests are being destroyed for firewood, lumber, and paper.

School Activities:

- Decorate the school lobby like a rainforest
- Display a fact a day about rainforests in the lobby
- Write a play based on a rainforest book
- Have a choral reading
- Serve rainforest fruits and nuts at lunch
- Collect pennies to buy a piece of land in the rainforest
- Hold a poster contest

Physical Education Game: Rainforest Obstacle Course

Obstacle 1: Jump Over the Amazon River. Place triangle mats face to face with two feet between them, wherein a drawing of electric eels and piranhas is placed.

Obstacle 2: Climb Up and Jump off a Waterfall. Stack mats four to five feet high, help students when they jump off, and provide mats for the landing area.

Obstacle 3: Wild Animal Walk. Scatter stuffed animals along a pathway and have students move through without disturbing them. Hang pictures of gorillas, monkeys, tigers, orangutans, and other endangered animals.

Obstacle 4: Deforestation Area Run Through. Set up cardboard and paper tubes painted brown and black, and have students run through them without knocking them down.

Obstacle 5: Snake Pit Crawl. Use high jump standards with a pole three feet off the floor. Hang paper snakes from the pole. The anaconda is a giant snake. Other kinds of snakes include the coral snake, tree snake, and boa constrictor.

Obstacle 6: Buttressed Roots Jump. Set up cones and place long twigs or sticks on top. The large fan of roots helps support trees.

Obstacle 7: Forest Canopy and Vines Run Through. Hang a parachute from the gymnasium ceiling, with brown crepe paper dangling from the ends. The top level of the forest is called the canopy. The middle level is the under story, and the bottom level is the forest floor. The vines are called lianas.

Obstacle 8: Crawl Through Termite Tunnels. Termites make long tunnels to their nests. Place crawl tunnels on mats for this effect.

Obstacle 9: Termite Mound Pass Through. Stack up foam shapes while maintaining an opening for the children to walk through. Have them move through without knocking the mounds down. Three million termites can inhabit one mound.

Each grade level can choose an area and decorate the gym with bats, colorful birds, animals (monkeys and gorillas are favorites), termites and termite mounds, tissue paper flowers, trees, leaves, vines, fish, snakes, and insects (see Figure 16.2).

OBSTACLE 1: JUMP OVER AMAZON RIVER

OBSTACLE 2: CLIMB UP AND JUMP OFF WATERFALL

OBSTACLE 3: WILD ANIMAL WALK

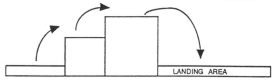

- SET UP PATH WITH JUMP ROPES
- PLACE ANIMALS ON PATH

OBSTACLE 4: DEFORESTATION AREA RUN THROUGH

OBSTACLE 5: SNAKE PIT CRAWL

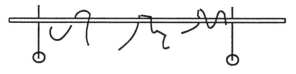

FIGURE 16.2: Rainforest Obstacle Course

OBSTACLE 6: BUTTRESSED ROOTS JUMP

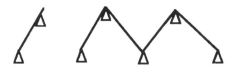

OBSTACLE 7: FOREST CANOPY AND VINES RUN THROUGH

OBSTACLE 8: CRAWL THROUGH TERMITE TUNNELS

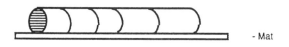 - Mat

OBSTACLE 9: TERMITE MOUND PASS THROUGH

 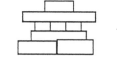 - Foam Shapes

FIGURE 16.2: Continued - Rainforest Obstacle Course

17

Using Narrative Stories in the Classroom and Gymnasium

Ellen M. Kowalski and Susan O. Kennedy

One approach to providing diverse play experiences is through the use of the obstacle course. Obstacle courses are an excellent medium for teaching concepts and skills, and they provide children with a wide variety of experiences and personal challenges (Kowalski, Kennedy, and Jackson, 1992). Obstacle courses are also economical, easily constructed, and a versatile means of providing activity that is challenging and creative. Equipment can include classroom furniture, old bed sheets, newspapers, and stepladders.

Narrative stories or story plays are another medium through which children can enjoy experiencing movement and self-expression. In story plays, children act out the characters of a familiar story (e.g., the *Tale of Peter Rabbit*), a fairy tale ("Beauty and the Beast"), or a real-life experience (visiting the circus, the zoo, or a farm). Acting out narrative stories can foster creativity and help reduce the hesitancy often felt by children when expressing themselves verbally and physically (Clements, 1991).

By combining these two instructional techniques, teachers can expose the child to a variety of movement experiences, as well as opportunities for creativity and self-expression, in a creative and imaginative medium (Kowalski, Kennedy, and Jackson, 1992). Children are given the opportunity to become part of the story through multisensory actions. These movement experiences can incorporate many instructional elements including balance and body awareness as well as math, spelling, geography and other academic subjects. Children can experiment with movement qualities such as force, flow, and time, and work on communication skills such as listening, following directions, auditory sequencing, and memory.

The story play obstacle course is an exciting concept because it can be used by anyone who teaches children, that is, classroom teachers, physical educators, adapted physical educators, and parents (Kowalski, Kennedy, and Jackson, 1992). Current trends in education support collaboration between teaching areas as well as multicultural and multisensory experiences. Narrative stories combined with the obstacle course give young children the opportunity to connect the motor, affective, and cognitive domains of learning in an enjoyable and novel manner.

We give one example of a story play obstacle course that can be easily modified to meet the needs of the young child. It can be constructed in the classroom, cafeteria, gymnasium, or living room. The following story play is based on Halloween, an exciting and festive time of the year for children. The haunted house provides children with the environment for creating many enjoyable, suspenseful, creative, and mysterious movement experiences.

THE HAUNTED HOUSE

Objectives: The child experiences the concepts over, under, through, and on. The child experiences crawling, climbing, jumping, maintaining dynamic balance while walking on tiptoes, riding a tricycle, balancing, and riding a scooter. (See Figure 17.1.)

Equipment Required: Balance beam, carpet squares, small ladder, newspaper, foam balls, jogger trampoline, accordion mats or Swedish box, hula hoop, tape, tissue paper, barrel, toy broom, tricycle, scooter board, small indoor slide, fishing line, incline mat, and a white sheet.

Story: It's HALLOWEEN NIGHT! Let's find a haunted house! I know where there is a deserted house. Look! Over there! There it is! OOOH, it looks scary. Let's go in!! First we have to **crawl under this fence to get onto the haunted house property (Obstacle 1).** Everyone under? O.K. Now we have to walk through all this overgrown brush. Swish, swish, swish, swish. Yuk! It's getting swampy! Squish, squish, squish. Now we've come to a stream. How are we going to get across? Look over there! There are big flat rocks that we can use as stepping stones! **Stay on your tiptoes and be careful not to fall in the water (Obstacle 2).** Whew! We made it! Here we are at the house. Ohh, it's old, falling apart. Everything is locked up and boarded up. How are we going to get inside? Look! There's an open window! **Let's put this ladder up against the side of the house. Be careful climbing the ladder and going through the window (Obstacle 3).** Hey, I think we're in what used to be the living room! Wow, here is an **old tricycle all covered with dust and cobwebs. Let's dust it off (cough, cough) and see if it still works. It works! We'll all take turns riding it around the living room (Obstacle 4).** Now that we've all ridden the tricycle, let's explore the rest of the house. YIKES!! There's a ghost! RUN! No, wait! The ghost is calling to us. He's a friendly ghost and his name is Jaimie. He wants to know if we would be his friend. Should we? All right! Hey, Jaimie wants to know if we'd like to learn to float like him? Yes, we do!! **We'll practice floating down this hallway (Obstacle 5).** Boy, that was fun floating. **Let's go see what's upstairs! Creak, creak. These stairs sure are rickety. We're almost at the top. Yikes! There's a trap door! AHHHHHHHH! We're sliding! (Obstacle 6).** Bump! Plop! Is everybody O.K.? I think we're in the basement. It sure is dark down here. **We'd better crawl on our hands and knees until we find a way out. Ugh! I just crawled into some cobwebs and bugs! What are these**

squishy things I feel? (Obstacle 7). I sure don't want to find out! Let's get out of here! **Here's a laundry chute! We'll crawl up it (Obstacle 8).** Hurry! WHOA! Oh look, we're in the kitchen! And over here is what must have been the dining room. What's that sound I hear??? It sounds like someone is laughing . . . it sounds like . . . oh no . . . it sounds like a wicked witch. YIKES! It is a wicked witch!! There she is flying on her broom inside the house! **We're not afraid of you, old witch!! We can fly and cackle just like you! OH NO! She's chasing us! (Obstacle 9).** Where is our friendly ghost? We'd better get out of here! Head for the window! **We go back through the window, down the ladder, across the stream, through the swamp and brush and back under the fence (Obstacle 10).** WHEW! We're safe.

Haunted House Obstacles:

- The child crawls under a balance beam, table, or chair and walks over foam sheets used in packing appliances.
- The child steps or leaps from one carpet square to another. Carpet squares are placed in random order between two long jump ropes laid on the floor to designate the water.
- A horizontal ladder is placed against stacked accordion mats or a Swedish vaulting box at an angle. The child climbs the ladder to the top of the mats. A hula hoop is taped vertically onto the top mat. The child crawls through and jumps down to the floor.
- The child rides a tricycle in a designated circle marked off by small cones.
- A white sheet placed over a barrel or trashcan serves as our friendly ghost. The child lies down on a scooter and pushes with both arms while trying to glide down a straight path marked by colored tape.
- The child climbs up the ladder of a small indoor slide and slides to the floor.
- The child closes his or her eyes and crawls on hands and knees among foam balls, bunched up newspaper, tissue, and unraveled fishing line or string. Newspaper taped onto the floor marks the boundaries of the basement.
- Two incline mats are placed back to back, forming a pyramid. The child crawls or walks, depending on the age level, up one side of the mat and down the other side to the floor. An alternative activity would be to use a carpeted barrel, a therapy tub, or a rolled mat that has been placed on top of a wedge mat and secured.
- The child jumps while holding a small broom handle to the side, or gallops with a small broom handle between his or her legs.
- The child returns to the starting place by climbing up the stacked mats, through the vertical hula hoop, and down the angled horizontal ladder, then leaping to each carpet square and crawling under the balance beam.

REFERENCES

Bailey, R., and E. Burton (1982). *The Dynamic Self: Activities to Enhance Infant Development*. St. Louis: C. V. Mosby.

Clements, R. (1991). Making the Most of Movement Narratives. *Journal of Physical Education, Recreation, and Dance*, 62(9), 57-61.

Dauer, V., and R. Pangrazi (1979). *Dynamic Physical Education for Elementary School Children*. Minneapolis: Burgess.

Kowalski, E., S. Kennedy, and S. Jackson (1992). Imagination in Action: A Story Play
    Obstacle Course. *Strategies*, 5(7), 16-20.

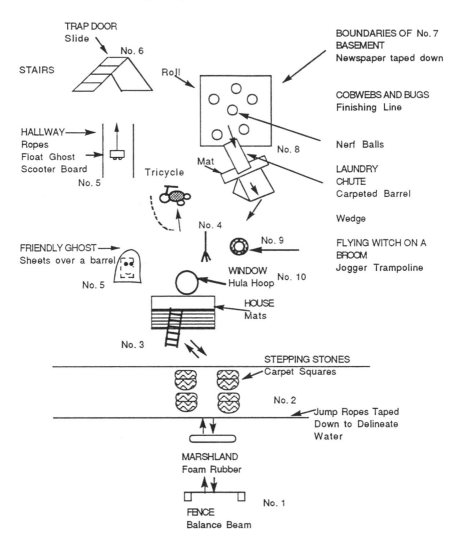

FIGURE 17.1: Haunted House Obstacles

18

Vegetable Stir-Fry:
A Creative Movement Game

Lorna J. Woodward

The following activity demonstrates how the understanding of nutrition can be incorporated into an enjoyable game activity for preschool through first grade children. To begin, the teacher discusses the types of vegetables found in a market or grocery store. Concepts related to shape, color, and texture should be identified. Photographs or picture books may help to reinforce these characteristics.

Ask the children to raise their hands if they have ever tasted stir-fried vegetables. Explain that raw vegetables that snap and crunch are cut or chopped into tiny bite-size shapes, which allows them to cook quickly. Fewer vitamins escape when vegetables are cooked quickly.

Begin the activity by asking the children to use their hands and arms to demonstrate a chopping motion. Challenge them to use their whole bodies to imitate the size and shape of a long, narrow stalk of celery, a tearful round onion, a thin cabbage leaf, a long, pointed carrot, a round green pepper, a tiny green pea, and a mushroom cap (by placing the hands on the head).

Explain that the class can move together and pretend to make a stir-fry recipe. Ask the children to imagine a large round frying pan in the center of the activity area. The children are challenged to make believe that their bodies are different vegetables in the middle of the frying pan (or wok) while they react to the following verbal commands:

a. Stir It Up—Move throughout the activity area in the shape of a favorite vegetable.
b. Heat Turned On—Move while quickly lifting the feet off the floor.
c. Heat Turned Down—Move slowly, making different pathways between and around classmates.
d. Heat Turned Off—Freeze motionless in space.

Complete the learning experience in the classroom setting by preparing a vegetable stir-fry for the children to sample, or by having the children model clay into shapes representing healthy vegetables and fruits.

19

Every Child a Winner Educational Games

Martha Owens and Susan Rockett

The Every Child a Winner project was originally funded to design and fieldtest a model physical education curriculum which would significantly improve the students' level of fitness and motor skill ability while also enhancing their self-esteem and academic performance in kindergarten through grade six. A three-year developmental grant was awarded the Irwin County schools in 1970. In 1974 the Joint Dissemination Review Panel of the United States Department of Education in Georgia validated the Every Child a Winner project as a national model. The National Diffusion Network of the U.S. Department of Education awarded a dissemination grant to provide training for schools throughout the United States to replicate the model. Over five thousand schools have adopted the program, and twelve national demonstration sites are available to view the developmentally appropriate model in operation.

CONTENT

The content of the Every Child a Winner instructional program is based on Rudolph Laban's system of analyzing human movement. A movement framework developed by using Laban's system provides structure for all experiences children receive in the Every Child A Winner program. Educational dance, educational gymnastics, and educational games are given equal emphasis. This chapter gives an overview of the Every Child a Winner instructional program in educational games.

In educational games children design their own games using the movement concepts presented during the current or previous lessons. Children are encouraged to participate in the decision-making processes that arise as the games are designed. Tasks are carefully structured to encourage maximum participation both mentally and physically. As a child's game develops, he or she is encouraged to add challenges and advance to the next stage of development.

Attention is given to children's development needs and their readiness to participate in the games they develop.

Competition occurs in many of the children's games. The desire for competition emerges at different age levels. In the Every Child a Winner program, competition is, always child initiated. When children initiate a competitive situation, tasks are carefully structured to encourage positive, realistic attitudes toward the importance of winning and losing in the games. Children are encouraged to do their best while experiencing winning and failing situations as an opportunity to learn, improve game skills, and build positive attitudes toward themselves and their opponents.

Children are asked to work alone or with others. Partners are not selected by the teacher for the child. Children may choose to work with just one other child or with several, but the decision is theirs. Socialization is handled developmentally following the child's lead.

THE IMPORTANCE OF MOVEMENT CONCEPTS

Children are often asked to play games that are not developmentally appropriate. In the Every Child a Winner program many factors are considered when structuring developmentally appropriate games lessons. Prime consideration is given to teaching the movement concepts of space awareness, body awareness, qualities of movement, and relationships as based on Laban's study of human movement. Each concept is taught sequentially from kindergarten through the sixth grade in games. A concepts-based program provides a decidedly different approach from an activities-based program, loosely organized around teacher designed games of varying complexity. Child-designed games are used in the program rather than teacher-designed games because they are found to be more developmentally appropriate. Children are encouraged to think, to interact, to solve movement problems, and to work cooperatively in games, as well as to compete. The teaching method is indirect rather than direct.

Outcome-based objectives provide accountability in the games program and give the direction and focus for each lesson. Years of field-testing have resulted in lesson plans rated developmentally appropriate by teachers and practitioners throughout the United States. In developing these outcome-based objectives, current research in motor development, perceptual motor functioning, and the mechanical principles governing a child's movement world are considered. In addition, teachers evaluate the lessons for content, age appropriateness, skill development, social development, and skill progression.

In Every Child a Winner educational games, the children's curiosity about their world and movement is stimulated through the orderly introduction of a variety of materials and movement tasks. When children are at what Jean Piaget called the stage of concrete operational thought, they are encouraged to learn primarily through tasks that allow exploration, experimentation, and personal discovery.

In every children's class there is a wide range of ability and interest in various aspects of games. In order to help teachers plan developmentally appropriate tasks, Mauldon and Redfern (1981) present 6 stages of games development which can be recognized at the primary level.

THE STAGES OF GAME DEVELOPMENT

The Every Child a Winner staff has found after twenty-two years of research that these stages consistently occur not only when children begin at the primary level, but also in older children when they first learn to develop their own games. In the first phase of games development, most young children are preoccupied with exploratory play. They are thrilled with the motion, color, and properties of the equipment. Many of their games involve repetition of one movement. Most will choose to work alone even when given an option. If other children are invited to intervene in play, they are allowed only to hold, carry, and return objects. Most would opt to play somewhere else without the teacher's intervention, but if this continues, the teacher should allow the children to think the situation through by asking questions to help them solve the problem of inactivity. Young children in this phase participate at each challenge they create for only a few minutes. This is not a concern for the teacher as long as the children are continuously selecting challenges that answer the movement task presented to them. Another frequent occurrence in the first stage is that a group of children may opt to play together in a way that gives some little chance to participate. An example is a kicking game where one child kicks, one pitches, and several stand in line waiting a turn. The child at the end of the line is usually unhappy with being inactive while waiting for a chance to kick. Carefully posed questions can assist the children in finding a solution that provides maximum participation opportunities for everyone.

In the second phase of games development, children become more aware of the importance of individual body parts and their ability to control objects that they manipulate through space. For example, using the instep of the foot suddenly becomes important in order for the child to manipulate a ball consistently in a low level while traveling through general space (dribbling). Often children select equipment not vital to the success of their games. The arrangement of the hoops, ropes, boxes, and so on overshadows the importance of designing a game in response to the movement tasks. This is an important developmental experience for children, who need to be allowed to move, touch, lift, and carry equipment of different weight, shape, and size.

In the third phase of games development, children become very interested in maximum participation. Although they are willing to involve others in their games, they are mainly interested in personal skill development. They strive to answer each movement task correctly, but they can easily be distracted into exploratory play.

By the fourth phase of games development, children want to perform each movement correctly. Being "skilled" becomes important to them. They have a desire to learn and improve at each task. Irrelevant equipment no longer appears in their games, and they concentrate on and spend more time practicing a given action. Cooperative games outnumber the competitive games children design during this stage. Rules, decided upon by the children, appear during this stage. These rules are designed to structure success rather than failure.

In the fifth phase children are very aware of the major sports and seek to emulate professional athletes in physical education class. The desire to share skills increases, and children begin to seek opportunities to display the skills they have mastered. Interest in making rules and keeping score becomes apparent, but the need to succeed daily is still more important. Therefore, they are lenient when penalizing infractions of the rules they have mutually agreed upon.

In the sixth phase the children develop a renewed interest in using a variety of equipment, and the process of introducing complicated rules to regulate participation is investigated. Excitement over their ability to maintain skill levels causes them to recognize and appreciate the organization of their games as well as the action occurring. The interest in professional sports increases, and there is a renewed interest in rules and regulations.

The concepts for the educational games lessons in the Every Child a Winner program are taken from the Every Child a Winner movement chart, with an emphasis on a different concept in each lesson. Children progress from low to high spatial levels, from the use of light to strong force, slow to fast time, small to large extensions in space; and from the exploratory participation of the newly involved games player to the skillful organized games player emerging at the sixth stage.

In summary, the educational games lessons in the Every Child a Winner model are based on concepts rather than activities, on child-designed games rather than teacher-designed games, on the indirect teaching method rather than the direct, on outcome-based objectives that provide accountability rather than on loosely organized objectives and subjective evaluation, and on current research and field-testing rather than guesswork. Children move generally through these six phases when working with educational games. As a result, those who have adopted the program report measurably improved fitness and motor skill as well as improvement in critical thinking, vocabulary, self-discipline, and self-esteem in kindergarten through grade six. The Every Child a Winner program encourages children to reach their personal potential, and winning occurs when they do their best.

SAMPLE LESSON ACTIVITIES FROM THE EVERY CHILD A WINNER PROGRAM

Goals are oriented toward space awareness, inculcating general space, personal space, and directions involving forward, backward, right, left, up, or down movements. Children in movement education, upon the completion of eight lessons, will, on the average, understand space awareness as evidenced by their ability to establish personal space in free space and in space occupied by individuals, groups, and objects. They will be able to travel among moving objects and individuals without touching them, and be able to move body parts in spatial directions.

Equipment Required: One yarn ball for every child, one long wand for every child

The Process: Can the children travel slowly through general space without touching one another, and gradually increase their speed? Allow them to travel only short distances between your stop signals, and draw their attention to free space before giving them the signal to begin moving. Can they indeed travel slowly through space without touching another person, and, as they travel, can they move quickly into the space observed around the playing space?

Movement Training

Can children find a place to work in space? Can they find their personal space? Questions can be asked such as how high their personal space is, or how low it is. For example, can the children explore moving body parts into every place in personal space? Have they stretched in front and behind their bodies? Are they always moving the same body parts? Can they expand their movements? Does bodily expansion increase the width of their personal space? Can they move to a new place in space? Can they re-establish their own personal space? Once they have established their personal space, and they move their base of support, does this personal space go with them? They have to keep their base still only when trying to establish a new personal space. Can they travel through space and avoid touching their peers' personal space? The teacher should use a signal to stop them to be sure they are observing others' personal space. They should not be able to touch another child even when stretching. There must be ample general space for children to use. Can they move a little faster and observe personal space? How fast can they move and still observe personal space? Stop the children frequently if maintaining personal space is a problem. Can they find a different point in space and establish personal space there? When they travel through space, what must they control in order not to get in someone else's personal space?

Given a signal, can they select a yarn ball and explore playing with it in different ways, keeping it in their personal space? What are some of the different things that can be done with each child's ball? Does the ball bounce? If not, then why not? What can be done to make the ball travel into someone else's personal space? Ask the child to return the yarn ball and select a ball that will bounce. Can the child bounce it so that it stays in his or her personal space? This inculcates height of space, force used, size of personal space, and body position that can best control the ball. Can students travel through space avoiding other people's personal space while keeping the ball in their own space? What must they watch as they travel? What must they try to control? Which is easier to control, the yarn ball or the bouncing ball? Can these children return the balls and establish a space beside one of the wands? Is the wand longer than it is wide?

Is the wand light or very heavy? Can the children pick up the wand slowly, keeping all of it in their personal space? How many things can the children explore with their wand and keep it in their personal space? When the child picks up a wand or any piece of equipment, it becomes an extension of his or her personal space and enlarges the area. Can the child hold the wand and move it slowly to establish a personal space? Can the children move through space with their wands at a medium level? Using the available equipment, can they create a game in which the equipment is maintained in personal space?

REFERENCES

Laban, R., and F. Lawrence (1947). *Effort*. London: Unwin Brothers.

Mauldon, E., and H. B. Redfern (1981). *Games Teaching*, 2nd ed. London: Longman.

Owens, Martha (1985). Developing and Disseminating a Curriculum Model—Implications for Professional Preparation. In H. Hoffman and J. E. Rink, eds. *Physical Education Professional Preparation: Insights and Foresights: Proceedings from the Second National Conference on Preparing the Physical Education Specialist for Children*. Reston, Va.: American Alliance for Health, Physical Education, Recreation, and Dance, 194-98.

Owens, Martha (1981). Mainstreaming in the Every Child a Winner Program. *Journal of Physical Education, Recreation, and Dance*, 52(7), 16-18.

Piaget, J., and B. Inhelder (1969). *The Psychology of the Child*. New York: Basic Books.

Rockett, Susan, and Martha Owens (1987). *Every Child A Winner Lesson Plans, Level I, II, III . . .: A Movement Education Curriculum for Today's Child*. ECAW–Lesson Plans, P.O. Box 141, Ocilla, Georgia 31774.

20

Designing Games for Fun and Learning in the Classroom

Lenore Sandel

The purposes for using games in the classroom are clearly defined in both learning theory and successful teaching practice. Although students frequently perceive a game as a means of play or diversion, the teacher's intent is to use this student view of play to motivate and reinforce learning, or to evaluate student growth through performance assessment. In other words, the reluctant student responds to a nonthreatening situation, and the teacher is able to assess the student's progress through the actual application of the lesson content in *playing the game*.

It is interesting to note that as early as 1693 John Locke wrote: "I have often thought that if playthings were fitted to learning, contrivances might be made to teach children to read whilst they thought they were only playing" (Garforth, 1964, p. 187). Locke was designing a game when he suggested that facts to be learned should be written on dice for motivation as play. Two thousand years earlier, Plato said, "Let your children's lessons take the form of play" (Garforth, 1964).

The distinction drawn between play and games is essentially that a game is play with rules. This distinction emerges from Piaget's classification of the most mature stage of play as "games with rules" (Garvey, 1977, p. 103). Inherent in this definition are the characteristics associated with games in the classroom. The activities are organized, are often competitive in nature, and contain rules that restrict and require a particular conduct of the play. This demands that the student be able to cooperate in competitive interactions, to plan and carry out activities with purpose, and to exercise self-control in attending to restrictions. Since these abilities are attributed in developmental theory to ages five and six years, the kindergarten or first grade classroom becomes the setting for organized play with rules. However, for those youngsters, even at this age, who have not reached the assigned developmental stage, Susan Isaacs (1933, 1935) proposes dramatic play to further children's intellectual and socio-emotional development.

Isaacs demonstrates how dramatic play within a "let's pretend" imaginary world projects the children into higher intellectual activity and achievement. Pestalozzi (1801; 1915) gives significance to developing imaginative powers, supporting Isaacs' "make-believe—let's pretend" as a means of advancing the child's educational progression. In essence, playing a game with rules requires the prerequisite abilities of self-control, cooperation, and reasoning.

Smilansky and Shefatya (1990) offered several suggestions to encourage the sequence of these developmental abilities through sociodramatic play activities. Using Smilansky's work as a guide, I have evolved a basic sequence of steps useful in designing developmentally appropriate classroom games. The steps are as follows:

1. Define the design objective.

    There may be a wide range of purposes, but the specific purpose of any game must ultimately reflect the teaching objective as determined by the teacher/designer.

2. Determine the scope of the game in terms of the issues to be examined, its setting in time, and its geographic area.

    Now the designer is defining the subject of the game, aware of what characteristics are recognized or recognizable by the intended players.

3. Identify key actors in the process, whether individuals, groups, organizations, or institutions.

    At this point, the number of players is a factor. With large groups, when it may be necessary to limit participation, ratios can be used.

4. Define the objectives of the actors in terms of wealth, power, influence, and other rewards.

    Where practical, player goals should be clearly identified. Is the goal, for example, to acquire material "wealth," "power," "rank," or "influence" for effective action? Here it is important to avoid any ideological objectives, since they are very difficult to define in this classroom context.

5. Determine the actor's resources, including the game information each receives.

    These may vary from tangible assets to intangible advantages, such as status or rank. Here we determine how many resources to begin with. How much information is needed to play? How many facts are necessary, for example, to recognize role profiles?

6. Determine the decision rules, or criteria, that actors use in deciding what actions to take.

    These basic decisions by the players constitute the foundation of the game.

7. Determine the interaction sequence among the actors.

    The need for communication is met through the interaction between and among the players.

8. Identify external constraints on the actions of the players.

    The constraints determine what the actors may not do.

9. Decide the scoring rules or win criteria of the game.

    The scoring rules are defined in terms of the objectives of the actors. In a game with a resource of money, for example, the winner may relinquish a specified amount of money as a penalty for responding to a question incorrectly. A correct answer, on the other hand, would be rewarded by a larger amount. The criterion here is to answer a question correctly. A guidebook, written by the game designer, defines the win criteria to decrease scoring problems.

10. Choose a form of presentation and formulate the sequence of operation. Two of many variations, for example, are game boards and role-playing.

Role-playing is an easier form of presentation since it provides for immediate response and involves the active attention of all participants. When a game board is used, several boards are better than one large board to encourage movement among the players. The sequence of presentation represents the rules of the game.

The sample game called "Lotto: Synonyms" demonstrates how the ten steps can be easily implemented.

Name of the Game: Lotto: Synonyms

1. **Purpose.** The purpose of this game is to extend vocabulary through knowledge of synonyms. (Lotto may also be designed for antonyms, homonyms, and multiple-meaning words.)
2. **Scope.** The players select a word on the lotto board closest in meaning to a word card drawn from the deck of synonym words.
3. **Players.** Limiting the number of players to two or three increases frequency of participation.
4. **Player Goals.** Each player will respond to as many stimuli as possible, with the goal of completing a vertical, horizontal, or diagonal row on the lotto board.
5. **Game Resource.** Each player will receive an adequate number of lotto counters for each game.
6. **Decision Rule.** Players will draw one card from the deck, and respond by selecting a synonym on the game board. When the line is completed, the player signifies by making an announcement. Answers are verified through review of stimuli (word cards with answers).
7. **Player Interaction.** Players take turns during each game.
8. **Constraints.** Players must select the synonym cards in order of the stack.
9. **Scoring.** The player who wins the greater (or greatest) number of individual games is the winner. The criterion of "winning" is completing a row before one's opponent(s).
10. **Form of Presentation:** Using a game board and a deck of synonym cards (synonyms for words on player boards).

Prizes for winners may be determined by players and/or the teacher. Lotto may be used as a small group or whole class activity if enough individual game boards can be prepared to avoid duplication.

Finally, it is important to include a few general pointers for introducing this chapter's conceptual framework to staff members involved in in-service training or students of preservice programs.

THE USE OF SUBJECT AREA GAMES

- In a subject area context, a game is used for reinforcement, not for teaching or reteaching. Students are often more willing to think, respond, and try to remember during instructional time if they are assured that they can use what they are learning in a game situation.
- After being taught and played in groups, many games can be played independently during free time. When accuracy is a major factor, provide supervision.

- Games should be designed so that all players must be alert at all times.
- The number of players should be limited to avoid awkward situations and to assure efficient use of time.
- When teaching games to young children, be certain that all directions (oral and written) are understood clearly by all the players.
- Design games that encourage students to apply the skills they have learned.

CONSTRUCTION OF GAMES

- Use manila file folders or colored railroad board. Colored card stock is fine for most game cards. Use cards in various sizes and an assortment of precut gameboards from an available supply when constructing a game quickly.
- Games that will be used frequently should be laminated or covered with clear contact paper.
- Keep a supply of assorted felt markers on hand. Color adds to the attractiveness and clarity of any game and often contributes to understanding through color association and distinctions.
- It is often possible to use materials from commercial games for different purposes, converting them to suit your needs. In these instances, the process of conversion must be the primary objective.
- Finally, when examining a commercial game (e.g., Monopoly or Bingo), apply the aforementioned procedures for designing games. You may draw your own conclusions about the appeal of some of the more popular games.

REFERENCES

Garvey, C. (1977). *Play*. Cambridge, Mass.: Harvard University Press.

Gordon, A. K. (1970). *Games for Growth*. Chicago: Science Research Associates.

Isaacs, S. (1933). *Social Development of Young Children: A Study of Beginnings*. London: Routledge and Sons.

——— (1935). *Intellectual Growth in Children*. London: Routledge and Sons.

Locke, J. (1964). *Some Thoughts Concerning Education*. F. W. Garforth, ed. Woodbury, N.Y.: Barron's Educational Services.

Pestalozzi, J. H. (1801, translated 1915). *How Gertrud Teaches Her Children*. Syracuse, N.Y.: W. Bardeen.

Smilansky, S., and L. Shefatya (1990). *Facilitating Play: A Medium for Promoting Cognitive, Socio-Emotional, and Academic Development in Young Children*. Gaithersburg, Md.: Psychosocial and Educational Publications.

21

Children as Partners in Creating Educational Games

Heidi Reichel

Educational games have been used successfully for years as an entertaining vehicle for reviewing and reinforcing information previously introduced. Involving children as partners in creating educational games takes this one step further. Here, the actual process of making the game becomes an additional positive learning experience through which information is reinforced and self-esteem is heightened.

POTPOURRI—THE GAME

Potpourri is designed to enable students to work on four different subjects as they create and later play the game. The choice of subjects is limitless. Virtually any body of knowledge about which questions requiring a definitive answer can be asked can be put into game form. The game-making process begins by giving each student (game maker) a copy of a blank gameboard. Each student is also given sources of information upon which to base the game questions. Entire worksheets, textbook chapter reviews, or examinations can be used for this purpose. It will be the job of the game makers to rewrite this information into game format.

Directions for Game Makers

Materials Required: Blank gameboard; index cards; red, green, blue, orange, and purple fine-tip and broad-tip markers; clear contact paper or laminating material

Procedure:

1. Color each of the squares on the gameboard red, blue, green, orange, or purple as shown in Figure 21.1 (use broad-tip markers).
2. Designate a subject area to correspond with the blue, green, red, and orange squares. The purple squares will be for potpourri.

3. Make question cards by using the fine-tip markers in the designated color for each subject. For example, all math problems could be in green, all science questions in orange, all social studies questions in blue, and all English questions in red. Write one question on the front of each index card. Write the answer to the question on the back of the same card. Select a few more questions in each subject and write them on index cards using the purple fine point marker. These will be the potpourri cards.
4. Cover the gameboard and question cards with clear contact paper or laminating material.

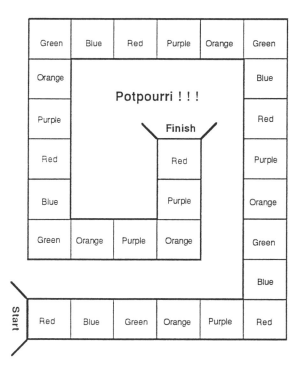

FIGURE 21.1: Potpourri Gameboard

Directions for Game Players

Equipment Required: Potpourri gameboard, question cards, one die, and colored pawn or button to mark each player's spot
Procedure:

1. Place the question cards in piles by color. Set the piles question side up around the outside edge of the gameboard.
2. Each player in turn will roll the die to see how many spaces to move his or her playing piece. Once the player has moved the playing piece, he or she will read the top question card written in the color that matches the color of the space he or she has landed on.

3. If able to answer the question correctly, the player moves ahead an extra space and the next player takes a turn.
4. Play continues until one student crosses the finish line.

22

Spell Hockey: A Creative Classroom Table Board Game

Joyce A. Zucker

The following activity combines the child's interest in sport activity with academic learning skills.

Name of the Game: Spell Hockey

Materials: Draw the gameboard on an 8" by 11" piece of cardboard. Cut out a puck and a hockey stick from a second piece of card-board. Laminate the entire gameboard with clear, self-sticking plastic.

Description: The game is for two or more players, on two teams. When teams play, players rotate turns to shoot, each getting a complete turn (see Figure 22.1). Teammates may assist in suggesting which letters to shoot for, and help select the longest word to make.

Place the puck in a shot spot and use the hockey stick to shoot the puck into a letter square above. The hockey stick must not touch the board beyond the shot line, or it counts as a foul. The letter inside *any* letter square that the puck touches may be used. Using dark, wipe-off crayons, write that letter in a space in the letter box. Each turn consists of seven shots. If a player fails to get seven letters, he or she must make a word out of the letters that were obtained. If the puck touches or enters the circles containing either bonus letter (the E and A circles in the center), that letter is used as any other letter, but the player receives an additional shot.

The area surrounding the bonus circles and the letter squares is the foul zone. The puck must be completely in the foul zone (not touching any box or circle) for the shot to count as a foul. If a player gets a foul, he or she gets one extra shot. If the puck goes foul on the extra shot, then the next team or player goes. The first player must make a word using as many of the letters that had been obtained as possible; if unable to make a word, the player receives zero points. At the end of a turn (after a student has taken seven shots or obtained seven letters), he or she uses as many of the letters as possible from the letter box to write a word in the word box. The individual or the team receives one point for each letter used. The highest score wins.

If an additional turn is due when the seventh letter has been obtained, the individual or the team gets one extra point. Erase the entire board after each turn.

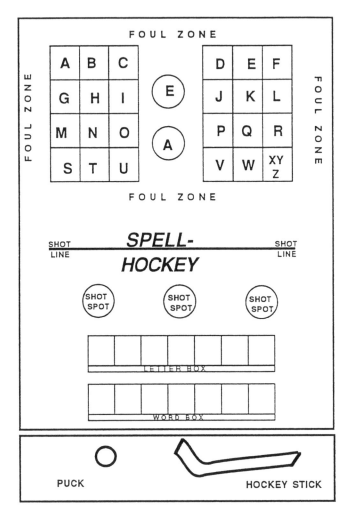

FIGURE 22.1: Spell Hockey

Part III

Games Reflecting Different Cultures

Part III opens with Ann Babcock Cella's chapter on five authentic activities of the North American Plains Indians. Georga Accola uses games and storytelling techniques to expand the student's knowledge of well-known individuals, groups, or events that influenced America's beginnings. In homage to our Native American legacy, Len Carolan explains how a homemade Alaskan Iditarod Race sled can be built and used in physical education classes to expand the student's knowledge of this popular sport. Mary McKnight-Taylor examines how popular jump rope skills and chants reflect African American culture. Similarly, Kirsten DeBear and Sara Kiesel relate how common culturally based street games containing rhythmic elements can be used to heighten the learning and physically challenged child's self-confidence through social interactions. Rhythmical activities are also used by Maria I. Ojeda-O'Neill in her selection of games and creative exercises common to Puerto Rico. Bess Ring Koval describes the game Thailand tag, which requires neither large spaces nor equipment when working with large or small groups. Susan M. Schwager and Ashley M. Hammond simplify the equipment needed to teach a modified version of the popular English game cricket. Teaching strategies related to throwing, catching, and striking are included. Birger Peitersen encourages American readers to place greater importance on the teaching of soccer. He explains how the Danish population has used soccer activities to articulate ideas and concepts while teaching children to become skillful movers. Donna R. Barnes examines seventeenth-century Dutch games, toys, and pastimes from the perspective of art and social hisotry, showing how this information is valuable to today's social and sport historians as well as teachers of children's games.

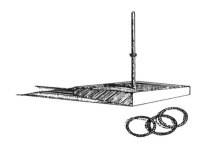

23

Selected Games and Dances of the North American Plains Indians

Ann Babcock Cella

Games and dance have existed in various forms since primitive times. In North America, Indian games and dance have reflected the history and culture of the people and have perpetuated values and skills needed for survival. Overtly, perceptual motor abilities and physical proficiency abilities were manifested in activities that simulated hunting, food gathering, fighting, and personal and tribal victories. Within the physical education setting, students can develop motorically, and at the same time achieve an understanding, awareness, and appreciation of the Native American culture. Two children's games and three dances of the Blackfoot Indian tribe are described here.

BLACKFEET GAMES

The children's games presented here were researched through interviews with elders, ethnology reports, books on the subject, and shared knowledge of the clan members of the Blackfoot Confederacy by Browning (Montana) Middle School students. These games emphasize cooperation and skill.

Name of the Game: Shinny

Blackfeet girls and women played this popular field game, similar to hockey. In the "dog days" before white settlers came, shinny was played by both males and females. Rules that included winning score and length of play were established by a tribal elder before play began. The object of the game was to score a goal by putting the ball through the goal posts at your opponent's end of the field.

Size of the Field: Any designated length

Goal Area: Goal posts of small tree shafts with feathers tied to the tops set about four or six feet apart at the end of the field, or a hide or a blanket laid on the ground

Length of Play: Any designated time or score

Number of Players: Any number

Equipment Required: Curved sticks about two to three feet in length made out of chokecherry wood, and a two- to four-inch ball made out of sewn buckskin on the outside and horsehair on the inside

Rules: Specific rules were designated by an elder. *Start of Play*: The game was started in the middle of the field with a "shinny." The judge would drop the ball between two opposing teams saying, "Shinny one, shinny two, shinny three" (drop ball), and play would begin. *Play*: The players would hit the ball with their sticks. The ball was not usually touched by any part of the body. *Rule Violation Penalty*: Players moved back at least three feet and the ball was put back into play with a shinny.

Name of the Game: Ring Toss

This game was generally played by young men or boys on an open field with goals at each end. The object of the game was to toss a ring into your opponent's goal after passing it from one team member to another down the field.

Size of Field: Any length

Length of Play: Any designated time or score

Equipment Required: Long sticks with hide or fur wrapped on the ends and a hoop ring large enough to fit around the stick

Rules: Any player in possession of the ring may not take more than three steps before tossing it. Each team must have attempted three tosses before scoring.

BLACKFEET DANCES

The Blackfeet dance has three major elements, rhythm, force, and space, but all are guided by the beat of the drum and style of dance. The dances are usually performed moving clockwise in a circle. The basic step, the Traditional Dance, and the Fancy Dance of the Blackfeet are described.

Name of Activity: Basic 1-2 Step
Females:

1. Weight is distributed equally on both feet.
2. As the drum beats, each foot slides forward then back, 1-2, 1-2.
3. The knees are bent to exaggerate the movement and add a slight bounce.
4. Arms and upper body are erect and straight.

Males:

1. Weight is distributed equally, with one foot slightly in front of the other.
2. As the drum beats, each foot moves forward, right then left, 1-2, 1-2.
3. The steps are larger and the knee movement is more exaggerated than for the females.
4. The upper body is flexed slightly forward, with elbows bent and pointing upward.
5. The head and eyes move in a percussive fashion, as if "looking for a wolf."

Name of the Activity: Blackfeet Traditional Dance

The Traditional is the classic of all the dances. It has a slower beat, and the outfits are the most authentic, with females wearing beaded buckskin and elk tooth dresses and males wearing one bustle.

Females:

1. The tempo is slower and the basic 1-2 step is performed, with very little movement other than knee bending.
2. Upper body remains erect with arms either straight down or in a shawl holding position.
3. The dance moves in a zig-zag pattern, with 3 steps zig, then 3 steps zag.
4. The body motion is graceful, fluid, and proud.

Males:

1. The tempo is slower and the basic 1-2 step is performed.
2. Arms are bent; the upper body flexes and extends.
3. The movement is proud and pronounced.

Name of the Activity: Blackfeet Fancy Dance

The Fancy Dance is performed to a fast beat of the drum. Each dancer has his or her own style with energetic footwork, spins, and arm movements. The dresses for the females are made of lighter, printed cloth, and women use a fringed shawl to accentuate the body movement. The males wear two colorful bustles made of fluffs, hackles, or eagle feathers.

Females:

1. The tempo is faster and therefore the 1-2 steps are performed faster, with a percussive hopping motion added.
2. The upper body leans slightly forward, the arms in a position to hold a shawl, with hands at the hips.
3. The shoulders move alternately forward and back.
4. Sliding, tapping, skipping, and hopping steps are performed.
5. Various body parts accentuate the beat.
6. Creativity is emphasized.

Males:

1. The tempo is fast, with the 1-2 step being more exaggerated and percussive.
2. The shoulders and head move back and forth, up and down, in a percussive and sometimes vibratory manner.
3. The foot and knee movements vary with the type of step performed—sliding, tapping.
4. The entire body goes through the realm of sustained swinging, ballistic, percussive, vibratory, and collapsing energies.
5. Various body parts accentuate the beat.
6. Creativity is emphasized.

REFERENCE

Browning Middle School Students. (1990). "Children's Native American Games: Blackfoot Confederacy and Plains Indians." Unpublished manual, Browning Middle School, Browning, Montana.

24

Bringing History to Life through Games and Storytelling

Georga Accola

History is made up of major events and famous people against the backdrop of everyday life. Children can readily identify with the daily routines and oral traditions of everyday life. Games and storytelling reflect these routines and help set the scene for the drama of history. Games and storytelling serve as a supplement to the regular history curriculum, engaging the children as active participants and setting the stage for the larger events of history. The beauty of introducing children to games of days past is that they will continue to play the games, tell stories, and keep folk traditions alive for generations to come.

Holidays, for example, provide an ideal opportunity to recreate historic experiences (see list of holidays below). Retelling or using excerpts from classic literature and poetry is also helpful when studying a particular period of history. Accounts of folk heroes and inventors as well as oral histories from living senior citizens can help set the tone of an era. Costumes, props, puppets, pictures, music, and games can complete the experience.

Three sample outlines are given here to assist teachers in bringing history to life through games. The information is intended for classroom teachers, physical educators, and recreation specialists who work with children six to nine years of age.

SAMPLE 1: A HOLIDAY PROGRAM

Concept: Holidays are reminders of events past. Creating an experience that encourages participation by children can bring the event and a slice of history to life.

Primary Objective: To focus on the story of Thanksgiving from a child's point of view. Puppets and/or costumes and props, games, and songs will be used throughout to ensure maximum participation.

Materials: Pilgrim and Native American costumes, created in collaboration with the art teacher or adapted from modern clothes with small touches like paper or cloth aprons, hats, vests, and headdresses. Pilgrim and Native American shadow puppets cut from oak tag paper and operated behind a sheet with overhead floodlighting

Activities:

1. The research and preparation of the puppets and props can be a lesson in itself.
2. The story of the *Mayflower* crossing and the celebration a year later can be told by the teacher and enacted by the children using puppets and costumes.
3. By focusing on the event from a child's point of view, everyday routines will be the main points of the story.
4. Begin by showing the ship at sea, using shadow puppets. Introduce the travelers, who have names like Patience, Fear, Love, Wrestling, and Oceanus.
5. Have the puppets lead the remainder of the class in a sea chantey like "Blow the Man Down" or "Three Times Round" (a song about a boat sinking). Talk about the dangers of sea travel.
6. Play the game pass the secret (known today as telephone), saying things that a child might have passed along while traveling to the new land, like "I miss England," "This boat makes me feel sick," and "Will we live in a house?"
7. Describe the landing and the hardships of the year to follow, including the lack of food and shelter, and fear of the Native Americans.
8. All class members might wear a hat or headdress at this point and mime the struggles of each group as they are described. The Native Americans hid in the forest, afraid of the strangely dressed new people and their guns. The new people ran out of food and were hungry. They had to build houses by chopping trees. The Native Americans wanted to chase away the new people who were taking over their land.
9. Focus on the coming together of the two groups, because the Native Americans taught the Pilgrims how to plant and prepare food and how to adapt to their new surroundings.
10. Play planting games like "Oats, Peas, Beans" and "Mulberry Bush" or the relay "Plant Corn Reap Corn." Appropriate hunting games would be grizzly bear tag or hide-and-seek.
11. The first Thanksgiving was a party celebrating the survival of the Pilgrims in the new land with the help of the Native Americans.
12. Games played at the first Thanksgiving included leapfrog, blindman's buff, and jump the stick.
13. As these games are played by the entire class, emphasize that Native Americans and the Pilgrims played the same games with different names, reinforcing the universality of games. Many children will comment on the similarities of these games to games they play today. Use this opportunity to explain how games are passed from generation to generation and transcend time.

List of Holidays

Holidays are celebrations that hold traditions passed down through time. The following list was created to serve as a reminder of the many dates that have historic significance and are fun to celebrate.

January 1	New Year's Day
January 15	Martin Luther King Jr.'s Birthday

February 14	Valentine's Day
February	Presidents Day Observed
March 11	Johnny Appleseed Day
March 17	St. Patrick's Day
March or April	Passover and Easter Celebrated
April 1	April Fools' Day
May 1	May Day
June 14	Flag Day
July 4	Independence Day
July 20	Moon Walk Day
August 14	National Senior Citizen Day
August 17	Davy Crockett's Birthday
First Monday in September	Labor Day
Fourth Friday in September	American Indian Day
October 12	Columbus Day
October 31	Halloween
November 11	Veterans Day
Fourth Thursday in November	Thanksgiving Day
December	St. Nicholas Day, Christmas, and Hanukkah

SAMPLE 2: THE LEGEND OF SLEEPY HOLLOW

Concept: A legend or an account of a folk hero, though fictitious, can set a tone for a period in history, giving many opportunities for incorporating authentic games and songs of the period. The story by Washington Irving is retold to highlight everyday life in a Dutch community in upstate New York in the late 1700s.

Primary Objective: The objective is to retell the legend, highlighting the everyday events each child can identify with, by using games, props, and a few costumes. By focusing on the life of Ichabod Crane in this active way, children should remember the legend and the essence of everyday life surrounding it.

Materials: This being a suspense story, it would be fun to have the teacher dress in a period costume and speak from the point of view of someone who lived through the event and knew Ichabod Crane personally.

- A costume for Ichabod Crane and hats for Brom Bones and Katrina Van Tassel
- A lap-size slate board and chalk
- A cloth handkerchief
- A maypole for circle dancing

Activities:

1. Ichabod Crane is a teacher in a one-room schoolhouse. Rebuses, which incorporate words and pictures, improve reading skills (see Figure 24.1). Have a child dress as Ichabod and use the slate board to make rebus sentences. Tongue twisters help improve diction, and such objective hiding games as "I Spy" improve observation skills. The teacher should lead these games.
2. Ichabod Crane loves Katrina Van Tassel. Chasing and courtship games have been played throughout time, and they show how matches were made. Have a girl wear a

hat as Katrina Van Tassel and have Ichabod drop a handkerchief behind her in a game of "Tisket a Tasket."
3. Brom Bones also loves Katrina. He and Ichabod are rivals. Dueling games like elbows and cock fighting were ways that boys showed off for girls. Choose a boy to wear the Brom Bones hat and have him challenge Ichabod in a cock fight by having both students stand on one foot with their hands behind their backs while trying to push each other off balance.
4. Katrina Van Tassel has a big party and everyone is invited. Party games and dances provide for maximum participation. The teacher can lead the entire class in circle dances with a maypole like "Loop-de-Lou," in partner dances such as "Skip to my Lou," and in line dances like "Oranges and Lemons" and "London Bridge."

FIGURE 24.1: Rebus

SAMPLE 3: A GUEST WHO CAN SHARE A PAST

Sample 3 includes several ideas for bringing the recent past to life. It is exciting to focus on inventors and their lives. The changes brought about by the invention or discovery of automobiles, the cotton gin, electricity, radio, railroads, television, and the telephone, for example, were tremendous. Children are surprised to learn that these conveniences have not always existed. They are even more amazed when they meet someone who has lived through a time when there were no television sets, or when there were streetcars, horses and buggies, and very few automobiles.

Concept: Learning from a person who has grown up in the immediate neighborhood and can share stories and observations of changes will add life to history.

Primary Objective: The children will ask preplanned questions to obtain an understanding of daily events in the guest's early years. The guest will prepare some anecdotes, songs, and games to share the past.

Materials: Personal photos and pictures of the neighborhood then, to compare with now; a tape recorder for recording the exchange.

Activities:

1. The guest is introduced and can open with a little background story. The children are invited to ask such questions as: "Did you go to school?" "Did you have a car or television when you were our age?" "How did you travel?" "What did you do for fun?"
2. If the guest has a special talent (singing, stitchery) or a passion (like baseball), he or she should be encouraged to share it.
3. The teacher should be prepared to lead the class in a block party or ice cream social while the children participate in street games such as kick the can, clapping rhymes, jump rope, and stoop games such as stone teacher and stoop ball.

REFERENCES

Angel, Jerome, and Jason Shulman (1981). *The Thanksgiving Book*. New York: Dell.

Boyd, Neva (1973). *Handbook of Recreational Games*. New York: Dover.

Brewster, Paul (1953). *American Nonsinging Games*. Norman: Oklahoma University Press.

Coney, Steven (1978). *Kid's America*. New York: Workman.

Hart, Jane, and Anita Lobel (1982). *Singing Bee: A Collection of Children's Songs*. New York: Lothrop, Lee and Shepard Books.

Opie, Iona, and Peter Opie. (1984). *Children's Games in School and Playground*. New York: Oxford University Press.

Vecchione, Glen (1989). *The World's Best Street and Yard Games*. New York: Sterling.

Willensky, Elliot (1986). *When Brooklyn Was the World (1920-1957)*. New York: Crown.

25

The Smithtown Iditarod

Len Carolan

This chapter describes an activity that can be used in physical education classes throughout the country, the Smithtown Iditarod Race. The idea stemmed from my oldest son's involvement in the Boy Scouts. At the winter camporee each troop was asked to build a dogsled to the specifications shown in Figure 25.1. My son, another scout, and I built the sled for the troop. Seeing how much fun the scouts had with the sled, it occurred to me that this activity could be used in my physical education classes for team races. To introduce the activity, I showed a videotape of the 1991 Iditarod Race. Discussion included how in 1925 a diphtheria epidemic in Nome, Alaska, made it necessary to carry medicine by dogsled from Anchorage. The Iditarod Race today follows much of that same trail. In the second class period, we selected teams of seven. This number can vary according to the class size. The rule was that there must be one person riding in the sled and one person pushing and steering at the back. We then spent time practicing how the teams would organize their members with the sled. This two-day preparation coincided with the Iditarod Race in Alaska, so that I was able to read and post newspaper articles covering the actual racing results.

The course selected followed the perimeter of a playing field and measured approximately one-third of a mile. Each team raced three times, and the combined times were used to calculate their overall standings. My grade seven class had six teams of seven students. The table demonstrates how the class performed.

Grade Seven Teams

TEAMS:	1	2	3	4	5	6
	3:38	3:12	3:30	3:06	2:48*	3.22
	3:21	3:05	3:53	2:59	3:01	3:13
	3:30	3:13	3:18	3:05	2:53	3:46
	10:29	9:30	10:41	9:10	8:42**	10:21

In addition to having a combined time champion (**) we also had an individual lap time champion (*). If a team member was absent from school, that team had to run with one less person pulling. (This is similar to the actual Iditarod Race. In fact, if a dog is injured or sick, it is left at a checkpoint and the rest of the team continues to race.) All students wore loose-fitting clothing and brought a change of sneakers.

This activity can also be expanded to involve other subjects. The students could build the sled in technology-related classes, or read books on dog sledding or the Iditarod Race in their English classes. During history classes, students could be challenged to study the original Iditarod in Alaska and the importance of dog sledding in the north country. Mathematical word problems and basic equations could be developed using the numbers from the physical education class races, and science lessons could explore how various loads and head winds would affect the race times.

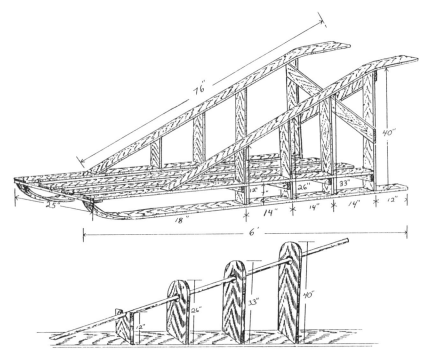

FIGURE 25.1: Iditarod Sled

26

African American Jump Rope Chants and Motor Sequences

Mary McKnight-Taylor

Dating back to ancient China, jump rope chants have maintained a universal appeal, reaching every culture and ethnic group. They are especially popular among African American children. One could surmise that the interest and participation in this complex motoric activity stem from at least two sources. First, a majority of African American children are reared in families where favorite rhythms such as rap, hip-hop, and spiritual pieces are heard daily from radios, cassette tapes, compact disc players, or television videos. Second, today's youths have been influenced by the tales and skills of previous generations of African Americans. Early literature is filled with the work songs of southern farmers, marching cadences of African American patriots, and pieces from spiritual choirs. In fact, the earlier generations were masters of rhythm. The motoric skills included hand clapping, thigh slapping, and tap dancing sequences. Subsequently, jump rope skills and chants are highly reflective of the African American heritage.

The following teaching progression and sample jump rope chant are intended to assist educators in offering this activity to students of all cultures.

1. Follow the progression of jump rope skills, which can be practiced individually or in groups of three children (see Figures 26.1-14).
2. Explain that many African call and response traditions are in the form of chants. Begin by assigning a leader to read a chant; alternately, the group as a whole may practice reading together. Apply the chant to rope skills. The rope turners chant while one child jumps.
3. Reinforce the idea that dialect and colloquialism are acceptable in chants. Many of the phrases stem from customs that were practiced to create a sense of group membership for individuals who knew a specific chant.
4. Expand the students' interest and knowledge by introducing vocabulary specific to a chant. The word jambo (jahm-bow), for example, means "hello."

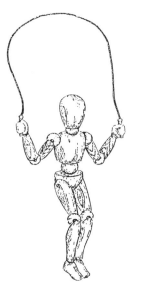

FIGURE 26.1: Double Bounce Forward Jump

FIGURE 26.2: Single Bounce Forward Jump

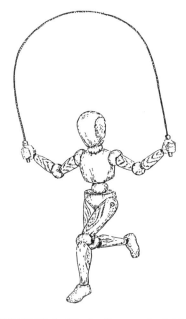

FIGURE 26.3: Single Bounce Right Foot Forward Jump

FIGURE 26.4: Single Bounce Left Foot Forward Jump

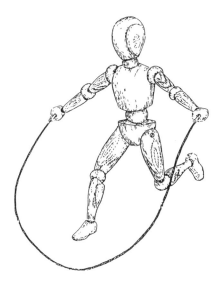

FIGURE 26.5: Double Bounce Right Foot Forward Jump

FIGURE 26.6: Double Bounce Left Foot Forward Jump

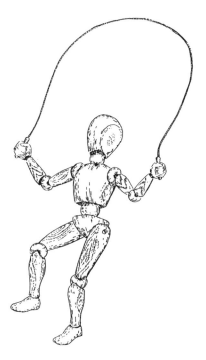

FIGURE 26.7: Double Bounce Backward Jump

FIGURE 26.8: Single Bounce Right Foot Backward Jump

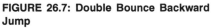

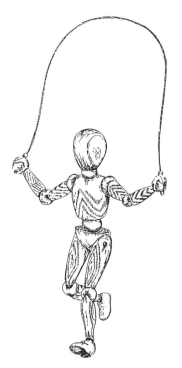

FIGURE 26.9: Single Bounce Left Foot Backward Jump

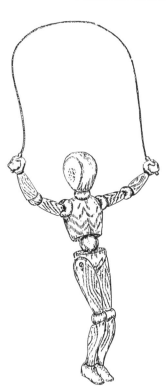

FIGURE 26.10: Single Bounce Backward Jump

FIGURE 26.11: Jog in Place Stepover

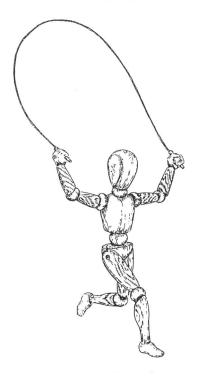

FIGURE 26.12: Moving Forward

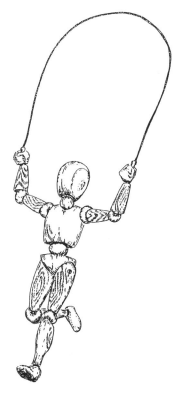

FIGURE 26.13: Double Bounce Left Foot Backward Jump

FIGURE 26.14: Double Bounce Right Foot Backward Jump

5. Stress to younger students that teasing and taunting are inappropriate between classmates. Help the children to understand that many of the phrases common to chants were intended to be performed in a nonthreatening way. Example:

Psycho-dilly
Your mama eats chili,
Bet you five dollars
She'll knock you silly.

REFERENCES

Abernethy, F. E. (1989). *Texas Toys and Games.* Dallas: Southern Methodist University Press.

Feelings, M. (1974). *Jambo Means Hello: Swahili Alphabet Book.* New York: Dial Books for Young Readers.

Opie, P. and I. Opie (1984). *Children's Games in Street and Playground* New York: Oxford University Press.

Shake It (1989). Gift box set—songbook and 26 song cassette of African, African-American, Creole, and Caribbean cultures. Available from J.T.G. of Nashville, 1024C 18th Avenue, South, Nashville, Tenn. 37212. Telephone (615) 329-3036. FAX (615) 329-4028.

Stone, V. W. (1943; reprint 1967). *Rope Jumping Rhymes in Backwoods to Border.* D. Day, ed. Dallas: Southern Methodist Press.

27

Helping Learning and Physically Challenged Children Acquire Rhythmic Skills through Street Games

Kirsten DeBear and Sara Kiesel

Many of the physical and linguistic abilities acquired in childhood are introduced through children's participation in rhythmic activities, including those customarily identified as street games. Games of this nature frequently combine repetitive actions with chanting, hand-clapping, rope-jumping, and ball-bouncing. These games may involve a solitary child, two children, or an extended group playing together or taking turns. Children with physical deficits or learning problems are not commonly given the opportunity to participate in these activities, and this deprivation may compound developmental difficulties. This chapter explains how rhythmic play can be used with disabled children. The suggestions are based on teaching performed at the Gateway School, a small private school for learning disabled children in New York City. Learning problems encountered among the students include language and social learning disorders, visual/spatial and perceptual difficulties, attention-deficit disorders, and other organizational deficits including mild motoric disabilities.

Games serve as ideal vehicles for social interaction at the Gateway School. They also present tangible skills for the child to strive for. Rhythmic games, in particular, encourage the acquisition of a well-coordinated movement system, as children acquire a sense of timing and the ability to integrate simultaneous inputs from a variety of sensory modalities. Since reciting rhymes and other types of communicative exchanges are often involved, they also foster the child's ability to engage with his or her peers socially. In brief, rhythmic games are not only appealing, they are also a functional means of approaching many vital goals.

THE VALUE OF RHYTHMS

It is important to facilitate a child's sense of rhythm for a number of reasons. First, everyone's life is governed by internal rhythms like the heartbeat and respiration, as well as the rhythms of daily activity. Most of these rhythms are not under our control. By and large, however, motoric and linguistic rhythms *are* subject to volition and provide a kind of metrical machinery for governing the subdivision and the management of time. That is, humans achieve a sense of controlled activity and organization. Children who can acquire a clearer perception of time should, therefore, feel more at home with the larger rhythms of their social environment.

The first goal of the Gateway games curriculum is to develop coordinated, fundamental motor patterns as the basis for internal rhythm. Our movement patterns must be efficient, consistent, and coordinated to allow a sense of rhythm to emerge. It is, therefore, necessary to plan activities that require the children to practice basic patterns. For example, both flexion and extension are encouraged by making it necessary for the child to stabilize him or herself while seated or lying prone on a scooter-board or swing. Rotational patterns are elicited during rolling activities. Weight-shifting occurs when the child is obliged to step over obstacles.

Creeping and crawling patterns are practiced during games, requiring the child to negotiate obstacles on all fours. Considerable emphasis is placed on jumping activities, since these require the child to learn spatial planning and the coordination of an ensemble of movements (especially if obstacles must be cleared). The acquisition of new skills is not attempted until the child can demonstrate efficiency, consistency, and reliability in the fundamental motor patterns.

A second goal is to help the child attend to and imitate others. Infants first experience socialization when they begin to imitate. Later, such experiences are heightened by the ability to synchronize one's behaviors with those of others. The children at Gateway are afforded ample opportunity to imitate the movements of their teachers and their peers. Nonverbal "follow me" activities represent a basic technique for teaching the children to attend to visual cues and to maintain attention levels.

A third curriculum goal is to connect words with movements and to develop a vocabulary of actions. Children must learn to internalize language so that they can use it in planning and establishing control over their actions. They must also learn to monitor their actions and to test them against internal goals. At the Gateway School, a great deal of attention is paid to the verbal concepts that accompany movement-oriented activities, and additional attention is given to resolving linguistic ambiguities. Since understanding prepositions and directional constructs is required for a child to follow spoken directions, it is essential that he or she be able to differentiate variant usages, such as "down" in phrases like "put down" and "slow down," or "up" as in "stand up," "lift up," "wind up," and "blow up."

A fourth curriculum goal is to facilitate the ability to learn sequences of movements. Skilled movement consists of complexes of simpler motor patterns combined, with the help of language, into longer sequences. According to Vygotsky in *Mind and Society* (1978), children acquire most skilled behaviors in the course of social interactions with adults and peers. Motor patterns are given a name, and so are behaviors. As these identifications are assimilated, the child begins to respond to directives. After units of behavior have been labeled and connected, the child is capable of practicing the sequence. Talking to oneself reinforces this learning process. If the sequence is consistent, it takes on an identity of its own in the way that *Swan Lake*, for example, comes to represent a specific sequence of movements to a dancer. Thus, a complex new behavior is acquired. In this respect, a child's experience with rhythmic games provides an ideal model for the learning of routine tasks. The process is facilitated by the pleasure implicit in the games and by the way in which language is used as an accompaniment (i.e., publicly, repetitively, metrically, and in a consistent, formulaic manner).

The fifth goal of the Gateway School curriculum is to develop competence in perceptual motor activities. Movement takes place in complex environments with multiple sensory stimuli. To move efficiently, children must learn to integrate what they see with the sensory information they receive from their skin, muscles, inner ears, and other organs. A coherent body image provides a perceptual base from which all movement may be planned. As the sense of balance increases, the child's awareness of laterality and directionality also increases. The movement patterns become more sophisticated. A positive body image and an improved sense of balance increase the child's spatial awareness. This in turn enables the child to better locate and negotiate obstacles in the environment. Such activities as moving through obstacle courses help the child to develop this sense of space.

Activities involving a swing help the child learn to focus on a stationary object while he or she is in motion. Many children experience a lack of visual or motor control during rotary movement. They must learn to focus their eyes on a specific point to regain stability. Specific rope activities (e.g., making "snakes" or "waves") encourage the child to track a moving object while he or she is stationary. Balloon tapping is also excellent for encouraging tracking.

DEVELOPING KINESTHETIC, AUDITORY, AND VISUAL RHYTHM

Before a child can join in the rhythm of others, he or she must have acquired a sense of timing. Normally, as the child gains experience in walking or running, he or she establishes an efficient pace and stride. In talking, the child establishes his or her own tempo; and in reading, there is a natural rate at which the eyes traverse the page. As the child develops consistency in the execution of basic movement patterns, he or she also develops the strength, endurance, and attention necessary to sustain the movements for longer and longer periods of time. Many of the children at Gateway, however, exhibit a common problem: though they may be capable of performing a desired movement, they often lack the ability to establish an efficient pace or to continue that action over time.

In running, for example, many of the children are disorganized by their own movements, and too easily distracted to run laps. They have difficulty moving in a goal-directed manner even though they may be physically capable. To counter this problem, visual movement targets and short-range goals must be established so that they can better monitor their own movements and stay in control. To encourage sustained running, for example, we may ask the child to perform a sequence of "tiger runs." This activity provides an easily visible endpoint and a limited duration. We also approach other tasks involving skilled rhythmic movement in a similar manner. We recognize that many of the children cannot independently practice new skills to the point where they experience a constancy of rhythm. We therefore provide external structure which enables them to carry on and gives them the incentive to continue.

FACILITATING THE EXPRESSION OF A RHYTHM
THROUGH TWO MODALITIES SIMULTANEOUSLY

Infants begin to demonstrate the rhythmic process by listening to music and swaying to it. Later, the child adds swinging movements, clapping, tapping, and banging to his or her repertoire of song and rhyme accompaniments. By nursery school age, the child can usually coordinate chants and simple movements by him or herself in games like "Five Little Monkeys." Often, the movements are not only descriptive (which helps the child to comprehend the rhymes), but also reinforce the cadence of the words so that the child gradually begins to sense how a spoken rhythm can be expressed motorically. As preschoolers, many of our Gateway children are unable to recite rhymes or sing, or to sing and move simultaneously. During circle play these children usually occupy the periphery, distract the group by refusing to sit still and participate, or simply lapse into inactivity. They are unable to integrate what they hear or see and act responsively.

In many cases, however, we have seen sufficient maturation by age five or six, after the child has been encouraged to participate in this type of expression. We cultivate this rhythmical awareness by offering activities in which the children's movements are matched to drumbeats. Gradually they become aware that they are in control of the rhythm. We urge them to invent new beats by altering their movements. This may be difficult for the impulsive child, but it is a cognitively challenging activity, and developmentally appropriate.

MATCHING THE CHILD'S ACTIONS TO EXTERNAL RHYTHMS

After children are able to sustain rhythmic movements, they are ready to attend to rhythms that call for a specific type of movement. This process usually involves music or drumming. The ability to start and stop at the appropriate moments increases, and the child achieves progressively higher levels of synchronization between the sounds and his or her own responses. The process is enhanced by encouraging synchronous rhythmic action in small groups.

As children attain the goal of synchrony, they slowly develop a sense of the group as a single, integrated organism rather than a collection of individuals. This can be an exhilarating process if care is taken to avoid undue frustration. The games must be simple enough to allow the children to stay in control and feel a sense of mastery. Instruction should be geared to the slower learners, since the end result depends on full participation by all the members of the group.

Considering that most of the children have difficulty integrating multiple information inputs, a slow, gradual learning process is warranted, with the pace adjusted for those who lag behind. At the outset, each child should be allowed to rely on imitation and verbal directions, with the rhyme added only as the movement patterns become relatively well established. The child gradually assimilates the movement sequence and begins to perform it rhythmically while synchronizing his or her own movements to fit the other children's. Recognition of partial successes is often helpful in encouraging this perception.

SAMPLE ACTIVITIES

The following sample activities are provided to assist teachers in their efforts to adapt rhythmic games for the learning and physically challenged child.

Jessica is a seven-year-old girl with low muscle tone and slow reflexes. She cannot run, skip, balance on one foot, or jump down from low platforms. She has difficulty catching balls. She displays anxiety when she experiences heights, fast movements, and inverted positions. Beth is a six-year-old girl with left hemiplegic cerebral palsy. She cannot balance on one foot, run, or skip, and has trouble catching a ball. She has visual/perceptual difficulties.

Hopscotch is modified for Beth and Jessica so as not to require hopping on one foot. The spaces in the hopscotch figure have been narrowed to challenge the girls to hop with the feet close together. For variety, a "No Stepping Here" square has been added in the places where children traditionally land on two feet. This requires them to make the space between their legs greater as they jump. The top has been divided into three spaces to allow them two 90° turns instead of one 180° turn, which they are unable to manage.

Since neither child is ready for jump-rope play, stick games have been created for them to combine jumping and chanting. In "Jack Be Nimble, Jack Be Quick," the children begin by stepping over sticks lying on the floor, then jumping over them as they are gradually raised. In "Around the World," they practice jumping over a stick spun around (at low speed) just above floor level. We chant, "Around the world *once*, around the world *twice*," and so forth, as they jump. In "Lumberjack," the children practice jumping over sticks as they are rolled toward them. The teacher chants, "Lumberjack, lumberjack, how many logs can you jump?" The children chant in turn as they jump over the sticks: "I can jump one, I can jump two," and so forth.

A soft, resilient Gertie ball suspended from the ceiling is ideally suited to many of our ball games. In "Roses," for example, the children pat the ball as they chant, "Roses are red, violets are blue; sugar is sweet and so are you." First time around they use their palms; second time, the back of the hand; third, the elbow; fourth, the shoulder. The children can be encouraged to incorporate other body parts.

Jessica can perform "Miss Mary Mack," a hand-clapping game, at a modest pace when the teacher adjusts her rhythm to Jessica's and allows time for visual imitation. Jessica is now learning more complicated games. Beth cannot use her two hands rhythmically together. She will also attempt to play "Miss Mary Mack," but the effort involved in getting the left hand to follow slows her progress. Therefore, we play one-handed rhythm games to allow her to experience regular and consistent cadences. "The Lion and the Unicorn," for example, calls for the following movements in a seated position: palm up on left leg; palm down on left knee; palm up on right leg; palm down on right knee; touch left shoulder; touch right shoulder; clap partner's hand.

These are simple games, but for Jessica and Beth they provide just the right degree of challenge. They experience success, feel greatly rewarded, and enjoy the excitement inherent in each rhythmic game. Like their peers, they become active learners within a social atmosphere.

REFERENCES

Kephard, Newell (1971). *The Slow Learner in the Classroom.* Columbus, Ohio: Charles E. Merrill.

Pennington, Bruce (1991). *Diagnosing Learning Disorders: A Neuropsychological Framework.* New York: Guilford Press.

Vygotsky, L. S. (1978). *Mind and Society: The Development of Higher Psychological Processes.* Edited by Michael Cole, Vera John-Steiner, Sylvia Scribner, and Ellen Souberman. Cambridge, Mass.: Harvard University Press.

28

Games Common to the Puerto Rican School System: Multicultural Approach

Maria I. Ojeda-O'Neill

This chapter describes several games and musical activities developmentally appropriate for children from five to eleven years old. These activities are considered childhood favorites by Puerto Rican children. They are also appropriate for use by elementary classroom teachers and community based organizations.

PUERTO RICO

The Commonwealth of Puerto Rico is the easternmost island of the Greater Antilles group of the West Indies. Puerto Rico is about forty miles west of the Virgin Islands and seventy miles east of Hispaniola. Roughly rectangular in shape, the island is about one hundred miles long and thirty-five miles wide. Although Spanish is the official language, English is widely used. The government-sponsored Institute of Puerto Rican Culture encourages the development of native art, handicrafts, music, and drama. Most of the people are descended from early Spanish settlers, and the remainder are mulattos and blacks descended from African slaves.

THE CULTURAL INFLUENCE

The following activities and games can be used to convey several multicultural ideas.

Activity 1: Warm-up
Suggested Grade Level: 2-6
Equipment Required: Cassette player; record player; drum music from Puerto Rico, Dominican Republic, Haiti, and/or Jamaica
Starting Formation: Scattered
Description: Instruct your students to walk freely around the room listening to the music beat. They should walk forward, backward, sideways, and diagonally

(in all possible directions except in a circle). As soon as the teacher lowers the volume, the students will face the teacher, but will keep marching in place. Challenge the students to perform a specific exercise every time they meet with another student. Examples include taking three jumps in place and then continuing to walk, or stopping and walking in different directions. Repeat the procedure by adding exercises to the ones already selected at the moment the teacher has lowered the volume.

Activity 2: Baile de los Pajaritos (Dance of the Little Birds)
Suggested Grade Level: 2-3
Equipment Required: Cassette player, music: *Baile de los Pajaritos*
Starting Formation: Circle, facing center
Description: Part I: When the chorus begins to sing, the following movements are performed:

a. "Pajaritos a volar"—hands elevated, placed at eye level; open and close fingers four times.
b. "Cuando acabas de nacer"—hands placed under armpits; four upward and downward movements with the elbows.
c. "Tu colita has de mover"—hands located at waistline; move hips sideways four times.
d. Clap four times.
e. Repeat every time chorus sings.

Part II: Walk forward eight steps.

f. Walk backward eight steps.
g. Repeat.
h. Repeat Part I: For Part II teach basic locomotor skills (i.e., run, skip, slide, and step kick).

Game 1: Endless Circle
Suggested Grade Level: K-3
Equipment Required: None
Starting Formation: Two single circles, facing center
Description: Children form two single circles, standing and facing center. The purpose of this activity is to participate in an organized rhythmic game. The teacher selects one initial leader from each circle. The selected students run, walk, or skip around the outside of the circle, until they return to their place and sit down. The students located to their right repeat the same activity, and so on until all students have run. The remainder of the class should clap to maintain rhythmical steps.

Game 2: Panuelo I (Handkerchief)
Suggested Grade Level: 1-3
Equipment Required: One handkerchief
Starting Formation: Single circle facing center
Description: One student stands outside the circle with the handkerchief. He or she runs around the circle and at any random moment drops the handkerchief

behind the back of a student standing in the circle. The student whom the handkerchief has fallen behind picks it up and runs in the opposite direction from the student who dropped the handkerchief. The objective of the game is to be the first player to return to the vacant space where the handerkerchief was dropped.

REFERENCES

Cadilla, M. (1940). *Juegos y Canciones Infantiles de Puerto Rico*. San Juan: Imprenta Baldrich.

Figueroa, J. (1976). *Algunos Juegos Infantiles del Chocó*. Bogotá: Instituto Caro Cuervo.

Gessell, A. (1974). *El Niño de Cinco a Diez Años*. Buenos Aires: Editorial Paidós.

Meduros, E. (1959). *Jogo para Recreacao na Escola Primaria*. Rio de Janeiro: Centro Brasileiro de Pesquisas Educacionais.

Vélez, C. (1991). *Juegos Infantiles de Puerto Rico*. Puerto Rico: Editorial de la Universidad de Puerto Rico.

29

Thailand Tag

Bess Ring Koval

Name of the Game: Thailand Tag
Equipment: None
Space Required: Playground or gymnasium
Starting Formation: Divide the class into two groups. A center line is identified in the gymnasium, or a center spot or line is marked on the playground.
Description: One player from Team A will cross the line into Team B's territory to begin to tag as many Team B players as possible. Player A must make a continuous, uninterrupted loud sound before crossing into the opponents' playing area, and then proceed to tag. Any kind of a continuous sound is acceptable. Player A must return to his or her territory without interrupting his or her sound in order to score. If Player A is successful, the number of players tagged is added to Team A's score. Should Player A not be able to sustain the continuous sound the total time in Team B's territory, including the crossing back into Team A's territory, Player A fails to score for his or her team. The game continues with a member from Team B crossing into Team A's territory to tag, making an uninterrupted sound. The game continues with a different member from each team taking a turn and moving into the opposing team's territory.

30

Hit and Run Cricket

Susan M. Schwager and Ashley M. Hammond

First played in England and currently played on most continents of the world, cricket is a striking/fielding game in which competitive play can continue from one to five days. A team consists of eleven players, with one substitute, called the twelfth man or woman. The basic game consists of two innings with ten wickets (i.e., outs) per team per inning. The winning team is the one who has scored the most runs, with both innings' scores combined. The batting team must face the bowler (pitcher), who bowls an "over" which consists of six deliveries (pitches), after which another bowler delivers six more balls from the opposite end. A team scores runs by hitting the ball away from the fielders and successfully running from one wicket to the other. When the two batsmen cross, one run is scored (see Figure 30.1). The fielding team keeps the batsman from scoring by catching the batted ball on the fly, or hitting the wickets directly from a delivery. In addition, a batsman may be out if a fielder hits a wicket while the batsmen are running. A batsman may cause him or herself to be out by hitting or standing on his or her own wicket, or by exhibiting unsportsmanlike conduct. Other ways in which the batsman can be put out include hitting the ball twice, obstructing the fielders, "being stumped," or being called out "leg before wicket."

DESCRIPTION

The object of both the traditional game and the version called hit and run cricket is the same; that is, the batting team may continue to score runs off pitched balls as long as the wicket is protected and a batted ball is not caught on the fly. In hit and run cricket, one batter (batsman) faces the pitcher (bowler), and to score a run, the batter must round a cone and return to the wicket (see Figure 30.2). A batter remains at bat until he or she is out by hitting a ball that is caught on the fly, or by allowing the wicket to be hit by the pitcher, as it is always the batter's responsibility to protect the wicket.

In the traditional game of cricket, the batsman is not obliged to run after hitting the ball. However, in the hit and run version, once a pitched ball is hit, the batter must run. Also, instead of playing two innings of ten outs per team, each team is at bat until all players have had an opportunity to hit and run.

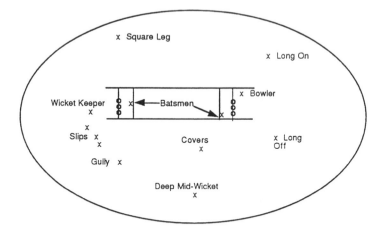

FIGURE 30.1: Traditional Cricket

This is a typical field setting for a righthanded batsman. Various other positions exist with equally strange names. All positions taken up by fielders are direct orders from the captain and bowler according to the speed and type of delivery to be used.

PREREQUISITE SKILLS AND STRATEGIES

Since American children have most likely been exposed to the skills related to baseball, the following practice drills are suggested in preparation for playing hit and run cricket:

1. The children should practice fielding grounders without gloves and returning the batted balls to the pitcher, since the most successful hits are those batted hard on the ground and are difficult to field.
2. The children should practice "batting" grounders that can travel in a variety of directions, especially those areas that have not been well covered by the fielding team.
3. Have the pitcher (teacher or well-skilled player) control the game by pitching easily to lesser skilled players, and by providing more challenging situations for better skilled children.

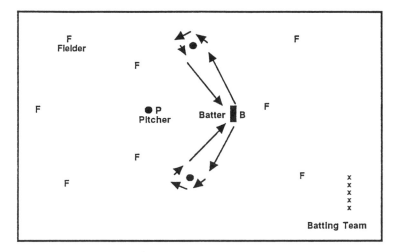

FIGURE 30.2: Hit And Run Cricket

ACCOMMODATIONS FOR INDIVIDUAL SETTINGS

The equipment in hit and run cricket varies. The batter may use a tennis racket or a homemade cricket bat. The wicket can be any oversized target (e.g., a large garbage can, a crate, or a carton). The ball may be a tennis ball or a whiffle ball, and the size of the field may be defined by the space available (indoors or out). When playing indoors, balls hit on the fly that rebound off the side walls may be caught one-handed and constitute an out. If the batter hits the back wall on the fly, the batting team is awarded a predetermined number of runs (e.g., six). If the ball hits the back wall after bouncing, a predetermined number of runs may also be scored (e.g., four). These are the only two situations when a batter is not obliged to run after hitting the ball.

The ideal number of players per team is proportionate to the size of the playing area. An average-sized gymnasium (approximately the size of a regulation basketball court) will accommodate teams of eleven to fifteen players each. When faced with small classes (fewer than twenty-two students), the teacher may create three or more teams, and can organize play so that one team is at bat and the remaining two or more teams combine forces to form the fielding team. With classes of thirty or more, three teams can be formed, with two teams at bat at any given time, and the third team responsible for fielding. The scores for each team are recorded separately.

INTERNATIONAL ELEMENTS

Hit and run cricket can also be used to add an international flavor to the elementary physical education curriculum. This is possible by conveying terms, demonstrating responses, and constructing equipment that is common to the

English version of cricket. "Being stumped," for example, refers to a situation in which the wicket keeper (catcher) catches a missed ball and hits the wicket while the batsman has stepped out of his or her crease (batter's box). "Leg before wicket" occurs when the ball strikes the batter's leg or leg pads without touching the bat. The bowler can then yell "owzat," and if the umpire decides that the ball would have gone to hit the wicket, he or she calls the batsman out "leg before wicket." A homemade cricket bat can be made from any hardwood (e.g., maple or oak). The length and weight of the bat should approximate that of a baseball bat appropriate for the age of the children playing. The shape, however, is quite different. To be appropriate for cricket, the bat should have a round handle (representing approximately one-fifth of the total length of the bat), and the hitting surface should be wide (approximately six inches) and flat.

31

Games as a Means for Development: A Scandinavian Approach to Teaching Soccer

Birger Peitersen

The 1994 World Cup in soccer championship was played in the United States. This sports event is the world's most popular. The fifty-two matches in the 1990 World Cup in Italy attracted 2.6 million spectators. Experts predicted that the global television audience for the finals might exceed 16 nillion viewers. In fact, it reached 31 million.

Soccer is the most popular sport in Denmark. The international success of the Danish teams during the 1980s challenged educators to find a way to combine the nation's hysteria with a balanced presentation of the joy and qualities of soccer in school physical education programs. American educators may soon face a similar challenge as enthusiasm for soccer reaches a new level.

Even though the United States women's soccer team has won the world championship, the game is unfamiliar to many Americans. This lack of appreciation may stem from the overwhelming popularity of baseball, basketball, and American football. These games provide high-scoring results, unlike the 0-0 results common to soccer.

American educators have a golden opportunity to introduce the game with new enthusiasm. If properly presented to children, soccer provides instant joy and positive involvement, and has great potential as an educational and recreational activity.

INTRODUCING SOCCER

When introducing children to soccer, the primary emphasis should be on the immediate challenge of kicking and controlling the ball. All introductory experiences should focus on those activities in an enjoyable atmosphere. Many well-known games can be modified and take on a new meaning when a soccer ball is added to the activity. The elements of the modified games should be used during the introduction of soccer skills.

Soccer is a passing and running game with unpredictable and constantly changing patterns, demanding an acute awareness of other players and an ability to make quick decisions and act upon them without delay. The game calls for physical training, psychomotor training, cooperative training, and cognitive challenges in relation to tactical aspects. The physical demands are obvious—players need strong legs and running ability. In general, endurance training is part of the game.

The passing combinations needed in the game must be viewed in relation to its basic tactical requirement: movement with or without the ball in decision-making situations. This means that basic technical and tactical skills should be developed in gamelike situations. For example, to work on technical skills with the foot, the main challenges would be balance, body control, and, of course, distal coordination. Perceptual abilities must be well established to then put these skills into a game situation. The kind of perception used in a soccer game is similar to that needed to drive a car in heavy traffic. General perceptual ability can be stimulated by putting various activities into decision-making game situations. For example, "Who is the best teammate to pass to?" or "Where will I run to be of any use after passing?" Questions such as these lead to the understanding and acknowledgment of team relations. By encouraging the students' personal self-concept and an awareness of their teammates' abilities, the executional resources of the individual are greatly increased. In order to stimulate these aspects, emphasis must be placed on the quality of play, both technically and tactically.

THE CORE GAME AND ITS ALTERNATIVES

Practice sessions emphasizing specific educational objectives can be used to stimulate these qualities. Groups of four will be used as the organizational units. For example, in K-6 classes, the teacher plays an important instructional role, gradually shaping the organizational units for the pupils. In grades seven and eight, the teacher should encourage the development of technical and tactical skills. The game situation chosen for this practice includes four players.

The first activity involves a one-on-one situation, with the objective being to kick the ball through the legs of the opponent. Challenges include determining which player scored the most goals in one minute. After one minute the goalie and the kicker change roles and the activity continues. This core game can encompass whatever objective the teacher has chosen for the exercise: physical, technical, tactical, or social. During practice, the teacher chooses one of the objectives listed in Figure 31.1, organizes the core game in a manner that will focus primarily on the identified objective, and indicates how to adapt the game to appropriately challenge both skilled and unskilled players. The following components can be stressed as needed:

1. Physical
   a. the distance between the two goals
   b. scoring opportunities at both goals (various alternatives)

2. Technical (dribbling, tackling)
   a. the two goals near to each other (even back to back)
   b. the width of the goals
   c. each player has his or her own ball
3. Tactical (covering, creating, and utilizing space)
   a. use one or two "goalies" as a passing alternative ("wall pass")
4. Social
   a. moving goals in relation to scoring opportunities
   b. loose marking
   c. verbal guidance from goalies

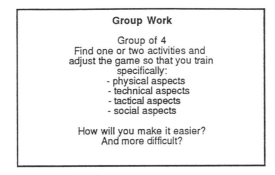

FIGURE 31.1: Core Game

SCHOOL EXPERIENCES

Physical education classes in Denmark seldom use worksheets in the actual teaching units, but recent experiences have shown promise. This approach stimulates the development of cooperation between groups of players and affords the opportunity to try out alternative suggestions from the players. The implicit understanding exists that a player's suggestions will be considered and perhaps eventually implemented.

DIDACTICAL CONSIDERATIONS

The teaching style combines problem solving with limited exploration and several teacher controlled styles (e.g., command or task style). This combination of styles is required in order to meet the objectives and actual needs of the players. Older players are required to devote periods of time to group work and present different approaches to playing the core game (Figure 31.1). This group work encourages reflection and assessment on the group's performance, including additional suggestions for improvement. It emphasizes how to articulate ideas and concepts, which is important in all areas of learning.

32

Dutch Games: Seventeenth-Century Dutch Depictions of Children's Games, Toys, and Pastimes

Donna R. Barnes

This chapter examines seventeenth-century Dutch artists' depictions of children's games, toys, and pastimes from two perspectives: art history and social history. It identifies the popularity of such images and discusses two major trends in art histori-cal interpretations. The artworks are also viewed as "visual documents" of social history, noting some questions that might be raised by those specifically concerned with the history of the games.

ART HISTORICAL CONCERNS
CATERING TO PATRON INTEREST IN "REALISTIC" WORKS

During the seventeenth century in the Netherlands, a time when Dutch people enjoyed unparalleled economic prosperity,[1] religious toleration, and a sense of political growth, Dutch artists found a ready market for images that today seem to us to be "realistic." Art historians have been careful to caution us about the seeming realism of Dutch artworks. Whether we are struck by realistic details in individual, group, or family portraits, landscapes of the countryside, still life arrangements of foodstuffs, floral bouquets, or birds, hares and game hunting trophies, river scenes or seascapes with small fishing boats or large merchant sailing ships, cityscapes showing important public buildings and squares in Amsterdam, or genre painting depicting aspects of daily life for village-dwelling peasants or city-dwelling bourgeois, the art historians claim that such realism must be seen as "contrived."

That is, painterly realism is not a "photographic" image of Dutch life, but, like all instances of painting, is a result of the artist having selected environmental details (real, remembered, or imagined) and skillfully combined them into created "pictures." Certainly, on occasion, a seventeenth-century Dutch artist might have taken a sketch pad into the countryside to make preliminary drawings, captured the expression on the face of a woman in the marketplace, quickly noted the drape of a man's jacket in a tavern, or sketched the movement of a child pushing a sled, but these on-site drawings (i.e., illustrations) were often later reworked into finished paintings, prints, or drawings. Far more often, painters did *not* copy from life, but posed people and objects in their studios, and sometimes copied or borrowed from the works of other artists.[2]

Dutch artists sometimes received commissions from individual patrons who were decorating their homes; from groups of leading citizens who were decorating municipal institutions (such as town halls, orphanages, hospitals, and company meeting halls); from groups of merchants and tradesman wishing to decorate their guildhalls; or from physicians honoring themselves and the science of medicine in "college" anatomy theaters. Commissioned portraits were always posed.

The works of Dutch artists were also sold on the open market—by art dealers who had shops where customers came to make their choices or place orders for paintings similar to ones on display, by printers and book-dealers who sold prints (etchings or engravings, available in multiple copies), by print hawkers at town fairs or on important market days, or by the artists themselves when clients visited them in their studios. Indeed, Dutch art was also sold by fanciers who copied certain artists' images onto tiles used in households as decorative wall moldings; many of those tiles depicted children playing.

THE IMPORTANCE OF MIDDLE-CLASS ART BUYERS

Royal patronage was fairly insignificant, as Holland's court life diminished with the country's freedom from Spain and the aristocracy was left in a weakened position. Ecclesiastical patronage was also insignificant, since Dutch Protestantism favored unadorned churches (to the extent of whitewashing the walls of formerly Catholic churches during the sixteenth century "alteration," when Protestantism became the dominant religion). Protestant churches did not contain images of saints or episodes from the life of Jesus. And painterly images of Old or New Testament episodes (known as "history paintings") were not hung in Protestant churches or owned by Protestant preachers. Instead they were found in the private collections of affluent families. Dutch Catholic monastic holdings had been dispersed in the sixteenth century; and while small Catholic churches continued to exist, providing priestly services to Dutch Catholics, they tended to be "hidden" and commissioned few new religious paintings during the seventeenth century.

Thus, for the most part, the images which we have of seventeenth-century Dutch daily life are ones for which Dutch artists found buyers. These buyers were often prosperous merchants, but they also included artisans and craftsmen working in the developing Dutch cities. What can be said about those images? They were responsive to Dutch popular tastes. Therefore, artists tended to depict Dutch people, Dutch towns, and Dutch activities in ways the Dutch people chose to see themselves.

Keep this in mind when considering seventeenth-century Dutch artworks as sources of information about Dutch children and their activities. It is not only that Dutch artists chose to represent some activities of children, but not all activities; it is also the case that there was a market for such depictions. Art historians encourage us to explore why. What did Dutch artists and perceivers "see" as they looked at children playing?

EARLIER ART DEPICTING CHILDREN AT PLAY

The tradition of showing children engaged in play activities, of course, was not new. Ancient Greek and Roman art sometimes depicted children playing with balls or pet animals; medieval European depictions of the Christ Child occasionally showed Him playing with birds or balls; and medieval European illuminated manuscripts, particularly books of the hours or calendars depicting the labors of the months, not infrequently showed children (or putti cherubs) playing games or musical instruments, dancing, or participating in seasonal feasts and festivals. Moreover, the sixteenth-century Netherlandish artist Pieter Bruegel the elder had created a large painting, teeming with little people engaged in more than ninety activities, called *Children's Games*. In fact, many of the "games" depicted by Bruegel[3] and played by the children of Flanders in the sixteenth century were carryovers from older traditions. Certainly many of them were played by Dutch children in the seventeenth century; some are still played by today's children—in Holland as well as America. Among others that still intrigue children are walking on stilts, playing dice or jacks, standing on one's head, shooting marbles, dueling on piggyback, guessing which hand, or swinging on a rail.[4] Games *were* popular activities for European people and themes for European artists prior to the seventeenth century.[5] The tradition both continued and was modified in seventeenth-century Dutch art.

SEVENTEENTH-CENTURY DEPICTIONS OF CHILDREN

What was new in seventeenth-century Dutch art was the *proliferation* of images of children, and the diverse ways that those images were treated. In talking about Dutch artists' depictions of children, Simon Schama notes that "Dutch art did not invent the image of the mortal child, but it was the first culture to make it impolite. Putti, by definition, cannot have dirty bottoms."[6]

Schama notes that Gerrit Dou depicts a mother wiping the beshitted bottom of a little child in the marketplace; a 1624 emblem book (by Johan de Brune) lamenting the transitoriness of life shows a woman sitting on the childbirth couch, wiping the dirty bottom of her child, and the legend above the print carries the message, "What is life, but stink and shit?"; in 1637 Jan Miense Molenaer treats the sense of smell in his allegorical series on the five senses by depicting a woman wiping the stinking bottom of a child while a man sitting nearby at a table, smoking and drinking, holds his nose.[7] Schama goes on to observe that these views are of "uncompromising earthiness." That is, the Dutch child was depicted without angelic wings and exhibited behavior that was sometimes more piercing than a cupid's arrow. It was a culture where children were viewed as having natural bodily functions and bed wetting actions, unlike the virtuous infant Jesus who was always seen as having glorious attributes. Furthermore, works that depicted a Dutch child being breast fed showed the child's face pressed deeply into the mother's bosom, unlike the Christ Child, who stares with a God-like view of being the Savior to all mankind.

Dutch art leaves the observer with a blatant realization that the "naughtiness" of young children runs the gamut from the more typical crying, shouting, screaming, yelling, and normal cacophony of sound, as well as horseplay and mischievous acts, to smoking, drinking, and stealing. These scenes included the destruction of playthings, thrown food, and smashed pottery. Surprisingly, the same children were also depicted by the same artist in different works as exhibiting moments of peace, and having the ability to fulfill simple household duties.[8]

ATTITUDES TOWARD CHILDREN

How did Dutch people feel about children? They enjoyed them. Again Simon Schama calls attention to the fact that children's "naughtiness" was often depicted and offers as one example the image of a child from Johan de Brune's *Emblemata* (where the child, in a temper tantrum, has thrown its toys—a doll, a miniature pot, a small spoon and glass, as well as a partially bitten apple—onto the floor). According to Schama, "The real engineer of all this angry chaos is shown in the form of a devil in the picture or mirror frame at the back."[9] He further notes: "But pictures of childish devilment of the kind that needed thrashing out, according to the fiercest Puritan doctrine, are very rare. More often, the naughtiness of children is represented as either an aping of adult inequities—as in the Steen scenes of 'As the old pipe, so the young sing'—or else as gleeful teasing."[10] And while Dutch moralists might have thought it irresponsible for parents to "spare the rod," clearly many Dutch parents were quite indulgent toward their children.[11] Travelers to Holland noted that corporal punishment was frowned upon by the Dutch.[12] Groups of Dutch children often played noisily in the streets. In some cases, boys played marbles on gravestones in the churchyard because they presented a smooth surface, and we know parents bought children toys.

Similarly, such indulgent attitudes about children also found their way into Dutch artworks. Children are not depicted as angels—far from it in many of Jan Steen's paintings. But Steen reminds parents that their examples of both excessive and prayerful behavior are important. It is the parental role of helping to shape children's behavior that is being underscored. Children naturally mimic the adults (and when Steen has children mocking adults, it is the adults who have themselves to blame). Consider, for example, the version of "the dissolute household" or "the old singing and the young piping." The girl child is stealing from the cupboard, a youngster smokes away on a long-stemmed Gouda clay pipe, the baby is tossing food about, the dog is eating up the pie on the table, and the dozing mother seems blissfully unaware of the whole scene. In the same picture, while father sings to the accompaniment of the boy playing the violin, a monkey mocks the activity; so does the pig standing next to the seated gallant and his tipsy female companion. However, it is the adults, not the children, who are culpable!

For the most part, whether children of poor peasants, fed tenderly by a father or amused by a mother holding a doll (in two works by Adriaen van Ostade), or children of a prosperous merchant seen in their carts or holding onto a rattle (in works by Frans Hals), children are *not* depicted as constantly in need of correction. S. Blankaart, who wrote about child-rearing in 1684 (*Verhandeling van de opvoeding en Ziekten der Kinderen*, published in Amsterdam), is cited by Simon Schama as one who "recognized that children could at times be little devils, [but] opposed such [corporal] punishment on the grounds that it made children grow up obdurate and stiff-necked." Instead, he said it was better "with a sweet admonition, to lead their thoughts to better ways." And Schama also notes that "at the other extreme, it was thought foolish to allow children's willfulness to go unchecked and unpunished. But the humanist emphasis on giving some rein to the natural instincts of the child and cajoling it into learning was so strong that notions of 'breaking the will,' apparently strong in more intensely Puritan and evangelical cultures, were almost wholly absent in the Netherlands."[13]

ATTITUDES TOWARD GAMES

What did Dutch artists and Dutch people think about children's games and activities? Dutch artists (and their clients) might well have attached moral significance to some of the particular games and activities in which children were engaged. That certainly seems to be the point explored by American and European art historians who have taken their lead in the past two decades from J. A. Emmens and Eddy de Jongh at the University of Utrecht. These art historians turn to the tradition of seventeenth-century Dutch literature (particularly the advice-giving emblem books of Jacob [Father] Cats or Johan de Brune), which saw some (few) games as likely to teach good habits of skill and forethought (such as chess); or playing with dolls as likely to teach little girls about their ultimate roles as wives and mothers. However, in the emblem books, many more games and activities were seen as either a waste of time or likely to lead to bad habits.

In 1988 Arthur K. Wheelock of the National Gallery of Art in Washington, D.C., discussed Dutch games and Dutch art at Hofstra University. Wheelock cited Jacob Cats' poem, "Kinderspel" (Children's Games), which appeared in his introduction to *Houwelyck. Dat is de gansche gelegentheyt desechten staets* (a treatise on marriage), published in Middelburg in 1625:

> Play, even if it appears without sense,
> Contains a whole world therein;
> The world and its complete structure,
> Is nothing but a children's game;
> Thus, after the frost thaws
> When you look at all that foolish youth does,
> You will understand on the street

How the whole world goes;
You will find there, I know it well
Your own folly in children's games.

And he observed that "Cats' attitudes towards play, thus, were essentially symbolic. Children's games, which he found frivolous, vain, and focused on transient pleasures, were in fact emblematic of adult behavior. For him the hoop symbolized a person whose life always follows one path and is in a rut."[14]

Mary Frances Durantini, in "The Child in Seventeenth-Century Dutch Painting," shares this interpretive perspective. In her chapter "The Child at Play: Reminders of Life and Death," she observes that literature of the time took the attitude that

games do not . . . contribute in a positive manner to the upbringing of children. To spend time at play is regarded as a means of corrupting children because it leads them away from serious concerns and introduces them to a world of frivolity and pleasure. The real danger, therefore, is that the vices learned in childhood are the precursors of those which appear in adulthood.[15]

Durantini goes on to catalog games and activities as falling into three categories: (1) reminders of the vanity and transiency of earthly matters; (2) depictions of qualities needed in order to live properly; and (3) images of vice, folly, and immorality. For example, a child blowing bubbles, according to her interpretation, would be perceived by Dutch observers as referring to the brevity of human existence; trying to chase or catch a bubble would be seen as a useless endeavor. Children or adults playing kolf (or golf) in an ice scene might represent the necessity to direct one's goal to a heavenly target and away from earthly concerns; yet sometimes the kolf club was also understood as an emblem of frivolity. Images had multiple interpretive meanings. And Durantini would argue that a child holding a mousetrap would be understood in the 1600s as a metaphor for punished immoderation; the mouse, who has yielded to the temptation of a brief moment of pleasure, reminds adult viewers of the dangers of lust.

There is no question that emblem books had wide circulation in Holland during the seventeenth century. People were almost as likely to have a copy of Cats' works as a family Bible. But whether the attitudes these authors expressed were subscribed to by all readers is a moot point. And whether artists and art patrons brought those emblematic interpretations to their interactions with visual artworks is also unclear. For example, in the emblematic literature cards and dice in the hands of children suggested their eventual ruination as adults through gambling. And since adults often gambled in peasant taverns, where smoking, drinking, betting on cockfights, and quarreling about the results also took place, some artists saw children's witnessing or participation in such activities as potentially corrupting or harmful. Jan Steen's *The Quarreling Card Players* can be used as an example. However, surely not all children playing with cards and dice ended up as reprobates; nor did every artist who depicts children with cards and dice see them as having one foot on the path to perdition. That is evident in the charming account by Dirk Hals in *A Boy and Girl Playing Cards, 1631* (in the Sterling and Francine Clark Art Institute in Williamstown, Massachusetts).[16] And while pictures of "merry companies" of young men-about-town enjoying music, women, drink, and tobacco showed them playing cards or tric-trac, as did any number of bordello scenes in which men often were cheated at cards by the whore, assisted by a wily procuress, there is no reason to assume that *every* Dutch person in the seventeenth century saw card-playing or tric-trac (a forerunner to backgammon) as morally corrupting for either adults or children. The games were simply too popular for everyone to take the moralizing preachers' view of them.[17]

An alternative way of interpreting seventeenth-century Dutch art has been suggested by the American art historian Svetiana Alpers. She questions the "emblematic" point of view by arguing that Dutch art is not as moralistic as certain readings of Jacob Cats and other authors of emblematic literature (utilized heavily by followers of the Utrecht theorists) would imply. Instead, Alpers argues, "pictures document or represent behavior. They are descriptive, rather than prescriptive. . . . [The aim of Dutch artists is] to portray each thing—be it a person, a flower, or a type of behavior—so as to make it known."[18] And yet anyone who has examined Jan Steen paintings in which children mock the foibles of their gluttonous, frolicking, drunken elders could not fail to see that children have sometimes been depicted as commentators on adult folly.[19] Surely that is the case in *The Effects of Intemperance*, where children mock the two besotted women who have had too much food, drink, and tobacco.

RESOLVING CONFLICTING INTERPRETATIONS

As art historians attempt to interpret seventeenth-century Dutch artists' images of children at play, they are necessarily second-guessing the artists' intentions and the perceivers' reactions. At best, art historians can hope to come to a plausible interpretation through induction. The evidence they have to draw upon is fragmentary at best. Only a few theoretical works by Dutch artists of the seventeenth century attempt to characterize the painter's task. Karel van Mander's *Schilder-Boeck* (*Book of Paintings*), printed in Haarlem in 1604; Cornelis de Bie's 1661-62 *Gulden Cabinet van de Edele vrij Schilder-Const* (*Golden Cabinet of the Noble Free Art of Painting*); and Samuel van Hoogstraten's 1678 *Inleyding tot de Hooge Schoole der Schilderkonst* (*Introduction to the Advanced School of Painting*) are notable examples. But these artists do not clearly set out a theory that could be used in the interpretation of the artists' intentions.

There is also one important account of the lives and works of different Dutch artists written early in the next century: Arnold Houbraken's three-volume *Groote Schouburgh de Nederlantsche Konstschilders en Schilderessen* (*Great Theatre of Dutch Men and Women Painters*), published between 1718 and 1721. While a source of information and impressions about many artists, and the reputations that individual ones then enjoyed, this cannot be fully corroborated.

Moreover, Houbraken gives little information about artistic intentions, repeating tales and gossip about artists. His work, characterized by Dutch art historian Bob Haak as the result of imagination given free rein, is nevertheless a major, indispensable information source.[20]

Seventeenth-century Dutch artists have not left letters or diaries in which they describe their works or what they intended to accomplish (with the notable exception of Rembrandt's letter to Constantijn Huygens, secretary to Stadholder Frederik Hendrik, who had commissioned two pictures, where Rembrandt describes his *Resurrection of Christ* and *Entombment of Christ*).[21]

For some artists, there are baptismal records, marriage documents, baptismal records for their children, listings of their names among those formally enrolled in the artists' guild (typically, the Guild of St. Luke) in a given town, occasional notarial copies of apprenticeship contracts as they either learned their trade from a master or took on pupils of their own, sworn testimony in court cases, bankruptcy proceedings, mention of paintings in auction sales notices or in the inventories of collectors who died, inventories of their own estates upon death, wills, and notices of burial. But these valuable and treasured documents, preserved in municipal archives in major cities throughout the Netherlands, do not tell today's art historian much about the inner thoughts, intentions, or ideas of the seventeenth-century Dutch artists.

Similarly, the owners of Dutch prints and paintings—the perceivers for whose eyes, and patronage, the artist worked—did not leave letters or diaries in which they discussed their interpretations of works they saw or purchased.

In the absence of such direct testimonial evidence, art historians have turned to emblem books, poetry, plays, sermons, and songs of the period for clues to help interpret the images. We need to be reminded that the interpretations, however intriguing or fanciful they might seem, are conjectures. In essence, we will probably never be certain why Dutch artists depicted children and adults playing certain games, engaging in particular pastimes, or amusing themselves with toys.

GAMES, TOYS, AND PASTIME

Today's social historians turn to seventeenth-century Dutch artworks as sources of visual documentation about the daily activities and special celebrations of Dutch people. Social historians notice the clothing people wore, the foods they ate, the houses they lived in, the markets where they shopped, the work and occupations of men and women, the kinds of transportation available on land and water, the musical instruments they played, the important geographical features of the countryside, and the architectural growth and expansion of cities. And some look carefully at Dutch artworks as sources of visual clues about children's activities, games, and toys. The social historian is less concerned with whether there is any hidden meaning in the artists' choice of games, toys, and pastimes to depict, asking instead, "What do the art works show us now in the twentieth century?"

To begin, one must ask, what games, toys, and recreational activities *do* we find represented in Dutch artworks? Many, many games and activities are captured in paintings, prints, or drawings. A partial listing includes: tennis (i.e., kaatsen, an open-air tennis game); kolf (golf), played on ice as a forerunner to ice hockey, on grass in the summer similar to golf, or on the street like a form of hockey; shuffleboard, played at an inn, using a disk on a long board; bowls or ninepins, played either in a lane or on a green; cockfights, falconing, birding, and bear-baiting; hunting rabbits, deer, or ducks; fishing through the ice or from boats, or by angling from a riverbank; horse racing, boating, iceboating, and sleigh riding; using goat or dog carts, sleds, and skates; pinwheels/windmills, marbles, hobbyhorses, hoops, and tops; singing, music making, dancing, and storytelling; outings and picnics via boats or wagons and partying in taverns; racing, on skates, horse, and foot; miniature household toys, dolls, and doll houses; drums and horns, soldier dress-up, mock sword fights, and bows and arrows; watching plays at fairs or markets; seeing comedians in costume dance at fairs or parties; goose-pulling game, herring catching game, and grabbing the eel; relationships with pets and animals such as dogs, cats, birds, and mice; and jumping rope, kite flying, blowing bubbles, and walking on stilts.

Holidays provided other opportunities to celebrate and participate in games. Examples of these activities include: St. Nicholas Day (December 6), when toys and sweets were left in shoes for good children, and switches to chastise the bad ones; Three Kings Day (January 6), when children dressed in paper crowns, paraded through the streets with paper lanterns, and sang, expecting cakes and gifts for their efforts, or joined the family in feasting, and jumped over lighted candles as a traditional game played at home parties; November slaughtering, when pig bladders were inflated and tossed around like large balloons; May festivals, when May Queens were chosen; Martinmas (November 11th), when in Amsterdam boat races were held on the Ij; wedding or birthday activities; and fairs or "kermisses," where toy booths would be set up for children eager to have hobbyhorses or pinwheels.

Teachers interested in the social history of children's games might pose the following questions about how games were depicted by Dutch artists:

1. Which games, toys, and activities seem to have been restricted to children?
   Answer: Goat or dog carts, hobbyhorses, blowing bubbles, pinwheels and whirligigs, storytelling, and jumping rope.
2. Were there games identified with just one sex?
   Answer: Boys were depicted playing tops, hoops, marbles, drums, soldier dress-up, playing with inflated pig bladders, nude swimming, kite flying, jumping ditches, walking on stilts, and using bows and arrows, whereas girls participated in female dress-up, acquiring doll houses and miniature household toys, and in being the May Queen on Pinkster Day.
3. Which games were played by adults in Dutch paintings? (At some point those games were learned, probably in childhood or during adolescence.)

    Answer: Shuffleboard, bowls or ninepins, cockfights, bear-baiting, iceboating, goose-pulling, grabbing the eel, herring catching, tric-trac (or backgammon), chess, lady come into the garden, and le main chaude.
4. Which activities were enjoyed by both children and adults (either together or apart)?
    Answer: Hunting, birding, fishing, tennis, kolf (golf), horse races, sledding, skating, sleigh rides, boating, singing, music-making, dancing, outings, races, plays at fairs or markets, the raising of pets and animals, card-playing, and the celebration of Three Kings Day, or Martinmas.
5. Which activities seem to be ones in which children were participants but adults were depicted as amused observers of their antics?
    Answer: St. Nicholas Eve and May or Pinkster Day celebrations.
6. Which activities were depicted as ones in which children observed adults?
    Answer: Partying to excess, quarreling and fighting over cards, and playing skittles.

THE IMPORTANCE OF WINTER SPORTS

Of all the games and activities depicted by Dutch artists, the most frequently occurring images focus on ice activities: kolf, skating, sledding, iceboating, ice fishing, visiting, flirting, and getting refreshments at temporarily constructed stands near the skating areas. When frozen in the wintertime, the canals, ponds, streams, and lakes in Holland provided places for these activities. Significantly, the ice was a place where the young and old, of both sexes, whether wealthy burghers or poor peasants, could play. Young couples courted while skating, neighbors visited each other, and games and competitive races were either planned or arose spontaneously. Some people took a tumble on the ice, and some fell in and needed to be rescued. Whether those potentially humbling episodes were meant to have deep emblematic meaning is not clear, but they were recorded by the artists.

Kolf, the forerunner to ice hockey, was played by both men and boys. It became such a popular activity that there were makers of kolf-balls (white leather balls filled with compacted cow hair and wool) in several Dutch towns. In 1631 three of these ballmakers, along with their families and apprentices, were recorded in the town of Goirle as having made 17,000 balls, a fair indication of the popularity of the sport. There were also specialized makers of kolf clubs or sticks in Middelburg, Leiden, Leeuwarden, Amsterdam, and Haarlem. By 1650 one enterprising Haarlem man had a sign on his house that proclaimed, "Praise God above all, here a man sells stick and ball."[22]

The players sometimes wore skates, but at other times played in their winter shoes or boots. Skate making became a specialized trade in the Netherlands during the seventeenth century; blades were fashioned of sharpened iron and steel and strapped onto the skaters' shoes. At least two prints depicting the making of skates were circulated in the seventeenth century, and it is clear from Romeyn de Hooghe's print that in the second half of the century adult male competitors began to outfit themselves with protective gear in addition to wearing skates. In fact, so popular was kolf that by 1659 the Dutch had brought the game to Fort Orange and the village of Beverwijk in Nieuw Nederland (now known as Albany, New York).[23]

CONCLUSION

Whether one turns to seventeenth-century Dutch artworks for their art historical interest or for their interest to social historians, there is no question that Dutch artists created for their customers a rich repository of images of children, as well as adults, playing games. Dutch portraiture frequently suggests a somber people; the images of people playing present the ludic side of seventeenth-century Dutch life. Games and pleasure activities were enjoyed by the young and the old throughout the entire year, as seen in winter skating as well as in summer activities such as crab-catching, swimming, or riding at the herring, or in children playing and celebrating May Day.[24]

NOTES

1. Of course, not all Dutch people were prosperous in the seventeenth century, as artists' accounts of wandering beggars, poor women and orphan children receiving food and clothing and sometimes shelter from church charity institutions, or alms-seeking inmates of leper hospitals and hospitals for syphilitics makes visually clear. Moreover, as van Deursen points out, Dutch sailors, small farmers, and workers in the textile trades in Leiden and Haarlem also had a hard time scraping by. See van Deursen's discussion of economic conditions and wages, "People of Little Wisdom and Limited Power," in *Plain Lives in a Golden Age: Popular Culture, Religion, and Society in Seventeenth-Century Holland* (Cambridge, England: Cambridge University Press, 1991), 3-31.

2. Copying or borrowing from the work of other artists by using prints, drawings, or paintings was acceptable in the seventeenth century. Indeed, such copying was a recommended means of training apprentices. That "borrowing" tendency was acceptable whether the seventeenth-century artist was utilizing works by contemporaries or by earlier masters.

3. Some ninety-one of them have been discussed by Sandra Hindman, "Pieter Bruegel's *Children's Games*, Folly, and Chance," *The Art Bulletin*, September 1981, 447-75.

4. According to Timothy Foote, *The World of Bruegel, c. 1525-1569*, (New York: Time-Life Books, 1968), 114-15, such games are still played. And even in a late twentieth-century world of complex computerized video games, there is still room for such outdoor activities for youngsters.

5. Philippe Ariès notes that from the medieval period onward, many games were played and activities enjoyed both by children and adults in Europe. (See his chapter focused on the history of games and pastimes, 62-99). Dutch artists sometimes give a glimpse of this in accounts where children accompany adults to village fairs (kermisses) or party with parents and grandparents at home or in taverns. Jan Steen's oeuvre is replete with such imagery.

6. See Simon Schama, *The Embarrassment of Riches: An Interpretation of Dutch Culture in the Golden Age* (New York: Alfred A. Knopf, 1987), 481.

7. Ibid., 481-83.

8. Ibid., 481-84.

9. Ibid., 552.

10. Ibid., 552-53.

11. Ibid., 485-86.

12. Ibid., 552.

13. Ibid., 556. The importance of a relaxed attitude toward children's natural instincts was further underscored in Schama's discussion. "Even in those areas of human function that seemed to call for drastic intervention, the orthodoxy was relatively gentle." On toilet training, writers of the seventeenth century would not have benefitted from Dr. Spock's theories. Young children should not be potty trained through methods of coercion. Nor should they be expected to perform on a parent's signal. Instead, the act of toilet training should be playful and carefree. The child should be offered favorite toys or musical instruments to help create a secure environment. Incidents of bed wetting should be treated with gentleness and understanding, since many children pass through this phase. It is also not uncommon for some children to urinate in their pants during school hours, because of a natural fear of being disciplined by the teacher. Blankaart added the comforting idea that it would be much worse if the child was unable to perform this function (Ibid., 557).

"In all this upbringing and education," wrote van Beverwijck, "children should not be kept on too tight a rein, but allowed to exercise their childishness, so that we do not burden their fragile nature with heavy things and sow untimely seed in the unprepared field of understanding. Let them freely play and let school use play for their maturing . . . otherwise they will be against learning before they know what learning is" (Ibid., 557, quoting J. van Beverwijck, *Schat der Gegondheid*, vol. 2, 192-93, published in Dordrecht, 1636).

14. Arthur K. Wheelock, Jr., "Games in Dutch Art: Innocent Pleasures or Moral Exemplars," paper presented at the Hofstra University International Symposium on 17th-century Dutch Art and Life, May 1988, 9-10.

15. Mary Frances Durantini, "The Child in Seventeenth-Century Dutch Painting," revision of Ph.D. thesis, University of California at Berkeley, 1983, 177.

16. See Christopher Brown's discussion in *Images of a Golden Past: Dutch Genre Painting of the Seventeenth Century* (New York: Abbeville Press, 1984), 166.

17. Ariès notes that ball games, sports, dancing, playing musical instruments and singing, festivals such as May Day, Shrove Tuesday, Martinmas (November) and Lenten masquerades, Three Kings Day or Twelfth Night, and card-playing enjoyed much popularity with people of all ages and in all classes in the sixteenth and seventeenth centuries. He answers his own question about the attitudes toward such activities by saying: "The vast majority accepted games indiscriminately and without any reservations. At the same time, a powerful and educated minority of rigid moralists condemned nearly all of them out of hand and roundly denounced them as immoral, allowing scarcely any exceptions. The moral indifference of the majority and the intolerance of a prudish elite existed side by side for a long time. A compromise was arrived at in the course of the seventeenth and eighteenth centuries which foreshadowed the modern attitude to games, an attitude fundamentally different from the old. It concerns us here because it bears witness to a new attitude to childhood: a desire to safeguard its morality and also to educate it, by forbidding it to play games henceforth classified as evil and by encouraging it to play games henceforth recognized as good." *Centuries of Childhood*, 81-82.

18. Svetiana Alpers, *The Art of Describing: Dutch Art in the Seventeenth Century* (Chicago: University of Chicago Press, 1983), xxvii.

19. Mary B. Durantini's *The Image of the Child in Seventeenth-Century Dutch Art*, as well as Simon Schama's *The Embarrassment of Riches* and Eddy de Jongh's *Tot Lering en*

Vermaak, give ample illustrations of such commentary, from Jan Steen and other Dutch artists. Eddy De Jongh, *Tot Lering en Varmaak* (Amsterdam: Rijksmuseum, 1976).

20. Bob Haak, *The Golden Age: Dutch Painters of the Seventeenth Century*, trans. Elizabeth Williams-Treeman (New York: Harry W. Abrams, 1984).

21. Paul Zumthor, who has an important discussion of Dutch recreational activities, comments that dancing was very popular. "Despite ecclesiastical condemnations, dancing remained popular throughout the century. Dancing schools and dancing masters flourished. No public holiday or private celebration was complete without a ball. There were two distinct styles of dancing, the rhythm and steps being inspired either by ancient folklore traditions or by recent importations. In the countryside and among the urban petty bourgeoisie, dances included 'raise the foot,' the 'hat-dance,' 'seven jumps,' 'Jimmy-be-still,' the 'clog-dance,' and many others, some of purely local usage. On the other hand, the gentry and aristocracy danced the minuet, the coranto, the scaramouch, the galliard, the beautiful bride, the *farlane*, the *alcide*, the kind victor, and so on; these dances were all known by French names, a sufficient indication of their national origin. But however elegant the ball, it would nearly always end with a round-dance." *Daily Life in Rembrandt's Holland*, trans. Simon Watson Taylor (New York: Macmillan, 1963), 170.

22. Jack Botermans, Nicolette Visser, and Tony Burrett note that as early as 1474, the making and selling of clubs or sticks and balls was authorized and regulated by the St. Nicholas peddlers guild in Middelburg. Ballmakers were listed by name in Amsterdam as early as 1543 and in Goirle by 1552. Between 1583 and 1601, some sixteen ballmakers were listed in the published marriage banns in Amsterdam. By 1610 ballmakers were established in Amsterdam on the St. Margrietenpad outside the city wall (near what is now the Elandsgracht); they were in Rotterdam by 1617. Records in Delft indicate that by 1626 the ballmakers belonged to the St. Michiel's Gild (along with the button makers) and had regulations governing their three-year apprenticeships. See *Timpen, hinkelen, and pierebollen: Spelen in de Lage Landen* (Houten: van Holkema and Warendorf, 1991) 22.

23. Ibid., 23.

24. It is not without significance that the Dutch have a museum of toys in Deventer and a skating museum in Hindeloopen. Collections of children's toys are also found in the Amsterdam Historical Museum, Rijksmuseum, Rotterdam Historical Museum, Alkmaar Municipal Museum, Simon van Gijn Museum in Dordrecht, and WestFries Museum. Those collections have very few play objects from the seventeenth century, but the ones there are treasured.

REFERENCES

Alpers, Svetiana (1983). *The Art of Describing: Dutch Art in the Seventeenth Century.* Chicago: University of Chicago Press.

Ariès, Philippe (1962). *Centuries of Childhood: A Social History of Family Life.* Trans. Robert Baldick. New York: Vintage Books.

Barnes, Donna R. (May 1988). "Educational Moments: Instructive Occasions Depicted in 17th-Century Dutch Paintings," paper presented at the International Symposium on Seventeenth-Century Dutch Art and Life, Hofstra University, Hempstead, New York.

———— (1991). *Street Scenes: Leonard Bramer's Drawings of 17th-Century Dutch Daily Life.* Exhibition catalog. Hempstead, New York: Hofstra Museum.

Botermans, Jack, Nicolette Visser, and Tony Burrett (1991). *Timpen, hinkelen, and pierebollen: Spelen in de Lage Landen.* Houten: van Holkema and Warendorf.

Brown, Christopher (1983). *Dutch Paintings: The National Gallery Schools of Painting.* London: National Gallery in Great Britain.

———— (1984). *Images of a Golden Past: Dutch Genre Painting of the Seventeenth Century.* New York: Abbeville Press.

de Jager, J. L. *Volksgebruiken in Nederland: Een nieuwe kijk oop tradities.* Utrecht/Antwerp: Het Spectrum.

Diekstra, Rene (1985). *Winter Aerdigheden, Winter Naerigheden: Recreation d'Hyver en Hollande.* Den Haag: Koninklijke Bibliotheek.

Durantini, Mary Frances (1983). *The Child in Seventeenth-Century Dutch Painting.* Ann Arbor, Michigan: UMI Research Press.

Encyclopedia of World Art, s.v. "games and toys," rev. ed., Vol. VI. New York: McGraw Hill Book Co.

Haak, Bob (1984). *The Golden Age: Dutch Painters of the Seventeenth Century.* Trans. by Elizabeth Williams-Treeman. New York: Harry W. Abrams.

Hallema, A. and J. D. van der Weide (1943). *Kinderspelen voorheen en thans izonderheid in Nederland.* The Hague: A. A. M. Stols.

Hofrichter, Frima Fox (1989). *Judith Leyster: A Woman Painter in Holland's Golden Age.* Doornspijk: Davaco.

Huizinga, Johan M. (1950; rev. ed. 1955). *Homo Ludens: The Play Element in Culture.* Boston: Beacon Press.

———— (1968). *Dutch Civilization in the Seventeenth Century and Other Essays.* Trans. Arnold J. Pomerans. New York: Frederick Ungar.

Kay, Marguerite (1969). *Bruegel.* London: Paul Hamlyn.

Mauritshuis (1982). *Dutch Painting of the Golden Age.* Exhibition catalog. The Hague: Royal Picture Gallery.

Nash, J. M. (1972). *The Age of Rembrandt and Vermeer: Dutch Painting in the Seventeenth Century.* New York: Holt, Rinehart and Winston.

Rafael, Valls, Ltd. (1988). *Recent Acquisitions.* Sales catalog. London.

Rijksmuseum Kunst-Krant, vol. 12(3) (1985-1986); vol. 13 (1986-1987). Amsterdam: Rijksmuseum.

Robinson, William W. (1991). *Seventeenth-Century Dutch Drawings: A Selection from the Maida and George Abrams Collection.* Lynn, Mass.: H. O. Zimman.

Schama, Simon (1987). *The Embarrassment of Riches: An Interpretation of Dutch Culture in the Golden Age.* New York: Alfred A. Knopf.

Schatborn, Peter, and Eva Ornstein-van Slooten (1984). *Bij Rembrandt in de Leer (Rembrandt as Teacher).* Exhibition catalog. Amsterdam: Rembrandtshuis Museum.

Slive, Seymour (1989). *Frans Hals.* Exhibition catalog. London: Royal Academy of Arts.

Stone-Ferrier, Linda (1983). *Dutch Prints of Daily Life: Mirrors of Life or Masks of Morals.* Exhibition catalog. Lawrence: Spencer Museum and University of Kansas.

Sutton, Peter C. (1984). *Masters of Seventeenth Century Dutch Genre Painting.* Exhibition catalog. Philadelphia: Museum of Art.

———— (1987). *Masters of 17th Century Dutch Landscape Painting.* Exhibition catalog. Boston: Museum of Fine Arts.

van Deursen, A. Th. (1991). *Plain Lives in a Golden Age: Popular Culture, Religion, and Society in Seventeenth-Century Holland.* Trans. Maarten Ultee. Cambridge: Cambridge University Press.

van Hengel, S. J. H. (n.d.). *Vroeg Golf en zign Ontwikkeling.* Pamphlet. Amsterdam: Historical Museum.

van Ostade, Adriaen (1987). *Country Life in Holland's Golden Age: Etchings by Adriaen van Ostade*. New York: Theodore B. Donson.

Wheelock, Arthur K., Jr. (May 1988). "Games in Dutch Art: Innocent Pleasures or Moral Exemplars." Paper presented at the International Symposium on Seventeenth-Century Dutch Art and Life, Hofstra University, Hempstead, New York.

Zumthor, Paul (1963). *Daily Life in Rembrandt's Holland*. Trans. Simon Watson Taylor. New York: Macmillan.

Part IV

Developmentally Appropriate Behavior through Games

Part IV begins with Bruce Grossman's chapter on play theories and the forces that interfere with the young child's spontaneous play behavior. The relationship between play and games is also explored. Karl E. Rohnke responds to the need for teachers and administrators to maintain a playful attitude and to participate in activities that have a great potential for fun. John LaRue's work serves as a foundation for readers unfamiliar with the nature of New Games. A brief comparison between the sport of baseball and a popular New Game is included. Deidre Burnstine interprets the concept of play as being physical education's authentic subject matter and suggests that New Games can accomplish student-initiated purposes within the physical education curriculum. Janis Bozowski presents eight ways to foster the New Games spirit in traditional lead-up games, and Janet M. Oussaty explores four myths about competition. Linda McNally describes a variety of games for three- to eight-year-old children. Each activity is intended to lay a foundation for learning rules, simple strategies, and playing tactics.

Kathy Pattak shows how students in grades five and six can work cooperatively in small groups, using previously learned skills to create their own games. Jim DeLine's five-step Dare to Care model can be used to teach students cooperative and prosocial behaviors. Techniques that give students opportunities to practice cooperative gestures and behaviors are included. Similarly, Jill Vomacka applies a point system to teach the value of sportsmanship in lessons developed for kindergarten through grade six. Susan Anne Sortino contrasts the extreme behaviors and actions commonly used to describe the traditional and nontraditional seventh and eighth grade learning environment, and Minna S. Barrett, Sheila Mardenfeld, and Rhoda Joseph identify a sample activity designed to help middle school students to express their feelings. Estelle Aden continues the theme of increasing self-expression by presenting a variety of creative theatre games that can be used to stimulate the elementary school child's constructs of thinking and imagination. Finally, Karen H. Weiller, Catriona T. Higgs, and

Betsy A. Brickell review the literature pertaining to gender socialization in elementary physical education. Strategies for eliminating sexist teaching behavior and practices are identified.

33

In Defense of Play:
Enhancing the Growth of Young Children

Bruce Grossman

CONFLICT BETWEEN PLAY AND EARLY SCHOOLING

Early childhood specialists generally agree that play is the primary way that children learn in the early years. A major threat arises when educators and parents contend that we must structure the learning experiences of preschoolers and toddlers in order to prepare them for later school experience. Proposals such as extending the school year and using workbooks for early learning experiences "steal" time from the young child's play periods. This time is already severely eroded by excessive amounts of television viewing. In conflict with this academic movement is a long tradition of play and social interaction as the mainstay of early education, dating back to the late nineteenth century and Pestalozzi. Since its inception in this country, early childhood education has emphasized the natural curiosity of children and the value of the preschool classroom as a place to explore social interaction as well as materials. These "traditional" early childhood classes encouraged creativity in a noncompetitive, "fun" atmosphere. The conflict between the advocates of a play curriculum and early schooling has existed at least since the Head Start program was introduced in the early 1960s.

While teaching children shapes, colors, letters, and numbers at an early age does offer the illusion of success, it can contain a built-in potential for disaster. By definition, play is self-motivated—the child does not play to please adults or to gain recognition. Play is not only a natural activity (meaning a spontaneous action), it is fun. Play may be facilitated and even guided by adults, but when the initiative is taken away from the child, a crucial source of energy is lost.

Fortunately for the play advocates who observed the power of play in early childhood classrooms, Jean Piaget's research became known in this country in the 1960s and 1970s. Piaget (1962) offered specific "scientific" evidence that play was a way for children to construct their world. Each new encounter produces a disequilibrium which in turn inspires internal mental images (schemata). Piaget not only confirmed that the young child learns best by doing and not by being told, he presented the theory to explain why this is so. Until his death in the 1980s, Piaget cautioned against structured learning. He was even opposed to a Montessori curriculum where activities had a built-in solution. Piaget stressed the role of an interesting play environment with objects and people available for children to explore as the best medium for learning. He insisted that it was important for the child's mind to make order out of the apparent chaos of experience and that this would eventually enhance the child's conceptual skills. He complained about his American colleagues, such as Jerome Bruner, who would attempt to rush this process or make it easier for children by prearranging their experience. According to Piaget, children need to make their own mental files.

How does Piaget's work underscore the value of play? Play is certainly an active encounter with the world. Through play children explore the nature of things, people, and themselves. As noted previously, play is *self-directed*, which is an important requirement for real learning, according to Piaget. It is interesting that this is the very ingredient necessary to breathe life into American education, according to many of those seeking solutions to the apathy often found in the classrooms of older children. As a clinical psychologist, I have learned that play is the best way to discover where a young child is "at" emotionally. It is also an excellent way to determine where a child is at intellectually, and, in fact, is often a better indicator of a child's intelligence than his or her performance on a standardized test. Especially for children who have difficulty trusting others or who lack confidence in themselves, play offers a sense of control and of freedom. Contrary to educators who insist that tightening teacher control is the answer to the reluctant learner, a play environment can create an atmosphere that is more conducive to learning.

Piaget (1969) has made another important point in defense of play. He notes, or rather *insists*, that play in young children corresponds to the sensory-motor period of development. Learning during this period requires manipulation of objects. This concrete representation prepares them for the ability to represent their world through thoughts and symbols. Piaget insists that this process *cannot* be rushed, and yet American educators and psychologists have consistently sought a way to do so. I believe that there are two major reasons for this: (1) in our desire to increase the child's learning we tend to lose sight of the stages of development, and (2) in our desire to ensure that things turn out the way we would like we are reluctant to give children the freedom to learn on their own. Let me briefly expand on these two notions. Concrete, sensory-motor learning like that obtained in a hands-on situation is helpful at any stage of development, but it is particularly critical before we have more advanced conceptual skills. It is what John Dewey (1933) termed "learning by doing."

Regarding the second point, we are often afraid when children are left to their own devices. We fear that they won't be productive, that they'll waste time, or worse, that they will do something "bad." Historically, in part because of this country's Puritan tradition, we have operated as if we believe that unless children are controlled and shaped, their inherent evil nature will prevail. While we may no longer believe this, and while we may no longer believe that idle hands are the devil's workshop, today's parents and educators look for structured programs with which to fill young children's free time. To a degree, we have moved away from the work ethic that prevailed in the past, but even when we maintain that play is "the child's work," we reveal our reluctance to support play for its own sake. Our modern point of view has also been clearly influenced by the behaviorist notion that if children are not instinctively "bad," they are at best blank slates (*tabula rasa*), and it is our responsibility to control and shape the learning process in order to meet society's demands.

Still another factor that accounts for our prejudice against play is a fear of our own rebellious and destructive inner impulses. This may sound rather ominous, or at least overstated, but there is a great deal of clinical evidence to support the psychoanalytic point of view that what we fear in our children are projections of impulses that we fear in ourselves. We need to control our children's behavior because we are afraid of losing control of ourselves.

Advocates of play must have faith in children. Fortunately, there is considerable scientific evidence to support this positive point of view. As noted, Piaget is perhaps the best known advocate of the power of play in children's intellectual development. Play allows children to explore and to develop their understanding of the world. From the point of view of adaptation, children's natural drive to reach out and to investigate the people and things around them contributes to their survival. Robert White (1959) has identified this natural tendency in children as a drive toward competency. White and other psychologists, observing infants as well as toddlers and preschoolers, have been impressed with their tenacity in their struggle to grasp and manipulate objects, to gain control of their own bodies, to imitate adults, and generally to master their world. The work of these researchers suggests that young children do not need to be *motivated* by behaviorist or Calvinist adults to learn. It is the inherent drive for competency and curiosity that supplies the motivation for early learning.

PLAY AND SELF-ESTEEM

Many authors, including Susan Isaacs (1966 [1933]) have linked play to the development of self-esteem. Isaacs and other psychoanalytically oriented writers point out that young children find themselves in a world dominated by adults who are not only more powerful and competent than they, but upon whom they are quite dependent. Pretend play in particular affords children a chance to move about in the world without the frustration and obstacles found in reality. Whether they are pretending to be super-heroes or simply "mommy" or "daddy," children can feel more powerful in play. At the same time, they are practicing behaviors and developing skills that contribute to their ego development and provide a legitimate base upon which to build self-esteem. The psychoanalysts point out that play specifically contributes to the process of identification. Identification contributes to dependent children's sense of security and well-being and, in turn, to their self-esteem. Identifying with significant adults in their lives helps children to share the power of these adults by forming an alliance with the people who protect and care for them. Identification is a powerful force in the socialization process that can be acted out in play. Meantime, children's cognitive, verbal, social, and even psychomotor skills are enhanced as they play, adding to their actual skills and to their self-esteem. In some respects play is a way of "thinking out loud." If the feedback is positive and contains words of praise, children feel good about their choices and about themselves. Erik Erikson (1963) speaks of the importance of the development of a sense of initiative during the early childhood period. Spontaneous play gives children an excellent milieu for making aesthetic and practical decisions as it builds their confidence in their own resources. This process promotes essential qualities of creativity, problem solving and decision making, along with heightened self-esteem.

PLAY AND GAMES IN EARLY CHILDHOOD

Since the central theme of this text is games, I think that it is appropriate to consider the relationship between games and play in young children. While we refer to a game as being "played," in some sense playing a game does not fall within the formal classification of play. By definition, play is spontaneous; it is not restricted by rules; it is self-defined and self- or intrinsically motivated. Usually the child at play is more concerned with process than with an outcome or product. Certainly, childhood play is not seen as concerned with keeping score or winning. On the other hand, many students of play, particularly Piaget (1962) and Brian Sutton-Smith (1971), have included games in their investigations. More recently, many students of infant-parent interaction have noted that almost from the moment of birth, exchanges are possible between babies and parents that take the form of games (e.g., Brazelton, 1982). In fact, Judith Van Hoorn (1987) recently studied parent-infant games in four cultures: Mexican, Filipino, Chinese, and U.S. Americans of European descent.

Van Hoorn observed that games such as peek-a-boo and pat-a-cake have their counterparts in virtually all of the cultures studied. These early games promote a sense of closeness between parent and child. They also serve as a source of stimulation and encouragement for the child. As Van Hoorn puts it, "They [the games] appeared to be culturally developed and 'field-tested' parenting programs" (p. 41). She suggests that a special feature of these early parent-child "games" is that they do not involve competition. They do involve rules or routines that may be learned even by very young children. These repetitive psychomotor and verbal exchanges are gently taught to infants by adults who perform most of the actions at first, but who respond with delight (reinforcement) when the children begin to anticipate and even to imitate the behaviors. Frequently, the adult guides the baby's hand as she repeats a sing-song chant. Given the universal nature of this phenomenon, one might conclude that this behavior has naturally evolved and has some adaptive value, and on this basis is worth preserving. In fact, as Van Hoorn points out, the activities she observed are part of the curriculum in home-based Head Start and other federally funded programs designed to enhance mother-child interaction.

The learning of repetitive patterns of behaviors seems to have a natural appeal for babies, even as they contribute to the babies' later development. Piaget (1962) notes that the child acquires object permanence as well as a sense of sequencing in these early games. Brazelton (1982) and others have emphasized how games played with very young children contribute to parent-child bonding and ultimately to a sense of "self" and "other."

Piaget observed how, as children mature intellectually, their ability to take the perspective of others, that is, to decline in egocentricity, enables them to follow rules. As anyone who has played games with children under seven years of age can attest, rules have no permanence or objectivity and tend to be biased in favor of the self-serving child. Playing by the rules requires an objectivity whereby the conditions for play are established by mutual agreement and usually remain the same throughout the play. This type of advanced thinking and ability to be less egocentric is clearly a desirable developmental achievement that is enhanced by children's participation in games. Needless to say, games with rules help to develop children's planning and decision-making skills and, at times, their creative ability. On a social-emotional level, games played with others (parents or peers) contribute to children's social development in a significant way. Yet, despite the advantages of playing organized or ritualistic games with children, I would caution that adults should not expect young children to be "fair" or to follow prescribed rules in the preschool years. In the long run, trying to impose social expectations on children before they are ready is usually more detrimental than helpful. As children enter the elementary school years, it could be useful for them to be reminded about the rules or even to express the preference that they play in a more consistent way (e.g., rules may be changed by mutual consent), but it could be harmful to generate a good deal of shame or guilt around a child's need to win in the early years. Like so many other things, playing by the rules can be better taught at a later point.

A final caution that I would offer for the use of games with young children is to be wary of competition. This is not a problem with infants and toddlers, but it is a comment on our culture that it has become an increasing problem with preschoolers and older elementary school aged youngsters. We are, after all, a competitive culture. Young children see competitive sports on television and observe their parents' and other adults' reactions to winning. Shouts of "Yes!" and "We're Number One!" are as familiar at home as is the "high five" sign. The children imitate these actions and the attitudes behind them. A three-year-old may ask, "Am I winning?" several times during a game of Chutes and Ladders, without really knowing what it means. Being a "winner" may be a nice feeling at times, but not when it takes the pleasure away from playing or makes you feel like a failure unless you're "number one." Children's activities such as Little League have demonstrated too frequently the destructive effects of playing only to win. This is why the concept of New Games is so necessary in recreational play, where everyone does not have to be a superstar to participate. Clearly, then, a premature emphasis on competition, even in organized games, only adds to the pressure in our culture to beat "the next guy."

COMMENTS

I have already cited two major forces likely to interfere with the spontaneous play of young children: premature emphasis on academic-style schooling, and excessive concern for competition. There are two other serious threats to play in young children: excessive television viewing and electronic and battery operated toys. Maire Winn (1977) has referred to TV as a "plug-in drug." She observes that extensive TV viewing not only tends to be addictive but that it has a narcoleptic quality that reduces brain function. The child who watches TV is likely to be more passive and less alert behaviorally. Neurologically, this reduced functioning can be detected by an electroencephalogram (EEG) as well as measurements of the autonomic nervous system. What about the specific effect of TV viewing on play? Most obviously, children who are watching have less time to devote to spontaneous play. After doing an extensive survey of children's viewing habits, Liebert, Sprafkin, and Davidson (1982) discovered that most preschool-aged children watch television between three and six hours per day. This leaves less time to play. As adults or even older children, we have the capacity to move the TV images around in our head—to conceptualize them and even to evaluate them. Children take what they see more literally. In addition they have less capacity for internal mental manipulation. These young children do their thinking by manipulating concrete objects. Television can be a source of information and stimulation for children, but it cannot be relied upon, as it often is, to be major contributor to their mental development. Television tends to provide ready-made fantasies rather than to encourage young children to take the initiative themselves. Advertisers bombard young children with attempts to influence their needs and values. As a result children learn from an early age about what they regard as valuable and necessary not from their parents or from themselves but from TV advertisers who are trying to sell their products and to make them sound "good" for children. As I noted above, play does just the opposite: it helps children to learn what is valuable and what they like and need for themselves.

Similarly, battery operated toys tend to take the initiative away from young children. I recall, with a touch of sadness, observing a three-year-old staring at an old-fashioned baby doll, saying, "How does this work?" I was baffled at first, but quickly understood as the child began turning the doll around and around, looking for the batteries. If I thought that battery operated toys were a threat to children's play, I did not anticipate the potential danger from computer games. At this point a child who does not have Nintendo is culturally deprived. Adults who were not brought up on this modern fare usually feel at a loss when children describe various cartridges that they own and have mastered. It may well be that video games contribute to perceptual-motor development, but I do not regard them as a substitute for play.

As noted at the beginning of this chapter, play is under siege, but not lost. Concerned adults can advocate free time to explore materials and for pretend play in early childhood classrooms and daycare centers. They can limit as well as monitor children's TV viewing. At home they can also encourage the use of nonelectronic toys that young children can use in a variety of ways. They can discourage competition and reinforce playing for fun. Parents can supply their young children with creative materials such as clay and paint, and take the time to do cooking and other chores *with* them rather than *despite* them. Even if parents are not particularly creative or do not have time to get materials together for a special experience, there are some good products on the market, such as the National Safety Association's Wings Program, which offers parents a series of noncompetitive, creative games to play with their young children that can also foster intellectual growth. In addition, parents can find books with suggested activities in the library and bookstores. All of this implies active parenting. It involves parent-child participation. Isn't it worth it?

REFERENCES

Avendon, E., and B. Sutton-Smith (1971). *The Study of Games*. New York: John Wiley.

Brazelton, T. B. (1982). Joint Regulation of Neonate-Parent Behavior. In E. Z. Tronick, ed., *Social Interchange in Infancy* 7-23. Baltimore: University Park Press.

——— (1983). *Infants and Mothers*. New York: Delacorte Press.

Dewey, J. (1933). *How We Think*. Chicago: Henry Regnery.

Erikson, E. H. (1963). *Childhood and Society*. New York: Norton.

Isaacs, S. (1966). *Social Development in Young Children*. New York: Schocken. (Originally published in 1933.)

Liebert, R. M., J. Sprafkin, and E. Davidson (1982). *The Early Window*. New York: Pergamon Press.

Piaget, J. (1962). *Play, Dreams and Imitation in Childhood*. New York: W. W. Norton.

——— (1969). *The Language and Thought of the Child*. New York: World.

Sutton-Smith, B. (1971). A Syntax for Play and Games. In R. E. Herron and B. Sutton-Smith, eds., *Child's Play*, 298-307. New York: John Wiley.

Van Hoorn, J. (1987). Games that Babies and Mothers Play. In *Looking at Children's Play: Between Theory and Practice*, 38-62. New York: Teachers College Press.

White, R. W. (1959). Motivation Reconsidered: The Concept of Competence. *Psychological Review*, 66, 297-333.

Winn, M. (1977). *The Plug-In Drug*. New York: Viking Press.

34

Serious Play:
Ten Suggestions for the Teacher

Karl E. Rohnke

I've made a successful career of professional funmanship. Organizations pay me a substantial consulting fee to teach them how to play *meaningful* games, but it's not the teaching per se that is covered by the fee, it's for a personal appearance by someone that can validate the play experience. "Karl's here, now we can play and have some fun." I am not being entirely facetious.

I added the word *meaningful* in between *play* and *games* above to emphasize a ludicrous juxtaposition. Administrators and teachers often feel obliged to make their play purposeful by verbalizing their way around fun. That's why I add an extra *n* on funn—functional understanding's not necessary. Please don't misinterpret my intentions. I am not advocating pure play for all situations, just making sure that the opposite doesn't take place simply to appease an office type who schedules and compartmentalizes fun, and determines that play must be validated, like a parking ticket.

I go out of my way to let fun find me; you don't find fun, just be open to it. And since I don't have a sure-fire "secret" to share about fun and games, consider the following four suggestions concerning playfulness:

1. Personal fitness is a large part of the play experience. Active play increases the likelihood that the individual will be able to take part in physical activities without hesitation, and be able to respond wholeheartedly without worrying about pulling muscles, feeling stiff, and all the other excuses that keep a person from experiencing the fun.

2. Don't wait for colleagues or family members to join you in recreational pursuits. Get out and do some potentially fun things by yourself. I'm not trying to turn you into a loner, but when you're just getting started it is difficult to know what you are going to enjoy. There's no use dragging someone else into this period of experimentation.

3. Do not schedule all of your planned recreation and leisure into one or two events. Try to establish a lifetime game plan that feeds fun doses at intervals. Fun should not be overwhelming, but rather an unplanned but expected series of rejuvenating interludes sandwiched between parent-teacher meetings and car pooling.

4. Avoid anything where you "must" take lessons or wear specialized clothing and shoes. Did you ever notice how much money and advertising space are devoted to activity footwear? Air soles, gel soles, and pumps—it's no wonder children are literally killing for the status that surrounds shoes. And if trophies are mentioned (particularly if they are all displayed on a table), get out quick. Find activities that you can learn through trial and error, where the errors are laughable, and where the necessary clothing is whatever you happen to have on.

The preceding considerations ultimately reflect the educator's mental attitude and adventure aptitude. If you have spent years doing a job and fulfilling family responsibilities, and would like to experience some of the fun that we learn about (I'm not talking about the heavily advertised aspects of smoking, drinking, and sexual involvement that are pitched as fun, but seem more like escape mechanisms and psychological crutches), you could skip all the preliminary suggestions and pursue the big A (adrenaline) event of your dreams by signing up for skydiving classes, scuba lessons, or high-speed driving lessons. It might be more beneficial, however, to initially commit to a weekend experience of hiking, canoeing, or square dancing. You should not risk life and appendages to experience adventure, play, and fun.

Age should have little to do with an individual's potential for play, but society does its best to make you feel irresponsible if you "have graduated" and continue to pursue playful situations. In our culture, growing up and aging are equated with being serious, responsible, mature adults. That's fine, but where's the fun?

It's difficult to remain "young" when people are always telling you to grow up and when a fun-loving attitude is regarded as a sign of immaturity and lack of seriousness. We read, quote, and extol the writings of great philosophers, because this defines us as mature, intelligent adults, then we ignore their maxims and teachings. Plato is quoted as saying, "I can learn more about a person in an hour of play than in a year of conversation," but for some, experiencing an hour of play is an unrealistic expectation; they don't know how. Play is unfortunately often defined as what children do, or on a higher, more competitive plane, as something adults pursue as sport. The following six suggestions are intended to reinforce the need for educators to pursue those activities and situations that have the highest potential for fun:

1. If the people you live with don't want to play, play by yourself or with similar-minded friends, and let the fun roll.
2. Don't plan activities where you have to consistently compete against yourself or someone else. It's hard to have fun when you're losing, and winning all the time isn't that rewarding either.
3. Become involved in something where joking and laughter are the primary means of communication.
4. Do things with people you like. Playing golf with a high-ranking school administrator might result in a salary increase, but you are not playing. You are playing at golf, but you are not playing. It's almost impossible to have fun if you are spending time with someone for a job-related purpose.

5. Find things that you like to do by yourself. I like to fly large kites with family members, but I also enjoy doing it alone. Give yourself a chance to get to know yourself.
6. Practice safety, stay healthy, and have some fun.

35

An Introduction to the New Games Approach

John LaRue

New Games offers an addition and new direction to traditional sports and games—a way of playing that is exciting and enjoyable and does not require exceptional athletic ability. The activities are challenging and combine competition with cooperation: each game emphasizes participation, not spectatorship. More than a list of games, New Games is an attitude toward play.

THE NATURE OF NEW GAMES

Several years ago, the New Games Foundation was purchased by the YMCAs of the USA. The last official New Games training was in June 1982. While no one else is able to use the registered "New Games" name and logo, several individuals still continue to spread and share the knowledge of cooperative-based play. This experience allows children to become their own leaders as they become empowered in the role of referee. New Games that are taught in the classroom do carry over to the recess activities, since they accommodate large groups of children and little (if any) equipment.

To better understand the nature of New Games, it may be helpful to think about baseball, America's pastime. The sport consists of batters, outfielders, umpires, bases, bats, balls, scoreboards, infield, outfield, foul territory, dugouts, backstops, right and left field lines, natural grass, artificial turf, uniforms, different styles of gloves, and of course, bubble gum and hot dogs! There are also numerous organizational factors that relate to strikes, balks, home runs, and stealing techniques. The point is that there is a very important scientific mixture of rules and conditions that are mutually agreed upon and can be "objectively" measured. The key is *objectivity*, which is the foremost criterion for measuring outcome.

New Games has many of the conditions mentioned in the preceding sport. New Games leaders call them players, environment, goals, roles, boundaries, equipment, interaction, action, scoring techniques, rituals, and/or fantasy, among others. The list can continue as long as the New Games motto is not compromised, that is, "Play Hard, Play Fair, Nobody Hurt." In brief, this concept allows players to change and modify any game so that it meets the users' needs. It is especially useful when teaching wheelchair, mobility impaired, or visual and speech impaired students and adults. Depending on the participants' developmental level (young, old, quick, slow, active, inactive), a game can be changed to meet the group's needs and interests. You simply change or modify one of the components. The following classic New Game is used to demonstrate this characteristic.

NEW GAME ACTIVITY: KNOTS

Components

Players:	A dozen or more works well. The fewer the participants, the less difficult the activity, but large groups can be accommodated.
Environment:	Anywhere! Indoors or outside, small or large facilities.
Goal:	The objective is to unravel your "knot" before other groups complete the task, or simply try to complete the activity in less time without letting go of hands.
Roles:	Essentially, each participant is a piece of rope . . . or a piece of spaghetti . . . or a piece of "?".
Boundaries:	All players should be clear of obstacles in the event that a participant looses his or her balance.
Equipment:	Just hands. Amputated players may use shirt sleeves or a handkerchief.
Interaction:	Intragroup function (prime directive); however groups may compete against each other.
Action:	Twisting, turning, moving over and under, maintaining a hand grip and periodically "surveying" the situation.
Scoring:	Scoring techniques are not necessary. In group play, the play leader can challenge the first group to complete the task to act as "technical specialists" to the other groups. A second method of scoring is to count the number of "Bandaids" needed when individuals momentarily release their hand grip.
Ritual:	Begin the activity with all players or groups of players standing in a circle, shoulder to shoulder. All participants place their hands toward the center of the circle and use them to make the movements of a washing machine (up, down, side to side) while keeping their eyes closed. On the signal "Hang on," the participants grab two different people's hands

across the circle to form the knot. The group maintains these hand grips while moving to untangle the knot into a long make-believe rope.

Fantasy: Ask the players what they represent. A long rope, a piece of spaghetti? In this example, success is measured by the level of the laughs, giggles, and jokes that occur during and after accomplishing the task, and the primary directive remains the same: Play Hard, Play Fair, Nobody Hurt!

36

New Ways with New Games:
Play with a Purpose

Deidre Burnstine

Children come to gym eager to play. For some reason physical educators shun the idea of "just letting children play," and feel compelled to incorporate structured learning theories to validate the lesson's purpose. In contrast, our colleagues within the classroom setting seek to use game and play theories to enrich the students' learning. This chapter argues that play is physical education's natural, authentic subject matter. We can and should use this concept to our advantage and extend those feelings into the larger educational community. A banner in the Indianapolis Children's Museum proclaims this thought: "Play is a happy activity that begins in delight and ends in wisdom."[1] At the very least physical educators need to convey the idea that children can and will learn in and through play that is structured to accomplish particular purposes. This philosophical basis could be viewed as the proverbial icing on our part of the educational cake, not something physical educators shun.

"New Ways with New Games" is about play with a purpose. This approach to using new games is based on the ability to determine one's purpose(s) and then select, invent, or adapt games and activities that foster them. The schema that follows reflects one formulation of potential purposes, along with an identification of particular games and activities that can accomplish these purposes. In most cases, the teacher will not need to make the connection between the purpose and the activity explicit for the students, and whenever possible the students should be encouraged to discover the connections for themselves.

Note that several games in this schema are listed under more than one purpose because of their ability to contribute substantially to each (see Figure 36.1). As teachers lead, play, and analyze games they are likely to discover or formulate additional purposes for many of them, and may identify more games that will serve other purposes. Such insights are often a benefit of reflective practice. The schema offered here is intended to stimulate the reader's thinking about new games. It is not an exhaustive compendium of matched games and purposes. I hope that this approach will help teachers move in directions that foster the concept of "play." The most desirable outcome will be the development of your own list of purposes and games. Ownership is critical to success.

FIGURE 36.1
Schema

I. New Games can be selected or modified to promote particular sport skills, strategies, and concepts.

Basketball/Team Handball

Aerobic Tag
Catch Up
Fox and Squirrel
Group Juggle
Smaug's Jewels
Trash Ball
Triangle Tag

Football

Aerobic Tag
Catch Up
Flag Grab
Fox and Squirrel
Rock Football

Soccer/Speedball

Catch Up
Frantic
Lilly Pad Soccer
Siamese Soccer

Volleyball

Blanket Ball
Boop
Catch Up
Infinity
Keep It Up
Rotation Ball
To and Fro
Trust Circle

Teamwork and Community and Strategy

Blind Polygon	Knots	Catch the Dragon's Tail
British Bull Dog	Trust Circle	Rock-Paper-Scissor
Frantic	Warp Speed	Stand Up/Group Stand Up

II. New Games can be selected or developed to provide active learning experiences leading to affective objectives.

Group Building and Cooperation

A Big Wind Blows
Build A Machine
Catch the Dragon's Tail
Frantic
Knots
Lap Circle
Living Sculpture
Prui
Stand Up/Group Stand Up
Team on a T-Shirt

Multicultural Awareness

Bone Game
Counting Group
Monarch
Samurai Warrior
Street Games
Yurt Circle

Trust

Car and Driver
Cookie Monster
Helicopter
Mine Field
To and Fro
Trust Circle
Trust Dive
Trust Fall
Trust Sit
Yurt Circle

Ecological Awareness

Clam Free
Eco-Ball
Trash Ball

III. New Games can be selected or developed to enhance creativity and problem solving abilities.

Creativity

Build A Machine
Create-A-Game
Living Sculpture
One on One

Problem Solving

Human Bomb
Knots/Loop
Monster
Octo Carry
Stand Up/Group Stand Up
Team on a T-Shirt
Traffic Jam
Warp Speed

IV. New Games can be selected or modified to provide variety for fitness development or maintenance.

Aerobic

Aerobic Tag
Can Can
Counting Coup
Everybody's It
Fun Run
Group Toe Tag
Imaginary Jump Rope
Line/Circle Aerobics
Monarch
Snake in the Grass
Toe Fencing
Triangle Tag

Flexibility

Horse Stretch
Partner Stretches
Sun Salute
Thread the Needle
Windmill

Agility

Ankle Biter Tag Games
Group Toe Tag
Samurai Warrior
Snake in the Grass
Toe Fencing

Balance

Stand Off
Stork Stand
Squat Thrust

Body Control/Coordination

Body Surfing
Caterpillar
Facial Exercise
Log Roll

Strength

Crab Tag
Dollar Jump
Lap Game (moving circle)
Popsicle Push Up
Trust Sit
V-Sit

V. New Games can be played to establish a playful spirit and to connect or reconnect people with the intrinsic values of joyful play.

Ice Breakers and Silly Games

Ah So Ko
Blob
Dizzy Dozen
Giants-Elves-Wizards

Hog Call
Touch Blue
Vampire

Note: The games and activities listed are described in one or more of the references provided. However, some of the games were learned as a participant, created by the author, or have been altered in name to reflect the changes in the game.

The ability to analyze game activities to determine if they coincide with desired purposes is of central importance. The following criteria can assist teachers in analyzing any new game or activity to determine which games to use or exclude for any given session. The criteria can be used as a deliberately written checklist, or they can become part of one's automatic screening process (see Figure 36.2). Suggested implementation options are included.

FIGURE 36.2
Criteria

Games Selection and Implementation Options

New Games can be selected and implemented within physical education programs in various ways.

Criteria for Games Selection

Purposes served: FUN and . . .
   Inclusion (nonelimination)
   Active Involvement: motorically, affectively, cognitively
   Activity level/intensity: high, moderate, low
   Space needed/available
   Number participants: needed/available
   Adaptability to needs of players
   Equipment needed/available: preferably minimal, novel

Implementation Options

   Separate unit
   Integrated with other units (e.g., sport themes, teamwork, etc.)
   Special days and/or to adapt to disruptions, holidays, etc.
   Episodes within lessons:
      "Warm Ups"
      Start of class
      End of class
      To address situations as they arise (e.g., need for cooperation, trust development)

CONCLUSION

The creative possibilities for programming are enormous and provide another purpose underlying new ways with new games: to recharge and invigorate physical educators by challenging them to create their own unique ideas for bringing the values of play into the lives of the children they teach.

NOTE

1. F. Caplan, and T. Caplan, *Creative Playthings, Inc.*, 1991. From Robert Frost's 1939 Preface (entitled "The Figure a Poem Makes") to *Collected Poems of Robert Frost* (New York: Henry Holt). Frost wrote: "It should be of the pleasure of a poem itself to tell how it can. The figure a poem makes. It begins in delight and ends in wisdom."

REFERENCES

Fluegelman, A. (1976). *The New Games Book*. New York: Doubleday-Dolphin.

———— (1981). *More New Games*. New York: Doubleday-Dolphin.

Orlick, T. (1978). *The Cooperative Sports and Games Book*. New York: Pantheon.

———— (1982). *The Second Cooperative Sports and Games Book*. New York: Pantheon.

Rohnke, K. (1984). *Silver Bullets*. Hamilton, Mass.: Project Adventure.

———— (1988). *The Bottomless Bag*. Hamilton, Mass.: Karl Rohnke.

———— (1989). *Cowtails and Cobras II*. Dubuque, Iowa: Kendall/Hunt.

Turner, L., and S. L. Turner (1984). *Alternative Sports and Games for the New Physical Education*. Palo Alto, Calif.: Impact.

Weinstein, M., and J. Goodman (1980). *Playfair*. San Luis Obispo, Calif.: Impact.

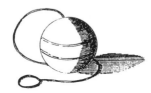

37

Old Sports and New Games: Rethinking Lead-Up Games

Janis Bozowski

Sports and sport-related activities have been the mainstay of physical education classes. Each year millions of children are exposed to a progressive series of sport skills and modified games designed to change them into skilled athletes. Viewpoints expressed by numerous adults suggest that many learned a different lesson: that they are unable to play games well; that sports are only for the athletically talented; that participation in sports is humiliating, hard, and uncomfortable; and that they prefer the role of spectator. In contrast, it seems that today's adults enjoy playing "New Games." Everyone has the opportunity to play, the rules are changed to serve the players, and winning does not seem important. In fact, these adults speak of the challenge, camaraderie, and pleasure. Old sports are not inherently evil, nor are New Games always appropriate. This chapter suggests a rationale, some criteria, and several components that educators may use to restructure activities into more developmentally appropriate and enjoyable learning experiences.

RETHINKING THE PROCESS

The decision to rethink sports teaching developed from a combination of values and observations. The rationale and some criteria for judging the appropriateness and effectiveness of redesigning lead-up games are explored below.

1. **All children deserve to experience the pleasure of movement**. This is fostered by promoting experiences that emphasize inclusiveness and accessibility, stress play *with* others, and challenge each individual at an appropriate level. These components are at the core of New Games.
2. **All students deserve to be active throughout a play session**. Children cannot develop their skills while they are spectators, waiting a turn, being eliminated, or standing in line. Games must be modified so that everyone can play all the time.
3. **The fewer players involved in one game, the more active each player will be**. In a game with twenty-two players and one ball, the majority of players at any given

moment will have little contact with the ball. Play the same game with four to six players, and the contact time for each player will dramatically increase.

4. **It is our responsibility to provide for the needs of all children, regardless of their skill level.** Given that each group of children will possess a wide range of skill levels, we must offer activities that will serve the needs of each child.

5. **Skills learned while performing drills seldom transfer effectively to games.** Drills often emphasize an isolated skill in a highly controlled setting. Actual sport situations are dynamic and unpredictable, requiring a versatility seldom required in drills. Observe children learning a game without the teacher's instruction. They play the whole game over and over, generally acquiring skill with each new attempt. The secret is that they keep returning to participate, not to learn a specific skill but to have fun.

6. **Competition does not foster learning as effectively as cooperation.** The effective educational use of competition involves challenging a player *after skills are mastered* and using the results of the competition as an affirmation of mastery and a tool for defining the next level of learning. Prior to mastery, the most effective style for learning is cooperative.

7. **If we expect students to cooperate, we need to directly teach cooperation skills, a combination of task skills (e.g., seeking information, pinpointing difficulties) and group skills (taking turns, encouraging, listening).**

8. **The ultimate purpose is to play with others.**

At least two different approaches can be followed when adapting or creating New Games that teach sport skills. The first involves using an actual New Game and changing its structure or emphasis to focus on sport skills. For example, Clean Out Your Backyard is a simple game in which two teams on either side of a line attempt to empty their side of all foam balls by tossing any ball over to the other side. To adapt this game to include specific sport skills, a teacher might increase the height or width of the line and specify the use of an overhand throw, designate and rotate "catchers" who can collect any caught ball in a "recycling bin" for their group, place targets on each side and challenge students to toss the "garbage" in their neighbor's garbage can, or use beach balls and incorporate volleying skills.

The second approach involves focusing on the sport skills we want the child to master, and designing a game that includes the qualities of a New Game to elicit the behavioral practice we want. Most often this approach involves an adaptation of a traditional sport or lead-up game and is more effectively used when students have the ability to handle more complex challenges. For example, if the goal is to track the children's basketball passing skills, they can be challenged to play two-on-two and score a point either by making a basket or by passing the ball three times without interception.

After identifying the skill we want students to learn and considering the most effective approach, several variables can be manipulated in adapting or designing games, including the number of players per team or game, the equipment (type, size, amount), the movement skills, the type of organization (random, circles, formations), what limitations will be imposed (rules, boundaries, time), and the type of scoring (cooperative, competitive). After designing a game, *try it*. Any problems will become readily apparent, and additional changes can be made to more effectively elicit the behaviors and skills the teacher is seeking.

A multitude of strategies can foster the New Games spirit in lead-up games. A critical one is that the more actively involved everyone is, the less attention they will pay to judging themselves or others. Find ways to challenge more highly skilled players without segregating them into a homogeneous group, like publicly identifying the person who has never been caught in a tag game, thereby instantly challenging him or her. Changing the method of scoring or winning is another powerful strategy. Teachers can award points for compliments or have the person who scored change teams, or require that each person score for a team to win, or ask a class to identify the skill they most want to reinforce and to suggest a scoring method to reward their performance of that skill.

"New Old Sport Games" is certainly not the only effective method for fostering skill learning in students while ensuring a quality play experience. Nor is it appropriate to advocate only one instructional strategy, given the variety of groups and skills that we teach. It is not a miracle cure. It does, however, offer alternatives and encourages teachers to reconsider the playfulness of the child's sports experience.

A SAMPLING OF "SOCCER" NEW OLD SPORT GAMES

Rush Hour

Give each student a ball to be foot dribbled throughout the room. On the teacher's "Stop" signal everyone should be close enough to his or her ball to stop it completely. Begin slowly, then challenge the students to move as quickly as they can while still controlling the ball. This allows them to test their skill, to function at their own skill level, and to acknowledge the value of some loss of control as a way to discover what one's limits are. As students increase their ball control skills, add that on "Stop" they must also be in their own space (i.e., far enough away from everyone else that they can touch no one). Challenge the students to move to spaces that are empty.

Variation: A Wonderful Rush Hour

Play the same initial game as Rush Hour, but now have students dribble the ball close to someone, pat him or her on the back, and say "Nice going!" without letting the ball touch the other's ball or body, and then move away.

Dribble Steal Tag

All students have a ball except for three or four students designated to be "it." The students in possession of a ball exhibit ball control skills while continuing to dribble. The students without a ball are going to try to secure one. Initially, students may steal a ball only when a classmate has kicked it far enough away that he or she is not in control. Allow the children to play for awhile, and then stop and ask what strategies they are using (e.g., pressuring someone by chasing him or her, or keeping the body between the ball and the challenger). As the group's skill level increases, incorporate tackling as an acceptable way to steal a ball. To ensure that everyone has a chance to be "it" and that the less skilled student does not remain in the "it" position for a long time, modify the activity so that the "it" person returns the ball to the dribbler and thanks the dribbler for his or her help in practicing the skills. The "its" are then reassigned.

Human Mixmaster

Every student in a large circle is given a ball. On the signal "Go," each student must try to cross to the opposite side of the circle by dribbling the ball without letting the ball or his or her body touch anyone else. Increase the challenge by decreasing the size of the circle. As the boundary of the circle becomes smaller, the teacher can add that when a student sees that he or she has a clear path to the edge of the circle, the ball may be kicked out of the circle.

Group Foot Juggling

Six to eight students form a circle. Establish a passing pattern that will be repeated by having one student kick the ball to anyone who is not immediately next to him or her. The receiving student passes the ball to a third, and so on, with the last student returning the ball to the first student. Challenge the students to repeat the pattern, calling out the name of the person who is to receive the ball. When the group has demonstrated control in passing one ball, add a second ball. Now the group must also avoid having the two balls collide. Continue adding one ball as a group demonstrates proficiency.

Group Foot Juggling on the Run

Three to four students form a circle and establish a kicking pattern in the same way described in Group Foot Juggling. After the groups have their pattern established, everyone is to begin moving throughout the gymnasium. The first person in each group is to dribble the ball until he or she can pass it to the second person in the group. This means that the second person must try to move into an open space before passing to the third person. Scoring could be based on the number of times each person in the group had possession of the ball.

Mine Field

Assign partners and give each pair one ball. Place a variety of "mines" (e.g., tennis balls, floor markers, or polyspots) throughout the playing space. The greater the number of mines, the greater the difficulty of the game. Around the perimeter of the facility, place X's low on the wall or position cones along each wall to serve as targets or goals. The objective is for each pair to pass the ball between them as they cross the room, without hitting any of the mines. When they have a clear shot to one of the perimeter goals, they attempt to kick for the goal by hitting the X or cone.

REFERENCES

Csikszentmihalyi, Mihaly (1982). *Beyond Boredom and Anxiety.* San Francisco: Jossey-Bass.

DeKoven, Bernie (1978). *The Well-Played Game.* Garden City, N.Y.: Doubleday.

Fluegelman, Andrew (1976). *The New Games Book.* Garden City, N.Y.: Doubleday.

———— (1981). *More New Games.* Garden City, N.Y.: Doubleday.

Johnson, David, and Roger Johnson (1975). *Learning Together and Alone: Cooperation, Competition, and Individualization.* Englewood Cliffs, N.J.: Prentice-Hall.

Morris, G. S. Don (1976). *How to Change the Games Children Play.* Minneapolis, Minn.: Burgess.

Orlick, Terry (1978a). *The Cooperative Sports and Games Book.* New York: Pantheon Books.

———— (1978b). *Winning Through Cooperation.* Washington, D.C.: Acropolis Books.

———— (1982). *The Second Cooperative Sports and Games Book.* New York: Pantheon Books.

Rohnke, Karl (1977). *Cowtails and Cobras.* Available from Project Adventure, Inc., P.O. Box 100, Hamilton, Mass. 01936.

———— (1984). *Silver Bullets: A Guide to Initiative Problems, Adventure Games, and Trust Activities.* Dubuque, Iowa: Kendall/Hunt.

Torbert, Marianne (1982a). *Follow Me.* Englewood Cliffs, N.J.: Prentice-Hall.

———— (1982b). *Secrets to Success in Sport and Play.* Englewood Cliffs, N.J.: Prentice-Hall.

Weinstein, Matt, and Joel Goodman (1980). *Playfair: Everyone's Guide to Cooperative Play.* San Luis Obispo, Calif.: Impact Publishers.

38

Games Children Shouldn't Play

Janet M. Oussaty

While most educators would agree that the "win at all costs" philosophy is not beneficial, few question the value of "good" competition. Alfie Kohn, the author of *No Contest: The Case Against Competition* (1986), found that after examining over 2,000 works, not one author supported this claim, thereby treating the benefits of competition as givens. He added that even if we reduce or eliminate our emphasis on winning, we are still competing; we are pitting one against another. Consistent with Kohn's findings, my examination of elementary school physical education textbooks revealed no support for stated claims, and all offered strategies to deemphasize competition (Gallahue, 1987; Graham, Holt/Hale and Parker, 1987; Logsdon et al., 1984; Nichols, 1990; Thomas, et al., 1988). Furthermore, not one textbook offered a cooperative approach exclusively.

Subsequently, this chapter takes issue with the claims of "good" competition and suggests that teachers use alternative, cooperative approaches to the design of children's games. It begins by offering Kohn's definition for competition and then examines four primary myths he associates with competition. A description of a cooperative approach to designing games and suggestions for redesigning competitive games follow.

PRIMARY MYTHS REFLECTING COMPETITION

Kohn defines competition as "two or more individuals trying to achieve a goal that cannot be achieved by all of them" (1986, p. 3). He explains that in order for one individual to succeed, the other needs to fail. He further explains that one individual can also "make" another individual fail, and that the belief and practice of competition are supported by four primary myths. Kohn states, "Once the myths justifying competition are behind us, the prospects are good for changing the structure that perpetuates it" (1986, p. 194).

Myth 1: Competition Is Innate

According to Kohn, there is no evidence to support the notion that competition is innate—that people have a natural instinct to be competitive. To support his position Kohn first clarifies the terms *natural selection* and *survival of the fittest*. Natural selection as conceptualized by Charles Darwin refers to adaptability to change. That is, an ability to adapt to change increases the probability of survival. The mechanism or tool for survival, however, is *not* mentioned by Darwin. The tool is assumed by many to be competition. Kohn points out that the term *survival of the fittest* was linked to natural selection by Herbert Spencer. He cites a number of studies that report cooperative behavior among animals, some of which conclude that some animals need to work with one another to survive. For example, it is better for some animals to migrate when in need of water than to compete for a watering hole. This strategy allows both species to survive. The authors of these studies stress that these cooperative behaviors are used when the need for survival is paramount, not just in times of prosperity (Kohn, 1986).

Cooperative behavior, however, is not inborn. Margaret Mead finds cooperation and competition to be dependent upon a society's particular emphasis. Cooperation and competition are therefore learned behaviors (Kohn, 1986). In studying the work of Terry Orlick and others, Kohn found that when children were taught cooperative activities, they not only voluntarily participated in them, they preferred them. Kohn concludes, "I am aware of no studies that found a preference for competition over cooperation, providing the subjects had experienced the latter" (1986, p. 32).

Myth 2: Competition Is Necessary for Productivity

There is also a belief that competition is a necessary incentive for productivity, goal attainment, and success. Kohn states that victory is not necessary to achieve success: "trying to do well and trying to best others are two different things" (1986, p. 55). In fact, "not only is competition not required for excellence; it usually seems to require its absence" (1986, p. 47).

There are three primary reasons why competition does not predict success. The first is that it causes anxiety. High levels of anxiety are correlated with low levels of performance. A high anxiety level may cause the individual to "choke" and not complete the task. Individuals who are over-challenged may not perform to their optimal level and can actually regress. The second factor reflects inefficiency. Individuals typically focus on winning rather than on the task at hand or even the quality of the performance. So, too, individuals who believe they will lose see little purpose in trying hard or producing; the children want to sit out. Finally, competition can undermine intrinsic motivation. When individuals find a task interesting in its own right and then perform it competitively for rewards, they may lose interest in it. In attempting to encourage success by offering external rewards, Kohn finds that curiosity, the "single most important predictor of success," is being undermined (1990, p. 17).

Kohn points out that cooperative activities involve productivity, intrinsic motivation, and low levels of anxiety. In his study of rural, urban, and suburban school settings, he finds that cooperation helps children learn complex tasks where problem solving and creativity are needed. When performing simple tasks requiring recall, competition works well.

Myth 3: Competition Is Necessary for Enjoyment

To some, activity without the possibility of winning becomes boring. Kohn warns that the zest that competition brings to the game can become a substitute for the pure fun of play. He uses the metaphor of someone who suddenly stops using salt with food; the food at first tastes bland. These feelings are sometimes experienced by individuals who stop competing. Participation may seem boring at first, but the need to compete becomes less important to the individual over time.

Myth 4: Competition Builds Character

Competition is believed to build character. Kohn's search of the literature, however, does not uncover a definition for character or evidence to support the claim that competition improves one's character. He uses the terms *self-esteem* and *self-confidence* in his critique, defining self-esteem as an acceptance of unconditional self-worth which is not dependent upon approval from others—a sign of a healthy personality. When individuals compete in order to prove their worth, it becomes conditional; how they value themselves becomes dependent on winning and how others see them.

The attempt to meet emotional needs through competition has further implications. Kohn points out that initially people are happy and may even gloat after winning. Later, however, they may experience slight depression, and feel a need to win again. He states, "The more we compete, the more we need to compete . . . it's like building up a tolerance to a drug" (1990, pp. 18, 189). He concludes that competition is not inborn and does not necessarily enhance productivity or enjoyment or build "character." In fact, it appears to have the opposite effect. Since cooperation and competition are learned, why not teach cooperation and unlearn competition? After all, schools teach the dangers of alcohol and drugs, so why not teach the dangers of competition?

One approach involves a shift in perspective for society, business, and education, from what benefits an individual to what benefits the group, and the use of negotiations and compromises. An individual benefits from a zero-sum situation, with one winner and one loser, or a negative-sum situation, with one winner and many losers. A group would benefit from a win-win situation. To do this, we go from a system where one individual has more power than others to one where members of the system are on an equal footing. When there is a conflict in hierarchical systems, individuals yield to what the individual in power desires; if they do not readily yield, threats and manipulation may be employed by the individual in power. When there is a conflict in an equal system, members negotiate possible solutions where everyone can benefit, meeting on common ground.

COOPERATIVE APPROACHES TO DESIGNING GAMES

A number of publications foster a cooperative approach to designing games. Terry Orlick has published over 300 games in his books *The Cooperative Sports and Games Book* (1978a) and *The Second Cooperative Sports and Games Book* (1982). He has also produced *Every Kid Can Win* (1975), *Winning Through Cooperation* (1978b), and *In Pursuit of Excellence* (1980). Other works include Deacove's *Co-op Games Manual* (1974), Fluegelman's *More New Games!* (1981), Sambhava and Luvmour's *Everyone Wins!* (1990), and Sobel's *Everybody Wins: Noncompetitive Games for Young Children* (1983). Cooperative approaches associated with initiative, trust, and problem-solving games can be found in Rohkne's *Silver Bullets* (1984) and in programs such as Project Adventure and Outward Bound. New Society Publishers, the Center for Educational Guidance, and Peace Educators are organizations that adopt a cooperative approach exclusively.

To look at one approach a little more closely, we can borrow from Orlick. His philosophy supports the notion that "everybody cooperates . . . everybody wins . . . and nobody loses" (Orlick, 1978a, p. 3). He emphasizes that games should be designed so that individuals play with one another, rather than against one another. He offers descriptions of a number of original games that are cooperative in nature, as well as games redesigned to eliminate the competitive element. He suggests considering four criteria when selecting or designing a game: (1) it is cooperative (people help one another); (2) there is no sense of losing; (3) everyone leaves happier; and (4) there is no physical or psychological hurt.

Orlick, for example, redesigns a conventional game of volleyball, naming it Blanketball. The following description of Blanketball indicates how each of these criteria are met.

Blanketball

In Blanketball, two groups face each other on opposite sides of a center line or net. The purpose of the game is for one group, while holding a blanket, to pass a ball that is placed on the blanket over the net to the other group, which is also holding a blanket. The groups then pass the ball back and forth, counting the number of successful catches. A variation could be to try to pass and receive using two balls. Still another variation involves no net. One group "pops" the ball up, then moves out of the way so that the other group can step in and receive the ball, and the action continues.

The first criterion (i.e., that the game be cooperative) is met in the manner that the ball is tossed—so that the other group *can* catch it. Another way to ensure that the groups are assisting each other's efforts is not to organize separate and distinct teams. In Orlick's redesigned game, for example, players rotate from one "team" to the other. In addition, teachers can structure the activity to work within a given time limit or other objective standard.

To meet the second criterion (i.e., there is no sense of losing), Orlick asks players to tally a collective score among the "teams" or groups. The third criterion, that everyone leave happier, is evidenced by the children's newly acquired sense of accomplishment. Finally, the fourth criterion, that the game cause no physical or psychological harm, is achieved because the children are not instructed to "hit" an "opponent" and cannot ridicule another player.

In conclusion, this chapter offers the etymology of the word *competition*, It comes from the Latin *competere,* meaning "to strive in common" (*com* means "together"; *petere* to "go toward," not against). The meaning and practice of competition has obviously drifted from its origination. After all, it has adopted the values of our Western society.

As physical educators, classroom teachers, and school practitioners, we can closely examine our practices, practices we typically perform automatically and without question. By examining and questioning them, we can determine if they are consistent with the meaning or intention of striving in common. Most of us are familiar with the cooperative learning efforts in education. Business is utilizing some of these principles by shifting to quality control management. These values are alive and we can keep them alive in *our* work.

REFERENCES

Brown, L., and S. Grineski (January 1992). Competition in Physical Education: An Educational Contradiction? *Journal of Physical Education, Recreation and Dance,* 63(1), 17-19.

Deacove, J. (1974). *Co-op Games Manual.* Perth, Ont.: Family Pastimes.

Fluegelman, A. (1981). *More New Games!—And Playful Ideas from the New Games Foundation.* New York: Doubleday/Dolphin Books.

Gallahue, D. (1987). *Developmental Physical Education for Today's Elementary School Children.* New York: Macmillan.

Graham, G., S. Holt/Hale, and M. Parker (1987). *Children Moving.* 2nd ed. Mountain View, Calif.: Mayfield.

Kohn, A. (1986). *No Contest: The Case Against Competition.* Boston: Houghton Mifflin.

——— (Spring 1990a). The Case Against Competition. *Journal of Noetic Sciences,* 14, 12-19.

Kohn, A. (Summer 1990b). The Case Against Competition, Part II. *Journal of Noetic Sciences,* 15, 21-23.

Logsdon, B., et al. (1984). *Physical Education for Children: A Focus on the Teaching Process.* 2nd ed. Philadelphia: Lea and Febiger.

Nichols, B. (1990). *Moving and Learning.* 2nd ed. St. Louis: Times Mirror/Mosby.

Orlick, T. (1978a). *The Cooperative Sports and Games Book.* New York: Pantheon.

——— (1978b). *Winning Through Cooperation: Competitive Insanity, Cooperative Alternatives.* Washington, D.C.: Acropolis.

——— (1980). *In Pursuit of Excellence.* Champaign, Ill.: Human Kinetics.

——— (1982). *The Second Cooperative Sports and Games Book.* New York: Pantheon.

———, and C. Botterill (1975). *Every Kid Can Win.* Chicago: Nelson Hall.

Rohnke, K. (1984). *Silver Bullets: A Guide to Initiative Problems, Adventure Games, and Trust Activities*. Dubuque, Iowa.: Kendall Hunt.

Sambhava, C., and J. Luvmour (1990). *Everyone Wins! Cooperative Games and Activities*. Philadelphia: New Society.

Sobel, J. (1983). *Everybody Wins: Noncompetitive Games for Young Children*. New York: Walker and Co.

Thomas, J. R., et al. (1988). *Physical Education for Children: Concepts into Practice*. Champaign, Ill.: Human Kinetics.

39

Teaching the Intrinsic Elements of Games to Three- to Eight-Year-Old Children

Linda McNally

Competition is viewed by many as an essential vehicle for education. It builds character, teaches responsibility and team spirit, and prepares children for the competitive world of adulthood. On a less favorable note, competition inevitably produces a winner and a loser, which can damage the less successful individual's self-esteem. The same qualities that competition seeks to encourage are the ones that can adversely affect many young children. Physical educators are sometimes guilty of failing to prepare students for the experience that should enrich their lives. Competition is a complex mixture of goals, rules, consequences, disappointments, and successes. Not only do children require specific physical skills to participate in sport, they also need the emotional and social skills to cope with the experience.

Children want to be part of a team and to feel that they are contributing to the group's effort. They must be able to identify the goals of the activity and to create strategies to achieve them. They need to understand the basic mechanics of games, such as spacing, offense, defense, marking, and dodging. They need to accept rules and appreciate fair play. Most important, they need to be able to share and to cooperate with others. One can cooperate successfully without competition, but competition without cooperation is not a positive experience. Young children play games for fun. Playing games is fun if everyone is given the opportunity to play and if everyone plays together while abiding by rules.

The activities and games described in this chapter highlight ways to introduce some of the intrinsic elements of sports. In order to increase the likelihood that the children will find enjoyment and become more effective movers, teachers must monitor the events. This is done by (1) selecting well-balanced teams even in games of low organization, (2) providing feedback to the group as well as to the individual, and (3) allocating a period of time in each lesson for closure. During this period, the teacher should identify the positive elements of the lesson that are directly connected with the children's progress in competitive activities. Teachers can congratulate a child who passed the ball to teammates frequently, and draw attention to a child who stayed in position throughout the game. They should praise the child who usually demonstrates poor behavior but managed to control his or her emotions. They should also highlight particular strategies that proved successful.

The following games help prepare children three to eight years of age for competitive game situations.

PRESCHOOL (THREE- AND FOUR-YEAR-OLDS)

Themes: Following rules, sharing, taking turns, cooperating, identifying goals and striving to reach them, and assuming roles.

Name of the Game: The Balloon Bump
Intrinsic Elements: Sharing and cooperating
Equipment Required: One 10" balloon for each group of three children
Rules: In groups of three, the children are challenged to keep the balloon up in the air for as long as possible. Everyone must have a turn. No one is allowed to catch the balloon or to run away with it. If their balloon bursts, a group must sit down and wait until the end of the game (i.e., action and consequences).

Name of the Game: Traffic Control
Intrinsic Element: Following directions
Equipment Required: None
Rules: On the teacher's command "Green," the children run around; on "Red" they must freeze exactly where they are; and on "Yellow" they must sit down.

Name of the Game: The Music Game
Intrinsic Element: Following instructions and responding to a whistle
Equipment Required: Musical instruments
Rules: The children are challenged to respond to musical instrument sounds by moving and stopping in different ways. The cymbals crashing means "Run"; the wooden blocks being hit means "Jump around"; the maracas being shaken means "Shake your body"; and an ascending scale on the xylophone means "Stand up," while a descending scale means "Sit down."

Name of the Game: The Mr. Men Game
Intrinsic Elements: Following directions, assuming roles
Equipment Required: None
Rules: Respond with actions to the challenges given by the teacher:

"Mr. Rush"—Run around
"Mr. Lazy"—Lie down on the floor
"Mr. Sneeze"—Make loud sneezing sounds
"Mr. Bounce"—Jump around the room on two feet
"Mr. Messy"—Wiggle and move in a crazy and messy manner

Name of the Game: The Dice Game
Intrinsic Elements: Taking turns and cooperating

Equipment Required: Six cards featuring pictures of actions (e.g., throwing an object, someone performing a locomotor skill) and an oversized die

Rules: Everyone sits in a circle with the playing cards lying face down in the center of the group. Each child in turn throws the die. Every time one child throws a six, he or she moves to the playing cards and selects one. That child shows the picture to the group, and everyone performs the action until they are called back to the circle to continue.

KINDERGARTEN

Themes: Following directions, monitoring one's own activities, learning different roles, taking turns, sharing, cooperating, identifying goals and striving to achieve them, beating the clock, and dealing with success and failure.

Name of the Game: Beat the Beanbags

Intrinsic Elements: Identifying a goal and striving to achieve it, and succeeding or failing

Equipment Required: Six beanbags, a hoop, a milk crate, and four mats or targets (see Figure 39.1).

Rules: On each occasion, a new person is selected to be "A." On the command "Go," all players run to touch each of the four targets and hurry back to sit cross-legged along the edge of the playing area. Meanwhile, "A" runs to collect a beanbag, returns to the hoop, throws the beanbag into the crate, then repeats the process until all the beanbags are in the crate or until all the runners are sitting down. If "A" completes his or her task before the runners, all the runners perform a teacher selected task. If all runners touch the four mats before "A" has completed the task, the game starts again with a new child as "A."

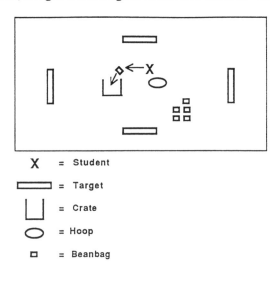

FIGURE 39.1: Beat The Beanbags

Name of the Game: The Tadpole
Intrinsic Elements: Following directions, cooperating, and learning different roles (e.g., offense and defense)
Equipment Required: Hoops and a foam playground ball (see Figure 39.2)
Rules: Group A makes a line with the first person standing in the hoop. Group B stands inside the hoops placed in a circle. On the command "Go," the first person in A runs around the circle created by B and tags the next person in line who has stepped into the hoop. Meanwhile, B is passing the ball around the circle, adding one point to the running score each time the ball is successfully caught. When every child in A has finished running, B must stop. The number they have reached is the number to beat next time. The groups then switch places.

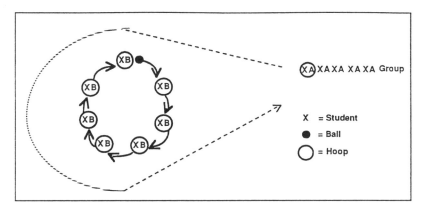

FIGURE 39.2: The Tadpole

FIRST GRADE GAMES

Themes: Offense-defense, spacing and playing positions, cooperating, competing, winning and losing, sharing, basic strategy, and identifying goals and striving to achieve them.

Name of the Game: Not Totally Tennis
Intrinsic Elements: Adapting to different roles, cooperating, sharing, and monitoring one's own activities
Equipment Required: Tennis balls and a lightweight, short-handled tennis racquet for each group of three children
Rules: Player A throws an underarm pitch which bounces once before it reaches Player B. Player B tries to hit the ball so it goes back to A. C acts as a catcher and fielder if B misses the ball or hits it past A. The idea is to cooperate to allow each person five attempts to hit the ball. Each time the group completes the exercise, they try to improve on their last attempt.

Name of the Game: Moving Islands
Intrinsic Elements: Cooperation, dealing with success and failure, identifying a goal and striving to achieve it
Equipment Required: Four small portable gymnastic mats (see Figure 39.3)
Rules: The class is divided into two groups. Both groups start on the "A" mats. Each group lifts the "B" mat overhead, puts it down closer to the finish line, and steps onto it. The process is repeated many times until the group has reached its destination. No player may touch the ground at any time during the event. The penalty for breach of this rule is returning to the starting point to begin again.

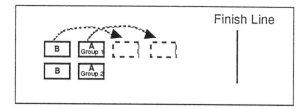

FIGURE 39.3: Moving Islands

Name of the Game: The Parachute Game
Intrinsic Elements: Cooperation, strategy
Equipment Required: Two parachutes, cones, and a large playing area (see Figure 39.4).
Rules: On the command "Get ready," both groups must be crouched down with their hands on the parachute and touching the ground. On "Go," both groups jump up and quickly try to move their parachute from their cone to the other team's cone. The first team to achieve this goal wins the round and the game repeats. Note: Group members should be encouraged to maintain their grip on the parachute during the game.

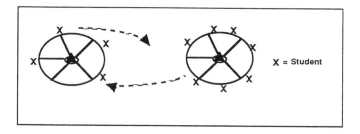

FIGURE 39.4: The Parachute Game

Name of the Game: Time Limit
Intrinsic Elements: Strategy, identifying a goal and striving to achieve it, and winning and losing

Equipment Required: One ball per student, a hoop, and a large bucket; all students start on one end of the activity area with the teacher positioned in the middle of the area

Rules: On the command "Go" all students must kick the balls from the start line toward line X (i.e., the opposite end of the activity area). They must then run to retrieve the balls and return them to the start line. They have five seconds to rest before they must begin again. The teacher keeps one foot inside the hoop at all times but is trying to intercept the balls as they are kicked. If a player's ball is intercepted, he or she must walk to line X and remain motionless. The teacher can use intercepted balls and tag individuals on the leg as they cross the playing area. Encourage the children to devise methods to get the ball past the teacher.

SECOND GRADE GAMES

Themes: Creating rules and adapting games, playing as a team, cooperating, strategies and creative answers, marking and dodging, offense and defense, and winning and losing.

Name of the Game: Fireball
Intrinsic Elements: Emphasis on offense, strategy, marking and dodging
Equipment Required: A playground ball and a confined clearly marked space such as a wrestling mat (See Figure 39.5)
Rules: There are no teams in this activity. A player is out if he or she steps or falls outside the boundary lines. In order to remove someone from the game, students must roll a ball and contact a player on or below the knee. If the ball goes out of bounds, one must wait for it to be tossed back in by a helper. When a player is out, he or she becomes a "helper." A helper stands outside the boundaries and must throw the ball back into play. A player holding the ball is not permitted to move his or her feet, but may throw a ball to a helper and move in closer. Note: Individuals are more successful when they actively use the helpers and try to get possession of the ball.

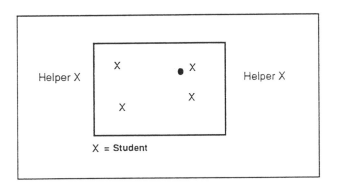

FIGURE 39.5: Fireball

Name of the Game: Three Kings
Intrinsic Elements: Marking and dodging, cooperation and spacing
Equipment Required: Three balls per group; two sets of benches or similar equipment that will lift the kings up about a foot from the floor (see Figure 39.6)
Rules: The first king for both groups (King 1) stands on the castle (i.e., designated area) at the opposite end of the room. The group members try to lob the ball to their king while attempting to intercept the balls being lobbed to the opposite king. If a ball is caught, the predesignated King 2 joins King 1. When another ball is caught, the third and final king joins his or her classmates. At this point, the kings have the power to get the opposing group out by moving a ball and hitting them below the knees. No ball can be used if it is dropped. When a student is out he or she stands behind the opposing king's castle. The objective is to get the other group out while trying to intercept the balls that could get your own group out.

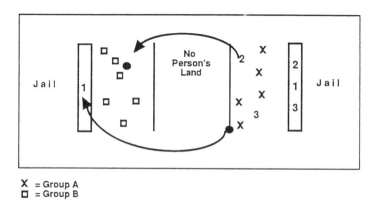

X = Group A
□ = Group B

FIGURE 39.6: Three Kings

Name of the Game: Dodgeball Rounders
Intrinsic Elements: Marking and dodging, spacing, cooperation and teamwork
Equipment Required: A sponge ball, a tennis racquet, and clear post markings (see Figure 39.7)
Rules: The group in the field scatters throughout the playing field and may not hinder the progress of the runner or the dodger. The batting group forms a line in twos. The first batter hits (or swings at) the pitched ball while the runner sets off to circle the bases. The runner begins to run even if the ball is not hit. The responsibility of the batter is to dodge away from the ball until his or her partner is safely home. The fielders may not run with the ball. If the dodger gets hit, the pair is out. A runner who returns home before the dodger is hit scores a point for his or her group, and the pair change roles.

Fielders are encouraged to pass the ball quickly in an attempt to get the ball closer to the batter.

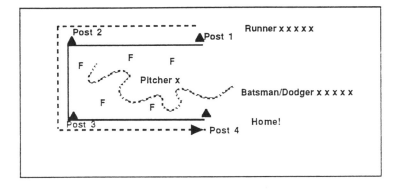

FIGURE 39.7: Dodgeball Rounders

40

Student-Created Games in the Fifth and Sixth Grades

Kathy Pattak

"This game's dumb. It's not fair. Why do we have to do it your way?" Comments like these led me to develop an original games unit for fifth and sixth grade students. I decided to give my students the opportunity to create games that they would teach to other members of the class.

I began by distributing student guidelines two weeks prior to the beginning of the unit. To encourage cooperation the students are permitted to work with small groups of friends.

When the groups turn in their game descriptions, they are reviewed for safety concerns and suggested changes are made. Each group participates in a teacher/student meeting and is given a teaching date. Usually the games that require the fewest suggested changes are scheduled first.

The groups are asked to arrive at the gymnasium a few minutes early to prepare the necessary equipment. When the daily stretches are completed, the students who are teaching explain their game to the remainder of the class. After answering any questions, teams (if needed) are selected. Whenever possible, teachers should not intervene unless safety is a concern.

Not every game is successful. The results are sometimes unpredictable due to a lack of originality and creativity. Oftentimes the least sophisticated games are the ones the students enjoy the most. Many games tend to use basketball skills in combination with other activities, perhaps because basketball hoops are readily available and obvious to the students who are seeking ideas.

At the end of the unit all students are asked to evaluate their lesson's objectives. In evaluating their own games they point out problems and make suggested changes. Occasionally a game is more popular with a class than a teacher realizes. When asked about problems that occurred while teaching, the students' comments were often related to the behavior of their peers rather than the activity itself. When asked what they learned from this experience, many students admitted that developing games wasn't as easy as they expected and that teaching takes patience and hard work. Finally, when asked how this experience would change their behavior as students, many responded that they would become better listeners, pay attention more, or not talk during an explanation. My favorite answer in recent years was, "I will never complain about a boring game again."

STUDENT GUIDELINES

- The class will be divided into groups of four or five students. Each group is challenged to create a new game and later teach the game to the entire class.
- Each group will have an entire class period to teach and play your student created game.
- It can be a combination of games you already know, such as basketball, soccer, or stick hockey.
- Safety is the most important concern.
- At least two-thirds of the class should be actively participating at any time.
- Most equipment is available for your use.
- If necessary, penalties should be included for those who do not follow directions.
- Rules and directions must be easy to understand and quickly explained.
- If someone in the group is uncooperative, tell the teacher.
- Groups will have two weeks to plan their game.
- Groups must turn in a written explanation of their game, including a list of needed equipment.
- Groups will teach their game to the class on dates that will be posted in advance.
- Games that are successful may be used during a play-day at the end of the school year. This will involve other classes.
- Games should take into consideration the skill level of all class members.
- Officiating should not be difficult, and the stoppage of plays should be kept to minimum.
- At the end of the unit all students will be asked to evaluate the teaching experience.

TIPS FOR TEACHING ORIGINAL GAMES

- Wait until the entire explanation is completed before dividing the class into teams.
- Specify the officiating responsibilities of all group members before the class begins.
- Have classmates seated during the explanation.
- If different teams have different activities (e.g., batters and fielders), explain each part separately.
- Use a stopwatch if timing is necessary.
- Explain the game to a friend before your class presentation to make certain that what you say is clearly understandable.
- Try to play the game ahead of time to see if it works.

SAMPLE GAMES

Name of the Game: Foam Hockey Basketball
Equipment Required: Eight foam hockey sticks, one foam ball (8"), and four basketballs
Description: The class is divided into four teams. Each team begins by standing behind a bench in one of four corners of the gymnasium. A basketball and two

foam hockey sticks are placed on each bench (see Figure 40.1). The first student on each team stands in front of the bench facing the opposite bench. On the teacher's signal, that player runs to get a basketball, dribbles the ball to the basket, and begins shooting. When the basket is made, the ball is returned to the opposite bench. That player returns to his or her home bench and picks up a foam hockey stick. He or she then runs to the center of the room and tries to hit the sponge ball under any other bench. At the same time the second player becomes the goalie. If a goal is scored under an opponent's bench before a basket is made by that team, the shooter is eliminated. After a team is eliminated no goals may be scored under that bench. Also, the goalie cannot defend the goal until the ball has gone through the hoop. Individuals have a time limit of two minutes and the round is stopped. Points are scored for each goal and basket. At this time, the goalie becomes the shooter and the third person becomes the new goalie.

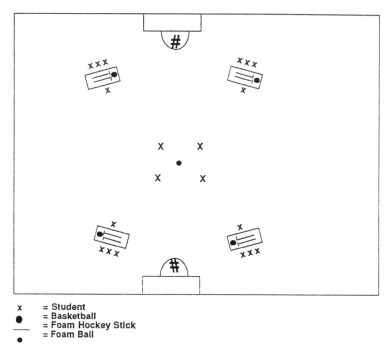

x   = Student
●   = Basketball
___   = Foam Hockey Stick
●   = Foam Ball

FIGURE 40.1: Foam Hockey Basketball

Name of the Game: Basket Wiffleball
Equipment Required: One wiffleball, one wifflebat, and one hula hoop
Description: Divide the class into two teams: batters and fielders. A student from the batting team is given a maximum of four pitches. He or she hits the ball and runs the bases. The fielder who gets the wiffleball throws it to the pitcher,

who places the ball in a hula hoop. A basketball is removed from the hula hoop and is thrown to another fielder, who shoots a basket (see Figure 40.2). The same fielder cannot shoot twice in a row, and no fielder can shoot more than twice per batter. If the batter returns home before a basket is made he or she scores one point. The batter is out after three strikes, or if he or she does not hit a fair ball by the fourth pitch, or if the fielding team makes a basket before he or she can return to home plate. All other softball rules apply.

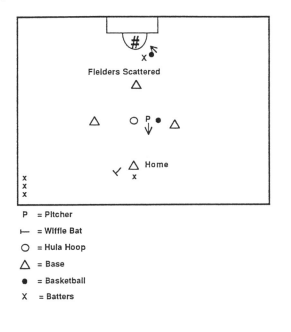

P   = Pitcher

⊢   = Wiffle Bat

○   = Hula Hoop

△   = Base

●   = Basketball

X   = Batters

FIGURE 40.2: Basket Wiffleball

Variations:

—Number off fielders; fielder #1 shoots when batter #1 is up, #2 for #2, and so forth.
—After each fielder shoots, he or she stoops down; no one can stand and shoot again until all have had one turn.

Name of the Game: Kickbowling
Equipment Required: One bowling pin, two safety cones, four bases, one foam soccer ball, and four tenequoit rings (see Figure 40.3).
Description: The class is divided into two teams: batters and fielders. Both teams organize themselves so that each team member has a different number. Six tenequoit rings are placed as shown in Figure 40.3. Two cones are set up as foul boundaries halfway between home and first and home and third. The batter stands in front of the bowling pin, which is placed behind home plate. The fielders assume regular softball positions. Fielder Number 1 becomes the pitcher, and the fielder with the last number is the catcher. The pitcher rolls the ball to

the batter, who kicks it into fair territory and then begins running around the bases collecting the rings as he or she passes each base. Meanwhile, the fielder who gets the ball passes it to the pitcher, who then rolls the ball at the pin. When the pin is knocked down, play stops and that batter's score equals the number of rings collected while running the bases. If the pitcher misses the pin, the catcher retrieves the ball and rolls it back to the pitcher for another try. If the batter gets all six rings and touches home before the pin is knocked down, the turn is over. As Batter Number 2 is ready to bat, Fielder Number 2 becomes the pitcher, Number 1 becomes the catcher, and the previous catcher moves back into the field. When everyone on the batting team has had a turn to bat, the teams change places, but the order is the same.

The batter cannot make an out. If the ball is caught on the fly, it is passed to the pitcher and play continues. When the batter is running he or she cannot interfere with the fielders, nor can they interfere.

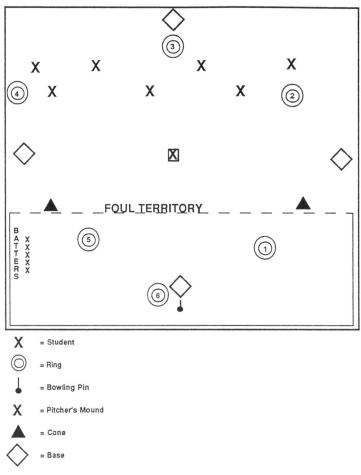

FIGURE 40.3: Kickbowling

41

Dare to Care: A Pedagogical Approach to Cooperative Physical Education

Jim DeLine

In very few physical education programs are cooperative skills specifically addressed, taught, and practiced. This does not suggest that efforts have not been made to foster cooperative behavior. Teachers do remind students that they must "get along," "be nice," or share things with others. However, these are temporary remedies that merely address symptoms and do little to cure the problem. Instruction is needed to specifically address and teach cooperative and prosocial strategies. This chapter briefly outlines a systematic pedagogical approach and an instructional model for teaching children cooperative strategies and prosocial behaviors.

The operative word here is *taught*. An abundance of cooperative games and activities already exist. Although intentions are genuine, these activities require students to use social skills they may have yet to master. Dare to Care approaches the concept of "learning to cooperate" as a skill. Educators do not expect students to learn difficult mathematical concepts without instruction, practice, and feedback. Beginning rope jumpers are not given a jump rope and expected to achieve mastery. Likewise, cooperative activities are meaningless without teacher guidance, instructional strategies, teaching cues, practice, and feedback. How can we realistically expect students to cooperate when they haven't received adequate and systematic instruction? Why don't all students cooperate? Maybe nobody has taught them how!

The ability to cooperate with others will greatly enhance any learning environment. In the gymnasium, students who are capable of and willing to work together, share equipment, wait their turn, trust their peers, communicate effectively, and play fair will learn with greater ease and enjoy themselves more. However, teaching students to acquire and utilize cooperative skills requires careful planning and systematic instruction. A Dare to Care unit adheres to the following instructional and behavioral objectives:

The teacher will:

1. Systematically introduce and define specific cooperative values and skills.
2. Teach and build a vocabulary that will allow students to identify and relate to a variety of cooperative skills.
3. Provide games and activities that demonstrate the benefits of being able to cooperate with others, and provide opportunities to practice cooperative skills and strategies.
4. Model, demonstrate, and reinforce the skills necessary to cooperate successfully with others.
5. Provide an environment where positive social interaction is demonstrated and cooperative expectations are clearly defined and understood.

The student will:

1. Recognize and identify specific cooperative skills.
2. Use verbal and behavioral strategies specific to each cooperative skill.
3. Practice the skill in a variety of group settings (i.e., partners, small groups, teams, and with the entire class).
4. Process each skill using a variety of peer reinforcement techniques.
5. Recognize opportunities and utilize cooperative skills outside of the physical education class.

DARE TO CARE COOPERATIVE SKILLS INSTRUCTIONAL MODEL

Teaching a cooperative skill is a five-step process. The process first involves skill identification, followed by strategies for its use. Next, carefully designed activities and games provide practice, and students are encouraged to process their ability to use the skill. Finally, students are given feedback, reinforcement, and continued practice.

Step 1: Identify the Skill

Identification of which skill to teach should be based on the particular needs of your students. If students yell or verbally abuse one another, communicating or talking nicely becomes the necessary focus of instruction. If students do not share equipment, sharing becomes a necessary social skill to practice. Once you have identified the skill, you must convey it to the students. This is a two-step process; first, define what the skill is, and second, explain why it is important.

Defining the Skill. Identify the skill as a focus-word (i.e., a cooperative skill that will be the focus of the lesson). Defining the focus-word simply involves a dictionary description of what it means. Write the definition on the blackboard or post it on a bulletin board. Read the definition aloud and begin the subsequent discussion by clarifying any unfamiliar words.

Establishing the Need. After defining and clarifying the focus-word, students need to understand its usefulness in terms of cooperating with others. Although this may be obvious to the teacher, students may not initially comprehend or accept the significance of the focus-word. Establishing the need involves a brief discussion of why the focus-word is important and when it could be used. Give examples of when students might use this skill at home or at school. Ask how they would feel if a peer did or did not effectively use this skill when working with them. Write these comments on the board under the definition. Emphasize that using the focus-word is necessary in order to accomplish the tasks in subsequent activities.

Step 2: Provide Strategies

Once the definition is clarified and the needs are established, the discussion shifts to *how* to use the focus-word. Through the use of a "T-chart," strategies are provided to identify *looks like* and *sounds like* behaviors (i.e., behavioral and verbal methods of using the skill). *Looks like* behaviors are things students can do, and *sounds like* behaviors are things students can say (see Figure 41.1). First give an example or two, then solicit student input. Generate ideas and list at least three strategies for each type of behavior. Once the list is made, state that the subsequent activity will require the use of these strategies. Establish the expectation that these behaviors will be seen and heard during the lesson.

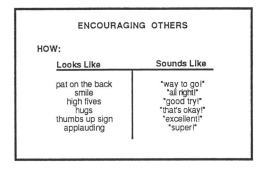

FIGURE 41.1: Strategies

Step 3: Practice the Skill

As with any skill, in order to achieve mastery, students must have many opportunities to practice. Structured practice with feedback, reinforcement, and processing is fundamental for cooperative skill acquisition. Dare to Care activities are designed to isolate the focus-word, thus giving students many opportunities to practice the cooperative skill. The emphasis of the activity is the individual's or group's effort to use the cooperative skill. Success is measured accordingly.

Cooperative skill acquisition is directly influenced by the types of activities selected and the requirements of the players when participating. The structure of the game or activity has a significant impact on the behavior and interactions of the participants. Selecting activities that isolate the focus-word and encourage participation is critical. Students will soon forget about the focus-word if competition is too intense or if winning is the sole criterion of success. Dare to Care activities adhere to the following guidelines: Competition is deemphasized.

Success is not measured by physical ability, winning, or losing, but rather by one's effort and ability to use the cooperative skill. All students will be actively engaged at all times. A student will never be eliminated from an activity. When possible, the activities concurrently emphasize motor skill and cardiovascular fitness development. Students have an opportunity to interact with many different partners or group members.

Step 4: Process the Skill

Processing incorporates strategies by which students reflect on their use of the skill, how it helped them and others, how it made them feel, and where in their daily lives the skill might be useful. Students respond to statements that illuminate the necessity for using the skill. Additionally, they discuss with peers their feelings, learning experiences, and ability to use the skill. Finally, processing provides gives the lesson closure and increases the possibilities for transfer of knowledge. Dare to Care uses a variety of processing techniques (e.g., Fun Check, Nice Time, Goal Setting, and Care-work).

The method of processing used will depend on such factors as available time, the nature of the activity, and student ability. However, central to all methods is the processing statement. In simple terms, the processing statement is a teacher-generated "fill-in-the-blank" statement by means of which students reflect on what happened during the activity. For example, "When our group encouraged me, I was able to ———." The blank requires students to discuss feelings, evaluate effectiveness, or plan new strategies. An exception to the use of a processing statement is Class Nice Time. This is done with the entire class during the last two or three minutes of each period. The intent is for students to praise each other by sharing with their peers nice things others did or said to them during the lesson.

Processing on a consistent basis enables students to develop and internalize a behavioral repertoire of cooperative skills. Students give and receive compliments, articulate their appreciation, and consequently hold one another accountable for cooperating. They become aware of how others feel about them when they cooperate, see that their effort did not go unnoticed, and thus develop a sense of pride and greater self-efficacy. Without processing, students merely engage in physical activity rather than learn how to cooperate. They become so involved with the enjoyment of the activity that processing is needed to direct attention back to the cooperative skill. In so doing, students may associate enjoyment with their ability to successfully use the focus-word.

Step 5: Feedback, Reinforcement, and Continued Practice

Steps 1 through 4 allow students to identify, practice, comprehend, and process the skill. However, complete mastery of the focus-word requires them to internalize the skill so that it becomes a natural component of their behavioral repertoire. The goal of Step 5 is to facilitate this process. Step 5 can either serve as a follow-up to the preceding four steps or be used concurrently with them. It embraces a broad spectrum of ideas, each intended to expedite the internalization process.

First, students need feedback about task performance. Feedback refers to how students are utilizing the cooperative strategies. If administered in the form of praise, feedback serves as a motivator. Furthermore, feedback acknowledges effort and makes them "feel good." Pats on the back, praise from across the gym, and group acknowledgment of an individual send messages that the performance is acceptable and the cooperative goals are being met. A short time for students to praise each other (Nice Time) also works well.

Second, seek opportunities to reinforce cooperative behavior whenever possible. Give certificates that read, "I Dared to Care," post the focus-words and Care-work. Do not confine the scope of reinforcement to physical education. In fact, students are frequently reminded, "The gymnasium is where we learn to care, outside is where we Dare to Care!" Praise students for being *thoughtful* when they open a door or help a peer pick up a dropped book. Acknowledge students who *share* a swing on the playground. Even praise a student for *being honest* because he or she remembered to sit in time-out without being asked. Opportunities to reinforce cooperative behavior are abundant. By illuminating the notion that cooperating with others is a lifelong skill and not simply a requirement of physical education class, students will become aware of how these skills are applicable to other areas of their lives.

Finally, the skill must be continually practiced. Although respective Dare to Care activities focus on a particular skill, they simultaneously reinforce other cooperative concepts. Illuminate these overlapping concepts. Periodically, provide "booster shots" of a particular focus-word. The activities are fun and students enjoy playing them again. Continued practice, reinforcement, and feedback will help them internalize cooperative skills. Strive to be consistent and generous in their application. Don't underestimate the effect this step will have on the effort of students to internalize these skills.

I have briefly presented a systematic method of teaching students cooperative skills and prosocial behaviors. These steps may appear time-consuming and difficult to administer. Initially, this may be so. Remember, however, that an initial investment pays great dividends in terms of students behaving more cooperatively, having more time allocated to activity, and to acquiring a lifetime skill (i.e., cooperating with others). Students who do not have a behavioral repertoire of cooperative skills can learn these skills only through instructional guidance, patience, and perseverance. An example of a Dare to Care model follows.

Focus Word: Honesty

WHAT: Being truthful, fair, and trustworthy. What do these three words mean?
WHY: Playing fair will help us to better enjoy the activity, and being trustworthy will help us to better get along.

HOW: Looks Like   Sounds Like
                  To tell the truth   "You got me"
                  Play fair   "I was out"
                  Follow the rules   "Tough"
                  Accept responsibility   "I did it"

WHEN: If you get tagged, tell the truth; when you are playing a game, play it fairly; and if you agree to do something for another person, accept the responsibility.

Name of the Game: Floor Fencing

Cooperative Objectives: The student will practice being honest while playing with a partner, honestly self-officiate his or her activity, respond positively regardless of the outcome, and analyze and discuss his or her ability to be honest.

Equipment: An activity wand per student

Physical Skills: Balance, agility, speed, gross motor coordination, and honesty

Cooperative Skills: Honesty and sportsmanship

Organization: Students are grouped in pairs, scattered throughout the activity area, and each student has an activity wand.

Description: Instruct the students that one end of the activity wand must slide on the ground at all times. The opening play begins when each student crosses the wand with his or her partner's. After gently tapping the wands together three times, the students begin "fencing." The object of this activity is for each student to touch his or her opponent's foot by sliding the wand across the ground. A "touch" is declared by a student when his or her foot is touched by an opponent's wand. The activity begins anew after each touch (i.e., crossing the wands and tapping three times). All touches must be declared verbally and honestly. When a student feels that his or her own foot has been touched by an opponent's wand, the student must declare "Touch!" or "You got me!" A touch may not be declared by saying, "I got you!"

Teaching Suggestions: Allow students the opportunity to practice sliding the wand on the ground before playing with a partner, to practice moving the wand back and forth or side to side in a circle and to spell vocabulary words, in geometric shapes. Have them practice sliding the wand on the ground while walking, skipping, or galloping.

Before a round of activity commences, have each pair of students shake hands and say, "Let's play fair!" or "Let's be honest!" and after the round shake hands again and say "Thank you!" or "I appreciate your honesty!"

Even though this is a combative, competitive activity, it can be structured so that all students can win. There are a variety of ways to keep score so that the criterion of success becomes the student's ability to be honest rather than his or her ability to defeat an opponent. For example, ask students to count how many times a partner honestly declares a touch, or when this partner has been honest three times to raise the partner's hand. Count how many times partners are able to be honest, and to raise their hands when together they have been honest ten times. Give a student a point if he or she touches a partner's foot, and a point if a student declares a "touch" honestly.

Safety Concerns: The obvious concern is that one end of the wand remain on the ground at all times. Stress that the wand must slide across the ground, and make sure that each pair of students is far enough away from walls and other groups. Encourage controlled movement.

Variations: Play with the nondominant hand. Play on one foot.

REFERENCES

DeLine, Jim (1991). Why Can't They Get Along? Because Nobody Has Taught Them How! *Journal of Physical Education Recreation and Dance*, 62(1), 21-26.

Dishon, Dee, and Pat Wilson (1988). *A Guidebook for Cooperative Learning: A Technique for Creating More Effective Schools*. Holmes Beach, Fla.: Learning Publications.

42

Developing Sportsmanship and Sharpening Skills through Games

Jill Vomacka

Motor skills are typically taught in a progressive order from the simple to the complex. Rules are introduced in a similar manner, beginning when the child is first asked to keep his or her body behind a specific line, and progressing to those involved in complex defensive and offensive strategies. This chapter makes suggestions and offers sample activities to help teachers implement a teaching progression related to the concept of sportsmanship.

Children with low self-esteem may not perform well in a competitive environment. If they fear making a mistake or not performing up to their expectations, they may develop behavior problems or withdraw from additional participation. Developing sportsmanship in physical education in a non-competitive, progressive manner will change the climate for the child. It will eventually become one in which students with enhanced psychomotor skills will naturally assist those with weaker abilities or at least praise their efforts.

Teachers can start the progression in kindergarten by asking children to talk about their feelings. Children should be asked to identify a variety of words, phrases, or statements that people use to make other people feel good about themselves and resist making statements that lead to negative feelings. These thoughts can be listed on a large poster board, or each thought can be written separately on an index card and placed on the gymnasium wall (see Figure 42.1). Continue this action in a low organizational game situation by having the children play for sportsmanship. That is, each group receives one point for saying something nice to members of their own group, as well as receiving bonus points for saying something nice to the opposing team.

This concept of introducing sportsmanship phrases is expanded in grades one and two by asking the children to compile a list of phrases that can be used when individuals do not perform well in an activity (examples: "Good try" or "That's O.K."). Sportsmanship points can be awarded for sitting quietly, passing a ball, sharing equipment, or waiting a turn.

Good Try	Great Pass	What a Shot
Great Catch	Good Pass	Great Stuff
Good Catch	Super Block	Nice Shot on Goal
Super Kick	Great Teamwork	Good Rebound
Good Kick	Nice Trap	Great Job
Good Throw	Great Set	Nice Offense
Great Play	Super Spike	
Good Defense	Nice Hit	

FIGURE 42.1: Sportsmanship Phrases

In grades three and four, place the emphasis on winning with grace and losing with pride. This behavior must be introduced at the beginning of the school year and reinforced by stopping the activities whenever necessary to review the concept. Individuals should be given a chance to voice their opinion and assist in the process of reorganizing the members of each team to keep the level of competition developmentally appropriate. This aspect is extended in grades five and six, where the students are encouraged to discuss penalties for unsportsmanlike behavior. These include losing one or more points or giving the other team a point every time a teammate uses inappropriate behavior, or replaying an activity if a disagreement cannot be settled.

The following games demonstrate how the preceding progression and point system can be implemented.

Name of the Game: Circle Trap Soccer
Description: The class is divided into two groups and situated around the outside of a circle (30' in diameter). Place two cones at opposite sides of the circle so that the students know where their group begins and ends along the circle. Each team is given several cloth rag soccer balls. On the word "start" the students try to kick the balls so that they cross the other team's half of the circle. They also try to trap the soccer balls coming toward their team's half of the circle. A point is given for every good trap, for every compliment, and for every ball that goes over the opposing team's half of the circle. All kicked balls must remain on the ground or below knee level. Rag balls or soft foam balls should be used. No student is allowed inside the circle to retrieve a still ball. Award points to the other team if a rule is broken. Hands are used only to protect the body from a high kicked ball.
Variation: To increase the level of competition, place two opposing players in the middle of the circle. The circle people trap the ball and pass it to their team's center player to score.

Name of the Game: Kong Pong (author unknown)
Description: Divide the class into two teams. Using a volleyball court and net, organize a front, middle, and back line of students for each team. The net should be touching the floor for younger students so that they can throw the ball over it. To start play, the student in the right back line position on Team A moves as

close as desired to the net and throws the ball over it. He or she then returns to the back line. Players on Team B try to catch the ball before it bounces four times. If they succeed, they throw it back over the net from their position or pass it to someone closer to the net. If Team B does not catch the ball before the fourth bounce, the next person in the back line of Team A serves the ball over the net. If Team B misses the ball, Team A gets a point. If Team A does not get the ball over the net on the serve or during play, Team B serves.

Use a foam ball, and progress to a beach ball or a regular volleyball. Rotate the teams by lines and then by individual positions. Give a point to the other team when a child moves out of his or her position. Arrange the team boy-girl-boy-girl on the lines.

Variation: Decrease the number of bounces as the child's skill level progresses. If a team catches a ball on the fly they receive a point. Give points for passing and good sportsmanship (e.g., if a student says "Good try!" or "Good catch!" give a point to that team). Play the entire game on good sportsmanship points.

Name of the Game: T-Ball Softball

Description: Divide the class into two teams. One team is given a batting order, while the other team is scattered in the outfield. Select a pitcher. Explain to the pitcher that he or she must stay on the pitcher's mound or the team at bat will receive one point. Place a large stanchion cone (30") on first base. A player on the batting team hits a whiffleball off a Batting T and runs to the cone. If he or she gets to first base before the fielders get the ball to the pitcher, the team receives one point. If the batting team does not throw the bat, they get another point. If the fielders get the ball to the pitcher without the pitcher missing the ball, they get a point. After every five batters, change fielding and batting position. As the game progresses, add a second cone (i.e., second base). If a batter makes it to second base before the fielders get the ball to the pitcher, the batter receives two points. As the skill ability progresses, continue to add bases.

Variation: To stop several children from running after the ball at the same time, assign each fielder to a batter, or bonus points can be given for sportsmanship phrases.

43

The Nontraditional Environment for Seventh and Eighth Grade Games

Susan Anne Sortino

To obtain an understanding of a nontraditional and developmentally appropriate environment for seventh and eighth grade games it is first necessary to clarify several definitions and assumptions. At one extreme, the mental images of the "traditional" physical education environment could include whistle blowing, skills testing, students standing in line formations, identical uniforms, platforms, and calisthenics. At the other extreme, the nontraditional environment can conjure images of circles, fluffy equipment, hand-holding, and multitudes of children skipping happily together. Neither image is accurate or helpful when searching for an appropriate definition. I propose a more neutral definition of the nontraditional environment, one where the individuals participating in an activity have priority and where it is the teacher's responsibility to create a "learner friendly" atmosphere. So, what do traditional and nontraditional mean in practical terms for a class of seventh and eighth grade students? To begin, we need to explore an object used to initiate and end games. It could be said that this object is a traditional symbol of physical education.

THE TEACHER'S USE OF THE WHISTLE

The whistle is a common tool of physical education teachers and officials alike. During the 1970s using the whistle was considered to be militaristic, insensitive, domineering, and, worst of all, traditional! Respected professionals asked, "Shouldn't we be talking with children rather than blowing at them?" The whistle, therefore, was seen as a symbol of the conflict between traditional and nontraditional, command-style versus cooperative learning. If a primary objective is to create an environment conducive to learning, teachers should explore their whistle-blowing behavior. Imagine fifty students participating in a traditional seventh grade physical education class. In order to learn the skills required to play any given game, the students may only move when the whistle is blown, and may only stop when it is blown twice. In this scenario, are the children a priority? Is it an environment in which they will learn to enjoy movement? Now imagine fifty students in a nontraditional physical education class. The noise level is astronomical, and the students do not listen to the teacher, who is attempting to get their attention. The class is in chaos and there is no way any game can be organized. The teacher refuses to use a whistle because of a philosophical point of view. In this situation, the same questions can be asked. Are the children a priority? Is this an environment in which they will learn to enjoy movement?

These obviously are two extreme examples; however, we all can agree that similar situations have been played out in gymnasiums. So, what would be the nontraditional, child-centered whistle-blowing technique in each case?

In the first situation, the children were commanded by the whistle when to start and stop moving. One could venture to guess that the skill being learned was how to stop and start quickly, as opposed to full concentration on the movement skill itself. The whistle became the focus, not the children learning. In this case, less whistle blowing would clearly be more nontraditional. In the second case, a quick toot of the whistle would seem to be appropriate in order to get things organized. Chaos is not learner friendly; therefore, if the whistle would help to create a learning atmosphere, then a toot, traditional though it may be, would help to create a progressive, less chaotic environment. In short, the use of the whistle is part of the environment and therefore has an influence on the playing and learning of sport skills. Whether that influence is positive or negative depends on the achievement of the child-centered, learner friendly objectives.

THE DEVELOPMENTALLY APPROPRIATE ENVIRONMENT

The elements that affect the environment seem to fall under three categories: class organization, game structure, and intangibles. It is important to explore each, while noting that the category is not limited by the examples given.

Class Organization

Class organization encompasses a myriad of different elements. One of the most obvious is whether or not a class is single-sexed or coed. Many teachers can remember when boys and girls were separated by walls, curtains, or different gymnasiums during instruction. The real barriers, however, may have been our own erroneous assumptions, discriminatory attitudes, and sexist behavior. We have come a long way in terms of combating sexist attitudes, but not far enough. It is not enough to simply have a coed class without putting in place systems that help the children become aware of and deal with prevailing attitudes.

I highly recommend that teachers eliminate the practice of organizing boys versus girls games. There is already animosity between the two sexes, and to sanction a confrontational situation through games or sport would serve to solidify that animosity. After all, we would never encourage one race to play a game against another race. Teachers already have the difficult task of changing attitudes about working together. Segregating the sexes for any activity should be discouraged.

Many television programs have depicted the negative aspects of the "classic" physical education classes of the late 1960s and early 1970s. Very often these episodes show two students standing in front of the single-sexed class, being forced by a dictatorial gym teacher to choose two teams. The selection process inevitably leaves the weakest players humiliated, standing alone in front of the entire class. This process does not treat the child as a priority, nor does it create a learner friendly environment.

An alternative to this practice would be to have a rotating system of two captains in the class. Each student would have the opportunity to be captain during the year. They could be given a class list and asked to select their teams. The students should be given the rationale behind the process and told that it is their responsibility to create equally matched teams. The system respects confidentiality.

Many traditional drills in physical education are very linear. Historically, physical education teachers seem to have gravitated toward orderliness and uniformity, resulting in rows of students doing the same thing at the same time. A circuit style of organizing the class is one alternative. Different skills can be practiced at the same time, and the students seem to enjoy moving from one station to another. The circuit method of organization eliminates boredom and encourages students to organize themselves as they adapt to the different activities that make up the circuit. A circuit can also be used to create several mini-game situations rather than one large game, which increases the time spent waiting for an opportunity to play.

Tournaments have long been a traditional culminating activity in most seventh and eighth grade teaching units. In the interest of keeping the individual as a priority during tournament action, I am a believer in awarding points for everything. If you actively participate, you score points for your team. If your team plays fairly and attempts to get everybody to participate, you get fair play points. In other words, the individual can score not only in the conventional sense, but also by participating and behaving in an appropriate manner.

I also believe that children should be given autonomy in a class. The amount of autonomy is determined by the readiness of the group; seventh and eighth grade students need an adult's guidance in order to achieve that readiness. It does not happen in a vacuum. One way to give the class some autonomy is to allow a choice day. The students learn to use and respect the democratic process while determining the choice day activity. Admittedly, problems or conflicts may arise, but the students must explore each other's ideas and solutions before the activity can begin.

Game Structure

The second category of elements affecting environment is game structure. The rules of the games can affect the environment of the class as much as the class organization. In a sense, it is a symbiotic relationship. Dodgeball is a traditional game that many teachers still use in the seventh and eighth grades. Unfortunately, the game is often played aggressively, and given a name like "bombardment." It is important to change several of the rules and to restructure the game and see what effect these changes could have on the symbiotic relationship among the group, the game, and the environment.

At the furthest extreme we could change the name of the game from "bombardment" to "poptart." Each student is playing for him or herself, so there are no antagonistic groups. You can help anyone you want, or play for yourself. There is also a very important equipment change. Red playground balls should never be used, only balls made from soft, "human being friendly" material. In addition, there are four possible ways to get back into the game after being hit. You sit down right where you are hit, and may get back into the game by (1) tagging a free player as he or she goes by—when that player goes down, you get up; (2) hitting a free player with a ball from your "down" position; (3) remembering who got you down; when that person goes down, you can automatically get up (mini-poptart); or (4) responding to the teacher's yell "poptart," when everyone can get up.

Clearly a multitude of variations are associated with this game. Part of the fun is having students originate variations. Although it can be played as a team game, it is important to be aware of how the rule changes affect the aggressive level of a game. The addition of teams usually escalates the aggression level, but there is no reason to hide from this fact. Use it as a teachable moment. Bring it into the students' awareness, and discuss why it happens. The bottom line, of course, is to insist that violent or aggressive play is never tolerated.

Teachers must also look at the modification of a sport. For example, if the students are playing basketball, it is very often necessary to put in a "no fast break" rule so that the more experienced players do not dominate the game. One could call it "half court courtesy," so that the offensive team must wait until the defensive team sets up its zone. Once again, the reasons for the rule modifications should not be a secret to the students and definitely should be discussed.

Intangibles

The third and final category I call intangibles. These elements stem from the style, personality, and sensitivity of the teacher; perhaps it is the most influential of all three categories. Humor is an example of one of the elements in this category. I am certain that most teachers have seen how humor, when used appropriately, can defuse a potentially difficult situation, especially with seventh and eighth grade students. It can certainly be used to set a positive, non-threatening tone in the class.

It all, therefore, comes full circle. The nontraditional environment for seventh and eighth grade games succeeds when the teacher implements methods and approaches to fulfill two important objectives: keeping the individual a priority, and creating a learner friendly atmosphere. It is, after all, that simple.

44

Helping Seventh and Eighth Grade Students to Express Their Feelings

Minna S. Barrett, Sheila Mardenfeld, and Rhoda Joseph

Journals, magazines, newspapers, and television all identify incidents of abuse, killings, and violent reactions to life situations. The media reinforce the reality that a segment of our society reacts to situations in ways that are not only self-destructive but also lead to dire consequences for those involved, including innocent bystanders. We hear of a father allegedly beating his child to death while the mother (also supposedly the victim of her husband's violence) stands by and fails to act. We remember the seemingly senseless mugging and rape of the Central Park jogger in New York, and the subway murder of a young man visiting from Utah. We recall the Texas murders perpetrated by a former postal worker who sought revenge on his superiors for perceived injustices. We hear of murders germinated by racism.

How do we get to the point where our behavior becomes violent? All violent acts begin with a set of feelings. These feelings lead to actions that may appear senseless to bystanders. For example, many people find it difficult to express love for their spouses. If we make ourselves vulnerable and the warmth is not returned, then what? Many parents manipulate their children, believing them incapable of taking responsibility for their feelings and actions, and therefore needing to be controlled by adults. In the same way, children often have tantrums or are self-destructive when parents deny them desired objects or freedom. In brief, humans have a rich emotional life with feelings that can change from one minute to the next.

Feelings are a natural part of everyday life. Learning to recognize, admit to, and gain healthy expression of those feelings is a complex process, partly because "handling feelings" is rarely taught at home or in school. Nonetheless, feelings are the foundation of behavior. Understanding how the actions of others make us feel and how we react when we experience certain feelings is an essential skill for preparing the individual for the many social interactions required throughout a lifetime.

Collectively, we have worked for over sixty years in the fields of early childhood and early elementary education, in university teaching, and in individual, group, and family counseling. Our experience has helped us to see that an appropriate expression of feelings requires learning or relearning, since the individual learns to react from people around him or her, and they, in turn, usually have not been taught to be open and expressive about their own feelings.

Our research indicates that the topic of feelings evaluation and expression will be a growth industry in the mental and physical health professions. Our culture has begun to recognize the high rates of child abuse, and other adult behaviors are now known to be a function of suppressing childhood feelings. Many people have little or no access to their feelings, and even less access to internal mechanisms for accurate, yet safe expression of those feelings. This is true for people of any age in our culture. Few of us feel comfortable telling a colleague or superiors how a particular decision or process will make us feel. Not having a legitimate place and safe people with whom to share them, however, is especially true for children and for seniors. These two groups of people are often unable to express their feelings because the consequences of that expression are, or at least appear to be, dangerous. Populations that could benefit from developing a clear relationship to feelings include families, hospital staffs, religious education groups, bereavement counselors, clinicians who work with children suspected to be victims of emotional, physical, and sexual abuse, teachers, children with special needs, adults in marriage and family counseling and addiction recovery, and seniors.

Educators who wish to use games and physical movement to help children learn to identify, express, and take responsibility for their feelings should have the following issues in mind. Help children communicate feelings to other people by encouraging them to recognize their feelings and to express them clearly, safely, and appropriately. Help children and parents to communicate feelings to each other, especially targeting adults who don't often feel they can take the time to listen. Help parents become aware of their children's emotional needs, and give adults a way to teach children how to express feelings in many different situations (e.g., going to the hospital, facing the death of a family member or a loved pet, or addressing sadness from physical, emotional, or sexual abuse, or enjoying a holiday or special visit).

DEMONSTRATING YOUR OWN FEELINGS

The following activity can be used to see how comfortable individuals are with identifying their own feelings. The activity is especially effective in grades seven and eight. Begin by asking the group the following questions: Do you know how you are feeling at the moment? If you can identify your feelings, are you able to express them safely for yourself and for others? Do you know what to do with your feelings? Individuals should feel free to participate as much or as little as they choose.

ACTIVITY

Divide the class into groups of four members. Ask the students to remember any feelings they have had since waking up that morning. Ask them to write down as many as they can remember. Encourage all group members who wish to do so to read their lists. Ask them to choose a partner and tell them how it felt to read the list aloud to the entire group. Have everyone return to their foursome, then ask them to select one of the feelings on their list. Encourage group members to explain where they think the feeling originated. In other words, what situation and thoughts led to the feelings? Individuals are asked to retain these feelings or to express different ones. Ask them to circulate in their group and act out the feeling. They are challenged to discuss what facial expressions go with a feeling, and what body positions and arm and leg movements are used to convey it. Individuals should be encouraged to exaggerate body expressions, but they may not use words. Let group members try to guess the feeling from the individual's expression and physical movement. Ask the class to select a third feeling from their lists. Circulate it throughout the room and let each member act out that feeling using facial expressions and body movement. Ask if each member uses the same body language, the same facial expression. Are there common elements in the way we all look when we have the same feeling? Discuss with each small group how it felt to act out their feeling. How did it feel when someone else was acting out a feeling on their list? How about when they were acting out a feeling on someone else's list?

ACTIVITY EVALUATION

Discuss what behaviors occurred during the exercise. Ask the class the following questions: Does this exercise allow you to see how you identify feelings? Did any feelings surface that you were not aware of? Were you upset or uncomfortable at any time? How did you feel about this activity? Can you see how to use nonverbal behavior to express your feelings?

45

Theatre Games:
Expressive Movement Activities

Estelle Aden

Many children who struggle to express themselves verbally find movement activities an excellent means of communication. The following theatre games were created for the child who has difficulty articulating thoughts and expressing him or herself. They can, however, be used for a variety of other purposes depending on the teacher's desire, time restrictions, the developmental level of the class, and the space provided.

Teachers are advised to resist the temptation to "overdirect" so that a nonjudgmental atmosphere of free-flowing responses can be achieved. The process by which the individual interacts, shares ideas, and explores different options is of greater importance than in the more common games where one team is declared the winner. After the children have been introduced to each activity, they should be encouraged to lead the activities without the teacher's direction. This self-direction builds confidence and helps to create a community of sharing and decision-making.

Name of the Game: Living Dictionary
Point of Concentration: Vitality of words, imagery of words
Rules of the Game: All students are sitting in a circle. This formation is always preferable. The object of the game is "to become" a word or to act out a word in mime. Talking is not permitted. The action can be performed individually or with several other students.
Variation: The choice of the word can come from the group. There can also be a "repetition of ideas" in any one category. For example, in the category of shapes, students can make a square-triangular-parallel-perpendicular form. In addition, the teacher can suggest other categories, such as words of emotion. The children's physical involvement makes the word meaning very graphic.

Name of the Game: Together We Can Make a Dragon
Point of Concentration: Spatial relationships, interdependency, analogy

Rules of the Game: All students are sitting in a circle. Student leaders suggest the size and diversity of the object, a fantasy monster or a machinelike monster. Their peers become moving parts of the selected object as the idea becomes more clear to the group.

The application of the activity may follow a storytelling session of *The Dragon Takes a Wife* by Walter Dean Myers or *The Fifty-First Dragon* by Heyward Broun.

Variation: Encourage the children to make other objects (e.g., a computer or a washing machine).

Name of the Game: Rhythm of Language

Point of Concentration: Appreciation of prosody, pitch/loudness/tempo/rhythm

Rules of the Game: All students are sitting in a circle. The teacher selects a word with more than one syllable, or the students may select a word to explore. While chanting the word, the children stress the quality of sound contained in the word. They may snap their fingers, clap their hands, or tap their feet. If the children are at their desks, they can beat out the rhythm on the desks, for example, Ti ger, Ti ger. This word can be extended into an action mime based on the poem "The Tiger" by William Blake.

Name of the Game: Opposites

Point of Concentration: Transformation, gradations of change

Rules of the Game: The children stand in a line, shoulder to shoulder, facing in one direction. Divide the class into Group A and Group B. Groups A and B move as one unit across the play area, which functions as a metaphor for change. The teacher or leader suggests a transformation, for example, light to dark. Groups A and B move simultaneously from a light place to a dark place. They respond to the environment and to the contrast. If desired, the leader may talk the groups through the transformation as the children move across the play area, changing from being in the light to being in the dark (e.g., "You are in a bright sunny place . . . a beach. The sun is hot and bright. You can see far off in the distance. Now you see clouds. It is getting darker and darker. You cannot see very well at all. You have to put your arm out to find your way back to the car").

Variation: Group A stands at one end of the play area facing Group B. {No narration is used in this variation, as it would be an intrusion.) The groups are at opposite ends of the transformation process. They move simultaneously and the lines pass by each other. In either option there is a complete experience of change. The advantage in having simultaneous activity is that everyone is moving, and there is more freedom when the child does not feel that he or she is the focus of attention.

Name of the Game: Birds Fly

Point of Concentration: Listening and categorizing

Rules of the Game: The teacher or leader selects an action verb, for example, fly, bend, or bounce. The leader identifies animals and objects that can fly, bend, or bounce. Students pantomime this action until the leader calls out an animal or an object that does not fit the category. Then the students stop moving and freeze very still. For example, the leader calls out "Birds fly—butterflies fly—airplanes fly—dinosaurs fly . . . Children freeze." In the older grades the children may create their own set and verbalize the combinations as the class responds to their directions. There is only one action verb to a set. The children should always join the action verb to a descriptive animal or object, such as birds *fly* or wrists *bend* or ice *melts*.

Name of the Game: In the Manner of the Adverb

Point of Concentration: Grammar, imaginative pantomime, nonverbal communication

Rules of the Game: The students sit in a circle. A student is chosen or volunteers to leave the group temporarily. The group selects an adverb, for example, quickly, carefully, or angrily. The student returns and challenges different members of the group to accomplish different tasks reflecting the adverb. Individuals continue to demonstrate actions reflecting the adverb until the correct adverb is identified. The teacher should expect many synonyms. This can be the beginning of a class thesaurus.

Name of the Game: Standing Scrabble

Point of Concentration: Spelling, familiarizing the alphabet, visualizing, interacting cooperatively

Description: The teacher prepares for this game by printing letters of the alphabet on 5 X 7 cards. Each card should have a safety pin for the child to pin the card to his or her sleeve. The cards are distributed to groups of approximately ten students. A complete set of alphabet cards from A to Z is given to each group. There should be an extra supply of vowels for the groups to use. This can be placed centrally in the activity.

Rules of the Game:

- The object is to have the students stand in a profile position so that the alphabet letter is visible. In this stance, the students form a line; as a group, they spell a word.
- Groups can vary in size depending on the words they choose to spell.
- The words can evolve from the group.
- One student can suggest a word and each of the others can take his or her turn suggesting a word.
- The class as a whole can create a word, a phrase, or a sentence.
- Replies can be formulated by the group. The quicker the reply the more enjoyment the children experience. At first the focus is on the spelling, but as the tempo changes, the structure of the words becomes the important factor.

Name of the Game: Half and Half

Point of Concentration: Listening, energy release, motor control

Equipment: A drum to cue the class for movement, or spirited music

Rules of the Game: Each child finds his or her own space. The leader instructs the group that they may move only body parts from the waist upwards. The feet are planted in a fixed position on the ground. The children begin to move when the cue is heard (i.e., either the drum beat or the music). When the music or drum stops, they freeze, holding their arms and upper torso in that position. When the music begins again, they hold that stance and begin to move only their feet and legs. The leg action can be a skip, hop, or some other locomotor skill. When the cue is given to freeze, they hold the position and repeat the activity, using their arms and upper torso. The exercise continues from upper action to lower action.

Many of these games can be enjoyed in ten- to fifteen-minute segments. They may be used out of context or adapted to a particular lesson. Young children's leadership qualities can emerge as well as their creativity and ability to express themselves.

REFERENCES

Blake, William (1953). "The Tiger," from *Songs of Innocence*. In *Collected Works of William Blake*, ed. Northrop Frye. New York: Modern Library.
Broun, Heyward (1985). *The Fifty-First Dragon*. Mankato, Minn.: Creative Education.
Myers, Walter Dean (1972). *The Dragon Takes a Wife*. New York: Bobbs-Merrill.
Spolin, Viola (1970). *Improvisation for the Theatre*. Evanston, Ill.: Northwestern University Press.

46

Eliminating Gender-Role Stereotyping in Elementary Physical Education

Karen H. Weiller, Catriona T. Higgs, and Betsy A. Brickell

Although changes have occurred in recent years, indications are that boys and girls still live in different social worlds, with boys more likely to be guided toward physical activity than girls (Greendorfer, 1980; Housner, 1981). This chapter gives an overview of the literature in the area of gender-role stereotyping and offers the elementary physical educator alternative games, activities, and strategies for eliminating sexist teaching behaviors and practices.

LITERATURE REVIEW

The most accepted global psychological theories used to describe the acquisition of gender-role behaviors stress the importance of reinforcement, observational learning, and modeling. Expectations of appropriate gender activities are inculcated into boys and girls at a very early age by significant others, particularly parents (Katz and Boswell, 1986). Positive and negative reinforcers teach children what behavior is appropriate and inappropriate in a variety of social situations. Greendorfer (1983) has indicated that early exploratory behavior, styles of play, and gross motor activities are sex-typed early in a child's life. Positive reinforcement is given to boys who are active and display aggressive tendencies in their play activities. Similar behavior in girls, however, is discouraged, and more passive activities promoted. "One result of such socialization is that boys are directed towards sport and girls are directed away from it" (Greendorfer, 1983, p. 18).

Observational learning and modeling theory contends that children learn appropriate gender-role behavior through observing and imitating the behavior of adults (Bandura and Walters, 1963; Perry and Bussey, 1979). "Children are shaped by external forces, particularly reference groups towards male and female roles" (Ignico, 1989a, p. 1067). The three major influences on a child's life, parents, peers, and teachers, provide children with gender-specific information regarding the appropriateness of an activity.

Children's toy selections and play experiences are both critical to later social development. A growing body of knowledge (Lever, 1978; Oglesby, 1978; Corbin and Nix, 1979; Brawley, Powers, and Phillips, 1980; Herkowitz, 1980; Jacklin and Maccoby, 1980; Sheldon, 1990) suggests that toys are often labeled by children according to gender and that these sex-typed toys are the result of parents' selections (Sheldon, 1990; Jacklin and Maccoby, 1980). Children spend a great deal of time engaged in play with toys, games, and activities.   The perception certain toys and games as gender appropriate influences how they are designed by manufacturers, marketed by advertisers, and selected by parents (Richardson, Albury, and Tandy, 1985).

In an essay related to sex roles and physical activities, Hoferek (1982) noted that physical activities were a strong socializing agent in our society.   Hoferek reiterated the rigidity of sex-role stereotyping and its effect on roles of girls and boys in physical education classes.   "Rigid sex-role stereotyping and its associated practices limit the vision people have of themselves and their options for behavior" (Hoferek, 1982, p. 73).   Teachers at the elementary school level are guilty of communicating their biases to students by labeling certain activities as gender appropriate, thus creating a self-fulfilling prophecy and limiting the variety of activities open to girls and boys.

Association of gender-specific appropriateness with physical activity excludes many children from potentially satisfying activities (Ignico, 1989b). It has been documented that boys' games are more competitive in nature and promote leadership skills, independence, and analytical thinking, whereas girls' games develop cooperative skills and indirect competition.   A gender label adds attraction to a game and may influence game performance (Montemayer, 1974; Lever, 1978; Greendorfer, 1980; Pitcher and Schultz, 1983). When one considers that a child can identify different sexes by the age of twenty-four months (Thompson, 1975) and that cognitive requirements for recognizing gender constancy are completed by the preschool period (Kohlberg, 1966), it is little wonder that children label activities according to gender (Thompson, 1975; Corbin and Nix, 1979) and learn gender appropriateness of activities early in the socialization process. Implementation of a gender-neutral curriculum requires deliberate and careful evaluation and modification of existing programs.

ELIMINATING SEXIST PRACTICES

Children enter the world of education with preconceived ideas regarding gender appropriate behavior and activities. Traditional physical education programs have perpetuated gender stereotyping just as other educational specializations have, by drawing upon practices and experiences long established in our society. Ignico (1989b) noted that "physical educators and teachers who handle their own physical education instruction frequently label activities and games in their curriculum according to gender and therefore perpetuate and reinforce stereotypical beliefs" (p. 23).

Practitioners are often left in a state of "void reality" when attempting to incorporate theory into viable classroom activities. When translating a program the physical educator must consider three areas: the educator's attitude and language; program planning and implementation of activities; and evaluation. Physical educators must provide a consistent message to all students that clearly avoids gender discrimination.

EDUCATOR'S ATTITUDE AND LANGUAGE

Numerous reports have consistently suggested that teachers demonstrate gender-differentiated attitudes and behavior patterns. This results in boys and girls being taught differently and being held to different expectations. Teachers may unknowingly reinforce gender-role stereotyping in their physical education classes as they provide different experiences for boys and girls (Ignico, 1989b). Such expectations can have potentially damaging effects on young students.

An educator's language can play a vital role in a child's perception of appropriate gender roles. The terms "he" and "man," although used with a gender-neutral intent, may be perceived as excluding females or assigning them lower status. If the pronouns "he" and "she" were truly analogous, being used only to distinguish sex, similar things could then be said regarding both males and females (Moulton and Korsmeyer, 1981). To acknowledge the dignity and unique attributes of each student, language used by physical educators must not assume or imply that certain activities and equipment are appropriate for one sex to the exclusion of the other. Expectations of gender differences are often verbally expressed by physical educators. To a young girl working on a skill a teacher might say, "That's okay, you tried hard; it is a hard skill," whereas a young boy might be told, "Don't worry, just concentrate and follow through; you'll get it" (Richardson, Albury, and Tandy, 1985). The two statements imply different expectations of achievement, setting the stage for differentiation of gender expectations.

In engineering an environment that gives all children equal opportunities to learn, physical educators must employ gender-neutral terminology applicable to students, people, athletes, players, or squad leaders. Statements such as "Squad leaders are responsible for posting their team rosters" rather than "Each leader is to post his team list" can be used to represent all class members. Such derogatory or exclusionary terms or phrases as sissy, tomboy, man-to-man defense, throwing like a girl, or girl's push-ups and boy's push-ups demean and discriminate against all children and send powerful messages that reinforce sexist expectations and behavior by both students and teachers. References to only one gender, exclusionary statements, and patronizing tones do not permit an egalitarian atmosphere. A gender-neutral physical education experience must be reinforced in language and attitudes that acknowledge contributions by both sexes.

PROGRAM PLANNING AND IMPLEMENTING ACTIVITIES

Differences in physical skill abilities prior to puberty are attributed to opportunity and cultural expectations rather than to any physical differences between the sexes. At the elementary level, it is vital for teachers to help all children develop an optimal level in a variety of skills and to avoid sexist stereotyping (Nichols, 1990). All children love to move, be involved, and have fun. Stigmatization, elimination, and rejection have no place in a gender-neutral physical education environment. Program planning by the physical educator should provide equal growth experiences for all participants. Even before skill development or movement activities begin, the physical educator should state clear, nonsexist expectations. For example, definitions of appropriate physical education attire for both boys and girls underscore and permit maximum participation by all students and set the tone for an androgynous curriculum (Ignico, 1989b).

Games and activities must provide equalization by offering all students the same opportunities to participate and grow. When choosing teams or grouping students for class activities, the physical educator should avoid division by sex and avoid allowing students to choose their own teams. Division of students may be accomplished by use of birth months, colors of clothing, stripes on socks, or eye color. For younger children, a game called Busy Bees may be enjoyed. Each student finds a partner and stands back to back. Each time "Busy Bees" is called, a new partner is found (Torbert, 1980). Older children can be grouped quickly by asking them to move into groups equal to the correct answer of a math problem given by the teacher. For group division, the physical educator can ask students to look at their hands. Those with palms up are in one group, palms down in another. Finally, physical education teachers can have students place one of their shoes in a pile in the center of the gym. The teacher then tosses randomly selected shoes to as many areas as groups are needed for class. Shoes found in each area will determine which children will be included in that group. Certainly, some activities will require specific group assignments; however, such assignments should not rely on sex as the criterion.

All too often team games and activities are labeled male and female appropriate and inappropriate. Similarly, creative and expressive activities are often perceived as only female appropriate. When teachers implement team games such as kickball and softball, both infield and outfield positions, including pitcher, should be equally shared by both boys and girls. A "boys" versus "girls" game should be avoided. Activities such as hopscotch and jump rope, often thought of as girls' activities, should be changed to coed activities. Coed tournaments can be held in which participation points toward fitness activity involvement are awarded. Housner (1981) advocated both teacher and peer modeling. Teachers can indicate by their modeling that all sports and physical activities are appropriate for both sexes. Reinforcing children who participate in nontraditional physical activities allows students to serve as valuable peer models.

Role modeling by male and female physical and classroom educators as well as students can be valuable and serve to reinforce gender-neutral ideas (Richardson, Albury, and Tandy, 1985; Ignico, 1989b).

In addition to changes in games and activities, a gender-neutral physical education curriculum might include a performance for students by male ballet dancers and a demonstration of basketball skills and techniques by members of a local high school or university women's basketball team. If live performances are not possible, videotapes or films can suffice. Physical educators can also display pictures of both male and female athletes in a wide variety of activities, stressing those often thought to be nontraditional for each sex (Ignico, 1989b). Through such events, children can come to appreciate a gender-neutral physical education environment.

EVALUATION

Children can learn who they are from interactions with significant peers, parents, and teachers. Periodically evaluating programs for gender bias and altering language, group division, activities, and presentations can help physical educators create an environment that maximizes personal achievement by both boys and girls. Such gender-neutral programs can eliminate stereotyping and help children feel confident in their physical endeavors.

Physical education classes should be fun and productive for all children. The need for children to see themselves positively means that any facet of a physical education program that diminishes a child's self-esteem must be re-evaluated and restructured to offer gender-neutral opportunities to learn skills and activities conducive to the physical and emotional growth of all children. Consistent, equitable modeling, program planning, and activity implementation on the part of the physical educator can ensure a smooth transition to a gender appropriate elementary physical education environment.

REFERENCES

Bandura, A. (1971). *Social Learning Theory*. New York: General Learning Press.
Bandura, A., and R. H. Walters (1963). *Social Learning and Personality Development*. New York: Holt, Rinehart and Winston.
Brawley, L., R. Powers, and K. Phillips (1980). Sex Bias in Evaluating Motor Activity: General or Task Specific Performance Expectancy? *Journal of Sport Psychology*, 2, 279-87.
Corbin, C. B., and C. Nix (1979). Sex-Typing of Physical Activities and Success Predictors of Children Before and After Cross-Sex Competition. *Journal of Sport Psychology*, 1, 43-52.
Greendorfer, S. L. (1980). Gender Differences in Physical Activity. *Motor Skills: Theory into Practice*, 4(2), 83-90.
——— (1983). Shaping the Female Athlete: The Impact of the Family. In M. Boutilier and L. San Giovanni, eds., *The Sporting Woman*. Champaign, Ill..: Human Kinetics.

Herkowitz, J. (1980). Social-Psychological Correlates to Motor Development. In C. Corbin, ed., *A Textbook of Motor Development*. 2nd ed. Dubuque, Iowa: William C. Brown.

Hoferek, M. J. (1982). Sex-Roles and Physical Activities: Evolving Trends. *Quest*, 34(1), 72-81.

Housner, L. D. (1981). Sex-Role Stereotyping: Implications for Teaching Elementary Physical Education. *Motor Skills: Theory into Practice*, 5(2), 107-16.

Huston, A. C. (1983). Sex-Typing. In P. H. Mussen, ed., *Handbook of Child Psychology*. 4th ed. New York: Wiley, 387-468.

Ignico, A. A. (1989a). Development and Verification of a Gender Role Stereotyping Index for Physical Activities. *Perceptual and Motor Skills*, 68, 1067-75.

——— (1989b). Elementary Physical Education: Color It Androgynous. *Journal of Health, Physical Education, Recreation and Dance*, 60(2), 23-24.

Jacklin, C. N., and E. L. Maccoby (1980). The Pinks and the Blues. Television program aired by KERA, Public Broadcasting Service, Dallas, Texas.

Katz, P. A. (1979). The Development of Female Identity. *Sex Roles*, 5, 155-78.

Katz, P. A., and J. Boswell (1986). Flexibility and Traditionality in Children's Gender Roles. *Genetic Social and General Psychology Monographs*, 112(1), 103-47.

Kohlberg, L. A. (1966). A Cognitive-Developmental Analysis of Children's Sex-Role Concepts and Attitudes. In E. E. Maccoby, ed., *The Development of Sex Differences*. Stanford, Calif.: Stanford University Press.

Lever, J. (1978). Sex Differences in the Complexity of Children's Play and Games. *American Sociological Review*, 43, 471-83.

Maccoby, E. E., and E. E. Jacklin (1974). *The Psychology of Sex Differences*. Stanford, Calif.: Stanford University Press.

Mischel, W. (1970). Sex-Typing and Socialization. In P. H. Mussen, ed., *Carmichael's Manual of Child Psychology*, Vol. 2. New York: Wiley.

Montemayer, R. (1974). Children's Performance in a Game and Their Attraction to It as a Function of Sex-typed Labels. *Child Development*, 45, 1152-56.

Moulton, J. and C. Korsmeyer (1981). The Myth of the Neutral Man: The Hidden Joke. Generic Uses of Masculine Terminology. In M. Vetterling-Braggin, ed., *Sexist Language: A Modern Philosophical Analysis*. Iotowa, N.J.: Rowman and Littlefield.

Nichols, B. (1990). *Moving and Learning*. St. Louis: Times Mirror/Mosby.

Oglesby, C. A. (1978). The Masculinity/Femininity Game. In C. A. Oglesby, ed., *Women and Sport: From Myth to Reality*. Philadelphia.: Lea and Febiger, 75-88.

Perry, D. G., and K. Bussey (1979). The Social Learning Theory of Sex Differences: Imitation is Alive and Well. *Journal of Personality and Social Psychology*, 37, 1699-1712.

Pitcher, E. G., and L. H. Schultz (1983). *Boys and Girls at Play: The Development of Sex Roles*. New York: Bergin and Garvey.

Richardson, P. A., K. W. Albury, and R. E. Tandy (1985). Mirror, Mirror on the Wall. *Journal of Health, Physical Education, Recreation and Dance*, August, 62-65.

Ruble, D. N. (1984). Sex-Role Development. In M. H. Bornstein and M. E. Lamb, eds., *Developmental Psychology: An Advanced Textbook*. Hillsdale, N.J.: Erlbaum, 325-71.

Sheldon, A. (1990). Kings are Royaler than Queens: Language and Socialization. *Young Children*, January, 4-8.

Thompson, S. K. (1975). Gender Labels and Early Sex Role Development. *Child Development*, 46, 339-47.

Thorne, B., C. Kramarae, and N. Henley, eds. (1983). *Language, Gender and Society.* Rowley, Mass.: Newberry House.

Torbert, M. (1980). *Follow Me: A Handbook of Movement Activities For Children.* New York: Prentice-Hall.

Part V

Fitness and Leisure through Games and Sport

Part V focuses on innovative physical fitness and leisure activities. Artie Kamiya gives examples of techniques teachers can use to keep students interested, and also describes favorite and newly developed partner and line dances to spark students' enthusiasm. Beth Goldin also recognizes that many teachers find it difficult to motivate elementary children to exercise. Her original games provide a stimulating means to promote health-related fitness. Mirabai Holland combines calisthenics with game activities within lessons emphasizing circuit training. Props such as hoops, elastic bands, and the parachute are used. Brenda Knitter increases the child's cardiovascular fitness through a continuous relay game called Catch-up. This activity is designed to accommodate sixty or more children using a circular formation. Paula Beach also finds the circle formation useful, serving as an effective way to organize students according to body size and height. Four circle games with differing levels of skill challenges are included.

William C. Payret presents a variety of stretch band activitives useful for increasing students' fitness level while they interact cooperatively with peers. Gerald J. Foley describes a progressive learn-to-swim program for children three years of age and older. Al Weidlein, using a simplified teaching progression, promotes golf activities as a fun and exciting challenge for seventh and eighth grade students, and Martin Joyce reveals how golf activities can be successfully used with physically impaired students. Louise Samaha McCormack and Lorence E. Moore propose several suggestions for teachers who want to teach gymnastic skills within the school setting. A progression of floor exercise skills is included. Seymour Lebenger covers several general principles for organizing activities in the recreation setting. An innovative leisure activity is presented.

A collection of field-tested games is included, beginning with David Oatman's chapter, which identifies vigorous as well as nonvigorous games. Darlene Bullock presents original manipulative skill games. Games created in several leading physical education teacher training programs add a new dimension. The volume concludes with Keith Gold's guidelines for purchasing equipment and supplies for school games.

47

Focusing on Fitness and Fun

Artie Kamiya

Teachers can use the following six activities to maintain student attention without destroying the "fun." A selection of creative line and partner dances for increased cardiovascular fitness is also included.

REFOCUS ACTIVITIES

Activity One: See This, Do This

Using your normal tone of voice say, "Children, if you can see this, . . . do this." Follow this request with a specific movement. Other examples include: "If you can see this, do this." (Movement: Pat yourself on the head.) "If you can see this, do this." (Movement: Put your finger over your lips.)

Activity Two: Knock, Knock

Using your normal tone of voice, say "Knock, knock!" The students who are listening would then say, "Who's there?" Repeat "Knock, knock!" until you have everyone's attention.

Activity Three: Clap to Quiet

Using your normal tone of voice, say "Everyone clap your hands" and quietly start to clap your hands. Continue doing this until all the students in class are clapping. Then say "Pat your knees" and direct the students to pat their knees. Then say "Rub your tummies" as you direct the group to rub their tummies. Now say "Fold your hands in place" as the students quietly fold their hands on their tummies.

Activity Four: Quiet Neighbors

Using your normal tone of voice, ask your students to see if there are any students near them who are listening closely or paying attention. Now ask them to raise their hand if there is a student next to them who is talking or not paying attention. If so, direct the quiet students to gently tap their noisy neighbor on the shoulder to remind them that it's time to be quiet.

Activity Five: Handshake Partners

This is a fast-moving icebreaker that can be used to direct the students through a series of partner challenges to interact and learn more about each other. To begin, the students are scattered throughout the activity area. The teacher asks individuals to find a partner and to perform a specific stunt (e.g., "Find a partner and shake hands"). The students are then asked to perform a high five with another partner. At this point the teacher challenges the group to use their short-term memory and try to find their orignal handshake partner. When they find their handshake partner, the partners shake hands. The teacher then proceeds to call out "high five partners!" The students will find their high five partners and do a high five. The activity continues with the students finding a third partner (low five partner). Other ideas for partners may include a "give-me-ten" partner, a "hug" partner, and a "smile" partner.

Activity Six: Leader's Change

The class is divided into groups of eight to ten students. Each group forms a large circle. One student from each circle is selected to be the leader at the start of the game. The leader moves to the middle of the circle. Music is selected that will set the tempo for the desired activity. Once the music begins, the leader is challenged to perform any activity that he or she desires, and the remaining students in the circle are challenged to imitate those actions.

On the command, "Ready—change," the leader returns to the circle. Each leader points to another student within the circle, and they change places. The new leader initiates a new activity. This process repeats itself until all students have participated or until the music stops.

Teaching Suggestions: Use music with a slower tempo for stretching, warm-up, or cool-down activity, and a faster tempo to encourage the students to be more active. Change leaders often, at least every fifteen seconds. Encourage students to do a different activity each time and not to copy the movements of their classmates.

LINE AND PARTNER DANCES

Level One

Amos Moses

(Select a country-western song from the recordings of Kenny Rogers or Juice Newton or others.)

Move the right heel forward and close.
Move the left heel forward and close.
Step forward with the right foot.
Step forward with the left foot and place behind the right foot.
Step forward with the right foot with a one fourth turn to the right.
Step with left foot closing beside the right foot.

Repeat sequence throughout the dance.

The Walk
(A nice record by Stevie Wonder works well!)

Step to the right with the right foot; touch left foot beside right foot.
Step to the left with the left foot; touch right foot beside left foot.
Walk forward with the right foot, left foot, then right foot, and make a one-fourth turn to the right; kick the left foot.
Walk backwards with the left foot, the right, the left, and the right.

Repeat sequence throughout the dance.

Grapevine
("How Will I Know" by Whitney Houston)

Use a grapevine step to the right (right, left, right, left).
Use a grapevine step to the left (left, right, left, right).
Step forward on the right foot and rock two times.
Step forward on the left foot and rock two times.
Make a one fourth turn to the left.

Repeat sequences throughout the dance.

The Freeze
("Ghost Busters" by Ray Parker, Jr.)

Use the grapevine step to the right and lift the left leg on the fourth beat (right, left, right, left).
Use the grapevine step to the left and lift the right leg on the fourth beat (left, right, left, right).
Walk backwards (right, left, right, left) and lift the left foot on the fourth beat.
Rock forward on the left foot and back on the right foot.
Make a one-fourth turn on the left foot and lift the right foot on the fourth beat.

Repeat sequence throughout the dance.

The Twelve Count Shuffle
("We Are Family" by Sister Sledge)

Step right to the side, close left.
Step left to the side, close right.
Step right forward.
Step left forward behind the right foot.
Step right forward with a one-fourth turn to the right.
Kick the left foot.
Step backward left, right, left, right.

Repeat sequence throughout the dance.

New York, New York
("New York, New York" by Frank Sinatra)

Step left to the side, kick right.
Step right to the side, kick left (repeat the two patterns twice).
Back up four steps: left, right, left, kick right foot.

Forward four steps: right, left, right, kick left foot.
Step left to the side (triple step: left, right, left).
Step right to the side (triple step: right, left, right) (repeat twice).
Take a four-step turn to the left: left, right, left, touch right.
Take a four-step turn to the right: right, left, right, touch left.

Repeat sequence throughout the dance.

Continental
("Break My Stride" by Matthew Wilder)

Grapevine right and left.
Take two steps forward right and left.
Do six kicks making a one-fourth turn to the right (R, L, R, L, R and cross in front of the
    left leg with the right and step on the right to side on sixth count).

Repeat sequence throughout the dance.

Salty Dog Rag

Take four step-hops forward (repeat these patterns once).
Go forward four steps and backward four steps (repeat).
Right heel forward and close.
Left heel forward and close.
Right heel forward and close.
Clap, clap, clap.

Repeat sequence throughout the dance.

Sweet Georgia Brown
(This is a partner dance using a double circle. The gentlemen are on the inside.
Select a blue grass tune.)

Walk forward four steps and face your partner (clockwise direction).
Back up four steps, forward four steps.
Two hand turn for four counts and couples walk forward four counts.
Right elbow turn for four counts, left elbow turn for four counts.
Each gentleman moves ahead to the next lady on four counts.

Repeat sequence throughout the dance.

L M Special
("Dancing on the Ceiling" by Lionel Richie)

Right arm out, palm down, point two times down on right side.
Left arm out, palm down, point two times down on left side.
Right arm out, palm up, point two times to right side.
Left arm out, palm up, point two times to left side.
Right thumb point two times over right shoulder (like hitch-hiking).
Left thumb point two times over left shoulder (like hitch-hiking).
Right hand point to left knee two times.
Left hand point to right knee two times.
Right hand slap left knee one time.
Left hand slap right knee one time.

Right hand slap right hip one time.
Left hand slap left hip one time.
Jump forward three times, jumping a one-fourth turn to the right.

Repeat sequence throughout the dance.

Popcorn
("Popcorn" by the musical group Hot Butter)

Use the grapevine step to the right (right, left, right, left).
Use the grapevine step to the left (left, right, left, right).
Step forward right and scoot, step forward and scoot on four counts.
Backup right, left, right and kick left.
Rock forward on left, doing two bounces.
Rock backward on right, doing two bounces.
Step left, right, left with a one-fourth turn to the left and lifting right.

Repeat sequence throughout the dance.

Level Two

Rise
("Rise" by Herb Alpert)

Step right, left, right, and touch left.
Step left, right, left and touch right (repeat sequence).

Step forward right, left, right, and hold for one count.
Step forward left, right, left, and hold for one count.

Step right sideways, and close left.
Step left sideways, and close right (repeat sequence).

Step backward right, left, right, and hold for one count.
Step backward left, right, left, and hold for one count.
Rock side to side, down four counts and up four counts.

Step on right forward, then one-fourth turn on left, counter-clockwise (four times).

Repeat sequence throughout the dance.

Bus Stop
("Celebration" by the musical group Kool and the Gang)

Walk back four steps, starting on the right foot (right, left, right, left).
Walk forward four steps, starting on the left foot (left, right, left, right—repeat sequence).
Use a grapevine step to the right and left.
Step right and touch or lift the left foot.
Step left and touch or lift the right foot.
Heels out and in.
Touch right toe forward (two times).
Touch right toe backward (two times).
Touch right forward, backward, sideways, cross and pivot one-fourth turn to left.

Repeat sequence throughout the dance.

Soul Walk
(Select a musical piece by the Pointer Sisters)

Step right to the side, close left, step right to the side and tap left.
Step left to the side, close right, step left to the side and tap right.
Tap right forward, tap right backward.
Step forward with a one-fourth turn right.
Tap left to the side and crossover right and step left.
Tap right to the side and crossover left and step right.
Step back on left.

Repeat sequence throughout the dance.

Hully Gully
("Invisible Touch" by Phil Collins)

Use the grapevine step to the right (right, left, right, left).
Use the grapevine step to the left (left, right, left, right).
Take two step-hops forward right and left.
Run forward right, left, right, kick left and pivot one-fourth turn right.
Back four (left, right, left, right).

Repeat sequence throughout the dance.

San Francisco Roller Coaster
("Billie Jean" by Michael Jackson)

Hustle right (right, left, right, left).
Hustle left (left, right, left, right) repeating the sequence with arms rolling up and down.
Step on right, kick left.
Step on left, kick right.
Step on right, kick left.
Step on left, full reverse turn, step on right.
Walk forward four steps (right, left, right, left).
Walk backward four steps (left, right, left, right).

Repeat sequence throughout the dance.

Level Three

There are two dances at Level Three. You can use most popular music and many country-western songs. "I Love a Rainy Night," "Louisiana Saturday Night," and "What Ever Happened to Old Fashioned Love?" are recommended.

Sidewinder

Heels out and together; do this twice.
Point the right foot to the side, behind, right, together; do this twice.
Point left foot side, behind, right, together; do this twice.
Right heel forward and together; do this twice.
Left heel forward and together; do this twice.

Right foot out, across the left knee, out, together.
Left foot out, across the right knee, out, together.
Step left foot forward and kick with the right.
Step right foot backward and kick with the left.
Step left foot forward and kick with the right.
Step right foot backward and kick with the left.
Left foot forward, make a one-fourth turn to the right, step behind the left with the right foot.
Step out to the left with the left foot and make a half-turn to the left, and then bring the right foot together with the left, with a stomp!

Repeat sequence throughout the dance.

Schwarzenegger Shuffle
("Jailhouse Rock" by Elvis Presley)

These activities are other ways to promote the idea of walking as a cardiovascular fitness exercise. Challenge the students to think of four different poses or balances that they will have an easy time remembering. For example:

1. Standing on the right foot
2. Flexing both arms as in a body building contest
3. Hands on hips
4. Kneeling on one knee

The students will practice their poses in sequence several times. Put on the record "Jailhouse Rock." There are four distinct phrases before the chorus "Let's rock" begins. Cue your students to perform and hold their four poses in order during the four distinct phrases. When the words "Let's rock" are played, the students will walk to the beat of the record around the room. As the record continues, you will be holding the four poses again and walking about the room when "Let's rock" is played. This will occur four times during the record. Halfway through the record, there is an instrumental "bridge" where the students can be directed to jump rope with an imaginary rope, or do ski hops from side to side. After this activity, remind them that while weight training develops muscular strength, they need to include aerobic fitness activities (like walking) to develop a lifetime of cardiovascular fitness.

Teaching Suggestions: Use a slower tempo music for stretching, warm-up, or cool-down activity, a faster tempo to encourage students to be more active.

48

Games that Are Fit to Be Tried

Beth Goldin

One of the most important goals of any effective physical education program is to promote the development of lifetime fitness. When children are told that they will be performing fitness exercises, however, many of them respond unfavorably. The response is very different when they are told that they will be playing a game. The seven fitness games described here are intended for the teacher who consistently seeks creative activities to motivate students to participate in the components of health-related fitness.

Name of the Game: Fitness Bonanza
Suggested Grade Level: 3-8
Equipment Required: Nerf or foam balls; cones; record, cassette, or compact disc player
Starting Formation: Students moving throughout general space
Description: The rules of this game are similar to those of dodgeball. That is, if a student is hit with the ball no higher than the chest, he or she will go to the "Fitness Center" (i.e., a designated area where the children can safely perform an exercise without interruption) and perform an exercise assigned by the teacher in order to return to the game. If a thrown ball is caught on the fly, the student who threw the ball must go to the Fitness Center to perform the exercise. Use one ball for every five students.
Variations:

1. Use balls of the same color, except for one of a different color known as the "exercise ball." If a student is hit with the exercise ball, he or she must go to the Fitness Center and perform an exercise. If the student is hit with a ball other than the exercise ball, he or she is out until the student who caused the out is hit by either the exercise ball or another ball.
2. Use two types of balls, designating one type as the exercise ball. With this variation, the teacher can use just one or several exercise balls.
3. At any time during the game, the teacher can say "Everybody back in," to allow all students to return to the activity.

4. Students can elect to do their favorite exercise at the Fitness Center.
5. Use different color balls and designate one exercise for each color.

Name of the Game: Fitness Hot Potato
Suggested Grade Level: 3-8
Equipment Required: Record, cassette, or compact disc player; beanbags and cones
Starting Formation: Students form circles of six or more
Description: Each circle is given a beanbag to be passed (not thrown) while the music plays. When the music stops, the student holding the beanbag steps out of the circle to the Fitness Center to perform a designated exercise. The game continues, and the student may return to the circle after completing the exercise. If the beanbag is dropped, the entire circle of students performs the exercise.
Variations:

1. More than one beanbag can be used if the circles are large.
2. The teacher can change the direction the beanbag is moving with either a verbal cue or a whistle.
3. Use different color beanbags and assign a specific exercise to each color.

Name of the Game: Watch Your Back
Suggested Grade Level: 3-8
Equipment Required: Record, cassette, or compact disc player; self-sticking labels; pencils or pens
Starting Formation: Students moving throughout general space
Description: Before play begins, each child is given an exercise description (e.g., fifteen jumping jacks) that has been written on a self-sticking label. This is placed on his or her back. The teacher selects two students to be the chasers. The remaining students move throughout general space. When a student is tagged, the chaser reads the exercise on the student's back, which is to be performed at the Fitness Center. Students who are tagged should jog to the Fitness Center, perform the exercise, and return to the game. The teacher should change the students doing the tagging frequently.

Name of the Game: Exercise Marks The Spot
Suggested Grade Level: 2-6
Equipment Required: Rubber spots or cones; record, cassette, or compact disc player
Starting Formation: Each student stands on a spot.
Description: The teacher prepares the same number of exercise descriptions (i.e., the name of an exercise on a small slip of paper) as there are students in the class. Round, plastic movement spots are scattered throughout the playing area, each concealing an exercise description. The spots should be far enough apart to allow the students to perform an exercise efficiently and safely. Students move in general space to music. When the music stops, they jog to a spot, and the teacher asks them to read the exercise description underneath their spot. Following this, the teacher gives the signal for a thirty-second exercise session to begin. At the

end of the thirty seconds, the teacher turns on the music and the students continue to move in general space. If possible, only one student should go to each spot, and not return there until he or she has moved to all of the spots on the floor.
Variation: Change the locomotor movements each time the music begins.

Name of the Game: Scarf-a-stenics
Suggested Grade Level: 3-6
Equipment Required: Juggling scarves; record, cassette, or compact disc player
Starting Formation: Students work in personal space while holding a scarf.
Description: In this game the teacher asks the students to toss the scarf, perform an exercise as many times as possible, and catch the scarf before it falls to the floor (e.g., "Can you toss the scarf, perform jumping jacks, and catch the scarf before it falls to the floor?" or "Who can toss the scarf, perform a squat thrust, and catch the scarf before it falls to the floor?"). Suggested exercises include jumps, hops, and side bends while holding the scarf.
Variations:

1. Ask the students to hold the scarf with one or both hands and perform stretches. This can be used as a cool-down after an activity.
2. Ask the students to hold the scarf and move in general space. Change the locomotor movements frequently.

Name of the Game: Copy Machine
Suggested Grade Level: K-4
Equipment Required: Record, cassette, or compact disc player
Starting Formation: Students work with a partner in personal or general space.
Description: One student will be the leader and perform an exercise or loco-motor movement. His or her partner copies the leader's movements, exercise, or locomotor skill. The teacher should signal the change of leaders by using a whistle or by stopping the music.
Variations:

1. Leaders should be encouraged to change the exercise every thirty seconds.
2. There can be more than one student who copies the leader.
3. The teacher selects the type of exercise that the leader should do (e.g., "The leader should perform a type of jumping exercise" or "The leader should perform a locomotor movement in general space").

Name of the Game: Exercise Match Game
Suggested Grade Level: 1-4
Equipment Required: Large hat; record, cassette, or compact disc player; paper; pencils or pens
Starting Formation: From a large hat or container, students take a piece of paper that identifies a specific exercise. They are then challenged to find their "match" or "matches" (i.e., the student or students who have the same infor-mation on their slip of paper) and find a space in the gymnasium where they can perform the movement. At this point, the students fold their papers and return them to the hat. When working with large groups, use several hats to avoid

waiting in line, or have the students jog in place while waiting to pick from the hat. The students can also perform two or three running laps together using a specific locomotor movement instead of performing an exercise.

49

Fitness Circuits for Fun

Mirabai Holland

Circuit training is an exciting way to introduce fitness concepts in a constantly changing and noncompetitive atmosphere. The two programs described here combine the principles of circuit training with noncompetitive games. Program One is designed for five- to seven-year-old children, and Program Two is developmentally appropriate for children eight through eleven years of age. Depending on the number of children in the class, each circuit has six to twelve stations addressing different components of physical fitness, including, among others, cardiovascular fitness, muscle endurance, flexibility, agility, and eye-hand coordination.

Each program begins with an active warm-up to get the core body temperature elevated, followed by several static stretches to prepare the body for the activity to come. Then the class session continues with a circuit program alternating with noncompetitive activity games. A class is completed with a cool-down activity to bring the heart rate to a normal resting level.

FITNESS PROGRAM ONE FOR FIVE TO SEVEN YEARS OF AGE

Balloon Warm-Up (5 Minutes)

Each child is given a balloon and is asked to walk slowly around the room, tapping or kicking it into the air, while music is played. When the music stops, the children freeze and catch or retrieve their balloon. The teacher can change the locomotor skills to jumping, hopping, or running. Each time the music stops the children touch the balloon to a different body part.

Stretching exercises include challenging the children to make their bodies as long as possible while reaching to touch the ceiling, or to make different body parts larger or smaller, or longer or wider.

Suggested Stations (30 Seconds at Each Station)

Repeat twice with an interval of parachute activity in between the first and second trial of the circuit.

1. Knee lifts
2. Jumping in and out of a hula hoop placed on the floor
3. Jumping jacks
4. Toe touches
5. Mountain climbers
6. Pretending to row a boat with the arms
7. Aerobic twists at the waist
8. Arm circles

Parachute Games: Merry-Go Round (5 Minutes)

Children hold onto the parachute in a circle while moving around and performing different locomotor movements such as walking, hopping, jogging, jumping, and running. Place two or three lightweight rubber balls in the middle of the chute and try to get them to bounce or to move around the chute in a merry-go-round fashion.

Cool-Down: Tight and Loose (3 Minutes)

Children can be sitting or lying down. Have them tighten or "squeeze" different body parts. Hold for a few seconds and then relax the tension.

FITNESS PROGRAM TWO: EIGHT TO ELEVEN YEARS OF AGE

Balloon Warm-Up (5 Minutes)

The children are challenged to perform different locomotor movements while keeping the balloon up in the air, and then quickly freezing into a balance on one body part. They should also be challenged to balance on two or three body parts. Other extensions include moving the balloon with the feet, elbows, nose, or head.

Partner Stretch (3 Minutes)

Individuals face a partner with their palms pressing against each other. On the teacher's signal they can stretch their legs and arms while helping to support and mirroring each other.

Suggested Stations (45 Seconds at Each Station)

Repeat the activities twice with an interval of Hoop Works between the first and second trial of the circuit.

1. Jumping jacks
2. Sit-ups
3. Crunches

4. Step ups
5. Agility run between two points
6. Jump rope
7. Dynaband resistance exercise
8. Push-ups

Hoop Works (5 Minutes)

The children are challenged to perform aerobic dance exercises while using a hula hoop to offer upper body resistance, agility, and balance.

Variation Activity: Rock, Scissors, and Paper (10 Minutes)

In this game, rock smashes scissors, scissors cuts paper, and paper covers rock. The class is divided into two teams with a center line between them. Each side has a designated spot. The teacher asks each group to form a huddle and secretly choose rock, scissors, or paper. When each group has decided and gives the thumbs-up signal, the teacher says "go" and each team puts their hands up in one of the following signals: a fist (for rock), a V (for scissors), or a palm with fingers pointing straight up (for paper). For instance, if one side chooses paper and the other side chooses rock, since paper covers rock, the paper crosses over to the rock side to tag as many of the rocks as possible before they get to their safe boundary spot. All the tagged players cross the line and are added to the winning side. Then the teams play another round, again deciding secretly to be rock, paper, or scissors. The object of this game is to try to get everyone on the same team.

Cool-Down: Stretching with a Dynaband (5 Minutes)

The children can use a dynaband or a bicycle inner tube to stretch different body parts. For example, they may stretch the band overhead and stretch to one side. Or they may lie down on the back and lift one foot to the ceiling with the band stretched across the sole of the foot and hold it for ten seconds. The children should be reminded to inhale and exhale while stretching the band.

REFERENCES

Brehm, Madeleine, and T. Tindell (1983). *Nancy Movement with a Purpose*. West Nyack, N.Y.: Parker.

Curtis, Sandra R. (1982). *The Joy of Movement in Early Childhood*. New York: Teachers College Press.

Hendricks, Gay, and Kathlyn Hendricks (1983). *The Moving Center: Exploring Movement*. Englewood Cliffs, N.J.: Prentice Hall.

Kirchner Glenn, Jean Cunningham, and Eileen Warrell (1970). *Introduction to Movement Education*. Dubuque, Iowa.: William C. Brown.

Kotnour, Mary (1990). *Physical Fitness Games and Activities Kit*. West Nyack, N.Y.: Parker.

Moore, Jane B. (1979). *Movement Education for Young Children*. Nashville, Tenn.: Broadman Press.

Orlick, Terry (1978). *The Cooperative Sports and Games Book*. New York: Pantheon.

Pangrazi, R., and V. Dauer (1981). *Movement in Early Childhood and Primary Education*. Minneapolis: Burgess.

Thomas, Jerry R., Amelia M. Lee, and Katherine T. Thomas (1981). *Physical Education for Children*. Champaign, Ill.: Human Kinetics Books.

Wheeler, Keg, and Otto H. Spilker (1991). *Physical Education Curriculum Activities Kit for Grades K-6*. West Nyack, N.Y.: Parker.

50

Catch-Up

Brenda Knitter

This chapter describes a continuous relay game called Catch-Up, which was initially introduced to me by a very creative elementary school principal. The activity can accommodate large numbers of students and actually works best with at least sixty students. Students are actively involved for an extended period of time.

Name of the Game: Catch-Up
Equipment Required: Four to eight cones, a whistle, four relay batons or rubber quoits, and pinnies for half of the students
Space Required: A 50-foot by 85-foot running space
Description of the Game: This running game begins with the students seated on the floor with their legs crossed, behind a cone (see Figure 50.1). In this formation, Team A will try to catch Team B, while Team C tries to catch Team D, and vice versa. They must run between the two cones, or outside if there is only one.

On the teacher's signal, the first runner for each team runs one lap around the cones and hands a relay baton to the next runner. After the handoff, the runner goes to the end of his or her line. Runners from all teams continue in this manner until the runner from one team catches up to another, legally passing him or her, and is clearly ahead.

When this pass has been made, the two teams involved are given a hand signal to stop. The two runners return to the beginning of their respective lines, and the teams are started again by a hand signal. The other two teams continue to compete as the first are stopped and restarted. If the whistle is sounded, all four teams stop.

The game is continued for twenty to thirty minutes. Teachers may find that it requires more time than usual to introduce the game to the group. Thus, some teachers have extended the game for two class periods, because the additional session allows students to receive more turns and develop a better feeling for the game.

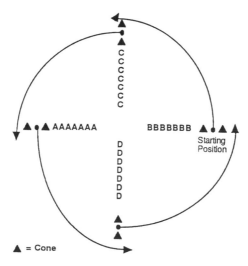

FIGURE 50.1: Catch-Up

TEACHING SUGGESTIONS

Several errors are commonly made during this large-scale game. Use them as "teachable moments" to reinforce safety rules.

The runner goes inside the cones on the handoff: The inner cone is the waiting line for runners. These students are all sitting cross-legged. Encourage students to keep moving their line toward the cone as consecutive runners take off. In this manner, no one can run through their space.

The passing person goes on the wrong side: The inside lane, the area near the inner cone, is reserved for the handoff team. If a runner is about to pass someone, he or she must do it on the outside. A runner should never pass on the inside of another runner. Teachers can award a point to the other team if the passing team goes on the wrong side, especially if the safety lecture has already been given on this rule.

The baton is dropped, resulting in a pass by the other team: Instruction can include how a student should get in a ready position for the handoff, keep the eyes on the baton, and not start running until the baton is in the hand. Remind students performing the handoff to complete their responsibility before moving to the end of the line. Remind students not to be critical of the person who dropped the baton. Accidents do happen.

The student hands off and turns to the right instead of the left: The student who hands the baton to the next runner should always go directly to the inside area, and to the end of his or her team's line. If the player goes to the right, he or she could move into the path of any runners nearby. This could be dangerous, and the student involved should be corrected immediately. This point should also be addressed when all four teams have stopped.

The value of a time-out: A time-out in the middle of the game is essential, not only to give students a rest, but also to assess the game's progress and to give praise.

51

Circle Games for Large and Small Groups

Paula Beach

Circle games have maintained their popularity since the early colonial period. The circle formation can accommodate large or small groups and is adaptable for kindergarten through eighth grade and can be used for effective class management. The game activity and the game's results are visible to all team players. Team players can be encouraged to cheer on their classmates, and an unlimited variety of games can be played using the circle formation (e.g., circle games, relays, and cooperative games).

The following four circle games are played by students moving around the perimeter of the circle or by players moving within the circle.

Space Required: A forty-square-foot game area that contains a circle thirty feet in diameter, within which is a ten-square-foot area. Each team designated by color (green, blue, red, or yellow) occupies one-fourth of the circle and a forty-foot square, as shown on the game circle formation (see Figure 51.1). Team color pins are five feet from the inner edge of circle and inner square.

General Guidelines for Participation:

1. Four teams of any number are arranged on the designated sides of the square.
2. For single-player contests around the game circle, players start on their color starting line (see figure) and perform the designated activity around the game circle in a counterclockwise direction, around their eighteen-inch line, and into the circle to pick up their color pin, which designates the end of the game.
3. For two-, three-, or four-player contests around the game circle, Player 1 starts on his or her color starting line; Players 2 and 3 wait within circle near the eighteen-inch passing line (see figure). As Player 1 rounds the circle in a counterclockwise direction, Player 2 enters the running lane for a pass of the beanbag (or a ring, ball, baton, or hoop) from Player 1 and moves around the circle, passing it to Player 3, who runs around the circle and around his or her eighteen-inch passing line, and into the circle for the team color pin, thus ending the game. Having passed the beanbag or other object, the student moves directly to the end of the team line, on the forty-foot square.

4. All players perform designated activities around and within the game circle unless going in for a color pin. Direction may be counterclockwise or clockwise.
5. Teams should be organized according to body size and height.

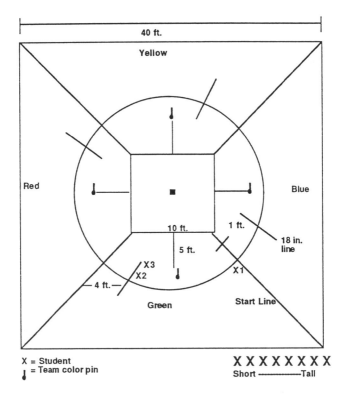

FIGURE 51.1: Game Circle Formation

Assigning Teams: Teachers have several options in selecting students for teams. The following three techniques are suggested.

1. Arrange all players according to height on the line, from the tallest to the shortest. Start at either end and assign the first four of the tallest or shortest students to four separate teams (i.e., green, blue, yellow, or red team) and continue to assign to the four teams. Make any necessary changes to equalize ability levels on teams.
2. Ask the students to form groups of four players of the same height and ability. The students assign each of the four individuals to a different color team line. Ask the students to do this within a time limit to encourage cooperative learning.
3. Ask the students to form four spokes of a bike tire with an equal number of players on each spoke radiating from the hub, with the tallest and the smallest near the rim. Assign the spokes to a color team line.

Note: The teacher has the right to exchange players at any time to equalize competition. "Floating" players may be designated by the teacher for that purpose.

GAMES AROUND THE GAME CIRCLE

Name of the Game: The Great Chase Relay
Players: Three per heat, with four teams
Equipment Required: Beanbags, baton, or balls
Space Required: Game Circle
Description: Player 1 begins on a color starting line, Players 2 and 3 begin inside the circle, near the eighteen-inch passing line (see figure). On the signal, Player 1 runs around the circle; as he or she nears the eighteen-inch passing line, Player 2 enters the running lane for a handoff, receives the beanbag, runs around the circle, and then hands it to Player 3, who runs around the circle, around the eighteen-inch line, and then into the circle for the team's color pin. The other team members standing on the team line call out their color when Player 3 grabs the pin. This designates the order of finish.

After the handoff, Players 1 and 2 go immediately to the end of the team line on the larger square. The object of the game is to get to the color pin first.

Name of the Game: Knock Down
Players: One or two players, four teams
Equipment Required: Plastic bottle, colored beanbags
Space Required: Game Circle
Description: Player 1 begins at his or her color starting line. On a signal, that person runs around the circle holding a beanbag and returns to the starting line. Standing behind the circle line and on the starting line, Player 1 throws the beanbag, trying to hit and knock down the plastic bottle which has been placed in the center of the circle. If Player 1 misses, he or she runs into the circle to retrieve the beanbag and returns to the starting line to throw again until successful. Play continues until a team player knocks down the bottle.
Variation: Limit the number of throws. Use two players, both of whom run together around circle, one throwing and the other retrieving, alternating responsibilities.

GAMES WITHIN THE GAME CIRCLE

Name of the Game: Four Way Tug
Players: Two per team, four teams
Equipment Required: Four-way tug rope, colored beanbags
Space Required: Game Circle and the inside square
Description: Two players from each team take hold of the four-way tug rope, using an overhand grip. Each player starts with one foot all the way to the center of the circle on the box. One beanbag is placed on the diagonal line one foot from the inside square corner. At the signal, all players pull the rope toward the beanbag on their team's diagonal line. The object is to pick up their team

beanbag while keeping one hand securely on the rope in order to score points for their team. While holding the rope, players may use their feet to draw the beanbag closer. The teacher may place the beanbag closer depending on the size and strength of players.

Name of the Game: Balloon Volley
Players: Two players per team, four teams
Equipment Required: One balloon
Space Required: Entire square
Description: Two players from each team stand in the center square. At a given signal, the balloon is tossed into the air at this center. Using the hands only, the players attempt to hit the balloon toward their own team's line. Play continues until the balloon crosses a team line. Kicking the balloon, roughness, pushing, and shoving are not allowed.

52

Mr. Rubberband:
Game Themes that Develop Fitness

William C. Payret

Teachers can become frustrated when searching for activities to increase the young child's level of physical fitness. Mr. Rubberband activities were developed to motivate young children to work together and become more physically fit. The program uses a large rubber circular cord fifteen to twenty feet in diameter. The activities are beneficial for both disabled and nondisabled children.

SAFETY CONSIDERATIONS FOR TEACHING GAMES AND FITNESS

Teachers should reinforce the need to have a firm grasp on Mr. Rubberband. All students should be evenly spaced while holding onto the cord. Teach a variety of games incorporating movement and fitness activities, and stress full range of movement. To help stimulate active participation, play music that has a lively tempo and beat. To help motivate the students, always participate in the activities, and assist them if they have difficulty using Mr. Rubberband. Use positive reinforcement and maintain a positive attitude during each activity.

EXAMPLES OF TEACHING DRAMATIC PLAY

Mr. Rubberband is very effective with preschool through first grade children. The object becomes a fictional character, enabling children to have fun, play games, and develop muscular tone. These are critical objectives for the young child's well-being. Here are some examples of dramatic play activities.

Activity: Rowing a boat in a lake or taking an exploratory trip down a river while looking for gold and lost treasure

The children pretend to row upstream against the current, with a change of tempo, from fast to slower rowing. These movements help to develop muscular strength and endurance in the shoulders and arms. The children may sit or stand while holding onto Mr. Rubberband and singing "Row, row, row, your boat gently down the stream." This rhyme enables children to perform the motion of rowing.

After the class "finds" the treasure, they can use Mr. Rubberband as a rope to pull the gold to shore.

Activity: Working on a Farm

This function lets children perform many of the activities associated with farming. Encourage the children to describe the farmer's daily routine and chores. The students begin to play act farm activities by using Mr. Rubberband. For example, demonstrate how the farmer plants crops by having the students bend their knees slightly, so that Mr. Rubberband becomes a hoe. Mr. Rubberband can also become the reins of the horse. This can be done while the children are galloping around the activity area steering and stopping with Mr. Rubberband.

Activity: Blast Off!

This involves an imaginary trip to the moon while students stand in a circle holding onto Mr. Rubberband. As the class counts backward from ten, the students should bend their knees, lifting Mr. Rubberband above their heads.

Activity: Pump It Up!

This involves having the children hold onto Mr. Rubberband at the waist. The knees should be slightly bent. The children pretend to inflate a tire by pushing the cord down to the floor and bringing it back up to their hips. Motivation is heightened by varying the tempo from fast to medium to slow.

Activity: Pedaling the Big Wheel

Ask the students to hold onto Mr. Rubberband with their hands extended outward. Alternate circling the arms while holding onto Mr. Rubberband. Explain that the faster they turn the wheel, the more distance they can travel. Add variation to the exercise by circling the arms backwards, forwards, and at different speeds.

Activity: Choo Choo the Train

Have the children use their bodies to be a train. All children form a single line inside the circle of Mr. Rubberband, while the teacher discusses the different parts of the train. The engine of the train pulls the boxcars and caboose along the tracks. The boxcars carry different types of animals and produce to the marketplace. The little caboose at the end of the train holds the train together. To start the activity, the teacher should take the lead position as the engine. The children are inside the circle in a single line. Mr. Rubberband is extended lengthwise so that the children can easily hold on with both hands at their sides. When the choo! choo! signal is given by the engine, the train moves forward. The children pump their arms and legs back and forth while holding onto Mr. Rubberband. When the train whistle blows, the children lift Mr. Rubberband above their heads with both hands. Include a movement theme of traveling to different parts of the town by using posters of different areas of the city. For example, the zoo, circus, supermarket, deli, and bakery can all be represented by posters or signs describing these areas.

Activity: Bouncing Ball

This activity involves the children in a circle holding onto Mr. Rubberband at their hips. The teacher explains that they are going to pretend they are bouncing balls. Fast and slow music is played. When the music starts, the children begin to jump up, while holding onto Mr. Rubberband with two hands. As the tempo is increased the children begin to jump faster and higher. If music is not available, a drum can be used to play lively beats.

Activity: Crossing the Swamp

This encourages the child to imagine a swamp between two parallel lines approximately two feet apart. Mr. Rubberband is used to make the boundary lines. The children are challenged to jump over Mr. Rubberband without landing in the swamp. Other creative types of locomotor movements can be incorporated. After the activity is completed, the children can begin rowing their way out of the swamp by using Mr. Rubberband.

EXPLORATORY MOVEMENT WITH MR. RUBBERBAND

Movement education is very important for young children. It helps them to develop body awareness and increases self-esteem. The following examples demonstrate this process, as the children grip Mr. Rubberband while standing in a circle.

1. Show me how fast you can shake Mr. Rubberband.
2. Show me how slowly you can shake Mr. Rubberband.
3. How far can you stretch Mr. Rubberband toward your feet?
4. How high can you lift Mr. Rubberband with one hand?
5. What ways can you stretch Mr. Rubberband with both hands?
6. Is it possible to stretch Mr. Rubberband across your chest?
7. Can you jump while holding Mr. Rubberband?
8. How many ways can you hold onto Mr. Rubberband behind your back?
9. See how many different shapes you can create with Mr. Rubberband.
10. Place Mr. Rubberband on the floor, and see how many ways you can jump over him.

Identification of Body Parts

The teacher can also play a body part identification activity with Mr. Rubberband. To begin, have the children hold onto Mr. Rubberband at their hips in a circle. Challenge the children to do the following:

1. Touch your legs with Mr. Rubberband.
2. Touch your knees with Mr. Rubberband.
3. Touch your toes with Mr. Rubberband.
4. Touch your hips with Mr. Rubberband.
5. Touch your stomach with Mr. Rubberband.
6. Touch your chest with Mr. Rubberband.
7. Touch your ankles with Mr. Rubberband.
8. Touch your nose with Mr. Rubberband.

9. Touch your hair with Mr. Rubberband.
10. Touch your chin with Mr. Rubberband.

A variation of the body game is to identify the different body parts by having the students sing a children's melody. For example: "This is the way we touch our hips, touch our hips, touch our hips so early in the morning." "This is the way we touch our stomach so early in the morning." This melody could be continued until all body parts are touched. The body game is an excellent activity for introducing gross motor movements while bending and stretching. It can also serve to prepare the body for vigorous activities during the course of the lesson.

Using Mr. Rubberband in the Swimming Pool

Mr. Rubberband is an excellent teaching tool for students with limited swimming abilities. The following activities can be implemented with the use of Mr. Rubberband.

Begin the lesson with Mr. Rubberband in the shallow end of the pool so that every child can stand in a circle comfortably. Have the children stretch their arms forward in front of the body as they blow bubbles in the water. **Blowing Bubbles** is a very important water adjustment skill and a way to practice breathing skills. **Cork Bobbing** involves all children holding Mr. Rubberband above the head in a circle. On the teacher's signal everyone begins to bob up and down in the water (i.e., by putting the face and lips under the water). **Row, Row, Row Your Boat Gently Down the Stream** asks the children to hold onto Mr. Rubberband with their hands extended in front of them. As the children sing the melody, "Row, Row, Row Your Boat Gently Down the Stream," they coordinate the arm movements of rowing a boat by using Mr. Rubberband as the oars. In **Rocketship** the boys and girls hold Mr. Rubberband at their hips. When the teacher counts 10, 9, 8, 7, 6, 5, 4, 3, and 2, the children bend their knees and sink down into the water. When the teacher says "1 . . . blastoff," they spring up, stretching Mr. Rubberband above their heads. In **Ring Around the Merry-Go-Round** the children hold onto Mr. Rubberband while facing sideways, so that each child is looking at the next person's back. The teacher explains to the students that they are going to make believe they are big whales bobbing up and down while moving around the merry-go-round. After two trials, the children select another sea creature and pretend to be it. Examples include dolphins, tuna, starfish, blowfish, and sharks. Other merry-go-round activities include singing the melody "Ring Around the Rosey" while holding Mr. Rubberband.

In **The Treasure Hunt**, the children hold onto Mr. Rubberband in a circle. The teacher tosses red golf balls or painted lightweight rocks to the middle of the circle and then selects two or three students to locate and retrieve as many pieces of treasure as possible. The recovered treasure is then thrown back to the center and the activity is repeated. The rest of the students hold Mr. Rubberband on the outside of the circle while bobbing up and down.

Fitness Exercises with Mr. Rubberband

Sherrill (1981) and Winnick and Short (1985) have shown that the muscular strength and endurance of the disabled individual are far below the average standard for physically capable individuals. One reason is that there are too few exercise programs geared to meet the challenges of the disabled. McGinnis (1987) has also reported that many elementary school children are not physically fit. A need exists for more community based fitness programs. Fitness activities incorporating Mr. Rubberband exercises can be used in community programs or in physical education classes by implementing the following activities.

Stretching Exercises

Shoulder and Arm Stretch: To develop flexibility in the arms, wrist, and shoulder girdle, Mr. Rubberband is lifted high above the head with two hands and held for a slow count of twenty to thirty seconds (see Figure 52.1).

Sit and Reach Stretch: To develop flexibility in the hamstring muscle groups and the lower back, the children keep the knees straight and the feet together while sitting on the floor. They then bend forward and reach for the toes using Mr. Rubberband. A modification of this exercise is to straddle the legs in a V split, stretching to the left foot and then to the right foot (see Figure 52.2).

Waist Bend Stretch: To develop flexibility in the lower back, upper back, shoulders, arms, and elbows while grasping Mr. Rubberband, the child stands with the feet astride and the hands fully extended. The upper trunk is bent forward with the knees bent slightly. The tension of the stretch cord stretches the back and arms (see Figure 52.3).

Muscular Fitness Exercises

Bent Arm Rowing: To develop the muscles of the arms, the biceps, triceps, and shoulder muscles, the child may sit on the floor with the arms fully extended. As soon as the arms are fully extended, Mr. Rubberband is pulled toward the chest. This movement is repeated for a set of fifteen to twenty times in a continuous motion. A modification of this exercise can be done while standing (see Figure 52.4).

Shoulder Press: To develop the deltoid muscles and triceps, the children can stand with the feet astride while grasping Mr. Rubberband at the chest level. The stretch cord is extended above the head and the action is repeated ten to twenty times (see Figure 52.5). One modification of this exercise includes the behind the back shoulder press. The child grasps Mr. Rubberband behind the back at shoulder level, then extends the stretch cord above the head ten to twenty times.

Double Arm Lifts and Single Leg Kicks: To develop the muscular fitness of arms, shoulder girdle, quadriceps, and hip flexor muscles, the child grabs Mr. Rubberband with two hands, stands with his or her feet astride, and lifts the cord above the head. This is performed while kicking one foot up (see Figure 52.6). This action is repeated on the left and right sides.

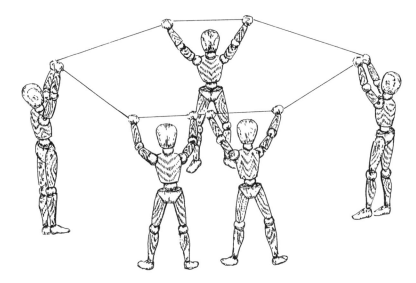

FIGURE 52.1: Shoulder And Arm Stretch

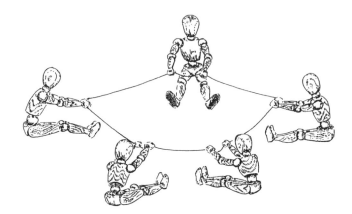

FIGURE 52.2: Sit And Reach Stretch

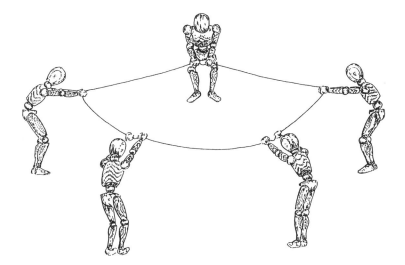

FIGURE 52.3: Waist Bend Stretch

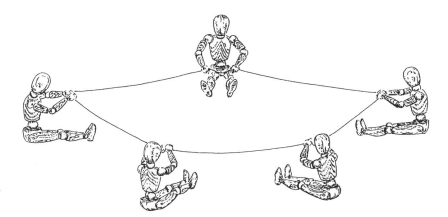

FIGURE 52.4: Bent Arm Rowing

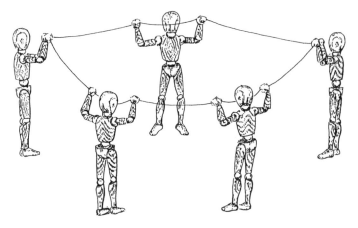

FIGURE 52.5: Shoulder Press

**FIGURE 52.6: Double Arm Lifts And Single
Leg Kicks**

Sit-Up: To develop abdominal muscles, the children should be seated on a mat or carpet square with their knees flexed. They grasp Mr. Rubberband with both hands approximately shoulder width apart and perform a series of sit-ups by lowering the body to the floor on their back and raising the body to the sitting position (see Figure 52.7). They should repeat this motion twenty times. A variation of this exercise is to add a right and left twist to the sit-up. This develops the oblique abdominal muscles.

Upright Rowing: To develop the deltoids, trapezius, and biceps muscles, the child stands and faces forward. Arms are shoulder width apart and extended downward while holding onto the stretch cord. Here the child pulls the stretch cord upward, nearly touching it under the chin. He or she holds for a count of two seconds before returning to the starting position (see Figure 52.8). Repeat the exercise slowly.

Regular Arm Curls: To develop the muscles of the biceps and forearms, have the child stand with the feet astride and grasp Mr. Rubberband with the palms up. The elbows are bent forward while bringing the stretch cord up to the shoulder. The child slowly lowers the arms to a starting position and repeats the exercise (see Figure 52.9).

Reverse Curls: To develop the muscles of the forearms, hands, and wrists, the child stands with feet astride and grasps the stretch cord with palms down. The arms are extended with the forearms bent forward (i.e., bending at the elbows). The stretch cord is brought forward toward the shoulders. The child slowly lowers the arms to the starting position and repeats the exercise. It is important to keep the body straight when performing the exercise (see Figure 52.10).

Sidebends: To develop the lateral muscles of the hips, the child stands sideways with the cord, bends all the way to the right, and then stands tall. The action is repeated on the other side (see Figure 52.11).

CARDIOVASCULAR EXERCISE WITH MR. RUBBERBAND

The development of the heart and the vascular system is an important component of the fitness program for the child's total well-being. Fox and Mathews (1981) have shown that when the cardiovascular system is healthy and strong, individuals have greater stroke volume, lower triglyceride levels, lower body fat, and more energy to enjoy life. By using Mr. Rubberband in developing the cardiovascular system, the teacher can adapt an exercise to the student's specific aerobic level. This is achieved by using a slow and gradual approach to the aerobic fitness program.

The teacher begins with the basic exercises described in the preceding fitness routine. As the students become accustomed to the exercises, the teacher can increase the exercise to twenty or thirty times. The exercises should be performed in a continuous flow, without interrupting the sequence of the routine.

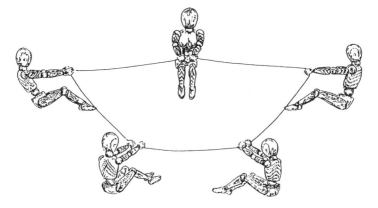

FIGURE 52.7: Sit-Up

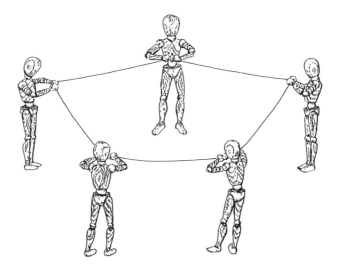

FIGURE 52.8: Upright Rowing

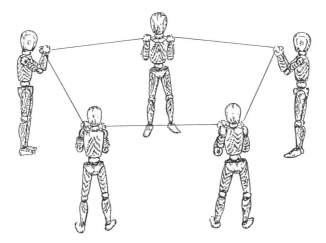

FIGURE 52.9: Regular Arm Curls

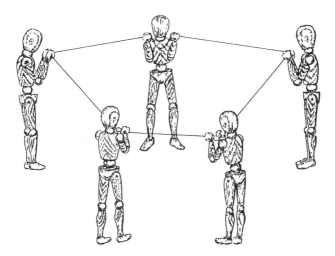

FIGURE 52.10: Reverse Curls

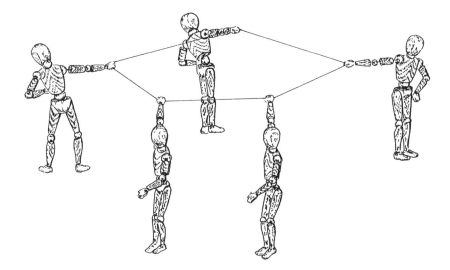

FIGURE 52.11: Sidebends

After the students master the routine without fatigue, the teacher is ready to begin Phase Two of the Mr. Rubberband aerobic program, comprised of walking, sliding, hopping, and jumping. The goal is to maintain ten to fifteen minutes of continuous movements using the large muscle of the legs and arms. Lively music is played to keep the group in continuous motion while holding Mr. Rubberband.

Specific Cardiovascular Exercises with Mr. Rubberband

Begin in a circle formation. The children pretend they are **Opening and Closing an Umbrella**, by grasping Mr. Rubberband, lifting it above their heads, and walking to the center of the circle. After the students face the center of the circle, they form a circle again and repeat the action eight to ten times. In **Walking Around the Ring,** the students grab Mr. Rubberband with one hand. Facing in the same direction, they slowly begin to walk clockwise in a circle formation. This activity can be modified to include the fundamental movements of skipping, sliding, hopping, and galloping. In **Good Morning Step-Up,** the students grasp Mr. Rubberband with two hands and face the center of the circle. Begin by doing step-ups in place as Mr. Rubberband is raised above the head with the knees lifted.

WORKING WITH SPECIAL POPULATIONS

Mr. Rubberband activities are an excellent way to mainstream special education with regular education classes. Analyze the group you are working with and determine the students' capabilities. Plan the program so that it increases the students' strengths. Give clear and specific verbal directions, and demonstrate the exercises and routines with Mr. Rubberband. Repeat and review movement routines. Show enthusiasm when teaching activities, and introduce music to coincide with the rhythm of the activity.

Considerations for Teaching Wheelchair Bound and Nonambulatory Individuals

Mr. Rubberband is an excellent activity in helping to mainstream nonambulatory individuals in a fitness program with able-bodied individuals. The nonambulatory individuals can sit in chairs while performing the exercise routines. Check to see that the wheelchair wheels' locks are on to prevent the chair from moving. Plan exercises that develop the upper body. Use carpet squares or mats for individuals who are sitting on the floor to prevent uncomfortable rubbing against it.

Considerations for Teaching the Visually Impaired Individual

Reinforce the need for all students to have a firm grip on the cord. Provide clear and specific instructions. Establish basic exercise routines when working with Mr. Rubberband. Provide tactile teaching when a student does not understand the routine. Stress proper posture and proper movement mechanics when performing exercises. Have students explore a variety of movements that can be done. Develop fitness routines that are vigorous and active. Use carpet squares as tactile floor spots for students upon which they can perform the exercises while sitting or standing.

Considerations for Teaching the Mentally Retarded

Use concise directions. Give a teacher demonstration of the activity first. Use the Mr. Rubberband program for a short teaching period, and repeat instruction whenever necessary. Change the activities often and plan in advance, and be prepared with back-up lessons to supplement the main lesson.

Considerations for Teaching Individuals Who Have Cerebral Palsy and Spastic Muscle Control

Use carpet squares or mats to perform the Mr. Rubberband exercises. Play slow-paced music and perform all exercises in a slow and gradual manner. Show an appreciation for what the student is able to accomplish with Mr. Rubberband.

REFERENCES

Fox, E. L., and D. K. Mathews (1981). *The Physiological Bases of Physical Education and Athletics*. 3rd ed.. Philadelphia: Saunders.

McGinnis, M. J. (1987). The National Children and Youth Fitness Study II: Introduction. *Journal of Physical Education, Recreation and Dance*, 58(9), 50.

Sherrill, C. (1981). *Adapted Physical Education and Recreation*. Dubuque, Iowa: William C. Brown.

Winnick, J. P., and F. X. Short (1985). *Physical Fitness Testing of the Disabled: Project Unique*. Champaign, Ill.: Human Kinetics.

53

Swimming Skills and Aquatic Games: Ages Three and Beyond

Gerald J. Foley

This chapter discusses a basic hand-foot method of teaching children to swim. It was developed with an understanding of the mechanical laws and kinesiological principles related to swimming by Charles E. Silvia of Springfield College more than thirty years ago.

RATIONALE

The Silvian method is used primarily for children age three and older. Teaching three- to five-year-old children requires some means of artificial support in order for them to practice conscious control of the hands and feet. This method advocates using a device such as the safety egg, which is made of highly buoyant material. The safety egg is strapped around the student's midsection and enables the young child to maintain a proper body position, prone or supine, while practicing skills. As students become older and physically stronger, they develop endurance and self-confidence, and the need for the egg gradually diminishes.

This method of teaching enables the beginner swimmer to concentrate on skills that involve propulsive movements. Once moving in the water, the children quickly develop self-confidence and overcome their initial fears and apprehensions. Silvia believes that the young child's progress in the aquatic environment is seriously retarded when instructors insist on having the student either submerge or place the face in the water. Many children experience anxiety. Those who experience a positive introductory experience are more likely to enjoy skills related to breath control.

SKILL PROGRESSION

Children should be instructed to wait on the bleachers or benches with their parents until the instructor calls them and fits them with a safety egg. The parents should remain in the general area while lessons are being conducted.

However, after the class has begun, parents should not be allowed on the pool deck unless summoned by the instructor.

The classes are divided into four ability groups. Generally, there should be about a 3:1 or 4:1 ratio of students to instructor, with one head instructor who supervises all groups. The children with the least swimming ability require more attention, and the instructors must be in the water, hence the lower student-teacher ratio. The students progress from one group to the next depending on their abililty to perform the prerequisite skills.

The students participate voluntarily when asked to perform skills. Instructors may speak words of encouragement and even cajole a student who is hesitant to perform the task. Instructors do not force students to perform any skill if they are apprehensive.

All classes end with a game activity. This reinforces a positive environment. The children remain happy and look forward to their next lesson.

GOALS OF ABILITY GROUPS

Level 1: Beginner

Students are dependent on the instructor for assistance and gain independence from their parents. New students in the program generally start here. All skills achieved in this group are performed with a safety egg.

Skills to Be Taught:

- Push and glide off the wall with assistance
- Flutter kick with a board one length of pool
- Swing and turn on front one length of pool
- Flutter kick on back one length of pool
- Swing and turn on back one length of pool

Level 2: Advanced Beginner

Students are independent of the instructor for help with the skills in Level 1. Most lessons use safety eggs. Students understand terminology related to skills being taught.

Skills to Be Taught:

- Push and glide off the wall front and back without assistance
- Butterfly kick—two pool lengths
- Butterfly arms—two lengths
- Bobbing
- Jumping with assistance into deep water

Level 3: Intermediate

Students are independent of the instructor for help with skills in Level 2. Most skills are still performed with a safety egg, but students have the endurance to swim for longer periods of time.

Skills to Be Taught:

- Swimming and turning on the front and back, becomes freestyle (front crawl) and backstroke (back crawl) progression—two pool lengths each
- Breaststroke kick—two lengths of the pool
- Breaststroke arms—two lengths of the pool
- Jumping without assistance into deep water
- Diving with assistance into deep water
- Survival floating with egg—on the front and on the back
- Controlling breathing
- Swimming one length of pool without the egg

Level 4: Pre-Team

Students are independent of the instructor for help with skills accomplished in Level 3, and all skills achieved in this group are done without a safety egg. Students completing this group are ready for the entry level on a swim team.

Skills to Be Taught:

- Individual medley, one length of each stroke continuous
- Swimming two lengths nonstop
- Kicking two lengths nonstop
- Breathing rhythmically
- Survival floating on the front and back
- Spatial awareness
- Having body control
- Shallow diving into deep water
- Streamlining
- Swimming underwater

CLASS ORGANIZATION

Since the vast majority of students do not possess any instructional experiences when they start, they need to practice skills that will enable them to progress to higher levels. This is done by swimming a series of feet (kicking), hands (pulling), and whole stroke (swimming) for each of the four strokes. Students' progress in the series is dependent upon their ability level. For example, an individual in Level 4 would swim two lengths of feet, hands, and whole stroke of all four strokes, a total of twenty-four lengths or six hundred yards. Since swimming is a repetition of skills, a series should provide maximum practice for the novice swimmer and maximum participation for all students. It is through this process of practicing skills and the instructor's concurrent verbal and physical feedback that the student learns best. It is important for the instructor to give continuous feedback and words of encouragement to his or her students. The more the students repeat the skills with positive feedback and quality instruction, the better they will perform those skills.

After students have become acclimated to the water, time should be allocated at the end of each class to let those who have safety eggs swim without them. This will prevent them from developing a dependency on the egg, for it is important that instructors remember that the safety egg is a teaching aid. However, it is more important for students to practice their skills correctly in a series by swimming up and down the pool by themselves with the safety egg than to swim incorrectly without the safety egg for only a few yards.

Getting Started

Teachers should begin the first lesson by explaining the correct method for entering the water. Ask the students to sit on the side of the pool. Reaching across their body, they place a hand on the wall and turn in, facing the pool wall. From that position they can lower themselves into the water. Once in the water the students should wait with one hand on the wall for the instructor's direction. Then teach students how to hold a kickboard properly. The arms should be straight, with the board flat on the water. Students can hold the sides or the front of the board as long as their arms are straight.

Teach a proper push off the wall with a glide. Beginners will not glide far and will not have their feet near the surface. They will quickly become vertical in the water. In order to make them mobile, simply ask them to run in the water. Some students may require the instructor to lead by placing a hand on the board and pulling them along. The normal progression for the student is to move from a vertical running motion to one that becomes increasingly horizontal in the water. Instruction includes teaching the child to point the feet and splash the water. Feedback phrases such as "toes up," "feet up," and "chin in the water" enable the student to achieve a more horizontal position. Learning how to kick is the first skill taught because it helps to keep the head raised and helps to reduce anxiety about getting the face wet.

After the children have found success with the kickboard, it is time to introduce them to the front crawl stroke or "swing and turn." This is done at first with the students sitting on the wall and having them move their hands in windmill fashion, making big circles with one hand. Then starting from the wall, instruct the children to enter the water and do a forward push-off. Some students will require the instructor to hold their hands as they initially try this skill. The instructor should stand in front of the students and encourage them to place their fingertips in the water in front of them and press back against it. Students quickly discover Newton's Third Law of Motion: "For every action there is an opposite and equal reaction." In other words, if students push against the water it will propel them forward. Teachers must reinforce the importance of having students turn the whole body to the side that the hand comes out. The key, according to the Silvian method, is to be as inertial as possible and as unmuscular as possible (i.e., having freedom of motion). With the beginner, the head will be above the surface of the water. As students progress, it is a natural transition for them to get their faces in the water and learn to breathe rhythmically. This action is the beginning phase of the front crawl or freestyle stroke. To assist students in the event they spin over, the backstroke is taught.

The backstroke poses a unique problem, namely, being on the back. Instructors must be sensitive to the students' needs and fears while swimming on their back. When the instructor tells students to do so, they should turn their safety eggs from the back to the stomach. After they learn how to get in and push off on their backs, the first skill taught is the flutter kick on the back. The instructor supports the swimmer from behind, palms under the armpits or holding onto the student's head. Initially, the instructor supports swimmers as they move away from the wall and challenges them to kick in the same fashion they did on their stomach. The feet need to be plantar flexed (pointed). Swimmers should be taught to kick right up to the surface without breaking the surface with the feet or knees. "Chin up," "chest up," "hips up," and "feet up" are the phrases that will help children attain the proper body position. As students show the ability to perform this skill on their own, the instructor allows them to hold onto the egg until they become confident enough to leave their hands at their sides.

To teach proper hand movements, use the same phrases employed while teaching the front crawl stroke, the "swing and turn." Have the beginner swimmers first demonstrate this at the wall while sitting. After swimmers are in the water, the instructor should stand behind them and grasp the arms to help demonstrate the proper motion. The instructor should teach a straight arm recovery with the thumb coming out of the water first, and should teach the student initially to sweep the hand toward the feet with a bent elbow about twelve inches under the surface rather than bringing the hands back underwater in a windmill action. The primary goal in the backstroke focuses on getting the child to keep his or her hands moving at all times opposite each other. It is especially important for the instructor to be close to the group during the backstroke performance. It is the teacher's responsibility to keep the swimmers away from the lane lines to prevent them from hitting their heads on the wall or from hitting each other.

The butterfly stroke is taught when a student has demonstrated his or her own mobility. The butterfly kick and the dolphin kick are done with both feet together with a down and up kick. It is initiated from the hips, with the knees slightly bent. While the proper butterfly foot motion cannot be taught in a vertical position, the hand action can. The instructor, either behind or in front of the student, grasps the student's arms near the elbows and then moves both hands simultaneously out to the sides and forward so that they enter the water in front of the shoulders. The next progression is to get the child to coordinate this with the foot action. As the stroke develops, the objective is to get the head down in the water as the hands enter. At this point a "kick, kick, pull" drill is very effective for teaching the proper timing.

The breaststroke kick is the most difficult kick to teach, and therefore the last of the competitive strokes to be taught. During the breaststroke the feet are held in a dorsi flexed position throughout the kick and pressure is applied with the instep of the foot and inside of the lower leg. With the student holding a kickboard, the instructor should grasp the student's feet from behind, with palms over the soles, and should dorsi-flex the feet. Move the feet in the proper circular pattern, emphasizing acceleration during the propulsive phase of the kick. The phrase "up, out, around, together" reinforces how to move the feet once the dorsi is flexed, and it helps the student learn the proper kick.

The breaststroke hand action is simple for these lessons. The students make circles with their hands in front of their faces while being horizontal. The phrases "sweep out" and "sweep in" serve as a reminder of what to do with the hands in helping students develop this circular pattern. The instructor can position him or herself in front of or to the side of the child to assist with the proper hand actions.

Little time is spent teaching a whole stroke coordination at the beginning of the instructional session. It is difficult for the child to think of coordinating more than one movement at a time. Instead, the instructor should let the hands dominate the child's thoughts. After a while the instructor may have to correct the timing slightly, but the vast majority of the students will work the foot movement by themselves.

The simplest method of developing conscious breath control is through bobbing. In its basic stage the student has both hands on the wall. The instructor encourages students to place their faces in the water and blow bubbles through the nose. At no time should the instructor force the head of the student underwater. Breath control is best taught in groups to help motivate the more apprehensive students. This skill should then progress to free bobbing away from the wall in shallow water, and then to deep water bobbing. After the students know how to use breath control, they can be taught to blow bubbles while swimming. The instructor should encourage students to put their faces in the water and blow bubbles while doing swing and turn on their front, as in freestyle swimming. The students can then quickly learn to rhythmic breathe during their strokes, requiring them to breathe every arm cycle. This progression is a natural development of unit movement. It is recommended that the instructor teach the student how to breathe bilaterally and thereby prevent one-sidedness in the crawlstroke. Similarly the instructor should teach students to use breath control while performing other kinds of strokes.

Survival floating on both the front and the back is an important skill to be taught at a young age. Students need to be instructed to keep as much of their body underwater as possible in order to get the maximum buoyant effect. Hands should be in positions where they are submerged and extended over the swimmer's head. The hands and feet may need to be moved in order to give the swimmer balance and to maintain a horizontal body position. Conscious breath control will increase the buoyant force, because the swimmer holds his or her breath for a portion of the time. While floating on the stomach, the students only need to push water downwards with their heads in order to lift them above the surface and breathe.

After the student has become properly adjusted to the water environment, jumping and diving are included in every lesson. As a safety precaution, all diving and jumping should be done at the deep end of the pool. Initially the beginner student learns a safety jump wherein the hands are extended to shoulder height and the toes are curled over the pool edge while flexing the trunk and legs. Students then jump into the water by pushing their legs upward and extending the body forward over the water. The feet enter the water first and the hands are kept away from the body, preventing the student from submerging. An instructor should be in the water to catch the fearful students, while another instructor should be positioned behind the students to assist them in jumping. Once a student has learned to jump into the pool without help, he or she is ready to learn how to dive. A simple method is to have students sit or kneel on the pool deck with the hands held over the head and arms outstretched. They should then be instructed to bend forward by extending the hip to push with the feet so that gravity pulls them into the water. The instructor can help timid students by holding their hands and pulling and guiding them into the plunge position. At this point the student progresses to diving from the standing position.

Swimming underwater is very natural after students have overcome their fears and are able to control their breath. A variety of strokes can be used to swim underwater. Students are taught how to move through the water with the least resistance, that is, to make a streamlined position with the hands extended over the head together and biceps pressing against the ear. The students learn to streamline off a wall on their front or back. They can also learn spatial awareness in the water and how to control their bodies by performing front and back somersaults. This serves as the first step in learning a proper flip-turn.

GAMES

Games are an integral part of the swim lesson program. Usually they are played at the end of the lesson to maintain a fun environment while helping students to practice the skills introduced in the lesson. Any game, song, or rhyme can be adapted. The *American Red Cross Infant and Preschool Aquatic Program* is an excellent source of games to help children learn certain aquatic skills. Some are included below.

Tube Rides

Using a big inner tube like that from a truck, three or four students hold onto one end and kick, while the instructor holds the other end and pulls them along. The faster and harder the students kick, the faster the movement.

Circus Hoops

Using several hula hoops, the students hold them beneath the water a few feet apart and are told that they are "circus hoops." The children are asked to pretend they are circus animals moving through hoops. Before the students push from the wall they must tell the instructor what animal they are and make that animal's noise. Then they submerge, pushing in a streamlined position, and swim through the hoops.

Ring Around the Rosie

The class is divided into groups. Instructors and students from one group join hands and form a circle. They sing the song "Ring Around the Rosie" and move together in a circle. When they get to the words "we all fall down," students and instructors submerge beneath the water. The beginner student will be apprehensive at first, so do not insist that all students submerge.

Red Light, Green Light

The instructor stands about ten yards away from the students with his or her back turned. When the instructor says "Red light, green light, one, two, three," the students swim toward the instructor. They must come to a stop when the instructor turns around. If the instructor still sees them moving, he or she sends the students back to the wall. The game is over when the students reach the instructor.

Choo-Choo Train

Students walk toward the deep end of the pool while grasping each other's shoulders or waist and forming a line.

Beach Balls

Beach balls can be used for a wide variety of aquatic activities. They are light, soft, and easy to move on the surface of the water. Have the students push the ball with their hands, alternating them while practicing swim and turn on their front.

Sharks and Minnows

This is a type of tagging game where one student is the shark and the rest are minnows. Establish two bases where the minnows are safe from the sharks. On the command "Minnows swim" the minnows must swim to the other base, trying not to get tagged by the shark. If a minnow is tagged, he or she becomes a shark. If a minnow makes it to the base without being tagged, it is safe. The game ends when only one minnow remains.

All Fishes Under

In this game of tag, one student is a shark and the remaining children are fish. The fish are safe when they are beneath the surface of the water or at a base. On the command "All fishes under" the fish swim under the water to a base. If the shark tags a fish while on the surface before reaching the base, the fish becomes a shark. The game ends when only one fish remains. This activity is very successful with more advanced groups.

Water Stunts

This is a choreographed activity. The concept is similar to synchronized swimming, except that one student performs at a time. For example, have the student jump in the pool at the deep end as if he or she were a pencil, with the hands at the side.

Dolphin Dives

Students jump off from the bottom of the pool in the shallow end and dive forward, pretending to be dolphins. They do this for about ten yards, moving steadily forward. This is a good introduction to the butterfly stroke and is enjoyable for advanced groups.

REFERENCES

American Red Cross Infant and Preschool Aquatic Program, Instructors Manual (1988). Washington, D.C.: American National Red Cross.

Ferris, Dave (1991). "Long Island Aquatic Club Lessons Program Instructors Guide." North Bellmore, N.Y.: Manuscript.

Silvia, Charles E. (1970). *Manual and Lesson Plans Basic Swimming and Diving.* Springfield, Mass.: Springfield College.

54

Middle School Golf Activities

Al Weidlein

There is a reason why so many people take up golf in their adult years; it's truly an enjoyable, relaxing, social, and competitive activity. A common lament among many people is that they wish they had received formal instruction at an early age. With proper instruction, middle school students can develop correct techniques and an early appreciation of the game. This chapter identifies a sequence of ten golf activities to assist teachers in presenting the sport as a fun and exciting challenge for middle school students. It also offers safety precautions to ensure a safe teaching environment, a simplified teaching progression of the golf swing, several golf games and lead-up activiites, and information related to an actual course design and tournament play.

ACTIVITY ONE

Equipment Required: Course description, list of safety precautions, a set of golf clubs, gloves, and tees

A. **Introduce the Game of Golf**
   1. Brief history (i.e., game objective and terminology)
   2. Description of the course (i.e., the tee, fairway, and green)
   3. Description of the golf clubs (i.e., woods, irons, putter, and angles of club faces)
   4. Introduce vocabulary list (see Figure 54.1).
B. **Discuss Safety Precautions** (see Figure 54.2).
C. **Introduce Holding the Club**
   1. Interlock
   2. Overlap
   3. Ten finger grip

ACTIVITY TWO

Equipment Required: Golf clubs (one club per person or one club per group), frisbees (one per group), and plastic golf balls (three per group)

A. Review Safety Precautions

Review holding the club and the three types of grips. Before making the first swing, skip a pebble across the water, throw a frisbee with the left hand, and note similarities between golf and different sports (e.g., tennis, baseball, and bowling).

B. Explain Terms Associated with a Swing

1. Backswing—the back is toward the target, and the chest is away from the target
2. Downswing—the chest is toward the target, and the back is away from the target
3. Follow-through—compare to other sports
4. Practice swing—with and without a club

FIGURE 54.1
Vocabulary

Tee box	The starting point toward each green's hole. This is the only area where a tee can be used.
Fairway	The central path from the tee to the green, the preferred location for balls to land.
Rough	The site on both sides of the fairway that consists of trees, shrubs, sand traps, and tall grassy areas.
Green	The site where each hole is, containing a flag and pin to serve as the target. (The cup has a four and one-half inch diameter hole, or cup down in the ground.)
Stroke	Each attempt to hit the ball (successful or not).
Par	The number of strokes designated for each hole.
Three par holes	They are 85-245 yards long.
Four par holes	They are 245-445 yards long.
Eight par holes	They are 245-600 yards long.
Birdie	One stroke under par for the hole.
Eagle	Two strokes under par for a hole.
Ace or hole in one	Is scored when only one stroke is used to hit the ball into the cup.
Bogey	One stroke over par for the hole.
Double bogey	Two strokes over par for the hole.

ACTIVITY THREE

Equipment Required: Golf clubs (one club per person or one club per group) and plastic golf balls (three per group)

A. Review the Grip and the Terms Used

B. Introduce Swing Progression
1. Stance—Make sure that each body part is correctly positioned. (Watch the knees, feet, shoulder width; weight toward toes; bend upper body at hip joint.)
2. Practice the mini swing for chipping and putting using minimum wrist movement. (Swing from 7 o'clock to 5 o'clock.)
3. Practice the half swing for pitching shots. Arms fold and hinge with more body movements. (Practice toe to toe swing from 9 o'clock 3 o'clock.)
4. Practice the full swing for fairway shots. (Use grass cutting exercise swinging from 11 o'clock to 12 o'clock.) Note: The easiest clubs to swing are those for shorter distances: the seven, eight, and nine irons.

FIGURE 54.2
Safety Precautions

Teaching golf in a modified facility requires planning to ensure a safe environment. Keep the following safety points in mind and reinforce them regularly to your students.
A golf club can be a dangerous weapon. It should never be swung near other people. No student should swing until he or she is in a designated area and all other students are safely positioned. Students should be careful in approaching a student who has a club down in an address position. Never position yourself or a student in the target line of a person who is swinging. Pair students so they share a golf club, so that one student becomes a "watchdog" for the other. No student should be allowed in front of an established hitting line, regardless of the type of ball being used. When the instructor is demonstrating or organizing, the students should hold their club at the clubhead end. This discourages swinging the club. Students should learn when to use the term Fore! They must be taught that this is not a substitute for following safety procedures. Teach your students the stop, look, and swing method they should use prior to each swing when playing golf. In play situations where close supervision is difficult, allow only half-swings. Half-swings incorporate all of the fundamental movements in a full golf swing.

ACTIVITY FOUR

Equipment Required: Golf clubs (one per person or one per group) and plastic golf balls (three per group).

A. **Review the Grip**
B. **Review the Three Step Swing Progression—the Mini, Half, and Full Swings**
C. **Explain and Demonstrate Aiming, Alignment, Ball Position, with Target Line Concept**

Key Points: For long shots the ball should be aligned with the student's front heel. When aiming, always set the club in position first, with the bottom edge of the club forming a T with the target line (imaginary line from the ball to the target). When aligning the body, aim the entire body, feet, knees, hips, and shoulders parallel to the target line. Shoulders will have the most important influence on the swing direction. Practice hitting balls in partner formation.

ACTIVITY FIVE

Equipment Required: Golf clubs (one per person or one per group), plastic golf balls (three per group), and cones

A. **Review the Ball's Position, Aiming, and Alignment**
B. **Organize the Class into Teams for Golf Games Competition**
    1. Chip pitch and catch with the mini swing
    2. Golf bocci, with the half swing and full swing

ACTIVITY SIX

Equipment Required: Golf clubs, plastic golf balls, and course material: cones, pieces of wood, rope, and spray paint
Design Your Own Golf Course by Utilizing the Existing Athletic Field and Available Equipment: When designing an open area golf course, arrange the holes in a counterclockwise position for safety. Space the tee areas to prevent potential danger. Divide the class into groups of four (foursomes) and place them at different holes. Remember to explain the proper sequence in hitting the golf ball before beginning to play. The ball furthest from the pin (the target area) will be hit first.

ACTIVITY SEVEN

Equipment Required: The same as needed for Activity Six
Keeping Score: Hand out score cards to each foursome. Students are responsible for bringing pencils. Collect the scorecards at the end of the class.

ACTIVITY EIGHT

Assessment:
    1. Have students review the key elements of the game for a written test.
    2. Organize a class tournament.

ACTIVITIES NINE AND TEN

Implement Test and Tournament:
    1. Give the students a written test.
    2. Arrange the gymnasium or playing field for a Death and Glory Golf Tournament.

OPTIONAL RAINY DAY ACTIVITIES

A. **Putting contests on carpet surfaces**
B. **Horseshoes**
    Equipment Required: A floor mat, a golf hitting mat or small carpet remnant, rope, tape, putting discs, chairs, and cones

Description: Putt two balls and score three points for a ball holed. The closest ball to a hole scores two points, and the next two score one point. A ball must be within the putter grip to score.

C. Ladder

Description: Students putt at one foot intervals from one to ten feet to cup, attempting to make each putt in succession. Individuals must start over at one foot after a miss. Score is the distance achieved.

55

Golf Activities for the Physically and Mentally Challenged

Martin Joyce

This chapter covers golf for the physically and mentally handicapped and explains how golf activities can be adapted for use in both indoor and outdoor physical education settings. Special emphasis should be placed on safety, skills acquisition, and competitive play. Suggestions are given for developing a golf unit in for physical education classes, especially for students who have problems adjusting to regular physical education units such as hockey or basketball.

The outdoor unit can take place on a soccer, softball, or baseball field, as long as the area is large enough to provide at least three holes, with a distance of about twenty-five yards from tee to green for each hole. The basic rules of golf are used. The physical disabilities of the student can range from cerebral palsy to cancer to Down's syndrome. As in any other class, students should be grouped with others of equal ability to increase the likelihood of success. This is possible by using a handicapping system. A handicap in golf is the allowance of a certain number of strokes given to a golfer competing against more skilled players. For example, if the hole is a par four, the more skilled player would have four strokes to make the par, while the less skilled player would get a two handicap, meaning that he or she would have six strokes to make par.

Teachers should also use modified equipment to increase student success. The selection of equipment should be based on the disability. Visually impaired students, for example, can use brightly colored or oversized balls as well as clubs with larger heads. Modifications should be made according to the student's need.

Golf activities for the physically and mentally challenged can also be moved indoors. Indoor golf emphasizes putting techniques to increase the eye-hand coordination skills of the participant. The game is played using the same rules as golf; scoring is the same, and the handicapping system is in effect.

The progression in fairway golf (outdoor) is as follows: driving range, chip shots, target aiming, and three holes of golf. Indoor or mat golf units progress from wall to wall, wall to putting cup, wall to obstacle, to three holes of golf. (See progressions at the end of the chapter.) As in fairway golf, competition and mini-tournaments can be used to motivate the students. With the use of the handicapping system, indoor golf should be fun for all.

These games are by no means novel ideas. Fairway golf is just a shorter version of chip and putt golf courses, and indoor golf is a shorter version of miniature golf. Both activities are purposeful because they allow physically impaired individuals to learn the game and to feel a sense of competition. Both games are also easy to organize, and with some imagination the courses can be made very challenging and provide repeated hours of practice and fun. The following information identifies a four-week unit in which classes meet two times per week.

FAIRWAY GOLF

Week 1

Lesson 1	Introduction to equipment, clubs
Lesson 2	Stance, grips, swing (practice)
Lesson 3	Swing
	Driving range (see Figure 55.1)

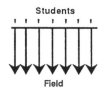

FIGURE 55.1: Driving Range

Week 2

Lesson 4	Swing
	Driving range
	Targets (sticks with flags) (see Figure 55.2)
Lesson 5	Driving range, one hole (see Figure 55.3)
	Targets
Lesson 6	Three holes

FIGURE 55.2: Driving Range With Targets

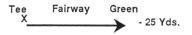

FIGURE 55.3: Driving Range, One Hole

Week 3

Lesson 7	Tournament—three holes
Lesson 8	Three-hole tournament
Lesson 9	Test (quiz)

INDOOR GOLF

Week 1

Lesson 1	Introduction to club and swing
Lesson 2	Swing
	Wall to wall practice (students hit from wall to wall trying to keep ball closest to target wall)
Lesson 3	Wall to wall (see Figure 55.4)

FIGURE 55.4: Wall To Wall

Week 2

Lesson 4	Wall to wall, wall to cup (Students putt from wall to cup 10-15 feet away) (see Figure 55.5)
Lesson 5	Wall to cup (varying distances)
Lesson 6	Wall to obstacles. Hit ball to miniature golf obstacles, then to cup; rotate every five minutes so students will use all obstacles (see Figure 55.6).

FIGURE 55.5: Wall To Cup

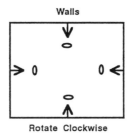

Walls

Rotate Clockwise

FIGURE 55.6: Wall To Obstacles

Week 3

Lesson 7	Play one miniature golf hole using many obstacles
Lesson 8	Play three-hole course
Lesson 9	Play three-hole course (see Figure 55.7)

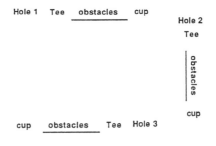

FIGURE 55.7: Three - Hole Course

Week 4

Three-hole Tournament

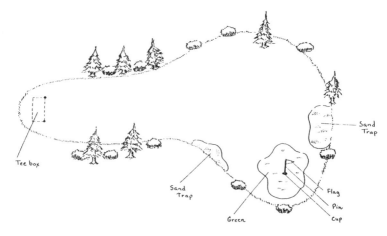

56

Do You Teach Gymnastics? Why Not?

*Louise Samaha McCormack
and Lorence E. Moore*

Interest in men's and women's gymnastics has increased significantly since the 1968 Olympics. Korbut, Rigby, Comaneci, Retton, Conner, and Zmeskal were household words during each of the Olympiads. The excitement, the competition, and the politics have allowed this sport to retain its glamour during the past few decades. The number of competitors is higher than ever before and continues to rise with each passing Olympiad. At some point, society must ask, "Where are these gymnasts receiving their advanced instruction?" Some might identify the private clubs or dance schools that are developing tomorrow's elite gymnast. Unfortunately, many professionals would not identify our public school systems.

ROADBLOCKS TO GYMNASTICS

Reasons for the decline in gymnastic instruction have not been studied. Could it be that some teachers dislike the hassle of assembling the equipment, or that they feel inadequate as gymnastic instructors, or that the school administration is concerned about the safety of gymnastics? This chapter suggests how to eliminate some of the obstacles that hinder the success of gymnastics.

SUGGESTIONS

Although setting up gymnastic equipment can be tedious and time consuming, the job can be made less cumbersome. First, consider changing the time of year that gymnastics is offered. Choosing a time when the gymnasium is not used for basketball or indoor hockey means that the gymnastic equipment can be assembled for long periods of time. Second, older students can help set up and tear down the equipment, thereby gaining an appreciation for the equipment and learning how to work with their peers. In any event, careful planning and cooperation can lessen the burden.

Overall, professionally trained teachers should not feel they lack the means to teach and demonstrate with confidence and reliability. Most instructors have acquired some degree of skill preparation. If the teacher believes he or she can no longer demonstrate proper execution, the student has been found to be an effective model influencing practice performance (McCullagh, 1987).

The issue of performance level is another concern for many teachers. Since gymnastics is an activity where technique is important, the skill must be accurately performed to ensure student learning (Magill, 1993). Therefore, if the teacher is uncomfortable with using student models to properly demonstrate advanced skills, using of visual effects (e.g., videotapes, filmstrips, and still pictures) is acceptable. In addition, teachers can explore the possibility of using local gymnastics coaches as resources as well as having professional organizations conduct clinics and workshops. There are a multitude of resources available if the teacher is willing to search.

This search for resources should also include the necessary information for the development of a K-12 gymnastics unit. Some form of skill progression must be identified to help define the expectations for each level. Numerous textbooks include photographs to assist the teacher in designing this written document. The cooperation and support of the staff and administrators are more easily obtained when a fixed curriculum is established, revised periodically, and conveyed to parents to reinforce program goals. Figure 56.1 shows a suggested progression of intermediate to advanced tumbling/floor exercise skills. Breaking down the various types of gymnastic skills can serve as the basis of a successful gymnastics unit.

ENSURING SAFETY

The overwhelming responsibilities related to safety have also become a stumbling block to the growth of programs. The implementation of spotting techniques is crucial to the success of gymnastics programs. Student spotters must know where to stand, when to grasp a wrist, and how much support is needed throughout the activity. The degree of support or "touching" should be introduced as "giving your friend a helping hand" in the early grades and used as a means of developing mutual respect in the older grade levels.

Teachers have a legal and a moral obligation to ensure that the student's body is properly prepared for exercise to prevent accidents and to develop strong safety habits (see Figure 56.2). A poll conducted by the National Association of Secondary School Principals raised concerns about gymnastics. Fifty-eight percent of the principals who responded had noted changes in their school-related programs traceable to liability concerns (Rothman, 1989).

Equipment must be checked and rechecked for wear and tear and proper setup. Cables, springs, and mats lose bounce over time and must be replaced. Since the equipment can be used by both competitive and intramural teams as well as physical education classes, the care of equipment should be a primary budget concern.

FIGURE 56.1
Participant's Ladder To Success

LEVEL 1—to move on you must have:
    a. fall into a backbend and up
    b. handstand
    c. front limber
    d. cartwheel

LEVEL 2—to move on you must have:
    a. one split
    b. one back walkover
    c. one front walkover

LEVEL 3—to move on you must have:
    a. two splits
    b. two back walkovers
    c. two front walkovers

LEVEL 4—to move on you must have:
    a. back limber
    b. round-off
    c. valdez

LEVEL 5—to move on you must have:
    a. three splits
    b. back handspring or front handspring

LEVEL 6—to move on you must have one of the following:
    a. back handspring and front handspring
    b. round-off back handspring
    c. round-off two back handsprings

LEVEL 7—to move on you must have two of the above

LEVEL 8—to move on you must have three of the above

LEVEL 9—to move on you must have one of the following:
    a. side aerial
    b. front aerial
    c. back somersault
    d. front somersault
    e. back somersault layout

LEVEL 10—to move on you must have two of the above

LEVEL 11—to move on you must have three of the above

LEVEL 12—to move on you must have four of the above

LEVEL 13—to move on you must have five of the above

FIGURE 56.2
Sample Warm-Up Activities

WARM-UP: 15 Minute Workout (Aerobic Exercise)
          100 Sit-Ups: Feet Down
                        No Hands
                        Hands on Shoulders
              Jumping: Two minutes—Knees Up

Stretching—NOTE: All stretching is done to a slow ten count—three repetitions for each exercise.

1. Stand with the legs apart. Pull your head through your legs, with the legs slightly bent.
2. Sit with your legs straight. Stretch forward, trying to touch your upper body to your legs; toes are pointed.
3. Same as above, but with your toes toward the ceiling.
4. Hurdle position. One leg is forward and the other is pulled back at a right angle. Stretch forward with your upper body, trying to touch the leg that is straight. The toes are pointed. Then lie back for the count of ten, leg kept in same position. Do the same for both the right and left leg.
5. With the legs back, lie on your back and pull one leg as far back as you can, keeping it as straight as possible and keeping your opposite leg as flat on the floor as possible. Do the same for both the right and left leg.
6. Lean back on your knees with the hips forward; lean back as far as possible with your hands out in front of you.
7. While sitting with the feet together, and knees out, push the knees down and try to get them flat on the floor.
8. Same as above, except try to touch your upper body to the mat as you press your knees to the floor.
9. Straddles. While sitting with your legs straight apart, try to touch your upper body to the mat in front of you. Eventually pull your legs farther and farther apart.
10. Backbend push-ups. Lie on your back and push up into a backbend until your arms are straight. Allow your head to touch the floor as you bend your arms, and then straighten your arms as you push back up into a backbend. Keep walking your arms and feet inwardly; try to get them as close together as possible. Try to work up to 20 repetitions.
11. Twist throughs. While on your hands and knees, try to twist at the waist to your right and place both shoulders to the floor. Repeat to the left.
12. Chest down. On your knees, place your chest on the floor with the hips up, and arch your back.
13. Rock and roll. In a backbend position with your arms straight, rock your hips back and forth toward your head and then your feet. Gradually continue to two minutes without letting your head touch.
14. Push-up. With the body as straight and tight as possible, push yourself up and down without letting your body touch the floor. Your body should get as close to the floor as possible by bending your arms.

STUDENT MOTIVATION

How can teachers best motivate their students? What can be done to ensure student interest? One way is to show students excerpts of Olympic competition. This will excite most of the avid gymnasts, while also demonstrating the concept of a routine to the less skilled participant (see Figure 56.3). An after school gymnastics demonstration can also heighten student participation. When organized correctly, all levels should be involved in the planning and participation. During class time, enlist upperclassmen to serve as aides. These additional assistants can greatly reduce the stress that often accompanies planning large-scale projects. During classtime, the station approach motivates many students to participate while maximizing practice time. Each station should contain daily written directions reinforcing the skills, techniques, and spotting procedure. The teacher should be positioned at the most complex station or at the station that requires the greatest spotting. Other station sites can include video camera, photographs (e.g., low beam work), stunt work, conditioning, and background music for skill routines.

FIGURE 56.3
Requirements For Floor Exercise

1. Use the complete mat by visiting all four corners.
2. Have good form by pointing the toes, etc. Walk and carry yourself like a gymnast.
3. Use three levels: floor, standing, off floor.
4. Show a change of mood and/or tempo.
5. Keep in time with the music; pick up the beat.
6. Have a beginning and a finish.
7. Use total body movement.
8. Use dance: original, modern, ballet, jazz, skating, and so forth.
9. Be original.
10. Develop a build-up to your finish.
11. Use combinations: three walkovers, walkover-back limber-cartwheel.
12. For advanced gymnasts have at least two tumbling runs, one at the beginning and one at the end.
13. Change direction.
14. Have a variety of movement.
15. Have a theme.
16. Show organization, by having a floor plan.
17. Smile and show expression.
18. Maintain eye contact.

Students can also be motivated when teachers stress the life skills through these lesson objectives. These life skills include experiencing self-testing techniques, goal setting, problem solving, using critical thinking skills, working together, and trusting one another. Social skills are also very important in this area, where students help each other and therefore may see each other in a different light. Many times people who are shy or clumsy in other activities do quite well in an activity such as gymnastics.

Student demonstrators, written plans, spotting techniques, and student motivation will enhance both student learning and enjoyment for continued success.

REFERENCES

Magill, R. (1993). *Motor Learning: Concepts and Applications*.   Dubuque, Iowa: William C. Brown.

McCullagh, P. (1987).   "Model Similarity Effects on Motor Performance." *Journal of Sports Psychology, 9*, 249-60.

Rothman, R. (1989, September 6).   "Fear of Lawsuits Spurs Districts to Cut Programs." *Education Week, 1*, 32.

57

Creative Games for Recreational Settings

Seymour Lebenger

This chapter identifies five programming axioms that seem to hold true when working with large groups of children in recreational settings. They are based on more than fifty years of programming experience involving a variety of populations of different ages, skill levels, ethnic backgrounds, and intellectual abilities. Each axiom is offered as a guideline to assist individuals in the development of creative games for recreational settings.

Axiom I: No one reinvents the wheel. All creative activities are based on decisions involving boundaries, equipment, tasks, and objectives. In brief, one person's crab relay is another person's Ninja Turtle race.

Axiom II: The process requires the developer to assume the personality of an army general and a stand-up comedian. A blah personality quickly destroys the creativity needed to design innovative activities that are both safe and fun.

Axiom III: Whenever possible, add novelty tasks that are not limited to the developmental skill level of a particular age group. Examples include crawling, walking in creative ways, balancing stunts, and tasks involving different uses of equipment.

Axiom IV: Game instructions must be carefully worded and easily understood. Avoid the possibility of placing the older participants in the role of interpreters for the younger children.

Axiom V: Create a game that fits appropriately into the scheduled time restraints. Nothing can spoil the screams of excitement faster than having to end the activity too abruptly. Include time for organization, questions, and dismissal. Children also need the opportunity to unwind.

To assist the reader in better understanding how the preceding axioms can be implemented, a sample activity developmentally appropriate for elementary children in grades five and six is provided.

Name of the Game: Super Challenge
Suggested Age Level: 11-12 years

Space Required: Several playing fields when organizing groups of 200 or more participants

Description: Individuals are placed in groups according to their age level. Each group is then divided into two or more groups of the same age until teams consist of eight to ten participants. Each group is assigned a letter of the alphabet as well as a number. Hence Group B1 challenges B2. Each group selects five activities from List A and five activities from List B. The students are guaranteed that they will participate in at least two of their choices from List A and two from List B. Their selections should be identified in order of preference ("Write a number 1 beside your first choice, a number 2 beside your second choice, a number 3, 4, and 5.") The play leader collects and collates all group selections. Organize each group's sequence of activities in an order that has the group participating in a novelty or nonactive event followed by an active skill-related event.

List A	List B
Hopscotch	Tug of War
Balance Beam Walk	Long Jump
Jump Rope	Football Toss
Snatch the Club	Run Around Bases (timed)
Bubble Gum Blowing	Kicking for Distance
Jacks	Modified Softball
Peanut Find	Basketball Throw
Hula Hoop Contest	Modified Volleyball
Simon Says	Frisbee Throw for Accuracy
Pyramid Can Knockdown	Soccer Kick
Limbo	100 Yard Dash

Outline the course of activities on paper. Include drawings to assist the groups in understanding where each event is being conducted. Have a neutral judge at each station to supervise the activity. This person records the scores for each group that competes at that particular station.

Ensure that all group members participate equally in each event by enforcing a rule that no group is permitted to move on to the next event until all group members participate. Scoring is as follows:

1. Hopscotch: How many participants can move through the seven-box hopscotch pattern without stepping on a line or having both feet touch the ground.
2. Balance Beam Walk: Cumulative score of the number of participants who cross the balance beam without falling.
3. Jump Rope: The number of participants that can jump rope ten times success-fully. Assistants turn the rope.
4. Snatch the Club: Best score wins. All numbers must be called.
5. Bubble Gum Blowing: Each contestant is given one piece of bubble gum. After chewing for thirty seconds, contestants attempt to blow the largest bubble.
6. Jacks: The number of individuals that pick up "onesie" successfully.
7. Peanut Find: The first group to find ten peanuts.
8. Hula Hoop Contest: The number of participants that can rotate a hoop around the hips are for five seconds.

9. Simon Says: The group with the most members remaining wins. Play two games. Cumulative score of both games wins.
10. Pyramid Can Knockdown: Each group throws until all cans are knocked off a bench. The group to use the fewest number of balls is the winner.
11. Limbo: All members of a group go under a pole. The winning team is deter-mined by getting the most players under the lowest pole.
12. Tug of War: Best two out of three trials.
13. Long Jump: Cumulative distance after all team members have jumped.
14. Football Toss: All group members throw for distance. The longest five throws of both teams are calculated to determine which group threw the farthest.
15. Run Around Bases: Best time wins. Each group can run twice.
16. Kicking for Distance: Kick a foam ball from a stationary position. Longest kick wins.
17. Modified Softball: Best score in three innings. Two pitches per participant.
18. Basketball Throw: All group members throw for distance. The longest three throws of both teams are added together to determine which group wins.
19. Modified Volleyball: Play four-minute games. Play three games. Compare each team's score for all the games.
20. Frisbee Throw for Accuracy: Place a marker the size of a garbage can 100 feet away from each team. The team throwing the closest to the marker wins.
21. Soccer Kick: Count the number of balls for each team that are kicked into a designated goal area.
22. 100 Yard Dash: Calculate the combined scores for each group. The group having the shortest time wins.

Reward all participants by including a scheduled ice cream cone break in which participants can reflect on their most successful event and receive ribbons or certificates for their role in Super Challenge.

58

Tried and Tested Games for Elementary School Children

David Oatman

The following games were selected from a larger collection of game activities. Each activity was field-tested by preservice teachers and was found to be effective in local elementary schools.

GAMES FOR THE CLASSROOM AND LIMITED SPACE

Name of the Game: Foxes and Squirrel
Description: Students either sit at their desks or form a circle while standing around the perimeter of the room. The teacher begins the activity by having the class pass three to five balls of one color (foxes) and one ball of a different color (squirrel). The object is not to get caught with the squirrel ball, which can be passed anywhere in the circle. The foxes can be passed to only one person at a time around the circle. Individuals try to catch someone with the squirrel ball while they have a fox.

Name of the Game: Hand Clasp Relay
Description: The class is divided into two groups, each forming a circle. Members join hands by slipping fingers through fingers as each person has his or her hands back to back with the person on either side. In this position it is possible to pick up and pass small objects in a cooperative effort from hand to hand. On the teacher's signal, the first student picks up a small object from a chair using the left hand and passes it to the right hand with the help of the person on the right. The object is passed around the circle from left to right, from student to student. If the object is dropped during the passing movements, it must be picked up without unclasping the hands. Players are challenged to maintain the hand grip throughout the game.

Name of the Game: Muro
Description: Partners stand facing each other, with their right hands behind their backs. They both call out a number between two and ten and put out a

number of fingers from one to five with their right hands. The player who calls the number that is the total of the fingers on both hands wins the game. The game continues if neither student had the total called.

Name of the Game: Circle Sit
Description: The students form a circle by sitting or standing. Several objects of various sizes and shapes are distributed among the students in the circle. The teacher selects one or two children to be "it," and they stand in the circle's center with their eyes closed. On the teacher's signal, the center students open their eyes and the players positioned on the circle start to pass the objects secretly from player to player. Fake passes are encouraged. The students in the center of the circle are challenged to guess who has the objects. A maximum of three guesses is allowed.

Name of the Game: Balloon Fooseball
Description: All students are sitting at their desks. One row sits facing in one direction, while the other row faces in the opposite direction. This sitting pattern is followed and maintained for as many rows as exist. The teacher begins the activity by tossing four to five balloons into the seating area. All students tap the balloons in the direction they are facing. The objective is for the players to move the balloons toward the end of the room that they are facing by cooperating with others facing the same direction. All students *must* remain seated throughout the activity.

Name of the Game: Card Toss
Description: The students are divided into two equal groups. Each group sits in a semicircle around a large bowl or wastebasket. Each of the two groups divides one pack of playing cards equally among their members. While standing behind a restraining line that is drawn by the teacher, one member of each team alternately tries to toss one card into the container. When all the cards have been tossed, those thrown inside the container are counted. The group with the greatest number of cards in the container scores one point.

Name of the Game: Toss and Spell
Description: The teacher places pieces of paper on the wall and on the floor. Each sheet has large letters printed on it. Using tennis balls, the children move from sheet to sheet and spell their name or a word by hitting the letter with the ball. The teacher can also use numbers to challenge the students to solve mathematical equations.

Name of the Game: Geography Jump
Description: The students stand or sit in a line at one end of the room. The first player names a geographical location. The next in line names a place that begins with the last letter of the previously named word. This can include cities, rivers, lakes, states, or countries. If a student is unable to name a place in a specified period of time, he or she must jump backward. The player who stays in the game the longest moves to the other side of the activity area and is the winner.

Name of the Game: Emotional Relay Race
Description: The class is divided into at least three groups standing at one end of the room. Each group is given one emotion (e.g., happiness, sadness, anger). On the teacher's signal one member from each group runs to the end of the room and demonstrates actions reflecting his or her group's emotion. All students are given a turn, and the relay is repeated using different emotions and locomotor skills.

GAMES FOR THE PLAYGROUND OR GYMNASIUM

Name of the Game: Ring of Fun
Description: Place hoops throughout the activity area. If the class is large, divide it into groups of no more than eight. Have each group gather around a hoop. All students in the group pick up the hoop at the same time. Make sure that all the participants understand that they cannot let go of it. Suggest different ways to move (e.g., jumping, skipping, and hopping, or moving at different levels). Take the group through doorways and other small areas. The group must work together to accomplish these feats.
Variation: Have the group put the hoop on the ground and pick it up with different parts of their body: elbows, right foot, left foot, and knees.

Name of the Game: Alphabet Relay
Description: The class is divided into two or more groups. A stack of shuffled alphabet cards is placed face up in front of each group. On the command "Go," the first player runs to a pile of cards and finds the letter A. He or she places the card above the pile, runs back to his or her group, and tags the next player. This player runs to the cards, finds B and places it next to A. The game continues with each player placing the next letter in the correct order. The first group to finish the alphabet is the winner.

Name of the Game: Ball of Glass
Description: This game involves partners passing a ball by using nontypical passing techniques and different body parts. For example, a student may choose to pass the ball to the next child by using only his or her head and one finger. The next student may choose to pass the ball by using only the chin and neck. The only stipulation is that the student receiving the ball has to return it the same way it was given. The teacher challenges the class to demonstrate a wide variety of passing techniques.

Name of the Game: Ready, Set, Go
Description: To begin this game, everyone stands in a line and every other child faces in an opposite direction. All of the players should squat or kneel down. The student at one end of the line is the first runner and may run around the others in either direction. The student at the other end of the line is the chaser and tries to tag the runner. On the teacher's signal, the chaser may run in any direction, but may not change direction after the running begins. The chaser

may, however, stop running. The chaser can tap the back of any squatting or kneeling player and shout "Go." With this action the chaser is replaced. The students who are squatting or kneeling should be encouraged to cheer and work together in order to capture the runner. When the runner is finally tagged, the student who caught the runner becomes the new runner, and the next student at the end of the line becomes the chaser.

Name of the Game: Traffic Tag
Description: Players divide into pairs—one person is designated as the car, while the other is the driver. Cars hold hands out in front (imitating headlights) and close their eyes. Drivers keep their eyes open and steer cars by standing in back and placing their hands on their partner's shoulders. One set of car and driver is chosen to be "it." As in the traditional game of tag, the person who is it tries to tag another player. In this game, cars tag only cars. Drivers carefully maneuver cars around other cars, trying to avoid getting tagged. Speeding is not allowed. When the car that is it tags another, the car that was tagged becomes the new it. Cars and drivers switch roles and the game continues.

Name of the Game: Jump to the Solution
Description: Develop a mimeographed or photocopied sheet of paper containing questions that can be answered mathematically. For example, the first question could ask the student to solve $12 \times 2 = ?$ The student responds by jumping rope 24 times.

Name of the Game: Jumping Syllables
Description: Teachers can add action and variety while students learn to count syllables in words. This is possible by saying a word and having the children jump rope as many times as the word has syllables. Hopping or skipping can also be used if jump ropes are not available.

Name of the Game: Nervous Wreck
Description: This game involves students "faking" throws. The game begins with a person holding a fluff or yarn ball. All other students form a circle and have their hands at their sides. The person with the ball can throw the ball to a classmate or fake a throw. If a student attempts to catch a fake throw by moving his or hands into a catching position, that individual is a "nervous wreck" and changes places with the student in the center.

Name of the Game: A Drop of Water
Description: In this game, one-third of the class is given the role of oxygen, while the other two-thirds assumes the role of hydrogen. One oxygen particle tries to tag two hydrogen particles in order to make water (H_2O).

Name of the Game: Diamonds and Gold
Description: Four hoops are arranged in the corners of the playing area. The distance between each hoop is twenty-five to thirty feet. Five or six pieces of diamonds and gold (i.e., beanbags) are placed in each hoop. The class is divided

into four equal teams, one behind each hoop. This is their home base. The objective is for each team to steal the treasure from other hoops and return it to the hoop that is their home.

In playing the game, the following rules are implemented:

1. A student can take only one beanbag at a time. That beanbag must be taken to the player's home base before he or she can return for another one.
2. Beanbags cannot be thrown or tossed to the home base, but must be carried over the vertical plane of the hoop before being released.
3. No player can protect the home base or its beanbags with any defensive maneuver.
4. Beanbags may be taken from any hoop.
5. When the stop signal is given, all players must freeze immediately and release any beanbags in their possession.

Name of the Game: Blazing Fire

Description: Divide the children into two equal groups. Those in Group One form a circle, and those in Group Two stand inside the circle. The children in Group Two are trees, except for one individual who is the ranger. Group One children walk, leap, gallop, or do other movements around the circle until the ranger says "Fire in the forest!" and steps in front of one of the trees. Members of Group One must quickly find a tree. The child left without a tree becomes the new ranger.

Name of the Game: Top Hat Tag

Description: The children are scattered within a designated area. One child is chosen to be "it" and another child is selected to be the runner. The runner and "it" each place a beanbag on their heads and are not permitted to use their hands to steady the beanbag. "It" attempts to tag the runner. The runner may transfer his or her beanbag to the head of any other player, who then becomes the new runner. Roles exchange when the runner is tagged.

Name of the Game: Catch the Dragon's Tail

Description: The class is divided into two groups (or three if the class is large), each of which becomes a dragon. This is done by having each group stand in single file and having all children in the group put their hands on the waist of the person in front of them. A sock is placed in the back pocket of the last student of each line. The objective is to have the dragon's head (i.e., the first student in each line) grab the tail (sock) of the other team's dragon without any part of the dragon becoming detached at any time. The game can be played for any length of time, changing the number of people in the dragon and the number of dragons.

Name of the Game: Human Obstacles

Description: The class is divided into two groups. Four children from each use their bodies as human obstacles. For example, the first obstacle sits on the floor, the second stretches the body like a bridge, the third squats, and the fourth sits on the floor. Each group's four obstacles position themselves in front of their group. On the teacher's signal, the first person from each group runs around the first obstacle, goes under the second obstacle, leapfrogs over the third obstacle, goes around the fourth obstacle, and runs back and tags the next player on their team. The action continues until all students from both groups have had a turn. Reinforce the need for safety to prevent injuries.

59

Manipulative Skill Games
for Elementary Children

Darlene Bullock

The following games emphasize manipulative skills for elementary children in grades two through six. Each game has been field-tested for its effectiveness in keeping all children actively involved.

Name of the Game: Rob the Nest
Suggested Grade Level: 2-3
Equipment: Four large hula hoops, playground balls
Space Required: Gymnasium or playground setting
Starting Formation: Four groups positioned into four lines
Description: This game can incorporate several manipulative skills such as catching, dribbling, rolling, striking, throwing, and kicking. Divide the class into four small groups. Each group will form a line behind a hula hoop, which is used to represent a nest. Each nest contains several balls or "eggs" (see Figure 59.1).

On the teacher's signal, the first in line from each group moves to any of the other three nests to snatch an egg. The child takes an egg out of a nest and performs a specified manipulative skill (e.g., dribbling) to get the ball back to his or her home nest. As soon as the child returns to the nest, the second group member is set free to snatch an egg, and so on. On a second signal, all children freeze and the eggs are counted for each nest. The team with the greatest number of eggs wins.

The students waiting for their turn may not protect the nest or impede the progress of the other children. Only one child is permitted to leave from the line formation at a time, and he or she is permitted to snatch only one ball (egg) at a time. The second child may begin only after the first child returns to the home nest. Place the nests close to each other to avoid students waiting for a turn.
Variations: Use various manipulative skills with locomotor movements (e.g., toss and catch with self when running back to the home nest, or manipulate the ball around the waist when skipping back to the home nest).

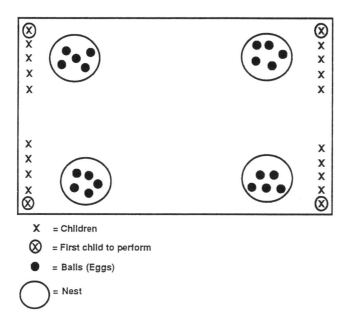

FIGURE 59.1: Rob The Nest

Name of the Game: Beach Ball Knockout
Suggested Grade Level: 3-4
Equipment: Two large beach balls, four cones, and a variety of foam footballs
Space Required: Gymnasium or playground setting
Starting Position: Two large beach balls are placed in the center of a 60-foot playing area. The class is divided into two groups. Each group is positioned on an endline designated by cones at least 30 feet from the center of the playing area.
Description: The object of this game is to force two beach balls to cross the opposing group's endline. This is accomplished by throwing foam footballs in order to direct the beach ball's path toward the endline. Each group stands side by side behind their endline (see Figure 59.2). Individuals may not step over the endline to throw the balls. No body part may be used to prevent a ball from crossing the endline. Each time a beach ball passes over the endline, a point is scored. Teachers may also use playground balls instead of footballs and incorporate the skill of kicking.

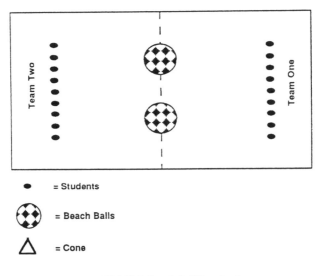

= Students

= Beach Balls

= Cone

FIGURE 59.2: Beach Ball Knockout

Name of the Game: Basketball Scramble
Suggested Grade Level: 3-4
Equipment Required: Two playground balls or two basketballs modified in size for elementary children; two basketball hoops
Space Required: Gymnasium
Starting Formation: Two groups are positioned on opposite sidelines; the first five players from each team form a line at the half court line.
Description: This game incorporates passing, catching, shooting, and teamwork. The class is divided into two groups. Each group is positioned along a sideline. The first five players from each group walk to the half court area and face their own basket (see Figure 59.3). The teacher starts the action by rolling two balls simultaneously at each of the two baskets, and blows a whistle. On the sound of the whistle, each group of five scrambles toward the rolling ball. The ball is picked up by one student, who passes the ball to his or her teammates until a total of five passes are completed. After the fifth pass is completed, the students attempt to make a basket by shooting the ball into the basketball hoop. The group continues to shoot until one basket is made, after which the round is over and both groups return to their respective sidelines. A point is awarded for each successful basketball shot. The next five players from each group move to the starting position at half court, and a new round is started.

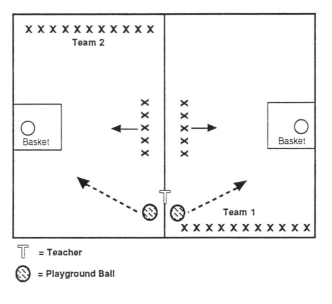

FIGURE 59.3: Basketball Scramble

Name of the Game: Four Skills Basketball
Suggested Grade Level: 5-6
Equipment Required: Ten cones, two basketballs, and two basketball hoops
Space Required: Gymnasium or playground setting
Starting Formation: The playing area is divided lengthwise. The class is divided into two groups. Four or five cones are positioned from the half court line to the opposite end of the basketball court.
Description: This game incorporates the basketball skills of passing, dribbling, shooting, and ball handling. Divide the class into two groups. One student from each group steps in front of the others and quickly chest passes the ball to each student while moving down the line. After completing the passes, the player dribbles around a series of five cones, then dribbles toward the basket and does a lay-up or a jump shot. The player continues to shoot until a basket is scored, then dribbles to the end of his or her group's line, where the ball is bounce passed down the line to the first student. After the first student in line receives the ball, he or she steps in front of the line, and the rotation continues (see Figure 59.4). The teacher should stress skillful passing in order to complete each group's rotation.

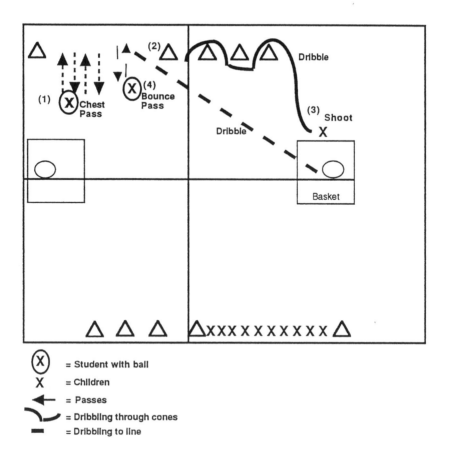

(1) Chest Pass

(2)

(4) Bounce Pass

(3) Shoot

Dribble

Dribble

Basket

= Student with ball

X = Children

= Passes

= Dribbling through cones

= Dribbling to line

FIGURE 59.4: Four Skills Basketball

60

A Compilation of Original or Modified Games for Elementary School Children

Invited Student Authors

These original or modified games were designed and field-tested by preservice physical education teachers and their mentors. Each activity is intended to motivate and enhance the elementary child's learning experience.

Name of the Game: Solar System Scramble
Suggested Grade Level: 4-6
Equipment Required: Prerecorded music and a tape player
Space Required: Gymnasium or playground setting
Starting Formation: Divide the class into two groups of students. Group One assumes the role of "planets" and forms an inner circle. Group Two surrounds Group One. Use chalk or tape to designate the formation of the two circles.
Description: Assign each student in both groups the name of a planet. Parts of nine songs with different rhythms should be prerecorded, each lasting about one minute, with twenty-second intervals between each. Two planet names are called by the teacher to be "it." As the music begins, the two planets orbit (using locomotor movements) in the center of the activity area around an imaginary sun. The outer orbiters walk just beyond them. When the music stops, the two planets try to tag those in the outer orbits before they can reach the outer limits. This safety area can be represented by a large outer line on the gymnasium floor or playground. Those tagged must spin and drop where they are tagged. Students in the outer orbit must continue walking until everyone is tagged or free in outer limits. Once everyone is tagged or free, two more planets will be called to orbit around the sun. The same process will be repeated as the music continues to start and stop. Have students change the direction of their orbits as different planets are challenged to be "it" (see Figure 60.1).

Call to the inner circle those students named Mercury and Venus, Earth and Mars, Asteroids and Jupiter, Saturn and Uranus, and Neptune and Pluto. Complete the activity by playing "The Secret of Life" (James Taylor).

Amber Crystal Ashworth
Elementary Education Major
Sponsor: Nanette Wolford
Missouri Western State College
St. Joseph, Missouri

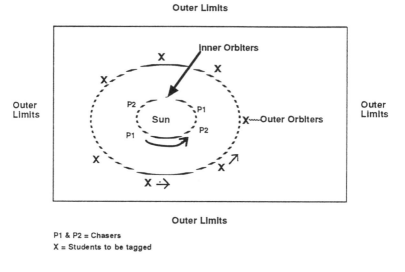

FIGURE 60.1: Solar System Scramble

Name of the Game: Launcher Scoop Ball

Suggested Grade Level: 4-6

Equipment Required: Eight plastic scoops, a small whiffle ball, four bases, a foot launcher, and a short tennis racquet

Space Required: Gymnasium or playground setting

Starting Formation: Eight players per team with the batting team behind home plate and the fielding team scattered throughout the field, with designated base persons

Description: Using the foot launcher, the batter sends the ball into the air and then hits it into the field using a hand paddle or a tennis racquet. The batter then circles the bases without stopping. Any fielder may catch or stop the ball with his or her scoop and then throw the ball to a second player who catches or stops it. The ball is then relayed to a third player. After a minimum of three touches by the fielding team, the ball is thrown to a catcher at home plate. If the batter completes the run around the bases before the ball is thrown home, the batter scores one run. If the fielding team retrieves the ball and successfully throws it to home plate before the runner can complete all bases, he or she is out. The entire batting team is given a turn at bat before switching sides. The completed number of runs constitutes the score of each team.

Variations: Advanced players can use a plastic bat to put the ball in play from the foot launcher. When playing with this bat, the fielding team must throw the ball to each base (first, second, third) as well as to home plate before the runner circles the bases and returns to home plate.

PHED 340—Contemporary Movement Environments
Margaret E. Elliot, Sponsor
Department of Health, Physical Education, Recreation
California State University
Fullerton, Calif.

Name of the Game: Pee Wee Handball
Suggested Grade Level: 3-4
Equipment Required: One six-inch coated foam ball for each group of eight students, and cones or other dividing markers
Space Required: Gymnasium or playground setting
Starting Formation: Each group of eight is divided into two teams of four. The activity area is divided into thirds cross-court, and each group is given its third. Players stand in a scattered formation in their group's area.
Description: This is a basic endline game in which a team's objective is to advance the ball to a teammate over their endline, or score through a goal set on the endline (see Figure 60.2). The game is played in a sequence over several classes, however, during which time the skills of team handball are gradually added. The skills progress as follows:

1. A throwing, passing, and scoring game, wherein the player with the ball cannot move or run forward.
2. A ball that can be advanced by basketball-style dribbling.
3. Air dribbling by tapping the ball upwards while a student is advancing.
4. Active defense in close proximity to the ball.
5. Adding additional specific positions such as offense, defense, and the goalie position.

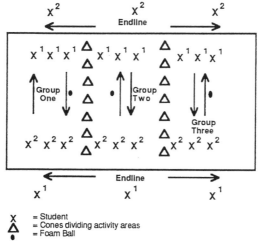

FIGURE 60.2: Pee Wee Handball

Name of the Game: "You Fix It"
Suggested Grade Level: 2-6
Equipment Required: Varies
Space Required: Gymnasium or playground setting
Starting Formation: Varies
Description: After participating in a game, the students are asked to suggest ideas to change the game and make it more enjoyable and more purposeful, thereby eliminating any reasons why the game should not be played in the future. Emphasis is placed on increasing individual skill development and participation. Group brainstorming and practice trials are encouraged. This approach can be used at the completion of any game.

Stacy Hunsley and Lori Liebentritt
Physical Education Majors
Sponsor: Robert M. Hautala, Ed.D.
University of Vermont
Burlington, Vermont

Name of the Game: HDL in the Blood
Suggested Grade Level: 3-4
Equipment Required: Beanbags and five hoops
Space Required: Gymnasium or playground setting
Description: Using four hoops, place one in each corner to make a square formation. A fifth hoop is placed in the middle of the playing space. Divide the students into four groups and position each group behind a corner hoop (see Figure 60.3). This hoop represents the group's blood vessel. Explain that fats are an essential part of the diet, but too much of the wrong kind can be bad for your health. Cholesterol is a waxy substance to which fats are attached that is carried around the body in the bloodstream. Most of the cholesterol in the blood is bound to a substance called LDL. The higher the LDL level, the higher the risk of heart disease. HDL protects against the risk of health problems. Explain that it is important to have HDL in the blood. Stress the concept that exercise increases HDL in the blood, which assists the body in getting rid of LDL. All the HDL (beanbags) is placed in the center hoop (i.e., the pool of HDL, which represents "good" cholesterol). On signal, the first child in each group runs to the large pool of HDL and grabs one HDL (beanbag). Individuals return to the group and place the HDL in their vessel. The next student runs to the center and picks up another HDL, and the game continues until all the HDL is returned to the vessels. Only one child from each group should run to the HDL at a time. The objective is to have the greatest number of beanbags or HDL.

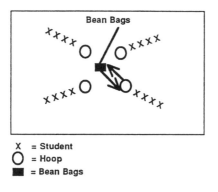

X = Student
O = Hoop
■ = Bean Bags

FIGURE 60.3: HDL In The Blood

Name of the Game: LDL in the Blood
Suggested Grade Level: 3-4
Equipment Required: One beanbag per child and four hoops
Space Required: Gymnasium or playground setting
Starting Formation: Teams of four
Description: Four hoops are placed an equal distance from each other in each corner of the activity area. Divide the students into four groups and give each student a beanbag. Each group has a designated blood supply or "pool of blood" (i.e., hoop on the floor). Upon signal, the entire class jogs outside the hoops, moving in the same direction (see Figure 60.4). The children should not pass in front of each other. As they continue to jog, they may drop their beanbags (LDL) in another group's blood supply. As they pass their own blood supply they should pick up an LDL from it. At the end of a designated time (e.g., two to three minutes), the class is asked to stop jogging and the LDL is counted in each pool. The objective is to have the fewest number of beanbags or LDL.
Variation: Permit individuals to pass their peers and vary the type of locomotor skill used to circle around the hoops.

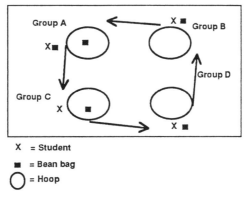

X = Student
■ = Bean bag
O = Hoop

FIGURE 60.4: LDL In The Blood

Name of the Game: King Cholesterol
Suggested Grade Level: 3-4
Equipment Required: Three foam balls
Space Required: Gymnasium or playground setting
Starting Formation: Single line at the end of the gymnasium
Description: Reinforce the idea that HDL carries bad cholesterol to the liver, which filters blood. LDL clogs arteries and causes problems in our heart.

Ask the players to form a line on one side of the activity area, with the exception of one child who is designated as "it" or King Cholesterol. King Cholesterol is given three foam balls and begins the game by yelling "flow cholesterol." The student's LDL objective is to run to the other side of the playing area (see Figure 60.5). King Cholesterol tries to tag the LDL with the foam balls as these students move across the playing space. If they are touched by a thrown ball, they must maintain a "freeze" position, for they have become captives of King Cholesterol. The LDL players are not permitted to move their feet, but they may try to tag other LDL players as they run by. The last LDL player to be tagged assumes the role of King Cholesterol.

Nannette Wolford
Department of Health, Physical Education and Recreation
Missouri Western State College,
St. Joseph, Mo.

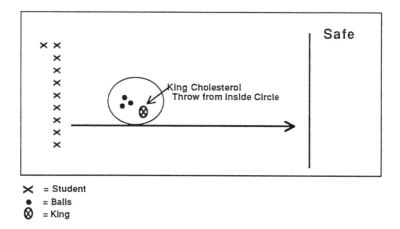

FIGURE 60.5: King Cholesterol

Name of the Game: Birdie Baseball
Suggested Grade Level: 3-4
Equipment Required: Four carpet squares for the bases; two used badminton rackets (one is a spare); two badminton birdies (one is a spare); and softball or baseball hats for each player on the nonbatting team
Space Required: The carpet squares should be placed in a softball diamond formation, with approximately twenty feet between bases
Starting Formation: Regular softball or baseball playing positions with additional fielders if desired
Description: To play Birdie Baseball the students bat by using a badminton racket and birdie, and use baseball hats to catch the birdie instead of baseball gloves. The hat should be held in the hand opposite the throwing hand. Carpet squares substitute for rubber bases. To add a little variety, incorporate skipping instead of running, or use scooters as a means to get to each base. To enhance individual motivation, select students to serve as radio and television sports-casters, newspaper reporters, and cameramen by taking Polaroid pictures. The results can be announced on the classroom bulletin boards or printed in the class newspaper.

Shirley Prater
Physical Education Major
Sponsor: Nanette Wolford
Missouri Western State College
St. Joseph, Mo.

Name of the Game: Be Nimble, Be Quick
Suggested Grade Level: K-1
Equipment Required: Several five-inch candles anchored in modeling clay in plastic bowls
Space Required: Gymnasium or playground setting
Starting Formation: Students in a file formation
Description: This game is based on the nursery rhyme "Jack be nimble, Jack be quick." The teacher begins the game by asking a student to perform a specific motor skill over or around the homemade candlestick. For example, "Tommy be nimble, Tommy be quick, Tommy jump over the candlestick," or "Abby be nimble, Abby be quick, Abby gallop around the candlestick." All other students then perform the skill. The teacher proceeds through the entire class, giving each student an opportunity to demonstrate a skill. Students are encouraged to chant along with the teacher.

Ask children having a native language other than English to recite the poem.

Lynn S. Vought
Elementary Education Major
Sponsor: J. Lisk
University of South Carolina
Aiken, South Carolina

Name of the Game: Hoop-A-Rama
Suggested Grade Level: 2-3
Equipment Required: Hula hoops, soccer-size foam balls
Space Required: Gymnasium or playground setting
Description: Divide the class into two groups. Individuals from one half of the class hold a hula hoop below the waist and to the side of the body. The remainder of the class dribble foam soccer balls throughout the activity area and use the instep kick to move their balls through the hoops. Individuals continue on to score as many points as possible during a teacher designated time period. All students should exchange roles and equipment in the following way:

The player with the hoop must roll the hoop to the player with the ball, while at the same time the player with the ball throws the ball to the player with the hoop (see Figure 60.6).

Chris Claditis
Patty Colao
Irene Negle
Judy Hodak
Michelle McCullough
Barb Huston
Kristie Hickinbottom
Physical Education and Education Majors
Sponsor: Jennifer E. Lindsay
Slippery Rock University
Slippery Rock, Pa.

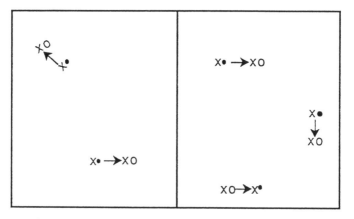

X● = Student with ball
X O = Student with hoop

FIGURE 60.6: Hoop-A-Rama

Name of the Game: Rolling Stone Tag
Suggested Grade Level: 3-6
Equipment Required: Cones or lines to mark boundaries; one large rubber playground ball for the student who is "it"; one tennis ball for each of the other players
Space Required: Gymnasium or playground setting
Description: The ball must be foot dribbled at all times. The player who is "it" must tag a player in possession of a tennis ball in order to switch roles. Once a player has been tagged, the newly tagged player and the one who did the tagging move to the opposite ends of the court to switch roles and balls by kicking the balls to each other. Play continues with the new tagger trying to tag another person. A time limit should be set at the beginning of the game.

Wendy Boben
Chris Detwiler
Tracy Duell
Paul Beck
Tonya Maglosky
Jennifer Moore
Andy Kerr
Physical Education and Education Majors
Sponsor: Jennifer E. Lindsay
Slippery Rock University
Slippery Rock, Pa.

Name of the Game: The Turtle and the Hare
Suggested Grade Level: 2-3
Equipment Required: One playground ball and one foam ball per ten players
Space Required: Gymnasium or playground setting
Description: The game is played by one student acting as a chaser ("it") and running to tag classmates with a foam ball, and one student having a playground ball and being the "freer." The "it" person must chase the other players, attempting to toss the foam ball underhand and tag the others below the waist. The person who is the freer cannot be tagged until all other classmates are frozen. The freer's position will change throughout the game to allow more students to have a turn at this role. Once players are tagged with the foam ball, they must drop to the floor and form a turtle position by arching their back so that the face is upward toward the ceiling. The freer must bring the ball over to player in this turtle position, and roll or kick it underneath them. After this action has been performed, the player is free to run like a rabbit by retrieving the ball and becoming the new freer. This action continues until every player is in the turtle position or until a two-minute time period is over for that round.

Jeff Fischer
Scott Pollock
Amy Perman

Georgia George
Dana Vitula
Brian Hudec
Tracy Kurelko
Physical Education and Education Majors
Sponsor: Jennifer E. Lindsay
Slippery Rock University
Slippery Rock, Pa.

Name of the Game: Mr. Pib
Suggested Grade Level: 5-6
Equipment Required: A lightweight bouncing ball and four cones
Space Required: Gymnasium or playground setting
Description: Mr. Pib is played with a ball and requires vigorous activity and little organization. It lets children practice a wide variety of skills. Begin by dividing the class into two teams of five to seven players. Four cones serve as goals, two at both ends of the court. The gymnasium is divided into three areas or courts. The game begins with one team gaining possession of the ball by winning the toss of a coin. The teams position themselves in front of their respective goals. Once a player has possession of the ball, he or she attempts to get it into the other team's goal. The player with the ball may score alone or with the aid of other teammates. The team without the ball must try to gain possession of it and protect their goal.
Rules:

1. In order to score, the player holding the ball must be moving at all times. While moving, he or she may throw the ball in the air and catch it, or pass the ball to another team member. The player moving with the ball can throw and catch it only three times, and then he or she must pass it to another team member. If the player tosses the ball more than three times, the other team gains possession.
2. When the ball is tossed to another team member and that person fails to touch it, the ball must remain on the ground until either:
   a. a goal is scored using footwork, or
   b. the ball is kicked into the air and caught by a player.
3. Teams substitute players every seven minutes.

Lisa Geyer
Valerie Sabota
Raymond Omer
Jeremy Thompson
George Wozniak
Ray Pranskey
Physical Education and Education Majors
Sponsor: Jennifer E. Lindsay
Slippery Rock University
Slippery Rock, Pa.

Name of the Game: Quick Pick Basketball
Suggested Grade Level: 5-6
Equipment Required: One basketball
Space Required: Basketball court
Starting Formation: Seven on offense and three on defense
Description: The objective is to score a basket using the following rules and format:

Each team consists of ten players, seven players on offense and three on defense. They are positioned at the start of the game as in Figure 60.7. Basketball rules apply with these modifications:

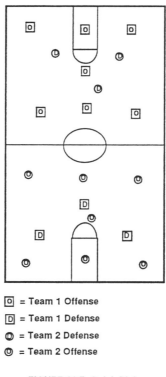

 = Team 1 Offense
= Team 1 Defense
= Team 2 Defense
= Team 2 Offense

FIGURE 60.7: Quick Pick
Basketball

1. An offensive player can move only when the ball is in his or her hands. He or she must dribble to move. Otherwise, the players must stay where they are and wait for a pass.
2. Defensive players can move throughout the playing space on their side of the court. They try to prevent the opposite team from shooting.
3. All players must stay on their half of the court.

4. With only three defensive players, the offense is naturally challenged to pass the ball to an open person rather than just dribbling. After defensive players gain possession of the ball, they dribble and pass the ball to their players on the other half of the court.

Variations:

1. No dribbling is allowed.
2. Every offensive player must touch the ball before shooting.
3. Put two or more balls into play.
4. Switch offense and defense roles frequently.

Willie Sleeth
Physical Education Major
Sponsor: Grace Goc Karp
Washington State University

Name of the Game: Heads and Tails
Suggested Grade Level: 1-2
Equipment Required: A coin
Space Required: Gymnasium or playground setting
Starting Formation: Two groups stand facing each other at two center lines between two baselines
Description: Heads and Tails is a variation of the popular children's game Crows and Cranes . The class is divided into two groups. Both stand on opposite sides of the playing area, at their group's center line (see Figure 60.8). One group is called Heads, the other Tails. A teacher or designated caller flips a coin and calls out which side of the coin is facing upwards. If the coin lands heads up, the Heads chase the Tails to their baseline. If the coin lands tails up, then the Tails chase the Heads to their baseline. Each group tries to avoid being tagged by the opposite group. When a player is tagged by a member of the opposite group, he or she becomes a member of the opposing group.

After each flip of the coin and tagging action, the groups position themselves on the center line and wait for the leader to flip the coin and call the chase again. The winning group is the one that has the greatest number of players. The game continues until all members of one group have been tagged. Hence, all the players are on the "winning team."
Variation: The groups may wear an item of clothing to distinguish themselves from the other team. For example, the Tails may tie a cloth belt around their waists as a tail, and the Heads may tie a cloth headband around their heads.

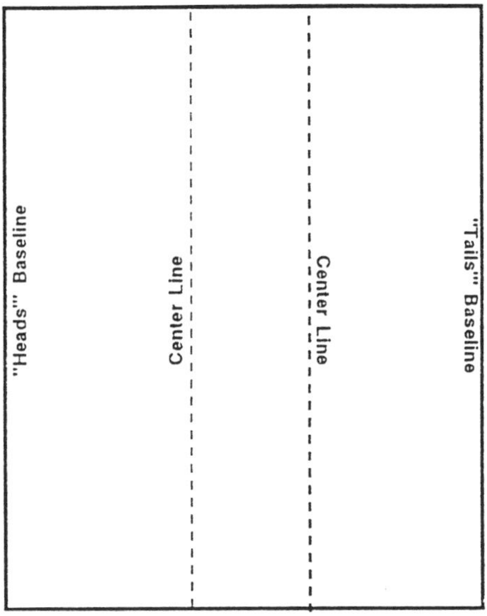

FIGURE 60.8: Heads And Tails

Name of the Game: El Lobo
Suggested Grade Level: 2-3
Equipment Required: None
Space Required: Gymnasium or playground setting
Starting Formation: Children standing in a circle surrounding a "wolf" in the center.

Description: El Lobo is a form of tag that originated in Peru. The object of the game is to avoid being tagged by "El Lobo" or the Wolf. The children ask the Wolf questions and the Wolf answers. A series of questions and responses proceeds. The Wolf decides when he or she is ready to change his or her response and chases the other players.

To begin, one child is selected to be the Wolf. This person stands in the center of the circle formation. The children call out, "Wolf, are you ready?" The Wolf replies, "No, I just got up. I have to put on my socks!," and pantomimes the action. Then the children call out again, "Wolf, are you ready?" The Wolf may answer, "I have to put on my shoes!" or "I have to brush my teeth!," and again pantomimes the action. The children's questions and the Wolf's responses proceed in this way until the Wolf finally shouts, "Now I'm ready! Here I come!" With that, the Wolf tries to tag the children before they reach the safety zone designated by the teacher. When a child is caught, he or she becomes the new Wolf. If the Wolf fails to tag a child, everyone reforms the circle and the game is repeated. The teachers should determine the length and width of the safety zone according to the number of children playing (see Figure 60.9).

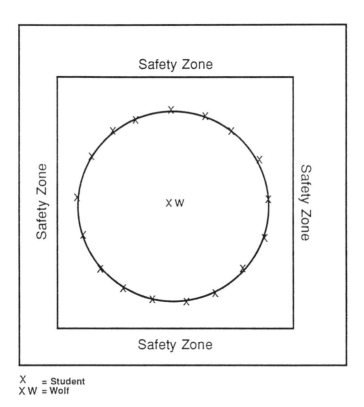

X   = Student
X W = Wolf

FIGURE 60.9: El Lobo

Variations: A facilitator may help children increase their awareness of directions by calling out "North," "South," "East," or "West," thus controlling which side of the safety zone children run to. In order to develop other locomotor skills, a leader may also wish to change *how* the children get to the safety zone (e.g., the leader may call out, "Crawl on all fours!" or "Hop!" or "Gallop!"). This variation can also be applied to the Wolf. He or she may be told to chase the children by crawling or hopping. Variations like these serve to balance the group's competitiveness.

Name of the Game: Help
Suggested Grade Level: 1-2
Equipment Required: None
Space Required: Gymnasium or playground setting
Starting Formation: Players are scattered throughout the activity area
Description: The game Help originated in Peru. One member of the class is selected to be "it." In choosing the "it," one player holds his or her hand out in front of the body with the palms facing upwards; the other players put their index fingers in that hand's palm. Without warning, the player whose hand is outstretched quickly closes his or her hand, and the other players try to pull their fingers away. The player whose finger is grabbed is "it." If all the players successfully get their fingers out of the hand before it closes, then the player whose hand is closed becomes "it."

Students immediately scatter throughout the facility while being chased by the "it." In order to avoid being tagged, a player shouts "Help!" In response, another player must come and hold hands with the person who shouted "Help!," thus making both players "safe." Neither player can be tagged while holding hands with a partner. The "it" must then move on and try to catch different players. When a player is tagged, he or she becomes "it." The game continues until the players decide to stop.
Variations: Boundaries can be changed to increase or decrease the size of the playing space. There can be more than one "it," and a rule can be made that players can only hold hands for a certain amount of time (e.g., three seconds).

Guthrie Morgan
Physical Education Major
Sponsor: Luz Cruz
San Francisco State University
San Francisco, Calif.

Name of the Game: Catch 22
Suggested Grade Level: 3-4
Equipment Required: Playground ball
Space Required: A tennis court
Starting Formation: Two groups are on opposite sides of the court with one group in possession of the ball
Description: This game's objective is to throw the ball over the net and have it land on certain areas of the court to score points. The front part of the court is worth one point, the middle part is worth two, and the backcourt three. Points can be scored only when the ball is thrown over the net and hits the ground before

being caught by an opposing player. Individuals on one team can pass to other teammates before propelling the ball over the net to the opposing group. The defending team's objective is to catch the ball before it lands on the ground. The area of the court in which the ball lands determines how many points are awarded for a throw. The game is played until twenty-two points are scored by either group.

Variations: Rotate the positions of the students from the front part of the court to the back, and add a second ball. This game can also be played by disabled children with the exception of the visually impaired.

Name of the Game: Good Vibrations
Suggested Grade Level: K-4
Equipment Required: None
Space Required: Gymnasium or playground setting
Starting Formation: Individuals stand facing each other approximately one arm's length apart
Description: In this game partners concentrate on achieving a cooperative range of motion. To do so, two individuals stand face to face an arm's length apart and touch hands. The students then close their eyes, separate their hands, turn around three times, and then attempt to get their hands back together with their partner's while keeping their eyes closed.

Variations: This activity can also be used by students with a variety of physical disabilities. For example, students in wheel chairs can wheel themselves back instead of spinning around.

Name of the Game: Beep Horseshoes for the Visually Impaired
Suggested Grade Level: 5-6
Equipment Required: Beeping marker and horseshoes
Space Required: Playground setting
Starting Formation: Two visually impaired participants stand approximately ten yards from the beeping marker. A sighted individual stands behind the participants and activates the beeper. The sighted individual also keeps score and retrieves the horseshoes after the two participants have thrown them.
Description: The objective is to get a horseshoe as close as possible to the beeping marker. The two players take turns tossing a horseshoe at the target. The player whose horseshoe lands closest to the target receives a point. Two points are awarded for a ringer. The sighted individual's responsibility is to give feedback and to assist the thrower in correcting inaccuracies. The game ends when one of the players reaches a specific score designated before the activity began.

Name of the Game: Tetraball
Suggested Grade Level: 7-8
Equipment Required: Cricket bat or flat bat, two bases, softballs, and lacrosse sticks
Space Required: Gymnasium or playground setting

Starting Formation: Nine players in the outfield are evenly dispersed at midfield, right field, and left field.

Description: This game's objective is for students to hit a softball into the outfield, run to second base, and return home without getting out. Each team consists of nine players. Three outs are allotted per team, and there are seven innings. In order to score a point the batter must hit the ball into the outfield after one bounce, using a cricket swing like a golf stroke. The pitch should be an overhand delivery, and the ball must bounce once before reaching the batter. The batter advances to second base and then returns home only if a player in the outfield does not raise the ball cradled in a lacrosse stick. One run is awarded only after the batter returns home.

The next batter is responsible for bringing anyone home that is on second base. Second base is located ten feet to the right of the pitcher. The batter is out if the outfielders pass the ball to the pitcher before he or she reaches home. The fielders must relay the ball to the pitcher using lacrosse sticks.

PPE 512—PE for the Disabled, Majors
Sponsor: Betsy Keller
Syracuse University
Syracuse, New York

Name of the Game: The Roly-Poly Adventure (Creative Movement Narrative)
Suggested Grade Level: K-1
Equipment Required: None
Space Required: Gymnasium or playground setting
Starting Formation: Scattered
Description: In this activity the child's task is to interpret the story and respond to the suggested actions through movement. Teachers many wish to read the story aloud before asking students to express themselves.
Narrative: There once was a roly-poly bug trying to hurry through the tall, tall grass. It was very difficult to travel forward because of all the high blades of grass. Finally, he made his way to a sidewalk where he could move on the smooth concrete and not worry about the grass. He merrily skipped along until he noticed a giant crack in the sidewalk. When he came to a crack, he crawled down into it and slowly pulled himself up the other side. After stopping to catch his breath, he scurried along. Suddenly the ground began to shake underneath him, and slowly the earthquake got stronger and stronger. The tremors nearly made him lose his balance. As he was about to fall, he looked up and saw a child towering over him. He knew it was the child's footsteps that had made the ground move. He stood as still as a statue and hoped that the child would not see him. A giant hand started reaching down, so he rolled himself up into a ball as tightly as he could to protect himself. As he peeked out of his shell, he watched the child pick a flower that was growing next to the sidewalk. After smelling the flower, the child turned around and skipped away, so the roly-poly bug slowly unrolled his body and scuttled along his way.

Note: Substitute *she* for *he* as desired.

Bobbi Henson
Physical Education Major
Sponsor: Shellie Myers
Southeast Missouri State University
Cape Girardeau, Missouri

Name of the Game: A Day in the Life of Lime Jello (Creative Movement Narrative)

Suggested Grade Level: K-1

Equipment Required: Visual aids—lime Jello and a clear bowl

Space Required: Gymnasium or playground setting

Starting Formation: Scattered

Description: Before reading the story, gather the class in a group and ask questions pertaining to the story. For example, "Does everyone know what Jello is?" "Can someone tell me what Jello looks like?" Read the story while the children sit and listen. Ask the students to use exaggerated movements to express the action of the story. The story should be read slowly, with emphasis on the action words.

Narrative: Your day begins as tiny granules which are poured very carefully into a bowl. Soon you change into a green watery mixture being whirled around by a long wooden spoon. You move around and around until you take the shape of the bowl. At this point, you are poured into a mold. Your body takes the shape of either a bunny rabbit, a flower, or a circus animal, and you fall fast asleep.

Suddenly you are awakened as a wiggly-jiggly mass moving back and forth in a bowl. Someone in the kitchen adds long banana slices and small round blueberries, and slices an apple which plops into your container. You are very happy when whipped cream is shaken in the can and sprayed all over you. Finally, a child shakes and wiggles the bowl and takes you to a special birthday party.

Joe Steiner
Physical Education Major
Sponsor: Shellie Myers
Southeast Missouri State University
Cape Girardeau, Missouri

Name of the Game: Underwater Captivation

Suggested Grade Level: Students should have passed the fourth level of the American Red Cross Learn to Swim program or a similar program.

Equipment Required: A pool at least four feet in depth and ten meters long (a desirable width is approximately fifteen meters). Two hula hoops, approximately eight balls (they may either float or sink), and a rope to mark off the playing area and hold the hula hoops in place. A space at least four meters square is needed to serve as the "dungeon."

Space Required: Pool

Starting Formation: Each team is positioned on opposite sides of the playing area in front of a hula hoop.

Description: Place four balls of the same color in one hoop and four balls of a different color in a second hoop. The objective is to capture the balls on the opposite side of the playing area without being tagged by a player on the opposite team. Players who are captured must swim to the opposite team's dungeon area. The only way to be freed from the dungeon is to have a teammate swim to the dungeon and make contact with the imprisoned student without getting tagged. Only one person may be freed from the dungeon at a time. Upon freeing someone, the rescuer has a free trip back to their team's area with the rescued person.

Any type of swimming stroke may be used, but swimming underwater is recommended. All passes should be aimed toward teammates and not thrown randomly across the pool. A person who is caught after passing a ball should proceed to the dungeon. The ball should be replaced inside the hula hoop. The ball may also be carried across the line by a player if the participant is not tagged by an opposing player. If so, the ball is replaced in the hula hoop. The game ends when one team has captured all four balls from the opposite team. A large number of participants can play if adequate space is available. A restraining line can also be added to prevent guarding.

Kayla Whiteside
Physical Education Major
Sponsor: Susan Miller
Washburn University of Topeka Kansas

Name of the Game: Catch the Bees

Suggested Grade Level: 2-3

Equipment Required: One large beach ball, one colored vest, and seven cones

Space Required: Gymnasium or playground setting

Starting Formation: The game begins with all participants standing in a circle formation. A beach ball is tossed into the air in the center of the circle and a number is called when the ball is in flight (see Figure 60.10).

Description: Each student is given a number to remember during the game. When the student's number is called he or she will step to the center of the circle as quickly as possible and catch the ball before it touches the ground. This student becomes the beekeeper. The other students assume the role of bees and fly away from the beekeeper. When the ball is caught, the beekeeper yells "Land on a flower," and the bees freeze in place. The beekeeper is allowed to take three steps in any direction toward any bee before rolling or tossing the ball at a bee. If a tossed ball is caught by the bee, the bee escapes the beekeeper, and an imaginary flower is pollinated. If the ball touches but is not caught by the bee, the bee moves to a designated beehive, where it becomes a worker bee and actively practices ball skills or fitness stunts. The beekeeper returns to the circle along with the rest of the bees and the ball. The ball is tossed again by the beekeeper, and another number is called to start the next round.

This game also incorporates a queen bee, who wears a yellow t-shirt or vest. Only the queen bee can free the caged bees. It is the last bee on the floor to be caught by the beekeeper. If the queen bee catches the ball from the beekeeper, all the bees are freed from the hive. If the ball is dropped by the queen bee, the game is over. The students may replay the game using different creatures and roles, such as a zookeeper and jungle animals.

Martin Brown
Physical Education Major
Sponsor: Rhonda Clements
Hofstra University
Hempstead, New York

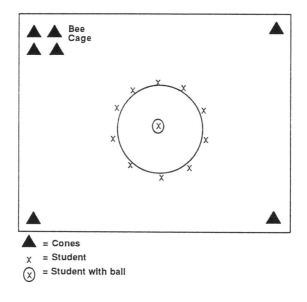

FIGURE 60.10: Catch The Bees

Name of the Game: Shipmates
Suggested Grade Level: K-1
Space Required: Gymnasium or playground setting
Description: The students stand on a line at one side of the playing facility, facing the teacher. The teacher asks the students to imagine that they are sailors on a large ship which is raging through the waves in the ocean. The children are challenged to follow the captain's commands to avoid being tossed into the frigid

sea. Various areas of the ship should be identified (e.g., the bow, the stern, the port and starboard sides); the teacher explains the following commands:

"Captain's coming"—children are to salute the captain without moving.
"Torpedo"—children will place both arms above their head and put hands together.
"Jaws"—children run as quickly as possible to the center of the ship.
"Hit the deck"—children fall forward to the floor, using their hands to break their fall.
"Hoist the sails"—children pretend to pull imaginary ropes using hand-over-hand movements.
"Mop the Deck"—children pretend to be sweeping or mopping a floor area.
"Bow"—children will run to the front of the ship.
"Stern"—children will run to the back of the ship.
"Port"—children will run to the port side of the ship.
"Starboard"—children will run to the starboard side of the ship.

The game is more challenging if the teacher tries to surprise the children by saying the commands while pointing in the opposite direction. Individuals who react incorrectly to the teacher's command must "swim" (i.e., run with a swimming motion) around the imaginary ship before continuing to play.

Robert Naylor

Name of the Game: Body to Body
Suggested Grade Level: K-1
Equipment Required: None
Space Required: Gymnasium or playground setting
Starting Formation: Scattered
Description: The children form a circle. The teacher says loudly, "Partner to partner." With this suggestion, the children move quickly and select a partner. After this selection, the teacher gives a command such as "Nose to nose." Partners touch nose to nose and stay in contact. The teacher gives another command (e.g., "Big toe to big toe"). In this example, the children must remain nose to nose while also touching big toe to big toe. When the positions become too complex, the teacher says "Partner to partner," and the children separate to find a different partner.
Variation: Instead of calling one body part, increase the challenge by saying two body parts (e.g., elbow to knee). The students must decide which partner uses which body part.

David Pezzella

Name of the Game: Bunny Freeze Tag
Suggested Grade Level: K-2
Equipment Required: Two hula hoops and ten to twenty beanbags
Space Required: Gymnasium or playground setting
Starting Formation: Scattered
Description: The students are scattered throughout the play area and one hula hoop is placed at each end to serve as an Easter basket. Eggs (i.e., beanbags) are

scattered throughout the area. Two students are selected to be "Mr. and Mrs. Farmer Jones," who try to tag the bunnies. On the teacher's signal the remainder of the children move like bunnies and jump with two feet throughout the playing area, picking up one "egg" at a time and placing it in either basket without being tagged. When a bunny is tagged, the child moves to an area designated as a garden. The bunny is challenged to toss a bean bag into the air and successfully catch it ten times before returning to the playing area. After the bunnies have collected all of the eggs, the game is repeated with different children playing the role of farmers.

Susan Huey

Name of the Game: Everyone Plays
Suggested Grade Level: 1-2
Equipment Required: Two foam soccer balls
Space Required: Gymnasium or playground setting
Starting Formation: Two groups scattered in separate playing areas
Description: Divide the class into two groups and the facility into two playing areas. Both groups scatter throughout their playing area and hold one hand in the air. One child starts the game by kicking the ball to a member from his or her group. That person may move one step to stop the ball. Once the player has received the ball, his or her hand goes down. The procedure continues until all teammates have their hands down. The last player with the ball yells "Everyone down," and the first group to have everyone sitting receives one point.
Variations: Use two basketballs and perform basketball passes, or use two footballs and perform football passes in the older grade levels.

Suzanne Verba

Name of the Game: Tag with a Twist
Suggested Grade Level: K-3
Equipment Required: None
Space Required: Gymnasium or playground setting
Description: This game is an extended version of tag. Two students are designated to be "it." The remaining students try to avoid being tagged. To increase this possibility the teacher identifies corners or areas in the gymnasium to be safety zones. In each of these areas the individual is required to perform a specific locomotor skill such as hopping or skipping, or a specific nonlocomotor skill like twisting, bending, or swaying. No student may enter a zone already occupied by more than five students. If a student is tagged, he or she becomes an additional chaser and assists in tagging others.

Shannon Marie Smith

Name of the Game: Bean Bag Crossover
Suggested Grade Level: 1-2
Equipment Required: Bean bags and two hula hoops

Space Required: Gymnasium or playground setting

Starting Formation: Two groups form a line on opposite sides of the gymnasium.

Description: Each student is given a bean bag. The objective is to have all the students from one group cross the gymnasium with their bean bags on their heads and place them in the hula hoop on the other side of the playing space. While each group is crossing the gymnasium, they may gently knock off each other's bean bag *if* their own bean bag has not fallen from their head. If a student drops a bean bag, then he or she must pick it up and toss and catch it five times before placing it back on the head and continuing to move across the activity area.

The first group to place all of their bean bags in the hoops receives one point. The game continues for several trials.

Yvonne Watkins

Name of the Game: Pit-Stop Kickball

Suggested Grade Level: 2-3

Equipment Required: One playground ball, one base (home plate), one jump rope, and one basketball

Space Required: Gymnasium or playground setting

Starting Formation: Two groups of students, one playing defense and one playing offense

Description: Divide the class into two groups. One group is at bat (Group A) and one group is in the field on defense (Group B). Group B rolls the playground ball to the first student kicking for Group A. The student at bat kicks the ball and runs to first base. At first base the student must bounce a playground ball five times and then move on to the second base. At second base, the student must jump rope five times. At third base, the student must perform five jumping jacks. There is no additional requirement at home plate.

Group B also has additional tasks to fulfill before tagging a student, which results in an out. After a player in Group B has stopped the kicked ball, Group B must then make three consecutive passes to different teammates before tagging the player. Each group has three outs.

Crystal Mallory

Name of the Game: Tom and Jerry Kickball

Suggested Grade Level: 3-4

Equipment Required: Eight cones and a playground ball

Space Required: Gymnasium or playground setting

Starting Formation: Divide the class into two groups.

Description: Students are divided into two groups, one named Tom and the other named Jerry, after the cartoon "Tom and Jerry." Remind the students that in the cartoon Tom, the cat, is always trying to catch Jerry, the mouse. The same concept applies to this kicking game. The batting or kicking team assumes the role of Jerry and is trying to run from Tom's team. Eight cones are used, four of which are placed in a diamond formation. The other four, placed approximately two feet from the first four, also form a diamond and are called mouse traps (see Figure 60.11).

The game begins with Tom's team scattered in the field. A student designated as the pitcher rolls the ball to the first member of Jerry's team. The remainder of the students are in line waiting to kick the ball. After the ball is kicked, the player runs through the first mouse trap and continues to run through the remaining three mouse traps to score a point. Tom's team has to throw the ball to each of the four basemen who are positioned on the outside mouse traps before the runner makes it home.

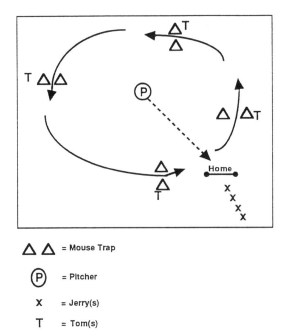

△ △ = Mouse Trap

ⓟ   = Pitcher

X   = Jerry(s)

T   = Tom(s)

FIGURE 60.11: Tom And Jerry Kickball

Each runner that makes it home before the other team can throw to all four mouse traps receives one point. After the kicking team makes three outs, the two teams exchange roles.

Variation: Change the size of the ball, and alter the distance of the mouse traps. When working with visually impaired children, place a bell on the ball.

Jean Marie Wagner

Name of the Game: Mixed Whistles
Suggested Grade Level: K-1

Equipment Required: A whistle
Space Required: Gymnasium or playground setting
Starting Formation: Scattered
Description: The students start in a scattered formation on half of the gymnasium. The teacher identifies one locomotor movement that the children will perform in general space. While the students do this, the teacher blows the whistle a specific number of times. Individuals count the number of times the whistle is blown and join hands to make a circle with that number of people. Groups formed with the incorrect number of people move to the other side of the gymnasium and continue playing the game. If any of these students form a group incorrectly, they will come back to the original side of the gymnasium. Hence, the students' goal is to stay on one side of the activity area as long as possible. Continue the activity having the groups hold hands and perform a different locomotor skill when connected at the hands.

Roy Reese

Name of the Game: Pairs
Suggested Grade Level: 2-3
Equipment Required: Vigorous music
Space Required: Gymnasium or playground setting
Starting Formation: Scattered
Description: One student is selected to be a runner and a second student is identified as the chaser. All other students are divided into pairs, and they interlock arms. On the teacher's signal "Go," the chaser tries to tag the runner. At some point the runner may hook up with another set of pairs. The individual farthest away from the runner becomes the new runner and breaks away, trying to avoid being tagged. This action is also true for the chaser, who may connect with any pair. (Example: Betty and Sally are partners. Being chased, Joey runs around and locks arms with Betty. Sally now has to take off running before she is tagged. She cannot go back and hook up with Joey and Betty; she must interlock arms with another partner group.)

Michelle Steigerwald

Name of the Game: Lacrosse Pinball
Suggested Grade Level: 4-6
Equipment Required: Tennis balls, Indian pins, lacrosse sticks, two hula hoops, four cones, and hockey sticks
Space Required: One-half of a regulation-size gymnasium
Starting Formation: The students are divided into a blue team and a red team. The blue team forms a line on the endline of the playing area, and the red team forms a line on the opposite endline of the playing area. Three students from each team play in the opposite half court from their teammates on the endline.
Description: This game's objective is to see which team can knock down the greatest number of Indian pins. The players on the endlines are given hockey

sticks. They attempt to hit the Indian pins with the tennis balls using a push pass. They must, however, stay behind their endline at all times. The only time they may cross their endline is to pick up an Indian pin that has been knocked over and put it in their goal. The goals of each team, designated by two hula hoops, are placed behind the two endlines (see Figure 60.12). The three players from each team positioned in the halfcourt area opposite their own team use their lacrosse sticks to block shots from the opposite team and supply their own team with tennis balls to shoot. These players can move about their designated half court area blocking shots. They may not cross the endline or the half court line. The teacher keeps score of each teams' goals. When all of the pins are knocked over, the three defensive lacrosse players replace three offensive hockey players. A natural rotation should continue until all of the players have played offense and defense. The teacher resets the Indian pins after each rotation.

Marc Speal

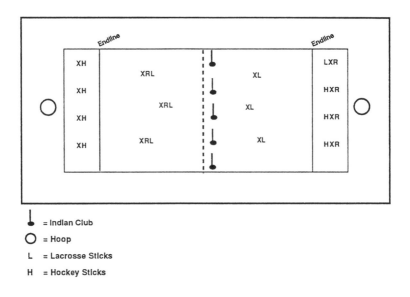

= Indian Club
O = Hoop
L = Lacrosse Sticks
H = Hockey Sticks

FIGURE 60.12: Lacrosse Pinball

Name of the Game: Mystery Volleyball
Suggested Grade Level: 4-6
Equipment Required: One volleyball, net, and poles
Space Required: Volleyball court
Starting Formation: Normal volleyball formation
Description: This game uses the regular volleyball rules except that the teacher selects one student from each side to be a mystery player. This selection is unknown to the opposite group at the beginning of the game. Each time the

mystery player comes in contact with the volleyball, the team receiving the ball is awarded one additional point. This increases the likelihood of the serving team trying to place the ball away from a key player.

Deborah Pyrcz

Name of the Game: Pass and Move
Suggested Grade Level: 7-8
Equipment Required: Football
Space Required: Gymnasium or playground setting
Starting Formation: The class is divided into two groups, each positioned on the sidelines. Five students from each group walk to the center of the playing area.
Description: The game is started with a jump ball, as in basketball. The team that receives the football from the jump ball must make a minimum of three passes of the football to the center players. Each pass must be made within three seconds. Teammates on the sidelines should be encouraged to count the number of passes and the seconds. If a team does not pass the ball within three seconds, a turnover occurs. The team playing defense guards the opposing group as in basketball. A point range should be set up by the teacher. After the three passes are made, five new students enter the playing area. The group that did not score has possession of the ball. If the ball touches the ground, a turnover occurs.

If the skill level of the group is advanced, the teacher may increase the number of passes needed in the time allotted.

Dan Grentz

Name of the Game: Power Line Soccer
Suggested Grade Level: 5-6
Equipment Required: Four cones, one playground ball
Space Required: Gymnasium or playground setting
Starting Formation: Two teams on both sides of the activity area
Description: Two cones are used as goals at both ends of the playing area. The cones are approximately four to six feet apart. Divide the class into two equal groups positioned on both sides (lengths) of the court. Each student on each team will be assigned a number (for example, Team 1, numbers 1-12; Team 2, numbers 1-12). A foam soccer ball is placed in the center of the court for the start of the game. The teacher calls out four numbers, and the students with the corresponding numbers from each team race for the ball. The game becomes four versus four. The players can pass the ball to their teammates or dribble the ball with their feet.

Players also have the option to pass the ball to their teammates on the sidelines, who then pass it back. The players on the court may not steal the ball from the players on the sideline, and the players on the sideline must remain on the line at all times.

Each group plays for one minute while trying to score as many goals as they possibly can. A running total of goals is kept in order to determine a winner.

David Lorenzi

Name of the Game: Socco-Ball
Suggested Grade Level: 4-7
Equipment Required: Cones, ball, goal
Space Required: Gymnasium or playground setting
Starting Formation: Two teams
Description: The objective of the game is for one team to score in the goal of the opposing team. This game is a combination of soccer, football, and basketball. It can be played with as many as five people on one team, although it works best with three on a side.
Rules:

1. A flip of a coin determines which team receives the ball first. The team that wins the coin toss puts the ball in play from the goal line, which is about 5 feet in front of the goal. The goal is about the size of a hula hoop. The individual who puts the ball in play kicks it to one of his/her teammates.
2. After the ball is kicked into play, the team must make at least two successful passes to another teammate before it can score. When moving down the court the ball must be dribbled. Unlike basketball, players can stop dribbling and then start again.
3. Students make as many passes as they like in order to get into scoring position. They can score from anywhere on the court, as long as they do not cross over the goal line. No player on either team is allowed to cross this line for any reason. If this rule is broken, the opposing team receives the ball at their own goal line.
4. If a shot on goal is taken by kicking, throwing, or bouncing the ball, and it either scores or misses, the opposing team puts the ball in play from the goal line.
5. When two players from opposite teams both grab the ball and are in a tie-up, a jump ball is taken.
6. When the ball is lost out of bounds, the team to touch it last loses possession, and the opposing team kicks it into play wherever the ball went out.

Amiee Whiteman
Jim Randza
Amy Sniezek
Jennifer Balla
Melissa Siget
Mickey Flood

Name of the Game: Good Guys/Bad Guys
Suggested Grade Level: 1-2
Equipment Required: Four cones
Space Required: Gymnasium or playground setting
Starting Formation: Three students, or Good Guys, are guarded by the Bad Guys at one end of the playing area. All other students or Good Guys are on the opposite endline.

Description: The students are divided into two groups. The Bad Guys are given the opportunity to chase the Good Guys until they successfully tag three members. These three members are positioned behind the endline of the Bad Guys' court. The object of the game is for the Good Guys to rescue their three members. This is possible by forming a football huddle and making a plan.

The Good Guy group should be encouraged to try different strategies, such as having one-half of their group run to the opposite side, followed by the other half, or by running down the sidelines. Teachers should stress "finding the best way" to rescue their teammates without being tagged by the Bad Guys. The Bad Guys may not move closer than half court. If a Good Guy group member is tagged while attempting a rescue, he or she joins the three students. If the Good Guys are successful in their attempts, the roles switch and the game is replayed with the students in opposite roles.

Phil Horning

Name of the Game: Clockwork Dribble
Suggested Grade Level: 5-6
Equipment Required: Basketball for each student, two cones
Space Required: Gymnasium
Starting Formation: One student stands on one end of the gymnasium with a basketball. The remainder of the class stands in a straight line on a baseline at the opposite end of the gymnasium.
Description: This game is a modified version of the popular game Midnight. To begin, all students are given a basketball. One student volunteers to be "it" and stands at the opposite end of the activity area. This person calls out a time ending with "o'clock," such as "six o'clock." With that action, the remainder of the class takes one step forward. "It" repeats the action, and the students take a step forward while dribbling their basketballs. "It" continues to call out different times until he or she feels that the participants are within tagging distance. At this point "it" yells "Midnight!!" While dribbling, "it" then tries to tag as many people as possible before they dribble to reach their safety zone, where they originally started dribbling. The students who were tagged join "it" in trying to tag the remainder of the students. The game continues until everyone has been tagged.
Variations:

1. A group of "its" can form a huddle and decide among themselves who will yell "Midnight!"
2. The safety zone can be moved to another space in the facility.

Barry Murray
(Previous 22 students)
Physical Education Majors
Sponsor: Darlene Bullock
Slippery Rock University
Slippery Rock, Pa.

Name of the Game: Crazy Clean-Up
Suggested Grade Level: 3-4
Equipment Required: That day's equipment
Space Required: Gymnasium or playground setting
Starting Formation: Small groups of children sitting or standing in a line formation
Description: The object of this game is to explore different methods of putting away the equipment. Begin by dividing the class into several groups. Ask the first individual from each group to walk to the equipment and to demonstrate a creative way of replacing it in the appropriate container or closet. When working with beanbags, for example, challenge the students to balance the beanbags on a different body part while collecting the objects. Small balls can be tossed, kicked, rolled, bounced, or manipulated around different body parts.

Stress originality while each student is performing the task.

Bob Starr

61

Purchasing Equipment for Elementary School Games

Keith Gold

This chapter reviews several important considerations that teachers or recreation leaders should assess when purchasing equipment or supplies.

PURCHASING EQUIPMENT

Three sources of equipment for school games are department stores, local sporting goods stores, and catalogs. Some items are best purchased from large department stores. Balls and plastic bats, for example, are sold in large quantities as "loss leaders" to attract the buyer to the store.

Local sporting goods stores are another source of equipment. If you can establish a good relationship with the proprietor, you may receive a large discount. However, since these stores typically mark up items 50 percent (more than most catalogs), and generally do not offer credit or carry long-term warranties, it is wise to buy only selected goods from them.

Generally, schools purchase from catalogs. The benefits of this method of buying are numerous: they extend credit, offer better warranties, represent many products in a wide range of categories, specialize in popular school products, are available to the buyer on a twenty-four-hour basis, offer products that are generally of institutional quality (and thus of better quality than most retail items), deliver to your school, have competitive prices, and create new activities aimed at developmentally appropriate student participation.

There are many factors to consider when determining which catalog to order from. All catalogers buy a certain percentage of their goods from the same manufacturers and sell them at approximately the same price. The remaining goods are proprietary to that catalog. It is sometimes difficult to distinguish between the two because most catalog houses sell their proprietary goods to each other. The key, then, is selecting catalogs that offer quality items at lower prices than their competitors. Look for creative items at affordable prices, for items that will last and have long-term warranties, for good customer service and quick, convenient delivery, and for a company that supports the purchaser through its professional organization.

Some time ago, a group of teachers working with budgets over $5,000 were asked if they received any privileges because of their above average budgets. One was mentioned consistently—they got a discount off catalog prices or freight charges. They may have failed to realize that the base prices in such catalogs were dramatically higher prices than similar items in other catalogs.

Also, seemingly similar products offered by "discount catalogs" at dramatically reduced prices are often of inferior quality, with short-term warranties. These discounted items offer short-term savings but have greater long-term costs because they need to be replaced sooner. In addition, you may have trouble returning products that fail to perform not because they are defective but because they are made from inferior materials.

This brings us to a major conflict that has developed between teachers and school administrators. Many schools are on the bid system, meaning that their needs list is sent to various manufacturers or catalog houses for price quotes. Competitive bidding should result in lower prices for the school, as vendors offer discounts off catalog prices and/or free freight on the order. Unfortunately, in their effort to win the bid, vendors often substitute similar goods of lower quality at a substantially lower price. Since the bid manager at the school either doesn't know the goods or does not have time to research all the goods submitted, the lowest bidder wins the order, and the teacher ends up with goods of low quality.

Is there any way to solve this problem? The best way would be to penalize the offending vendor. This grievance, however, is very difficult to prove. The next best solution is for the teacher and the bid manager to work together, being as specific as possible when describing the items they send out for bid. Instead of just listing, for example, "soccer ball, hand-sewn, synthetic leather, #5" (for which there are tremendous quality differences among manufacturers), the bid should specify "soccer ball, hand-sewn, butyl bladder, PU synthetic leather, #5, two year warranty." Stipulate that the school will not accept substitutes that do not match these specifications.

PRODUCT KNOWLEDGE

The question remains, how does one select the best equipment? Teachers need to know what to look for in terms of materials, quality, construction, and safety when buying equipment for their classes.

Most balls are constructed of vinyl, plastic, rubber, leather, or synthetic leather. However, there are many grades of materials within these categories. For example, playground balls are made with a combination of natural rubber and synthetic materials. Generally speaking, the more rubber there is in a playground ball, the better it is. Teachers can usually determine this by the brightness of the coloring and the feel of the ball. Synthetic leather balls use many different chemically made leathers, such as PVC (polyvinyl-chloride) or PU (polyurethane). These synthetics also come in different grades. Generally, PU balls feel more like real leather. With chemical improvements it is becoming more difficult to tell the difference between good quality PVC and PU. Leather may be either full grain or split grain. Full grain is of higher quality because it consists of a whole piece of the outer skin of an animal, while split grain consists of underlayers of skin pieced together.

These outer coverings protect the bladder, which holds the air in a ball. Most sport balls have a bladder (e.g., basketballs, soccer balls, and volleyballs). Bladders are made of either synthetic fibers like latex or natural fibers like butyl. Latex has a better feel and creates a softer ball, but does not have long-term air retention. Butyl bladders hold air for up to six months. Most molded balls use butyl bladders, as do most institutional balls. Latex bladders should ideally be used for hand-sewn competition balls.

Safety concerns among balls relate to their feel and degree of inflation. All balls have a suggested inflation range. Practitioners should never exceed this range as balls can and will explode if overinflated. Balls come in many textures, from supersoft gertie or flyweight balls to medicine balls. It is very important to select a ball suitable for the teaching conditions in which it will be used.

When buying other plastic products, it is easy to become confused. Various materials are used to create plastic items, including PE (polyethylene), which is fairly flexible; PVC (polyvinylcarbonate), which is a bit stiffer; and ABS plastic, which is quite stiff. Strength is determined by the material and by the thickness of the plastic walls of the product. Unfortunately, many vendors do not know the specifics of a given product. They should, however, know the type of plastic used, the bladder type in a ball, and the cover material of a ball.

Safety standards must also be considered when purchasing equipment. Many new products are designed for "safe play." Most are effective, and many have been created by teachers and coaches. The National Federation of State High Schools Association (NFSHSA) has a product safety testing arm named National Operating Committee on Standards for Athletic Equipment (NOCSAE) which offers ratings on various "impact sport" products. This information is available through the organization, which does not judge items, but merely rates them against a standard for safe use. For example, the RIF baseball and softball are 92 percent less likely to cause serious injury than a regulation baseball, yet they play to within 10 percent of the flight of a regulation ball. The regular Little League baseball is a harder ball and can cause greater injury than a regular big league or major league baseball. Other safety products include baseball bases that pop up or slide on impact, thus reducing the chance of ankle and knee injury; the double first base, which protects both the first baseman and the runner from collisions; softer footballs, which decrease tip injuries to students; lightweight, oversized volleyballs, which reduce the fear of striking the ball; and scooters with handles for reducing hand injuries.

In summary, with some diligent research into the advantages and disadvantages of purchasing from various equipment vendors, the nature and quality of the equipment, and its safety features, teachers should be able to make wise selections that match their budget allocations and their students' needs.

General Index

Activities Index

About the Editor and Contributors

RHONDA L. CLEMENTS is the Coordinator of the Graduate Physical Education Degree Program in the Department of Health, Physical Education and Recreation at Hofstra University. Her research interest includes preschool movement activities, and she recently co-authored a handbook entitled *Let's Move, Let's Play: Developmentally Appropriate Movement and Classroom Activities for Preschool Children.*

GEORGA ACCOLA is a child life specialist at Caledonian Hospital in Brooklyn, New York, and has worked as an arts specialist at Yale Hospital. She is also an early childhood consultant at Brooklyn's Children Museum, a circus arts drama teacher, and a storyteller.

ESTELLE ADEN is Professor of Drama and Speech at Hofstra University, Hempstead, New York. She actively participates in creative drama workshops at the Long Island Institute of Studies and at Teachers Centers of Learning in North Bellmore, Oceanside, and Farmingdale, New York.

CAROL L. ALBERTS is Chairperson of the Health, Physical Education and Recreation Department at Hofstra University. She has consulted extensively with school districts, law firms, and bar associations in the area of student and teacher rights.

DONNA R. BARNES is Professor in the Department of Administration and Policy Studies at Hofstra University. In addition to curating several seventeenth-century Dutch art exhibitions for the Hofstra Museum, she has organized two international interdisciplinary symposiums focused on seventeenth-century Dutch art and life and has presented papers on educational, culinary, and monetary aspects of Dutch life as depicted by artists.

MINNA S. BARRETT is a certified psychologist and consultant to various state, local, and private counseling agencies. She is Associate Professor and the

Chairperson of the Psychology Department at SUNY, Old Westbury, New York.

GARY T. BARRETTE is Professor in the Department of Physical Education and Human Performance Sciences at Adelphi University in Garden City, New York. He is a noted writer and presenter of innovative approaches to pre-professional physical education teachers concerning issues which have been discussed on the state, national, and international levels.

PAULA BEACH is Assistant Professor of Physical Education at Le Tourneau University in Longview, Texas. She has also held appointments at Concordia College, Northwestern College, Texas A&M University, and Philadelphia College of Bible, where she taught courses in teacher preparation.

SVEA BECKER is Associate Professor in the Department of Exercise and Movement Sciences at William Paterson College in Wayne, New Jersey. She has conducted numerous classes and workshops in movement education, modern dance, and aerobics.

JANIS BOZOWSKI has been teaching elementary physical education since 1977 and is currently at South Brunswick Township Schools, New Jersey. She has made several state and local presentations focusing on Project Adventure techniques and programs by which physical educators can become more involved in developing schoolwide community projects.

BETSY A. BRICKELL teaches at Franklin High School in Pennsylvania. She has made several state and local presentations on youth fitness and is currently enrolled in a doctoral program at Temple University.

DARLENE BULLOCK is Methods Instructor in the Department of Physical Education at Slippery Rock University in Pennsylvania. She has designed and implemented a community partnership between the university and Slippery Rock Area School District, which involves over 200 children in each grade level participating in extracurricular programs of gymnastics, basketball, track and field, and mini-olympic events.

DEIDRE BURNSTINE is Associate Professor at East Stroudsburg University, Pennsylyania, in the Department of Movement Studies and Exercise Science. Her principle interests include cooperative and new games, educational applications of adventure activities, and strategies in teacher preparation.

LEN CAROLAN is a physical education teacher at the Smithtown Middle School in Smithtown, New York. He has taught for twenty-two years and has made numerous presentations at the state and local level.

ANN BABCOCK CELLA is an adapted physical education specialist for Browning Public Schools in Browning, Montana. She has conducted numerous dance classes and demonstrations to promote an understanding and appreciation of the American Indian sports and games culture.

KARA CHRISTIAN is Assistant Professor and Coordinator of the Teacher

Preparation Program in the Department of Health, Physical Education and Movement Science at Long Island University/C. W. Post Campus in New York. Her current research interests include cooperative movement activities and innovative teaching approaches.

KIRSTEN DeBEAR is a pediatric occupational therapist in private practice who specializes in treatment of developmental delays in preschool children. She is Adjunct Professor at the Bank Street College of Education in New York City, where she teaches courses on developmental delays, and a consultant at the Gateway School for learning disabled children.

JIM DeLINE is currently the physical education instructor at Barbara Jordan Elementary School in Austin, Texas. He has made numerous presentations and workshops on games and activities directed at increasing the elementary child's cooperative attitudes and physical behaviors.

SARAH DOOLITTLE is Assistant Professor in the Department of Health, Physical Education and Recreation at Hofstra University. She has extensive experience as a physical education curriculum and teaching specialist for teachers in urban, suburban, and rural public and private schools in New York and Massachusetts.

LEAH HOLLAND FIORENTINO is Clinical Professor in the Department of Physical Education and Human Performance Sciences at Adelphi University. Her current research and program directions focus on improving teacher preparation utilizing school-university collaborations.

GERALD J. FOLEY is the Director of Aquatics and head swim coach at Adelphi University. He is also the head coach of the Long Island Aquatic Club, where he has successfully employed strategies related to exercise physiology, biomechanics, and nutrition.

LOUISE M. GERBES is a physical education teacher at the Discovery Elementary School in Deltona, Florida. She has an in-depth background in the area of integrated learning theories and implementation techniques.

KEITH GOLD is Director of Marketing and Product Development at Flaghouse, Inc. in Mount Vernon, New York. He has conducted workshops in the United States and Europe on sport and play equipment innovations, safety awareness, and equipment design.

BETH GOLDIN has been a featured lecturer on fitness activities and concepts for professional teacher preparation programs. She is also the creator of the "Fit Kid" Fitness Program at the Berkeley Carroll School in Brooklyn, New York, where she is the Director of Elementary Physical Education.

BRUCE GROSSMAN is Professor of Child Development at Hofstra University, where he teaches a course on play and imagination. He is an accomplished presenter and the author of *Your Children—Your Choices, Helping Children*

Grow, Early Childhood Administration, and numerous journal articles.

ASHLEY M. HAMMOND was formerly a professional soccer player in England and is now a professional soccer consultant in the United States through the U.S. Soccer Federation and the British Football Association. He is currently developing youth soccer programs through the Montclair United Soccer Club in Montclair, New Jersey.

CATRIONA T. HIGGS is Assistant Professor in the Department of Physical Education at Slippery Rock University in Pennsylvania. She is a noted speaker on the topics of women in sports, sexism in sport, and gender-related issues.

MIRABAI HOLLAND is the president of Holland's Fitness, located in Demarest, New Jersey. She has written extensively on creative fitness activities and programming for preschool through grade eight elementary children, and is the author of *All Winners Cooperative Fitness Play Programs For Kids: 3-5 Years of Age*.

PAT HUBER is Associate Professor in the Department of Exercise and Movement Sciences at William Paterson College, Wayne, New Jersey. She is a specialist in curriculum and teaching physical education with an emphasis in the supervision of preservice teachers.

SHEILA L. JACKSON is Assistant Professor in the Department of Health Promotion and Kinesiology at the University of North Carolina in Charlotte. She is currently conducting research in biomechanics and perceptual motor development.

RHODA JOSEPH is a poet and reading specialist in Long Island, New York. She has received several awards for her children's radio activities and programs.

MARTIN JOYCE is an adaptive physical education specialist at the Mineola Public School District in Mineola, New York. He has conducted numerous workshops on the state and local levels identifying creative teaching techniques for physically challenged students.

ARTIE KAMIYA is currently editor of the Great Activity Publishing Company in Durham, North Carolina. He is the physical education consultant for the Department of Public Instructions for the State of North Carolina, and is the author of *The Elementary Teacher's Handbook for Indoor and Outdoor Games* and co-author of *Fitness and Fun for Everyone*.

SUSAN O. KENNEDY has nineteen years of experience as a public and university physical educator, focusing primarily on developmental/adapted physical education and biomechanics and sports medicine. She has taught at the University of North Texas; Chadron State College, Nevada; Regional School District 7 in Oregon; and Regional School District 1 in Connecticut.

SARA KIESEL is an adapted physical education specialist at the Gateway School in New York City. She has also served as a creative dance and movement specialist for several theatre dance centers for children.

BRENDA KNITTER has eighteen years of experience teaching elementary physical education in a number of states including New York, Illinois, and Texas. She is currently teaching grades one through six in the Fairfax County Public Schools in Springfield, Virginia.

BESS RING KOVAL is Professor Emeritus of Dance from SUNY-Cortland, New York. She has also taught at Ohio State University, University of Puerto Rico, Kent State University, and Women's College, Greensboro, North Carolina.

ELLEN M. KOWALSKI is Assistant Professor in the Department of Physical Education and Human Performance Science at Adelphi University. She has made numerous presentations on topics related to motor learning, developmental assessment, and sensory integration techniques for the motorically challenged child.

JOHN LaRUE is a certified recreation therapist for Kompan/Big Toys Northeast, Inc., in New York. He was also a training assistant for the former New Games Foundation and has facilitated over 300 workshops and play sessions throughout the United States.

SEYMOUR LEBENGER is Assistant Dean for Hofstra University's College of Continuing Education. He has more than forty years of administrative experience in the area of recreational summer camp programming and activity implementation.

LILKA LICHTNEGER is a physical education teacher at the Tooker Avenue School in West Babylon, New York. She has worked extensively field-testing all activities for the grant-funded H.O.P.E. Project, which strives to increase the elementary child's environmental awareness in the gymnasium as well as the classroom.

SHEILA MARDENFELD has been working in professional social work practice involving youths, adults, and families. She is the originator of the PMS support line and has worked with several school systems and youth councils in New York State.

LOUISE SAMAHA McCORMACK is Associate Professor in the Health, Physical Education and Recreation Department at Plymouth State College, where she is the Coordinator of Student Teaching. She is the former director of gymnastic judges for the State of New Hampshire and former gymnastic coach at Brooklyn College.

MARY McKNIGHT-TAYLOR is Associate Professor in the Department of Counseling, Research, Special Education and Rehabilitation at Hofstra University. Her specialty areas include training teachers in advanced curriculum strategies to facilitate language and learning.

LINDA McNALLY is currently the development manager at the Farrington School in Chislehurst, Kent, England. She is also the coordinator of sport facilities for the school and is involved in the operation of the school's day camp programming.

LORENCE E. MOORE is the supervisor of the Health and Physical Education Program, a physical eduction teacher, and an elementary gymnastics coach for the Central Berkshire Regional School District in Dalton, Massachusetts. He has conducted numerous gymnastic clinics throughout Massachusetts, Vermont, Rhode Island, and Connecticut, as well as at several Eastern District AAHPERD Conferences.

SUZANNE MUELLER is Associate Professor at East Stroudsburg University, Pennsylvania, in the School of Health Sciences and Physical Education. Among other accomplishments, she has been a featured speaker on topics related to creative motor development activities and educational gymnastics.

BEVERLY NICHOLS is Associate Professor of Physical Education in the Department of Human Development Studies at the University of Vermont in Burlington. She is a noted scholar in the area of teacher training experiences and is the author of *Moving and Learning: The Elementary School Physical Education Experience*.

DAVID OATMAN is Associate Professor in the Department of Health, Physical Education, and Recreation at Southwest Missouri State University in Springfield. His research interests include innovative approaches to teacher education and classroom discipline and management techniques.

MARIA I. OJEDA-O'NEILL is Assistant Professor in the Department of Physical Education at the University of Puerto Rico in Rio Piedras. She specializes in motor learning theories and multicultural research as they apply to physical education settings.

JANET M. OUSSATY is Assistant Professor in the Department of Physical Education at Kean College, New Jersey, where she coordinates the physical education program. She was formerly the coordinator of the teacher education program at Rutgers University and for eight was an elementary and middle school physical educator.

MARTHA OWENS is a director of the Every Child a Winner project based in Ocilla, Georgia. During this twenty-year experience she has co-authored training booklets, lesson plans, and audiovisual materials used by the schools participating in the project throughout the United States and Canada.

KATHY PATTAK is currently an elementary health and physical education teacher at the Stephen Foster School, Mt. Lebanon School District in Pittsburgh, Pennsylvania. She has published articles reflecting creative activities in several elementary education and physical education journals.

WILLIAM C. PAYRET is a physical education teacher at Simon Baruch Junior High School in New York City. He is also the coordinator of a specialized gross motor program for students and the community at Manhattan College, New York.

BIRGER PEITERSEN teaches courses in sport and physical education at the Danish State Institute of Physical Education in Copenhagen, Denmark. He is a noted international scholar who has made numerous presentations on the topics of sport pedagogy, sport socialization, and teacher training techniques.

LISA M. QUIRK is director of physical education and athletics and swimming coordinator at the Grace Church School in New York City. Her creative teaching approaches have focused on interdisciplinary techniques and cooperative learning strategies.

HEIDI REICHEL is an educational consultant and learning disability specialist with a private practice in Huntington, Long Island. She is also on the faculty at Dowling College, New York, and has written numerous articles on topics related to special education.

SUSAN ROCKETT is program director of the United States Department of Education's National Diffusion Network Project, Every Child a Winner Project, based in Ocilla, Georgia. She is co-author of five books as well as numerous articles and training visuals.

KARL E. ROHNKE has twenty-three years of experience in the role of educational consultant and author for Project Adventure Inc., in Hamilton, Massachusetts. His Adventure curriculum clinics have been presented in Australia, Hong Kong, New Zealand, Ireland, Canada, and Japan.

LENORE SANDEL is Professor Emeritus of Reading at Hofstra University. She has performed extensive research in the area of whole language and has numerous publications related to increasing the elementary child's writing and socialization skills.

SUSAN M. SCHWAGER is Associate Professor in the Department of Physical Education, Recreation, and Leisure Studies at Montclair State College in Upper Montclair, New Jersey. She is a noted writer and presenter in teacher preparation, curriculum and program development, and in-service teacher development.

PHILIP DUHAN SEGAL is Associate Professor in the Department of English at Queensborough Community College. Among other accomplishments, he was honored as Visiting Professor of American Literature at Hiroshima University in Japan, and has been a recipient of the Ford Foundation Teaching Fellowship.

LYNETTE C. SHOTT is a third grade academic teacher at Timbercrest Elementary School in Deltona, Florida. She has extensive experience in implementing whole language and integrated curriculum designs.

SUSAN ANNE SORTINO is a physical education teacher at Columbia Grammar and Preparatory School in New York City. She has extensive physical education teaching and athletic administration experience in the private, independent school sector, as well as coaching girls' volleyball, basketball, softball, and track and field.

JIM STILLWELL is currently Chairperson of the Department of Human Performance Studies at the University of Alabama in Tuscaloosa. Author of three books, including *Making and Using Creative Play Equipment*, and more than fifty articles in a variety of journals, he frequently serves as a featured speaker on the topic of developmental movement activities for elementary children.

JILL VOMACKA is a physical educator at the John Street Elementary School, Franklin Square, New York. She has served as an adaptive physical education consultant to numerous local school districts and on the Adapted Physical Education Committee for the New York State Department of Education.

AL WEIDLEIN is an experienced varsity golf coach and physical educator at the Mineola Public School District in Long Island. He is also Vice-President of the Nassau County Golf Coaches Association and is actively involved in promoting junior golf throughout New York State.

KAREN H. WEILLER is Assistant Professor in the Department of Kinesiology, Health Promotion and Recreation at the University of North Texas. She is a certified professional counselor, and has conducted research as well as numerous presentations and workshops focusing on gender-related issues in physical education.

AMELIA MAYS WOODS is Associate Professor in the Department of Physical Education at St. Olaf College, Northfield, Minnesota. She has published works on teaching effectiveness and has presented research implications at the state, national, and international levels.

LORNA J. WOODWARD is a certified home economics and elementary classroom teacher. She is currently a freelance writer of children's books focusing on historical accounts of early home and family living practices.

NANCY WORONOWICH is currently a fourth grade elementary school teacher and has taught gifted and talented classes for grades four and five at the Tooker Avenue School in West Babylon, New York. Her knowledge of environmental concerns has been a major force behind the grant-funded H.O.P.E. Project.

JOYCE A. ZUCKER is a certified art teacher for kindergarten through twelfth grade. Her specialty is creating educational games, songs, and stories, which are presented in workshops for parents, teachers, universities, and other places of learning.